Cambridge IGCSE® and O Level

Business Studies

Fifth edition

Karen Borrington

Peter Stimpson

HODDER
EDUCATION
AN HACHETTE UK COMPANY

Orders: please contact Bookpoint Ltd, 130 Park Drive, Milton Park, Abingdon, Oxon OX14 4SE. Telephone: (44) 01235 827720. Fax: (44) 01235 400401. Email education@bookpoint.co.uk Lines are open from 9 a.m. to 5 p.m., Monday to Saturday, with a 24-hour message answering service. You can also order through our website: www.hoddereducation.com

IGCSE® is a registered trademark

© Karen Borrington and Peter Stimpson 2018

First published in 1999 by
Hodder Education
An Hachette UK Company
Carmelite House, 50 Victoria Embankment, London EC4Y 0DZ

Second edition published 2002
Third edition published 2006
Fourth edition published 2013
This fifth edition published 2018

Impression number   5 4 3 2 1

Year   2022   2021   2020   2019   2018

Cover photo © Shutterstock/Lesia_G

Third edition typeset in ITC Officina Sans 11.5/13 pts. by Aptara Inc.

Illustrations by Oxford Designers and Illustrators Ltd and Aptara Inc.

Printed and bound in Slovenia

A catalogue record for this title is available from the British Library

ISBN 978 1 5104 2123 3

Contents

Introduction iv

How to use this book iv

Exam preparation and technique vi

SECTION 1 Understanding business activity
1 Business activity 2
2 Classification of businesses 11
3 Enterprise, business growth and size 19
4 Types of business organisation 35
5 Business objectives and stakeholder objectives 51
Case study 61

SECTION 2 People in business
6 Motivating employees 63
7 Organisation and management 76
8 Recruitment, selection and training of employees 92
9 Internal and external communication 114
Case study 129

SECTION 3 Marketing
10 Marketing, competition and the customer 132
11 Market research 143
12 The marketing mix: product 158
13 The marketing mix: price 170
14 The marketing mix: place 178
15 The marketing mix: promotion 185
16 Technology and the marketing mix 197
17 Marketing strategy 203
Case study 212

SECTION 4 Operations management
18 Production of goods and services 214
19 Costs, scale of production and break-even analysis 228
20 Achieving quality production 241
21 Location decisions 248
Case study 262

SECTION 5 Financial information and financial decisions
22 Business finance: needs and sources 265
23 Cash flow forecasting and working capital 281
24 Income statements 293
25 Statement of financial position 303
26 Analysis of accounts 311
Case study 323

SECTION 6 External influences on business issues
27 Economic issues 326
28 Environmental and ethical issues 340
29 Business and the international economy 351
Case study 362
Index 364
Acknowledgements 368

Introduction

This book has been written for all students of Cambridge IGCSE® and O Level Business Studies. It carefully and precisely follows the syllabus from Cambridge Assessment International Education. It provides the detail and guidance that are needed to support you throughout the course and help you to prepare for your examinations. It will also prove to be of great use to anyone who wants to learn more about the key concepts of business.

This book will prove to be valuable to students of Business Studies whether you are:

>> studying the subject for the first time through your school or college and need a comprehensive and clearly written textbook
>> revising the subject before your examinations and need a study guide to help you with key definitions, techniques and examination advice
>> learning the subject on your own through distance or open learning and need a complete programme of supportive questions, activities and suggested answers to these.

Building on the successful formula of the previous four editions, this fifth edition updates all existing chapters including removing material which is no longer in the syllabus and adds new subject material with additional chapters and new features.

How to use this book

To make your study of Business Studies as rewarding and successful as possible, this Cambridge International endorsed textbook offers the following important features:

Learning objectives
Each chapter starts with an outline of the subject material to be covered and ends with a checklist to confirm what you should have learned and understood.

Organisation
The content is in the same order as the syllabus: chapter titles and chapter section headings match those of the Cambridge IGCSE and O Level Business Studies syllabuses.

Approach
The subject material is written in an informative yet lively way that allows for complete understanding of each topic to be gained.

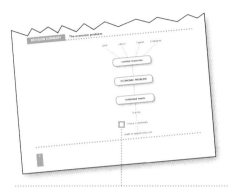

Revision summary

Revision summaries in the form of helpful 'spider diagrams' that highlight key topics and issues.

Revision checklist

This checklist lists the key concepts and topics you have covered in the chapter and the key points you'll need to know for an exam.

Study tips

Tips to help you make key points when answering questions.

International business in focus

Case studies of businesses from around the world and discussion points to help cement understanding.

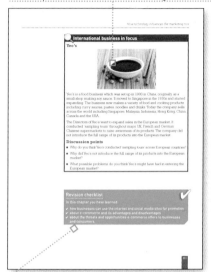

Definitions to learn

Definitions of the key words you need to know are given, with terms highlighted in the text.

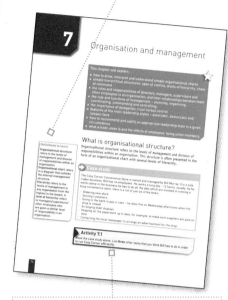

Activity

Numerous activities support your learning and check your progress at each important stage of every chapter.

Key info

Key info boxes provide further explanation of the key concepts you need to know with real world examples.

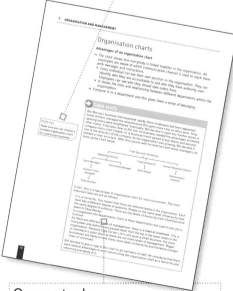

Case study

Case studies based on a range of international businesses/examples put concepts into a real world context to help you understand and think about how they work in practice

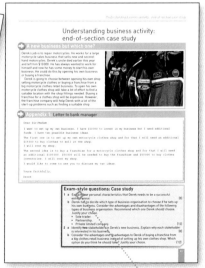

Exam-style questions

Further case study examination-style questions at the end of each group of chapters provide practice for a specific section of the curriculum content.

Chapter review questions

Examination-style questions at the end of each chapter allow you to gain essential practice at answering questions to the required standard.

Exam preparation and technique

Revision

You should be able to perform to the best of your ability if you:

» ensure that you have worked through all of the activities and examination-style questions in this book
» revise thoroughly before the examination – allow plenty of time for this and avoid leaving it until the last minute.

You can also help yourself greatly if you take the following steps.

» Obtain a copy of the syllabus. You should also be able to obtain past examination papers and mark schemes. It is very important that you check the progress of your learning and revision by 'ticking off' each topic against the syllabus content.
» Make sure that you know the number and length of each of the examination papers you will have to sit. The style and nature of the questions often differ between papers so you must be quite clear about the type of questions likely to appear on each paper.

For Cambridge IGCSE® and O Level Business Studies the examination papers are:

	Length	Type of paper	Type of questions
Paper 1	1 hour 30 mins	Data response	Four data response questions based on four different businesses. The questions are structured a) to e)
Paper 2	1 hour 30 mins	Case study	Four structured questions (i.e. a) and b)) all based on a case study

In the examination

Make sure you check the instructions on the question paper, the length of the paper and the number of questions you have to answer. In the case of Cambridge IGCSE® and O Level Business Studies examinations you will have to answer every question as there will be no choice.

Allocate your time sensibly between each question. Every year, good students let themselves down by spending too long on some questions and too little time (or no time at all) on others. You will be expected to spend longer writing an answer to a question worth 12 marks than you would when writing an answer worth 8 marks.

Remember that the most common 'prompt' words are 'identify', 'explain', 'consider' and 'justify'. The following guide should help you.

Key command words you need to know

Define
This is asking you to clearly show the examiner that you know what a term means. A single sentence answer is nearly always sufficient.

Identify

As in 'Identify **two** factors that could influence the price of a product.' Identify means write down, without explanation or discussion, the required number of points.

So the answers to the question above might be:

1 Costs of production.
2 Prices of competitors' products.

Calculate

As in 'Using the figures provided, calculate the break-even level of production.' This means 'using the figures provided, work out the following'.

Explain

As in 'Explain **two** ways in which the hotel could promote its services'.

Here the examiner is asking you to give more detail than just identifying points. Your answer must also be *applied to the business in question – in this case, a hotel*. So, advertising on TV would not be appropriate for one hotel given the high cost of TV time. A better answer would be:

1 The hotel could contact all guests who have stayed at the hotel before by email to give them details of a special offer.
2 The hotel could also use a colourful and effective website to promote its services to customers who book hotel accommodation online.

Consider

As in 'Consider whether the car manufacturer should reduce prices to increase demand.' This is asking you to show advanced skills. The best approach to answer this type of question is to explain the advantages and disadvantages of reducing car prices – using any case material about the business to help you. You should then weigh up these advantages and disadvantages *applied to a car manufacturer* and compare them before making a final conclusion.

Justify

As in 'Recommend to TelCom the best way to expand – taking over a phone manufacturer or a chain of shops selling mobile phones? Justify your answer/ recommendation.'

In questions like this you need to consider both options for expansion, giving advantages and disadvantages for both. Finally, you should weigh up the points for and against each option and come to a final decision based on the most important points. For longer questions also justify why the alternative(s) was rejected.

State

As in 'State two examples of promotion for XYZ company.' This question only requires two examples to be given and no explanation is required.

Outline

As in 'Outline two benefits to Jameel of operating his business as a sole trader.' This is asking you to set out two benefits of operating as a sole trader and how they relate to Jameel and his business.

Finally...

Learning Business Studies should be both rewarding and challenging. We hope that this textbook will help you overcome the challenges of the Cambridge IGCSE® and O Level courses so that you can achieve the success you are seeking. In particular, we want the book to encourage you to develop a real interest in – even a passion for – finding out more of how the world of business really works. Business activity is so crucial to the future wellbeing of us all and it offers great opportunities for all well-motivated students. Success in Cambridge IGCSE® and O Level Business Studies can help you take the first important steps towards playing a leading role in managing and directing business activity in your country. We are confident that this book will fully support you during your course.

Wishing you all the best in your studies,

Karen Borrington

Peter Stimpson

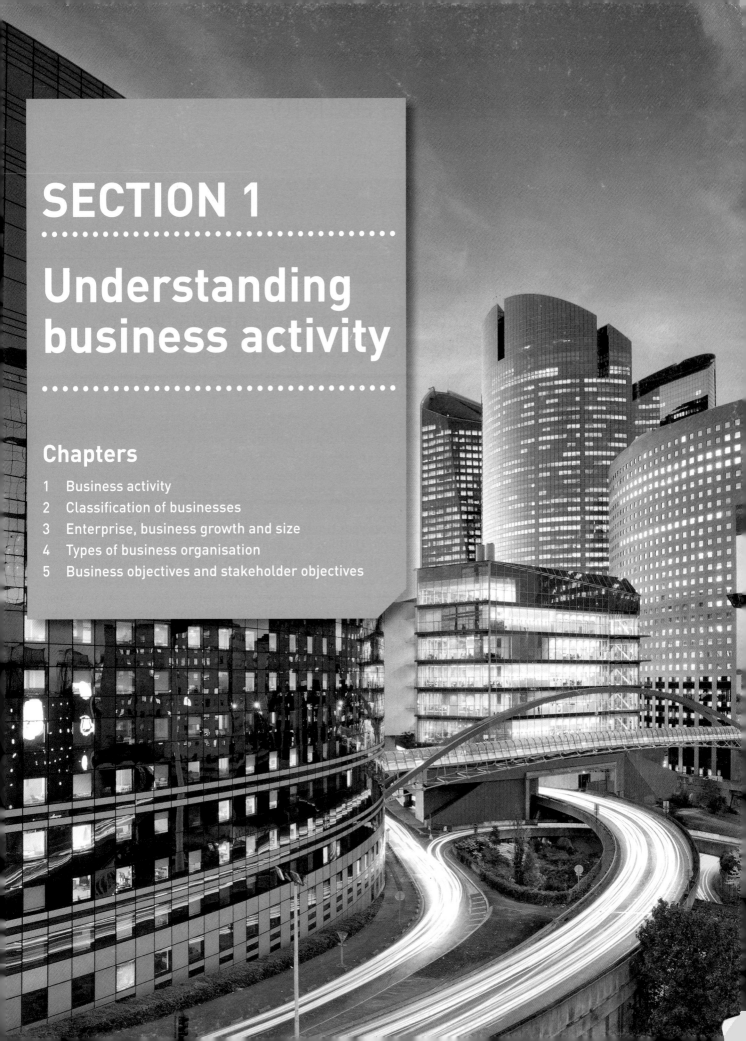

SECTION 1

Understanding business activity

Chapters

1 Business activity
2 Classification of businesses
3 Enterprise, business growth and size
4 Types of business organisation
5 Business objectives and stakeholder objectives

1 Business activity

This chapter will explain:

★ the concepts of needs, wants, scarcity and opportunity cost
★ the importance of specialisation
★ the purpose of business activity
★ the concept of adding value and how added value can be increased.

The economic problem: needs, wants, scarcity and opportunity cost

Activity 1.1

Make lists of:

a your needs – those things you think are necessary for living
b your wants – things you would like to be able to buy and own.

For example, on your needs list you will probably include clean water, and on your wants list you may include a luxury house.

Definitions to learn

A **need** is a good or service essential for living.
A **want** is a good or service which people would like to have, but which is not essential for living. People's wants are unlimited.
The **economic problem** – there exist unlimited wants but limited resources to produce the goods and services to satisfy those wants. This creates scarcity.

What do you notice about your two lists? Probably the really important items are on the **needs** list – water, clothing for warmth and protection, food and some form of housing or shelter. And on your **wants** list? That will be up to you and your interests and tastes, but you could probably have written a very long list indeed.

Do you already own all of the items on your wants list? If you do, then you must be very lucky and very rich! Most people in the world cannot afford to buy everything they want because our wants are unlimited. In many countries, some people cannot afford to buy the things they need and they are likely to be very poor.

Why are there so many wants and needs that we cannot satisfy? Why are millions of people living in poverty in many countries around the world? Most people will answer these questions by saying, 'Because there is not enough money.'

Is the real **economic problem** caused by a shortage of money? An example may help to show you why more money is not the answer to the problem of many people's wants and needs not being satisfied.

Case study

The government of a small country is worried about large numbers of people who cannot afford the basic needs of life. Even those citizens with more money are always complaining that the country is not producing enough of the luxuries that they want to buy. The government decides to try to 'solve' these problems by printing more bank notes, doubling everyone's incomes.

Has the government solved the economic problem of the country? Are there now more goods for the people to buy? More houses? More schools? More cars? Improved standard of living of the population?

The answer to all of these questions is 'No'. Printing more money does not produce more goods and services. It will just lead to prices rising so more goods cannot be afforded – you just pay more for the same amount of goods.

The economic problem – the real cause

The real cause of the shortage or scarcity of goods and services is that there are not enough **factors of production** to make all of the goods and services that the population needs and wants.

There are four factors of production:

» **Land** – this term is used to cover all of the natural resources provided by nature and includes fields and forests, oil, gas, metals and other mineral resources.
» **Labour** – this is the number of people available to make products.
» **Capital** – this is the finance, machinery and equipment needed for the manufacture of goods.
» **Enterprise** – this is the skill and risk-taking ability of the person who brings the other resources or factors of production together to produce a good or service, for example, the owner of a business. These people are called entrepreneurs.

In any one country, and in the world as a whole, these factors of production are limited in supply. As there is never enough land, labour, capital or enterprise to produce all of the needs and unlimited wants of a whole population, there is an economic problem of **scarcity**.

▲ The real cause of the economic problem

Limited resources: the need to choose

We make choices every day. We have to, as we have limited resources but so many wants. We therefore have to decide which wants we will satisfy and which we will not. All choices involve giving something up – this leads to **opportunity cost**. Should I take a bus to school or use the money for a new pen to write clear Business Studies notes? Do I buy a new pair of trainers or spend the money on a new smartphone?

We do not have the resources to satisfy all our wants, so the next best alternative that we give up becomes our opportunity cost. This problem of 'what to give up' exists not only for consumers like us but for governments and businesses too. In making choices we need to consider carefully the opportunity cost to make sure it is not worth more to us than the item we are buying.

Individual	Business	Government

| Holiday or car? | Machine A or Machine B | New road or new school? |

The individual chooses to buy the holiday, so the car becomes the opportunity cost

The company decides to buy Machine A, so Machine B becomes the opportunity cost

The government chooses to build the road so the school becomes the opportunity cost

▲ Examples of opportunity cost

REVISION SUMMARY   The economic problem

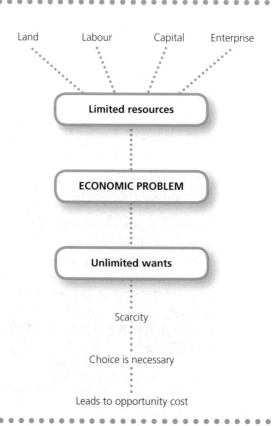

Land   Labour   Capital   Enterprise

Limited resources

ECONOMIC PROBLEM

Unlimited wants

Scarcity

Choice is necessary

Leads to opportunity cost

The importance of specialisation: the best use of limited resources

In all societies the factors of production are in limited supply. It is therefore important to use these resources in the most efficient ways possible. The ways in which these resources are used have changed greatly in the last 250 years. Very few products are now made just by the efforts and skills of one worker. Nearly all workers specialise in particular skills and many businesses specialise in one type of product. **Specialisation** is now very common because:

>> specialised machinery and technologies are now widely available
>> increasing competition means that businesses have to keep costs low
>> most people recognise that higher living standards can result from being specialised.

➡ Case study

This is how Joe Sharma, a carpenter, went about making a table 250 years ago:

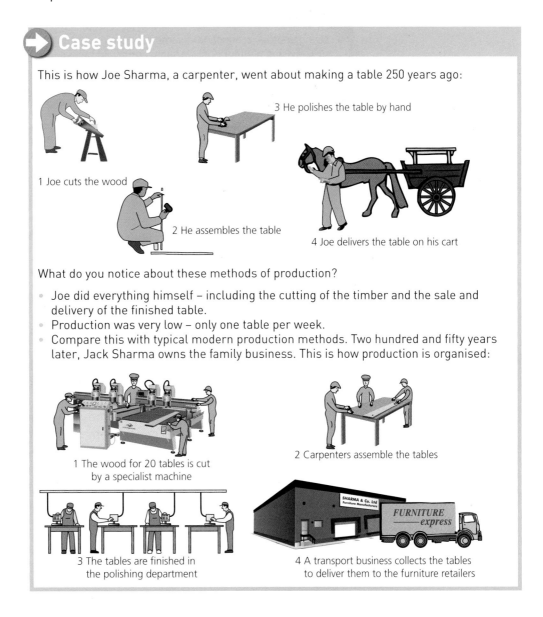

1 Joe cuts the wood

2 He assembles the table

3 He polishes the table by hand

4 Joe delivers the table on his cart

What do you notice about these methods of production?

- Joe did everything himself – including the cutting of the timber and the sale and delivery of the finished table.
- Production was very low – only one table per week.
- Compare this with typical modern production methods. Two hundred and fifty years later, Jack Sharma owns the family business. This is how production is organised:

1 The wood for 20 tables is cut by a specialist machine

2 Carpenters assemble the tables

3 The tables are finished in the polishing department

4 A transport business collects the tables to deliver them to the furniture retailers

Specialisation and the division of labour

Jack Sharma is using the principles of specialisation and **division of labour**. He is dividing up the making of tables into different jobs and making each worker a specialist at just one task. Division of labour has advantages and disadvantages:

Advantages	Disadvantages
• Workers are trained in one task and specialise in this – this increases efficiency and output	• Workers can become bored doing just one job – efficiency might fall
• Less time is wasted moving from one workbench to another	• If one worker is absent and no one else can do the job, production might be stopped
• Quicker and cheaper to train workers as fewer skills need to be taught	

Activity 1.2

a Using another product, for example, bread or clay pots, explain, with simple illustrations, how division of labour or specialisation could be used to make the product.
b Explain the possible advantages/disadvantages of using division of labour (or specialisation of labour) to the business you chose.

The purpose of business activity

We have identified the following issues:

» People have **unlimited** wants.
» The four factors of production – the resources needed to make goods – are in **limited supply**.
» Scarcity results from limited resources and unlimited wants.
» Choice is necessary when resources are scarce. This leads to **opportunity cost**.
» **Specialisation** improves the efficient use of resources.

So far, we have hardly mentioned **businesses** and yet this is the purpose of this book!

Where does business activity fit into the ideas we have already looked at?

The purpose of all businesses is to combine the factors of production to make products which will satisfy people's wants. These products can either be goods – physical items such as cars and shoes which we can touch and see – or they can be services, such as insurance, tourism or banking.

Businesses can be small – just one person, for example – or large. Some businesses employ thousands of people with operations in many different countries. Businesses can be privately owned or owned by the state/government. They can be owned by one person or by thousands of shareholders.

Whatever their size and whoever owns them, all businesses have one thing in common – they combine factors of production to make products which satisfy people's wants.

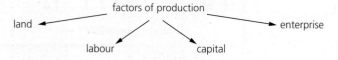

Farms

Factories

Offices

▲ Businesses in all sectors of industry produce goods and services by combining factors of production

What would life be like without business activity? In simple, undeveloped economies, businesses do not exist. Everyone attempts to do everything for themselves – they are self-sufficient. With their own plot of land and by their own efforts, such as hunting, they attempt to survive and produce enough for their own needs. This is a very basic existence and living standards are low.

By a slow process of specialisation, people began to concentrate on what they were best at. They then traded those goods for others made by people who had different skills. In this way, businesses began to be formed, and trade and exchange of goods expanded. In today's world, most people specialise by working in one job for a weekly wage. With this money, they are able to purchase a wide range of goods and services produced by many different businesses – specialising in different products.

Business activity therefore:

» **combines scarce factors** of production to produce goods and services
» **produces goods and services** which are needed to satisfy the needs and wants of the population
» **employs people** as workers and pays them wages to allow them to consume products made by other people.

Added value

This is a very important idea. All businesses attempt to **add value**. If value is not added to the materials and components that a business buys in, then:

» other costs cannot be paid for
» no profit will be made.

Definitions to learn

Added value is the difference between the selling price of a product and the cost of bought-in materials and components.

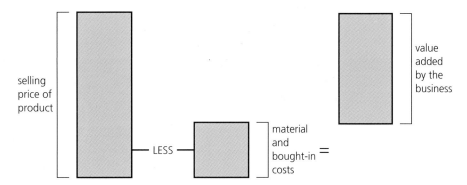

selling price of product — LESS — material and bought-in costs = value added by the business

▲ Diagram showing value added

Study tips

Adding value is not easy for many businesses – if it was, every business would be very successful! When some businesses try to increase added value it can lead to serious disadvantages. For example, just increasing the price of the product can lead to lower sales and, perhaps, lower profit.

Study tips

You should take every chance to apply your answers to the business in the question. A jewellery shop is likely to add value in different ways to a hotel business or a soft drinks manufacturer.

Example:

» The selling price of a newly built house is $100 000.
» The value of the bought-in bricks, cement, wood and other materials was $15 000.
» The added value of the building firm was $85 000. This is not all profit – out of this the builder must pay wages and other costs too.

Why is added value important?

Added value is important because sales revenue is greater than the cost of materials bought in by the business. This means the business:

» can pay other costs such as labour costs, management expenses and costs including advertising and power
» may be able to make a profit if these other costs come to a total that is less than the added value.

How could a business increase added value?

There are two main ways in which a business can try to increase its added value:

a Increase selling price but keep the cost of materials the same. This might be possible if the business tries to create a higher quality image for its product or service. If consumers are convinced by this then they might be prepared to pay higher prices and buy the same quantity as before the price rise. A jewellery shop could employ very experienced and knowledgeable sales staff, decorate the shop to look luxurious and use high-quality packaging. Note though: other costs might increase when trying to create this quality image.

b Reduce the cost of materials but keep the price the same. A building firm could use cheaper wood, bricks and other materials when constructing a home or shop. If the price charged to customers stays the same then a higher added value will be made. Note though: lower priced materials might reduce the quality of the product. Will customers be prepared to pay the same price for a product that they believe is of lower quality?

REVISION SUMMARY

Adding value

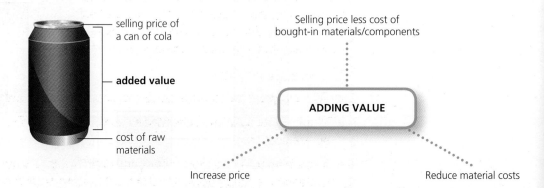

selling price of a can of cola

added value

cost of raw materials

Selling price less cost of bought-in materials/components

ADDING VALUE

Increase price

Reduce material costs

Case study: Rakesh's bakery

Rakesh owns a small bakery selling bread, cakes and biscuits. His business is just making enough money to survive. His wife, Neeta, had the idea of serving customers tea and coffee at two small tables that could be fitted into the bakery shop. 'Customers will pay more for each cake and biscuit if we sell them with tea or coffee – just like a little café.' Rakesh bought some second-hand café equipment and

furniture and tried what Neeta had suggested. She was right! Some of his customers not only bought teas and coffees but they paid higher prices for the cakes and biscuits they bought as they were served them on a plate!

Rakesh had increased the value added to the flour, sugar and butter he used to make these cakes and biscuits.

Activity 1.3

Refer to the case study above.

a If the best-selling cake in this bakery uses 30 cents' worth of flour, sugar and butter and Rakesh sells each one for $1, calculate the value added.
b If customers are prepared to pay $1.50 when this cake is served on a plate at a table within the bakery, what is the new value added per cake?
c Does the opening of the small café mean that Rakesh must have increased his weekly profit? Explain your answer.

International business in focus

Division of labour at McDonald's

The cooking of food in all McDonald's restaurants is broken down into small, repetitive tasks. These include serving customers, pouring drinks, cooking French fries and cooking burgers. These separate tasks allow workers to become very efficient and skilled in them. All workers are given much training in the tasks that they will become skilled at.

The speed and efficiency of McDonald's workers means that customers are served very quickly with freshly cooked food. Costs are kept very low and this helps to keep prices low.

McDonald's and other fast-food restaurants often make great efforts to reduce the high labour turnover in this industry; this means they are trying to reduce the high number of workers that leave the industry each year.

Discussion points

● Why do you think a large business such as McDonald's uses specialisation?

● Think about as many advantages as you can to McDonald's of using specialisation.

● If you owned a fast-food restaurant, consider **two** ways in which you could increase the value added to the food bought in by the restaurant.

Exam-style questions: Short answer and data response

1 Gowri plans to start up her own business using her savings. She wants to produce fashion clothes for women. She is a very good clothes designer but she does not like stitching clothes together. Two friends have offered to help Gowri. Abha is an experienced material or fabric cutter – she can cut lengths of material or fabric for clothes with very little wastage. Aditi is quick at sewing fabric together.

   a Define 'business'. [2]

   b Identify **two** factors of production that Gowri will need for her new business. [2]

   c Outline **two** possible opportunity costs that Gowri may have from her decision to start her own business. [4]

   d Explain **one** advantage and **one** disadvantage to Gowri's business of using division of labour in making clothes. [6]

   e Do you think that Gowri's business will be able to sell all of the clothes that it makes? Justify your answer. [6]

2 Mohammed owns a bakery. He makes bread and cakes. He employs three workers who help him mix the dough for the bread and cakes, put the dough into tins, bake the bread and cakes, and serve customers. Mohammed has calculated that the 'added value' of his business is low. His customers complain when he tries to increase his prices. 'We can buy the same bread and cakes at lower prices,' they tell him.

   a Define 'added value'. [2]

   b Identify the opportunity cost to Mohammed of buying a new oven. [2]

   c Outline **two** benefits to Mohammed's business of all of his workers being able to do all of the jobs in the bakery. [4]

   d Explain **two** ways in which Mohammed could increase the value added of his bakery business. [6]

   e A friend told Mohammed, 'Your business would be more successful if you only served in the shop and let your workers make the bread and cakes.' Do you agree? Justify your answer. [6]

Revision checklist

In this chapter you have learned:

✔ the difference between wants and needs
✔ why scarcity of resources results in choices and opportunity cost
✔ why specialisation is important
✔ the purpose and nature of business activity
✔ how businesses can try to increase added value.

NOW – test your understanding with the revision questions in the Student etextbook and the Workbook.

2 Classification of businesses

This chapter will explain:

★ the differences between primary, secondary and tertiary production
★ the reasons for the changing importance of business classification, for example, in developed and developing economies
★ the differences between public sector and private sector business enterprises in a mixed economy.

Stages of economic activity

As you read this book you are probably sitting at a desk or table. Most tables are made of wood. How many different types of businesses might have been involved in converting the wood into a finished table ready to be sold to a final consumer? What stages of production has the wood passed through to arrive at the finished table?

The diagram below shows the most likely stages in the production and sale of a wooden table.

stage	activity	business involved
primary		woodcutter
secondary		furniture maker
tertiary		retailer

▲ The stages involved in making and selling a wooden table

Definitions to learn

The **primary sector** of industry extracts and uses the natural resources of Earth to produce raw materials used by other businesses.

You will notice that there are three main stages from the cutting down of the timber to the sale of the completed table. These stages are typical of nearly all production and they are called the levels of economic – or business – activity.

Stage 1 is called the primary stage of production. This stage involves the Earth's natural resources. Activities in the **primary sector** of industry include farming, fishing, forestry and the extraction of natural materials, such as oil and copper ore.

Stage 2 is called the secondary stage of production. This stage involves taking the materials and resources provided by the primary sector and converting them into manufactured or processed goods. Activities in the **secondary sector** of industry include building and construction, aircraft and car manufacturing, computer assembly, bread baking.

▲ Examples of activities in the different sectors of industry: rice farming in Vietnam, clothes production in China and retailing in Kenya

Stage 3 is called the tertiary stage of production. This stage involves providing services to both consumers and other businesses. Activities in the **tertiary sector** of industry include transport, banking, retail, insurance, hotels and hairdressing.

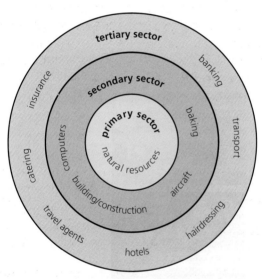

▲ The three types of business activity

Activity 2.1

Copy this table. Indicate with a tick which sector of industry each business is in.

Business	Primary	Secondary	Tertiary
Insurance			✓
Forestry	✓		
Coal mining	✓		
Computer assembly		✓	
Travel agent			✓
Bakery		✓	
Car showroom			✓

Relative importance of economic sectors

Which sector of industry is most important in your country? This depends on what is meant by 'important'. Usually the three sectors of the economy are compared by:

» percentage of the country's total number of workers employed in each sector

or

» value of output of goods and services and the proportion this is of total national output.

In some countries, primary industries such as farming and mining employ many more people than manufacturing or service industries. These tend to be countries – often called developing countries – where manufacturing industry has only recently been established. As most people still live in rural areas with low incomes, there is little demand for services such as transport, hotels and insurance. The levels of both employment and output in the primary sector in these countries are likely to be higher than in the other two sectors.

In countries which started up manufacturing industries many years ago, the secondary and tertiary sectors are likely to employ many more workers than the primary sector. The level of output in the primary sector is often small compared to the other two sectors. In economically developed countries, it is now common to find that many manufactured goods are bought in from other countries. Most of the workers will be employed in the service sector. The output of the tertiary sector is often higher than the other two sectors combined. Such countries are often called the most developed countries.

 Case study: Comparing the three economic sectors – India and Papua New Guinea

The relative importance of the three economic sectors in India is very different to that in Papua New Guinea. India does not have large reserves of primary products (natural resources), whereas Papua New Guinea is rich in mineral deposits including copper, gold and oil and also has extensive forests covering much of the country producing timber products. Extracting these valuable resources makes a huge contribution to the economy of Papua New Guinea.

India's textile, steel and car manufacturing industries are rapidly growing, but the secondary sector in Papua New Guinea is small – palm oil processing, plywood production and wood chip production are the most important secondary industries. If Papua New Guinea developed a furniture industry making tables and chairs from the timber extracted from its forests, secondary production could increase.

The tertiary sector is expanding in both countries – tourism is starting to gain importance in Papua New Guinea but it is still in its early stages of development and its main service industries are linked to the transport and export of its minerals. Providing IT services to businesses all over the world is India's largest service industry.

% of total national output 2017	Primary	Secondary	Tertiary
Papua New Guinea	35	13	52
India	17	26	57

Activity 2.2

Refer to the case study above.

a Explain what 'tertiary production' means by using examples from the case study.

b Explain **two** reasons why the primary sector is relatively more important to Papua New Guinea than to India.

c In 2017, it was estimated that 47 per cent of Indians worked in the primary sector – mainly in agriculture. Why was this sector the least important of the three in terms of output?

d Discuss the likely impact on Papua New Guinea if its copper and gold mines become exhausted (the copper and gold runs out!).

Key info

South Korea is one of the best examples of a country which has experienced changes in the importance of industrial sectors. In the 1950s the economy was dependent on agriculture. By 2017 agriculture and other primary industries accounted for just 4% of GDP, with manufacturing (secondary) responsible for 42% of output. Service industries (tertiary) produced 54% of total output.

Key info

Mexico now has nearly 25 per cent of its labour force employed in manufacturing and it is making a major contribution to the changing economy of the country. Its secondary sector produces over a third of its $2.2 trillion GDP. It is now the USA's second-largest export market and third-largest source of imports. The main secondary industry is car manufacturing, as it cannot only export to the USA but also to Asia, Australia and New Zealand from ports on the Pacific coast. However, aerospace manufacturing is growing at 20 per cent per year, it is the fifth-largest exporter of medical devices in the world, and its domestic appliances such as refrigerators, washers and TVs make up half of all retail sales of appliances sold in the USA.

Changes in sector importance

In the UK and other developed economies there has been a decline in the importance of manufacturing industry – or the secondary sector – since the 1970s. The tertiary sector in the UK now employs well over 75 per cent of all workers. Many workers who lost jobs as factories closed have found it difficult to obtain work in the service industries. The decline in the manufacturing or secondary sector of industry is called **de-industrialisation**.

In China and India, the relative importance of the secondary sector has increased since the 1980s, compared to the primary sector. However, in both countries, many of the tertiary sector industries are now expanding more rapidly than those in both the primary and secondary sectors. There are several reasons for changes in the relative importance of the three sectors over time:

» Sources of some primary products, such as timber, oil and gas, become depleted. This has been true for Somalia with the cutting down of most of its forests.
» Most developed economies are losing competitiveness in manufacturing to newly industrialised countries such as Brazil, India and China.
» As a country's total wealth increases and living standards rise, consumers tend to spend a higher proportion of their incomes on services such as travel and restaurants than on manufactured products produced from primary products.

Case study: Bangladesh – the importance of economic sectors over time

In 1970, Bangladesh had an economy largely based on agriculture. A high proportion of the population worked in farming, either to produce crops for their own consumption or to sell in local markets. Secondary manufacturing activities were not very important and the tertiary sector was also small as incomes were very low and people had little spare cash to spend on 'services'.

By 2017, Bangladesh had undergone significant changes. Although 40 per cent of the workforce still works in agriculture, primary production of goods such as jute, tobacco and food has fallen in relative terms. Manufacturing industries – mainly food processing and clothing – have expanded rapidly. Tertiary services such as telecommunications, transport and finance now contribute approximately half of total national output.

Economic sectors in Bangladesh – World Bank estimates of % share of GDP

	Primary	Secondary	Tertiary
1970	53	15	32
2017	15	29	56

Activity 2.3

Refer to the case study above.

a Explain **two** possible reasons why the relative importance of primary output has fallen.
b Would workers who formerly worked in agriculture find it easy to obtain jobs in the secondary or tertiary sectors of industry? Explain your answer.
c What do you expect to happen to the relative importance of tertiary industries if incomes continue to rise in Bangladesh? Explain your answer.

Mixed economy

Nearly every country in the world has a **mixed economy** with private sector and a public sector:

» Private sector – businesses not owned by the government. These businesses will make their own decisions about what to produce, how it should be produced and what price should be charged for it. Most businesses in the private sector will aim to make a profit. Even so, there are likely to be some government controls over these decisions and these are explained in later chapters in this book.

» Public sector – government (or state) owned and controlled businesses and organisations. The government, or other public sector authority, makes decisions about what to produce and how much to charge consumers. Some goods and services are provided free of charge to the consumer, such as state health and education services. The money for these comes not from the user but from the taxpayer. Objectives of private sector and public sector businesses are often different (see Chapter 4).

Which business activities are usually in the public sector?

In many countries the government controls the following important industries or activities:

» health
» education
» defence

» public transport
» water supply
» electricity supply.

> **Activity 2.4**
>
> For each of the examples of key industries or activities listed above, suggest three possible reasons why the government of a country might decide to own and control that industry or service.

> **Activity 2.5**
>
> Find out whether, in your own country, the government owns and controls the following businesses:
>
> a railway system
> b local bus services
> c water supply
>
> d electricity supply
> e TV and radio stations
> f hospitals.

Mixed economies – recent changes

In recent years, many governments have changed the balance between the private sector and the public sector in their economies. They have done this by selling some public sector businesses – owned and controlled by government – to private sector businesses. This is called privatisation. In many European and Asian countries the water supply, electricity supply and public transport systems have been privatised.

Study tips

The advantages and disadvantages of the private sector are useful to remember.

Why have governments done this? It is often claimed that private sector businesses are more efficient than public sector businesses. This might be because their main objective is profit and therefore costs must be controlled. Also, private sector owners might invest more **capital** in the business than the government can afford. Competition between private sector businesses can help to improve product quality.

However, a business in the private sector might make more workers unemployed than a public sector business in order to cut costs. A private sector business is also less likely to focus on social objectives.

Changes in the balance between the private sector and the public sector are likely to continue in many mixed economies.

Study tips

Do not confuse 'privatisation' with 'converting a sole trader into a private limited company'. Sole traders and private limited companies are both examples of private sector businesses (see Chapter 4).

> ### Activity 2.6
>
> Your government is considering the privatisation of your country's postal service. You decide to write to the government minister in charge, explaining your views on this matter and stating your opinion. Your letter should contain:
>
> - an explanation of the difference between private sector businesses and public sector businesses
> - the possible benefits of the postal service being in the private sector
> - the possible disadvantages of the postal service being in the private sector
> - your recommendation to the minister on whether to keep the postal service in the public sector or not.

REVISION SUMMARY   Sectors of industry

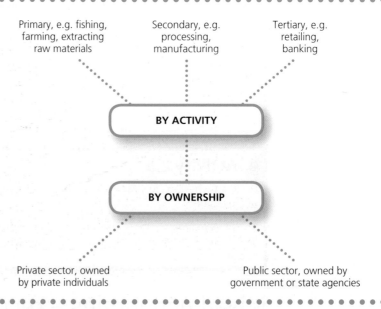

Primary, e.g. fishing, farming, extracting raw materials

Secondary, e.g. processing, manufacturing

Tertiary, e.g. retailing, banking

BY ACTIVITY

BY OWNERSHIP

Private sector, owned by private individuals

Public sector, owned by government or state agencies

International business in focus

Tourism in Mauritius

Mauritius is a small island in the Indian Ocean with a land area of just 2000 km². The Mauritian economy is dominated by the tertiary sector. In 2017, tourism, finance and other services accounted for 74 per cent of total national output (gross domestic product). In contrast, the secondary sector accounted for 22 per cent and primary industries – mainly sugar production – just 4 per cent. The government is planning for 2 million foreign visitors and the number of tourists is increasing by 9 per cent per year. These tourists spend a great deal of money on food, drink, travel and holiday gifts.

Air Mauritius is one of the businesses that has benefited greatly from the expansion of tourism in the country. The airline is partly owned by private owners and the Mauritian Government. It has won the 'Indian Ocean's Leading Airline' prize ten times in recent years.

Air Mauritius not only has an extensive network of air routes but it also offers services to other airlines operating in the region and owns holiday companies such as Mauritian Holidays UK. There are hundreds of hotels and guesthouses in Mauritius and these employ many local workers. Some of the largest hotel groups in the world operate in Mauritius, such as Radisson and Le Meridien.

Discussion points

- Why do you think the primary sector of the Mauritian economy is relatively small?

- Explain **three** ways in which tertiary sector industries contribute to the Mauritian economy.

- Do you think that increasing numbers of tourists will bring only benefits to Mauritius?

- Why do you think the Mauritian Government still owns a part of Air Mauritius?

Exam-style questions: Short answer and data response

1 Ade's Engineering Company (AEC) makes parts for cars and trucks. These are sold to car manufacturers in many countries. The parts include metal brake components and rubber seals to fit around windows. AEC operates in Country X, which, until a few years ago, had an economy dominated by agriculture and coal mining. Over the last 20 years the relative importance of the primary sector has declined. To be successful AEC requires natural resources to make car parts and services provided by other businesses. Consumer incomes are rising rapidly in Country X.

   a Define 'primary sector'. [2]

   b Identify **two** examples of services that a business such as AEC requires. [2]

   c Outline **two** reasons why a business such as AEC could not be successful without other firms providing natural resources. [4]

   d Explain **two** likely reasons why the relative importance of the primary sector of Country X's economy has declined. [6]

   e A government minister in Country X recently said: 'The secondary sector of industry will always be more important than the tertiary sector to our economy.' Do you agree with this view? Justify your answer. [6]

2 The government of Country Y owns and controls many businesses. 'The public sector always produces goods and services more efficiently than privately owned businesses,' a government minister recently said. Other ministers disagree and want to privatise many state-owned businesses. The private sector businesses in Country Y produce 55 per cent of total output – mainly in services such as transport, tourism and finance. The secondary sector of industry produces 35 per cent of total output.

   a Define 'public sector'. [2]

   b Identify **two** industries in the secondary sector. [2]

   c Outline **two** reasons why the tertiary sector of industry is becoming more important in most economies. [4]

   d Explain **two** possible reasons why some ministers want to privatise some businesses in the public sector. [6]

   e Do you agree with the government minister's view that: 'The public sector always produces goods and services more efficiently than privately owned businesses'? Justify your answer. [6]

Revision checklist

In this chapter you have learned:

✔ the differences between the three sectors of economic/business activity
✔ the reasons why these sectors vary in importance between countries
✔ the reasons why these sectors vary in importance over time
✔ the differences between the private sector and public sector in mixed economies.

NOW – test your understanding with the revision questions in the Student etextbook and the Workbook.

3 Enterprise, business growth and size

> **This chapter will explain:**
>
> ★ the benefits and drawbacks of being an entrepreneur
> ★ the key characteristics of successful entrepreneurs
> ★ the contents of a business plan and how plans assist entrepreneurs
> ★ why and how governments support business start-ups
> ★ the methods of measuring business size
> ★ the limitations of the methods of measuring business size
> ★ why the owners of a business may want to expand the business
> ★ different ways in which businesses can grow
> ★ the problems linked to business growth and how they might be overcome
> ★ why some businesses remain small
> ★ the causes of business failure
> ★ why new businesses are at a greater risk of failing.

Enterprise and entrepreneurship

What will you do when you leave school or college? Maybe you will go to university or get a job. Some of you may decide to take the risk of setting up your own business – this could be full- or part-time. If you do decide to do this then you will become an **entrepreneur**!

What are the benefits – and possible disadvantages – of starting up your own business?

Benefits of being an entrepreneur	Disadvantages of being an entrepreneur
• independence – able to choose how to use time and money	• risk – many new entrepreneurs' businesses fail, especially if there is poor planning
• able to put own ideas into practice	• capital – entrepreneurs have to put their own money into the business and, possibly, find other sources of capital
• may become famous and successful if the business grows	• lack of knowledge and experience in starting and operating a business
• may be profitable and the income might be higher than working as an employee for another business	• opportunity cost – lost income from not being an employee of another business
• able to make use of personal interests and skills	

For many successful entrepreneurs, starting up their own business has led to great wealth and fame. How many of these business leaders have you heard of? They all started out as entrepreneurs with their own business idea.

Entrepreneur	Nationality	Main business interests
Richard Branson	UK	Virgin group of companies including airline, mobile phone and train services
Dhirubhai Ambani	India	Reliance group of companies including chemicals, IT and retailing
Pan Shiyi	China	Property
Carlos Slim	Mexico	Telecommunications
Mark Zuckerberg	US	Social networking site Facebook
Jerry Wang	Taiwan/US	Yahoo
Vera Wang	US	Fashion designer

▲ Mark Zuckerberg   ▲ Sir Richard Branson   ▲ Vera Wang   ▲ Jerry Wang

Case study: 'Believe in Your Ideas!' – an entrepreneur's success story

Justina Kavale is a young entrepreneur who has found a new passion in soaps and cosmetics and turned it into a success story. She recently started a small business in Namibia that will focus on manufacturing soaps, detergents and cosmetics. Running her business part-time, Justina hopes to be able to eventually focus on growing her business and leaving her regular nine-to-five job. Her dream is to become a full-time entrepreneur and she is on her way to business success!

'I wanted to offer a service or product that helps in meeting a basic need. I also wanted to be unique in a way, so I avoided areas like catering, décor, entertainment, etc. I really aspired to create a business where I focus on making my own product and not buying and re-selling. Eventually I want to be able to offer employment opportunities to others and make a difference in our economy.

'I just think the time has come to have Namibian-made products as I think we heavily rely on imports and have very few products made locally. I thought soaps and cosmetics have not really been explored in Namibia as I know of less than four companies that do soaps in Namibia. It is a market not really explored as almost all big retail shops have soaps from other countries.'

Source: https://africanentrepreneurshipaward.com/entrepreneur-success-story-in-namibia

Characteristics of successful entrepreneurs

Would everyone make a good entrepreneur? Probably not – some people do not like risk or working independently – they might prefer to be an employee of a large business instead.

Characteristics of successful entrepreneurs	Reasons why important
Hard working	Long hours and short holidays are typical for many entrepreneurs to make their business successful
Risk taker	Making decisions to produce goods or services that people might buy is potentially risky
Creative	A new business needs new ideas – about products, services, ways of attracting customers – to make it different from existing firms
Optimistic	Looking forward to a better future is essential – if you think only of failure, you will fail!
Self-confident	Being self-confident is necessary to convince other people of your skills and to convince banks, other lenders and customers that your business is going to be successful
Innovative	Being able to put new ideas into practice in interesting and different ways is also important
Independent	Entrepreneurs will often have to work on their own before they can afford to employ others. Entrepreneurs must be well-motivated and be able to work without any help
Effective communicator	Talking clearly and confidently to banks, other lenders, customers and government agencies about the new business will raise the profile of the new business

REVISION SUMMARY   **Entrepreneurs**

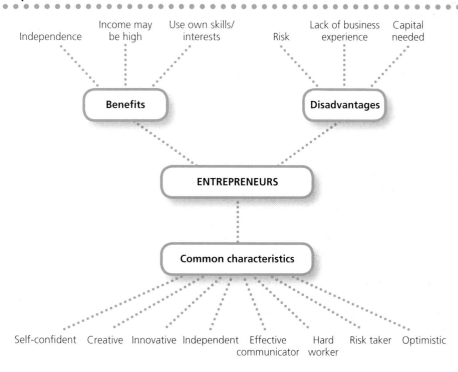

Definitions to learn

A **business plan** is a document containing the business objectives and important details about the operations, finance and owners of the new business.

Contents of a business plan and how business plans assist entrepreneurs

A bank will almost certainly ask an entrepreneur for a **business plan** before agreeing to a loan or overdraft to help finance the new business.

By completing a business plan (most banks are able to give business owners a ready-printed form to fill out) the entrepreneur is forced to think ahead and plan carefully for the first few years. The entrepreneur will have to consider the following:

» What products or services do I intend to provide and which consumers am I 'aiming at'?
» What will be my main costs and will enough products be sold to pay for them?
» Where will the firm be located?
» What machinery and how many people will be required in the business?

Every business plan might be different, but generally business plans contain similar headings. The contents of a business plan will usually include the following:

1 **Description of the business**
   Provides a brief history and summary of the business, and the objectives of the business.
2 **Products and services**
   Describes what the business sells or delivers, and strategy for continuing or developing products/services in the future to remain competitive and grow the business. This section may also include full details of the product and how it is to be manufactured and distributed.
3 **The market**
   Describes the market the business is targeting. The description should include:
   • total market size
   • predicted market growth
   • target market
   • analysis of competitors
   • predicted changes in the market in the future
   • forecast sales revenue from the product.
   There should also be a marketing strategy (which is considered in Chapter 17). Market research data should also be included.
4 **Business location and how products will reach customers**
   Describes the physical location if applicable, internet sales or mail order. Also describes how the firm delivers products and services to customers.
5 **Organisation structure and management**
   Describes the organisational structure, management and details of employees required. It usually includes the number and level of skills required for the employees.
6 **Financial information**
   Includes:
   • projected future financial accounting statements for several years or more into the future; these should include income statements and statements of financial position

- sources of capital, for example, owners' capital, revenue, bank loans and any other funding sources
- predicted costs – fixed costs and variable costs
- forecast cash flow and working capital
- projections of profitability and liquidity ratios.

7 Business strategy

Explains how the business intends to satisfy customer needs and gain brand loyalty. A summary should be included to bring together all the points from above that should demonstrate the business will be successful.

Without this detailed plan, the bank will be reluctant to lend money to the business. This is because the owners of the new business cannot show that they have thought seriously about the future and planned for the challenges that they will certainly meet. Even with a detailed business plan, the bank might not offer a loan if the bank manager believes that the plan is not well completed (for example, poorly forecasted cash flow).

An example of a business plan is shown on page 24. It was completed by two entrepreneurs planning to open a takeaway pizza restaurant.

REVISION SUMMARY **Business plans**

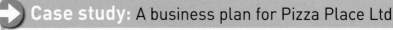

Case study: A business plan for Pizza Place Ltd

Name of business	Pizza Place Ltd
Type of organisation	Private limited company
Business aim	To provide a high-class takeaway pizza service including home delivery
Product	High-quality home-cooked pizzas
Price	Average price of $8 with $2 delivery charge
Market aimed for	Young people and families
Market research undertaken and the results	Research in the area conducted using questionnaires
	Also, research into national trends in takeaway sales and local competitors
	Results of all research in the appendix to this plan
Human Resources plan	The two business owners to be the only workers to be employed initially
Details of business owners	Peter Yang – chef of 15 years' experience
	Sabrina Hsui – deputy manager of a restaurant for three years
Production details and business costs	Main suppliers – P&P Wholesalers
	Fixed costs of business – $50 000 per year
	Variable costs – approximately $2 per unit sold
Location of business	Site in shopping street (Brunei Avenue) just away from the town centre
	Leasehold site (10 years)
Main equipment required	Second-hand kitchen equipment – $6000
	Second-hand motorbike – $3000
Forecast profit	See financial appendix to this plan
	Summary: In the first year of operations the total costs are forecast to be $75 000 with revenue of $105 000
	Predicted profit = $30 000
	Level of output to break even – 10 000 units per year
Cash flow	See financial appendix to this plan
	Due to the high set-up and promotion costs there will be negative cash flow in the first year
Finance	$10 000 invested by each of the owners
	Request to bank for a further $15 000 plus an overdraft arrangement of $6000 per month

Activity 3.1

Read the business plan for Pizza Place Ltd above. Explain why, if you were a bank manager reading this plan, each of the following would be important to you before you gave the entrepreneurs a loan:

- market research results
- experience of business owners
- forecast profit.

> ### Activity 3.2
> Draw up another business plan. It should be based on your own idea for a business that is operated within your school or college (for example, a stationery shop, confectionery store or cake shop).

> ### Activity 3.3
> Research the background and business activities of **two** well-known entrepreneurs in your own country. Identify the personal characteristics that you believe each entrepreneur has which have helped them to succeed. Write a brief report on each one and be prepared to present your reports to the rest of your class.

Why governments support business start-ups

Most governments offer support to entrepreneurs. This encourages them to set up new businesses. There are several reasons why this support is given:

>> To reduce unemployment – new businesses will often create jobs to help reduce unemployment.
>> To increase competition – new businesses give consumers more choice and compete with already established businesses.
>> To increase output – the economy benefits from increased output of goods and services.
>> To benefit society – entrepreneurs may create social enterprises which offer benefits to society other than jobs and profit (for example, supporting disadvantaged groups in society).
>> Can grow further – all large businesses were small once! By supporting today's new firms the government may be helping some firms that grow to become very large and important in the future.

How governments support business start-ups

Business start-ups need:	Governments often give support by:
Business idea and help	Organising training for entrepreneurs that gives advice, and support sessions offered by experienced business people
Premises	'Enterprise zones', which provide low-cost premises to start-up businesses
Finance	Loans for small businesses at low interest rates
	Grants, if businesses start up in depressed areas of high unemployment
Labour	Grants to small businesses to train employees and help increase their productivity
Research	Encouraging universities to make their research facilities available to new business entrepreneurs

Methods of measuring business size and limitations of these methods

Businesses can vary greatly in terms of size. On the one hand, firms can be owned and run by a single individual. At the other extreme, some businesses employ hundreds of thousands of workers all over the world. Some firms produce output worth hundreds of dollars a year, while the biggest businesses sell goods valued at billions of dollars each year.

Who would find it useful to compare the size of businesses?

» Investors – before deciding which business to put their savings into.
» Governments – often there are different tax rates for small and large businesses.
» Competitors – to compare their size and importance with other firms.
» Workers – to have some idea of how many people they might be working with.
» Banks – to see how important a loan to the business is compared to its overall size.

Business size can be measured in a number of ways. The most common are:

» number of people employed
» value of output
» value of sales
» value of **capital employed**.

They each have advantages and limitations.

> **Definitions to learn**
>
> **Capital employed** is the total value of capital used in the business.

Number of people employed

This method is easy to calculate and compare with other businesses.

Limitations: Some firms use production methods which employ very few people but produce high output levels. This is true for automated factories which use the latest computer-controlled equipment. These firms are called capital-intensive firms – they use a great deal of capital (high-cost) equipment to produce their output. Therefore, a company with high output levels could employ fewer people than a business which produced less output. Another problem is: should two part-time workers, who work half of a working week each, be counted as one employee – or two?

Value of output

Calculating the value of output is a common way of comparing business size in the same industry – especially in manufacturing industries.

Limitations: A high level of output does not mean that a business is large when using the other methods of measurement. A firm employing few people might produce several very expensive computers each year. This might give higher output figures than a firm selling cheaper products but employing more workers. The value of output in any time period might not be the same as the value of sales if some goods are not sold.

Value of sales

This is often used when comparing the size of retailing businesses – especially retailers selling similar products (for example, food supermarkets).

Limitations: It could be misleading to use this measure when comparing the size of businesses that sell very different products (for example, a market stall selling sweets and a retailer of luxury handbags or perfumes).

Value of capital employed

This means the total value of capital invested into the business.

Limitations: This has a similar problem to that of the 'number of people employed' measure. A company employing many workers may use labour-intensive methods of production. These give low output levels and use little capital equipment.

There is no perfect way of comparing the size of businesses. It is quite common to use more than one method and to compare the results obtained.

▲ A capital-intensive and a labour-intensive business

Activity 3.4: Comparing business size

You are employed by Company A, which makes motorcycles. You have been asked to write a brief report to the Managing Director comparing the size of your company with three others in the same industry. Use the following information in your report. State the benefits and drawbacks of each of the ways of comparing business size.

	Workers employed	Capital employed ($m)	Value of output ($m)
Company A	20 000	50	100
Company B	5000	150	300
Company C	3000	60	160
Company D	15 000	180	150

REVISION SUMMARY **Comparing business size**

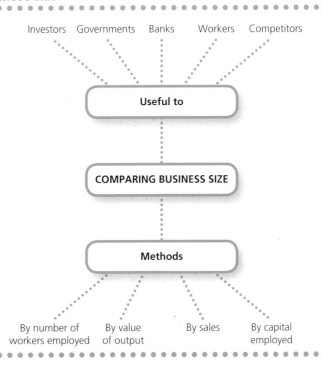

Investors   Governments   Banks   Workers   Competitors

Useful to

COMPARING BUSINESS SIZE

Methods

By number of workers employed   By value of output   By sales   By capital employed

Why the owners of a business may want to expand the business

The owners of businesses often want their business to expand. What advantages will a business and its owners gain from expansion? Here are some likely benefits:

>> The possibility of higher profits for the owners.
>> More status and prestige for the owners and managers – higher salaries are often paid to managers who control bigger businesses.
>> Lower average costs (explained in Chapter 19, page 231, *Economies of scale*).
>> Larger share of its market – the proportion of total market sales it makes is greater. This gives a business more influence when dealing with suppliers and distributors, and consumers are often attracted to the 'big names' in an industry.

Different ways in which businesses can grow

Businesses can expand in two main ways:

>> By **internal growth**, for example, a restaurant owner could open other restaurants in other towns – this growth is often paid for by profits from the existing business. This type of growth is often quite slow but easier to manage than external growth.
>> By **external growth**, involving a **takeover** or a **merger** with another business.

Three examples of external growth are shown below.

>> Horizontal merger (or **horizontal integration**) – when one firm merges with or takes over another one in the same industry at the same stage of production.

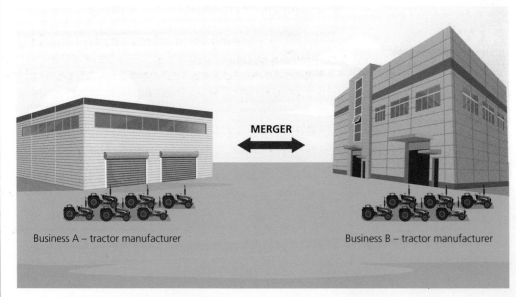

Business A – tractor manufacturer   Business B – tractor manufacturer

▲ An example of horizontal integration

>> Vertical merger (or **vertical integration**) – when one business merges with or takes over another one in the same industry but at a different stage of production. Vertical integration can be *forward* – when a business integrates with another business which is at a later stage of production (closer to the consumer) – or *backward* – when a business integrates with another business at an earlier stage of production (closer to the raw material supplies, in the case of a manufacturing business).

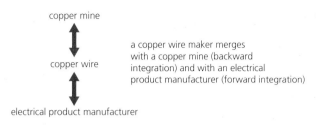

▲ Backward and forward integration

» Conglomerate merger (or **conglomerate integration**) – when one business merges with or takes over a business in a completely different industry. This is also known as **diversification**.

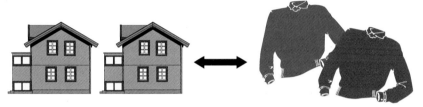

▲ A business building houses merges with a business making clothes

You should notice that the three examples of integration are very different, even though they all involve two businesses joining together.

The likely benefits of integration

Horizontal integration

» The merger reduces the number of competitors in the industry.
» There are opportunities for economies of scale (see Chapter 19).
» The combined business will have a bigger share of the total market than either business before the integration.

Forward vertical integration

For example, a car manufacturer takes over a car retailing business.

» The merger gives an assured outlet for its product.
» The profit margin made by the retailer is absorbed by the expanded business.
» The retailer could be prevented from selling competing models of car.
» Information about consumer needs and preferences can now be obtained directly by the manufacturer.

Backward vertical integration

For example, a car manufacturer takes over a business supplying car body panels.

» The merger gives an assured supply of important components.
» The profit margin of the supplier is absorbed by the expanded business.
» The supplier could be prevented from supplying other manufacturers.
» Costs of components and supplies for the manufacturer could be controlled.

Conglomerate integration

>> The business now has activities in more than one industry. This means that the business has diversified its activities and this will spread the risks taken by the business. For example, suppose that a newspaper business took over a social networking company. If sales of newspapers fell due to changing consumer demand, sales from advertising on social network sites could be rising at the same time due to increased interest in this form of communication.

>> There might be a transfer of ideas between the different sections of the business even though they operate in different industries. For example, an insurance company buying an advertising agency could benefit from better promotion of its insurance activities as a result of the agency's new ideas.

Activity 3.5

Identify the form of business growth which is used in each of these situations.

a A garage agrees to merge with another garage.
b A bicycle retailer expands by buying a bicycle shop in another town.
c A fruit juice business buys a fruit farm.
d A business making electrical goods agrees to join with a business with retail shops specialising in electrical goods.
e A mining company takes over a company supplying mining equipment.
f A construction company buys a holiday company.

Activity 3.6

In each of the cases in Activity 3.5, explain the likely reason(s) for the expansion.

▲ Hsu Fu Chi International produce

Case study: Nestlé takeover of large Chinese sweet maker

Nestlé is the largest food and confectionery manufacturer in the world. The company made the decision to take over Hsu Fu Chi International (based in Guandong, China). This Chinese company makes sweets and snacks. The takeover cost US$1.7 billion. It will now be easier for Nestlé to sell its products in China. There should also be cost savings from the takeover. Some consumers are worried that there might be less choice of sweets and snacks than before the takeover. Also, perhaps Nestlé might increase prices as there will be less competition in the sweet and snack market.

Activity 3.7

Read the case study above.

a Is this takeover an example of horizontal or vertical integration? Explain your answer.
b Explain **two** possible reasons why Nestlé took over the Hsu Fu Chi company.
c Do you think consumers in China will benefit from this takeover? Explain your answer.

　How businesses grow

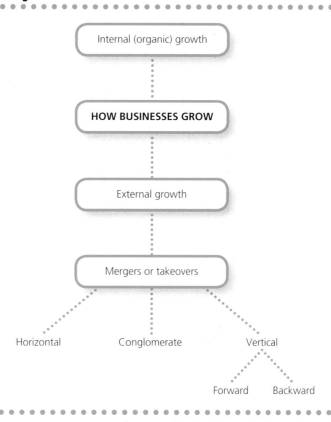

Problems linked to business growth and how these might be overcome

Not all business expansion leads to success. There are several reasons why business expansion can fail to increase profit or achieve the other objectives set by managers.

Problem resulting from expansion	Possible ways to overcome problem
Larger business is difficult to control (see also *Diseconomies of scale*, Chapter 19)	Operate the business in small units – this is a form of decentralisation
Larger business leads to poor communication (see Chapter 9)	Operate the business in smaller units Use latest IT equipment and telecommunications – but even these can cause problems
Expansion costs so much that business is short of finance	Expand more slowly – use profits from slowly expanding business to pay for further growth Ensure sufficient long-term finance is available (see Chapter 22)
Integrating with another business is more difficult than expected (for example, different management styles or 'ways of doing things')	Introducing a different style of management requires good communication with the workforce – they will need to understand the reasons for the change

Why some businesses remain small

Not all businesses grow. Some stay small, employing few people and using relatively little capital. There are several reasons why many businesses remain small, including:

» the type of industry the business operates in
» the market size
» the owners' objectives.

The type of industry the business operates in

Here are some examples of industries where most businesses remain small: hairdressing, car repairs, window cleaning, convenience stores, plumbers, catering. Businesses in these industries offer personal services or specialised products. If they were to grow too large, they would find it difficult to offer the close and personal service demanded by consumers. In these industries, it is often very easy for new businesses to be set up and this creates new competition. This helps to keep existing businesses relatively small.

Market size

If the market – that is, the total number of customers – is small, the businesses are likely to remain small. This is true for businesses, such as shops, which operate in rural areas far away from cities. It is also why businesses which produce goods or services of a specialised kind, which appeal only to a limited number of consumers, such as very luxurious cars or expensive fashion clothing, remain small.

Owners' objectives

Some business owners prefer to keep their business small. They could be more interested in keeping control of a small business, knowing all their staff and customers, than running a much larger business. Owners sometimes wish to avoid the stress and worry of running a large business.

> ### Key info
>
> There were 5.5 million private sector businesses in the UK in 2016. Small businesses accounted for 99.3 per cent of all these private sector businesses. Total employment in these businesses was 15.7 million, which is 60 per cent of all private sector employment in the UK. How many small businesses are there in your country? A small business here is referring to one with fewer than 250 employees.

> ### Activity 3.8
>
> In groups, visit or research the central area in your nearest town or city. List the main businesses in this area. Which of these are large businesses and which are small businesses? You may be able to identify this by whether they are part of a chain of shops or businesses or single individual businesses. What products or services do the small businesses offer? Can you conclude what makes these businesses small?

Causes of business failure

Not all businesses are successful. The rate of failure of newly formed businesses is high – in some countries, over 50 per cent close within five years of being set up. Even old-established businesses can close down because they make losses or run out of cash. The main reasons why some businesses fail include the following:

» **Lack of management skills** – this is a common cause of new business failures. Lack of experience can lead to bad decisions, such as locating the business in an area with high costs but low demand. Family businesses can fail because the sons and daughters of the founders of a business do not necessarily make good managers – and they might be reluctant to recruit professional managers.
» **Changes in the business environment** – failure to plan for change is a feature in many of the later chapters. This adds to the risk and uncertainty of

operating a business. New technology, powerful new competitors and major economic changes are just some of the factors that can lead to business failures *if* they are not responded to effectively.

» **Liquidity problems** or **poor financial management** – shortage of cash (lack of liquidity) means that workers, suppliers, landlords and government cannot be paid what they are owed. Failure to plan or forecast cash flows can lead to this problem and is a major cause of businesses of all sizes failing.

» **Over-expansion** – as was seen above (page 31), when a business expands *too* quickly it can lead to big problems of management and finance. If these are not solved, the difficulties can lead to the whole business closing down.

Why new businesses are at greater risk of failing

Many new businesses fail due to lack of finance and other resources, poor planning and inadequate research. In addition, the owner of a new business may lack the experience and decision-making skills of managers who work for larger businesses. This means that new businesses are nearly always more at risk of failing than existing, well-established businesses.

> ### Activity 3.9
> Using the internet, research one business you know that has stopped operating or gone bankrupt. Try to find out why it failed. Share your findings with the rest of the class.

International business in focus

Tata grows through takeovers

The Tata group is one of the largest companies in Asia, measured by value of output. It is a conglomerate as it operates in many industries, including electricity, steel, cars, chemicals, hotels and – tea!

Much of Tata's growth has resulted from takeovers of other businesses. For example, it bought out Daewoo's truck division in South Korea and Jaguar Land Rover in the UK. Tata car making uses many products, such as steel and plastics, produced by other Tata factories.

Each division of the vast Tata empire is given much independence in how it is managed – this means more decisions are not taken centrally at head office.

The success of Tata's car division is in great contrast to SAAB, the Swedish car maker. This business failed and stopped making cars. Its new models were too expensive and did not meet car customers' changing needs – and the business simply ran out of cash.

Discussion points

● What are some of the benefits to Tata of being a 'conglomerate'?

● Why do you think Tata's managers have used takeovers as a method of growth?

● If the Tata car division was to take over a chain of garages selling cars, what form of integration would this be? Do you think this would be a good idea?

▲ Tata's cars

Exam-style questions: Short answer and data response

1 Sabrina was bored with her job in a clothing factory. Her main passion was fashion and she had always been good at selling since helping her father on his market stall. She encouraged her parents and some friends to invest in her idea for opening a shop selling good quality women's clothes. Sabrina, as the entrepreneur behind the idea, was prepared to risk her own savings too. She had some exciting ideas for the shop layout and presentation of clothes.

   a Define 'entrepreneur'. [2]

   b Identify **two** benefits to Sabrina of starting her own business. [2]

   c Outline **two** characteristics that Sabrina seems to have that might lead to the success of her business. [4]

   d Explain **two** benefits to Sabrina of keeping her business small. [6]

   e 'I think I should draw up a business plan before I start,' said Sabrina to a friend. 'I think it would be best if you set the business up now – you don't need a plan as the shop will be so small,' said her friend. Which view do you agree with? Justify your answer. [6]

2 TelCom owns a phone network and provides phone network services to many consumers. The business does not manufacture phones and it does not own retail stores selling them. Senior managers at TelCom are considering a takeover of either a phone manufacturer or a chain of phone shops. TelCom employs 4000 workers and, last year, recorded total sales of $300 million. In contrast, the largest manufacturer of mobile phones, PhonTec, has 450 workers and recorded total sales last year of $1200 million.

   a Define 'takeover'. [2]

   b Identify **two** other ways, apart from takeovers, that a business might grow. [2]

   c Outline **two** reasons why external groups would be interested in measuring the size of businesses such as TelCom. [4]

   d Explain **two** possible reasons why senior managers at TelCom want to expand the business. [6]

   e How should TelCom expand – taking over a phone manufacturer or a chain of shops selling mobile phones? Justify your answer. [6]

Revision checklist

In this chapter you have learned:

✔ what an entrepreneur is and what characteristics successful entrepreneurs have
✔ the needs of a new business
✔ the importance of a business plan
✔ the support business start-ups get from government
✔ how size of businesses is measured and the limitations of these methods
✔ the different ways in which a business can grow and why this is desirable
✔ possible problems resulting from business growth
✔ reasons why some businesses remain small and why some businesses fail.

NOW – test your understanding with the revision questions in the Student etextbook and the Workbook.

4

Types of business organisation

This chapter will explain:

★ the main features of different forms of business organisation: sole traders, partnerships, private and public limited companies, franchises and joint ventures
★ the advantages and disadvantages of each of these forms of business organisation
★ differences between unincorporated businesses and limited companies
★ the concepts of risk, ownership and limited liability
★ how appropriate each of these forms is in different circumstances
★ business organisations in the public sector.

Business organisations: the private sector

There are several main forms of business organisation in the private sector. These are:

» sole traders
» partnerships
» private limited companies
» public limited companies
» franchises
» joint ventures.

Sole traders

Sole trader is the most common form of business organisation. It is a business owned and operated by just one person – the owner is the sole proprietor. One of the reasons it is such a common form of organisation is because there are so few legal requirements to set it up. There are only a few legal regulations which must be followed:

» The owner must register with, and send annual accounts to, the Government Tax Office.
» The name of the business is significant. In some countries the name must be registered with the Registrar of Business Names. In other countries, such as the UK, it is sufficient for the owner to put the business name on all of the business's documents and to put a notice in the main office stating who owns the business.
» In some industries, the sole trader must observe laws which apply to all businesses in that industry. These include health and safety laws and obtaining a licence, for example, to sell alcohol or operate a taxi.

What are the benefits and disadvantages to sole traders of running their own business rather than having other people join in with them? If you wanted to set up your own business, why might you choose to create a sole trader organisation? We can answer these questions by looking at the following case study.

> **Definitions to learn**
>
> **Sole trader** is a business owned by one person.

35

Case study

Mike decided to start his own taxi business. He set up the business as a sole trader. These are the advantages to Mike of being a sole trader.

Advantages of being a sole trader

- There were few legal regulations for him to worry about when he set up the business.
- He is his own boss. He has complete control over his business and there is no need to consult with or ask others before making decisions.
- He has the freedom to choose his own holidays, hours of work, prices to be charged and whom to employ (if he finds that he cannot do all the work by himself).
- Mike has close contact with his own customers, the personal satisfaction of knowing his regular customers and the ability to respond quickly to their needs and demands.
- Mike has an incentive to work hard as he is able to keep all of the profits, after he pays tax. He does not have to share these profits.
- He does not have to give information about his business to anyone else – other than the Tax Office. He enjoys complete secrecy in business matters.

After operating the business for several months, Mike realised that there are also some disadvantages to being a sole trader. He made a list of them.

Disadvantages of being a sole trader

- I have no one to discuss business matters with as I am the sole owner.
- I do not have the benefit of **limited liability**. The business is not a separate legal unit. I am therefore fully responsible for any debts that the business may have. **Unlimited liability** means that if my business cannot pay its debts, then the people I owe money to (my creditors) can force me to sell all of my own possessions in order to pay them.
- I want to expand the business by buying other taxis – but I do not have enough money to do this. The sources of finance for a sole trader are limited to the owner's savings, profits made by the business and small bank loans. There are no other owners who can put capital into the business. Banks are often reluctant to lend large amounts to businesses like mine.
- My business is likely to remain small because capital for expansion is so restricted. My business is unlikely to benefit from economies of scale. I cannot offer much training or opportunities for my workers' future careers.
- If I am ill there is no one who will take control of the business for me. I cannot pass on the business to my sons – when I die the business will legally not exist any longer. This is because there is no continuity of the business after the death of the owner.

Definitions to learn

Limited liability means that the liability of shareholders in a company is limited to only the amount they invested.

Unlimited liability means that the owners of a business can be held responsible for the debts of the business they own. Their liability is not limited to the investment they made in the business.

These disadvantages are typical for all sole traders. Did Mike take the correct decision to set up a sole trader business? He still thinks so. He would recommend a sole trader structure to people who:

» are setting up a new business
» do not need much capital to get the business going
» will be dealing mainly with the public, for example, in retailing or providing services like hairdressing – personal and direct contact between the customer and the owner is often very important for the success of these businesses.

But, as his business began to expand, Mike wondered if another form of business organisation would now be more suitable.

Partnerships

Definitions to learn

Partnership is a form of business in which two or more people agree to jointly own a business.

A **partnership agreement** is the written and legal agreement between business partners. It is not essential for partners to have such an agreement but it is always recommended.

A **partnership** is a group or association of at least two people who agree to own and run a business together. In some countries, such as India, there is a maximum limit of 20 people. The partners will contribute to the capital of the business, will usually have a say in the running of the business and will share any profits made.

Partnerships can be set up very easily. Mike could just ask someone he knows to become his partner in the taxi business. This would be called a verbal agreement. Mike would be advised to create a written agreement with a partner called a **partnership agreement** or deed of partnership. Without this document, partners may disagree on who put most capital into the business or who is entitled to more of the profits. A written agreement will settle all of these matters.

Case study

Mike offered his friend Gita the chance to become a partner in his taxi business. They prepared a written partnership agreement which contained:

- the amount of capital invested in the business by each partner
- the tasks to be undertaken by each partner
- the way in which the profits would be shared out
- how long the partnership would last
- arrangements for absence, retirement and how new partners could be admitted.

The two partners signed the agreement. After the partnership had been operating for some time, it became clear to Mike that it had several advantages over being a sole trader.

Advantages of a partnership

- More capital could now be invested into the business from Gita's savings and this would allow expansion of the business. Additional taxis could now be purchased.
- The responsibilities of running the business were now shared. Gita specialised in the accounts and administration of the business. Mike concentrated on marketing the services of the taxi firm and on driving. Absences and holidays did not lead to major problems as one of the partners was always available.
- Both partners were motivated to work hard because they would both benefit from the profits. In addition, any losses made by the business would now be shared by the partners.

Although the taxi business expanded and profits were being made, Gita became worried about what would happen if the business failed, perhaps because so many new competitors were entering the market. Gita explained to Mike that although their partnership was working well, this form of business organisation still had a number of disadvantages.

Disadvantages of a partnership

- The partners did not have limited liability. If the business failed, then creditors could still force the partners to sell their own property to pay business debts.
- The business did not have a separate legal identity. If one of the partners died, then the partnership would end. (Both sole traders and partnerships are said to be **unincorporated businesses** because they do not have a separate legal identity from the owners.)
- Partners can disagree on business decisions and consulting all partners takes time.
- If one of the partners is very inefficient or actually dishonest, then the other partners could suffer by losing money in the business.
- Most countries limit the number of partners to 20 and this means that business growth would be limited by the amount of capital that 20 people could invest.

Mike and Gita discussed these points with their solicitor. They agreed that partnerships were very suitable in certain situations, such as:

- when people wished to form a business with others but wanted to avoid legal complications
- where the professional body, such as medicine and the law in some countries, only allowed professional people to form a partnership, not a company
- where the partners are well known to each other, possibly in the same family, and want a simple means of involving several of them in the running of the business.

Gita and Mike made it clear that they wanted to expand the business further but wanted to reduce personal risk. They wanted to protect their own possessions from business creditors in the event of failure.

▲ As partners, Mike and Gita often discuss important business issues together. They share their ideas on how to run the business

The solicitor advised them to consider forming a private limited company. She explained that this type of business organisation would be very different from a partnership and would have its own benefits and drawbacks.

Activity 4.1

Your friend, Amin, is an expert computer engineer. He currently works for a large computer manufacturer that operates in an expanding industry. He thinks that he could run his own successful business. He has no experience of running a business. He has very few savings to invest into a business.

Amin has a rich uncle who knows nothing about computers! He is a retired businessman. He is friendly but rather bossy as he always thinks he knows best.

Amin asks for your advice about whether he should set up his own business and what form of organisation he should choose. He asks for your help on three issues that are worrying him.

a Explain **two** advantages and **two** disadvantages to Amin of running his own business rather than working for the computer manufacturer.
b Do you think he should set up a sole trader business? Explain your answer.
c His uncle would like to become his partner in the business if Amin decides to go ahead. Explain **two** advantages and **two** disadvantages to Amin of forming a partnership with his uncle.

Limited partnerships

In some countries it is possible to create a Limited Liability Partnership. The abbreviation for this new form of legal structure is LLP. It offers partners limited liability but shares in such businesses cannot be bought and sold. This type of partnership is a separate legal unit which still exists after a partner's death, unlike ordinary partnerships that end with the death of one of the partners.

REVISION SUMMARY   **Sole traders and partnerships**

Private limited companies

<table>
<tr>
<td>

Definitions to learn

Incorporated businesses are companies that have separate legal status from their owners.
Shareholders are the owners of a limited company. They buy shares which represent part-ownership of the company.
Private limited companies are businesses owned by shareholders but they cannot sell shares to the public.

</td>
<td>

There is one essential difference between a company and an unincorporated business, such as a sole trader or partnership. A company is a separate legal unit from its owners – it is an **incorporated business**. This means that:

» a company exists separately from the owners and will continue to exist if one of the owners should die
» a company can make contracts or legal agreements
» company accounts are kept separate from the accounts of the owners.

Companies are jointly owned by the people who have invested in the business. These people buy shares in the company and they are therefore called **shareholders**. These shareholders appoint directors to run the business. In a **private limited company**, the directors are usually the most important or majority shareholders. This is usually not the case in a public limited company, as we shall see in the next section.

</td>
</tr>
</table>

 Case study

Mike and Gita asked the solicitor to list the benefits of forming a private limited company.

Advantages of a private limited company

- Shares can be sold to a large number of people (in some countries there is a maximum number). These would be likely to be friends or relatives of Mike and Gita – they could not advertise the shares for sale to the general public. The sale of shares could lead to much larger sums of capital to invest in the business than the two original partners could manage to raise

themselves. The business could therefore expand more rapidly.
- All shareholders have limited liability. This is an important advantage. It means that if the company failed with debts owing to creditors, the shareholders could not be forced to sell their possessions to pay the debts. The shareholders could only lose their original investment in the shares – their liability is limited to the original investment. Shareholders in a company have less risk than sole traders and partners. Limited liability encourages people to buy shares, knowing

that the amount they pay is the maximum they could lose if the business is unsuccessful. It is important that the people and other businesses that deal with a private limited company know that it is not a sole trader or a partnership. Creditors, for example, need to be aware that if the business does fail, then they cannot take the owners to court to demand payment from their savings. For this reason all private limited company names must end with 'Limited' or 'Ltd' as an abbreviation. In some countries, although not the UK, this title is amended to 'Proprietary Limited' or '(Pty) Ltd'.

- The people who started the company – Mike and Gita in our example – are able to keep control of it as long as they do not sell too many shares to other people.

The legal adviser was keen for Mike and Gita to know exactly what they would be committed to if they formed a private limited company, so she also listed the disadvantages.

Disadvantages of a private limited company

- There are significant legal matters which have to be dealt with before a company can be formed. In particular, two important forms or documents have to be sent to the Registrar of Companies.
  - *The Articles of Association* – this contains the rules under which the company will be managed – the rights and duties of all of the directors; rules concerning the election of directors and the holding of official meetings; and the procedure to be followed for the issuing of shares.
  - *The Memorandum of Association* – this contains very important information about the company and the directors. The official name and the address of the registered offices of the company must be stated. The objectives of the company must be stated as well as the number of shares to be bought by each of the directors.

- Both of these documents are intended to make sure that companies are correctly run and to reassure shareholders about the purpose and structure of the company. Once these documents have been received by the Registrar of Companies, a Certificate of Incorporation will be issued to allow the company to start trading.
- The shares in a private limited company cannot be sold or transferred to anyone else without the agreement of the other shareholders. This rule can make some people reluctant to invest in such a company because they may not be able to sell their shares quickly if they require their investment back.
- The accounts of a company are less secret than for either a sole trader or a partnership. Each year the latest accounts must be sent to the Registrar of Companies and members of the public can inspect them. Mike and Gita have to be prepared to allow more information about their business to be known to other people.
- Most importantly for rapidly expanding businesses, the company cannot offer its shares to the general public. Therefore it will not be possible to raise really large sums of capital to invest back into the business.

Private limited companies – how suitable is this form of organisation?

Mike and Gita were impressed by the benefits of a private limited company form of organisation. The legal adviser told them it was a very common form of organisation for family businesses or partnerships when the owners wished to expand them further *and* wanted to reduce the risk to their own capital. Private limited company status allows more capital to be raised – and this is often sufficient for all but the largest businesses. The legal adviser offered to help Mike and Gita fill out the necessary legal forms to turn their business into a private limited company.

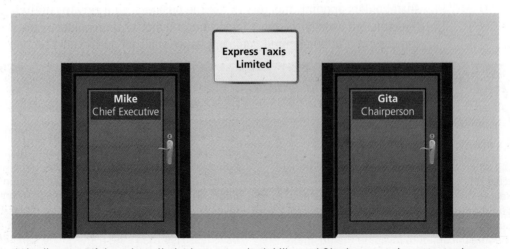

▲ As directors of the private limited company, both Mike and Gita have very important roles

Private limited companies

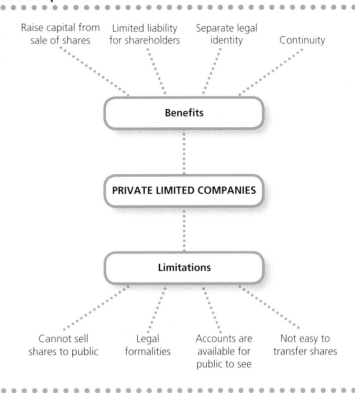

Study tips

When answering questions that refer to 'companies', the business must be either a private limited or public limited company. The term 'companies' should not be used when referring to sole traders or partnerships.

> ## Activity 4.2: Amin forms a limited company
>
> Read Activity 4.1 (see page 38) again. Amin decided not to form a partnership with his uncle. Instead, five years after setting up his business, he is thinking of forming a private limited company. Amin would sell shares in this new company to friends and relatives but he wants to keep most shares himself. He is very busy repairing computers and fitting new computer systems for the large number of customers who appreciate Amin's IT skills and like the personal service he offers. He wants to raise capital to pay for a bigger workshop and two new vans. He plans to employ at least two other IT engineers. Amin is also thinking of recruiting a manager to help him deal with customers and the accounting side of the business. Amin has been told that when he creates a private limited company his 'personal risk will be reduced but that he will still own most of the business'.
>
> **a** Explain **two** advantages and **two** disadvantages to Amin of converting his business into a private limited company.
> **b** Do you think that a private limited company is the appropriate form of organisation for Amin's business? Justify your answer.

Public limited companies

Definitions to learn

Public limited companies are businesses owned by shareholders but they can sell shares to the public and their shares are tradeable on the Stock Exchange.

This form of business organisation is most suitable for very large businesses. Most large, well-known businesses are **public limited companies** as they have been able to raise the capital to expand nationally or even internationally.

Students often make two mistakes about public limited companies:

1 Public limited companies are not in the public sector of industry, as many students believe. They are not owned by the government but by private individuals and as a result they are in the private sector.

2 The title given to public limited companies can cause confusion. This is why in the UK, public limited companies are given the title 'plc' after the business name, for example, J Sainsbury plc. In other countries, the title 'Limited' is used. This must not be confused with the UK use of 'Limited' which refers only to private limited companies.

The table below might help.

Private sector companies

	Private limited companies	Public limited companies
UK	Limited or Ltd	plc
South Africa and some other countries	Proprietary Limited or (Pty) Ltd	Limited

Do not worry about the different terms used; any questions will make it clear what type of company is being referred to.

Case study

Express Taxis Ltd had been operating and expanding for many years. The two directors, Mike and Gita, still owned most of the shares. The company owned 150 taxis and had diversified into bus services. It owned 35 buses. The government had recently announced the privatisation of all bus services in the country. Both Mike and Gita were determined to expand the business further by buying many of these bus routes from the government. Many new buses would be needed. A huge investment of around $90 million would be needed. Although profitable, the private limited company could not afford this sum of money. Mike and Gita went to see a specialist business financial consultant at a large bank. The consultant was impressed by the directors' plans and advised them to convert their company into a public limited company. He explained the procedure for doing this and the benefits and drawbacks of this change.

Key info

In 2015 the total number of publicly listed companies in the world was 45 508. The average number of listed companies on stock exchanges in different countries was 560 companies. The highest number of companies was in India: 5835 companies, closely followed by the USA with 4381. The lowest number was in Kuwait, where there were 0 companies listed.

A public limited company has certain advantages and disadvantages

Advantages of a public limited company

» This form of business organisation still offers **limited liability** to shareholders.
» It is an **incorporated business** and has a separate legal identity to the owners or shareholders. Its accounts are kept separately from those of the owners and there is continuity should one of the shareholders die.
» There is now the opportunity to raise **very large capital sums** to invest in the business. There is no limit to the number of shareholders a public limited company can have.
» There is no restriction on the **buying**, **selling** or **transfer** of shares.
» A business trading as a public limited company usually has high status and should find it easier to attract suppliers prepared to sell goods on credit and banks willing to lend to it than other types of businesses.

Disadvantages of a public limited company

» The **legal formalities** of forming such a company are quite complicated and time-consuming.
» There are many **more regulations** and **controls** over public limited companies in order to try to protect the interests of the shareholders. These include the publication of accounts, which anyone can ask to see.

» **Selling shares to the public is expensive.** The directors will often ask a specialist merchant bank to help them in this process. It will charge a commission for its services. The publication and printing of thousands of copies of the prospectus is an additional cost.
» There is a very real danger that although the original owners of the business might become rich by selling shares in their business, they may **lose control** over it when it 'goes public'. This is an important point which we will investigate further.

Control and ownership in a public limited company

In all sole trader businesses and partnerships the owners have control over how their business is run. They take all the decisions and try to make the business achieve the aims that they set. This is also the case in most private limited companies which have relatively few shareholders. The directors are often the majority shareholders so they can ensure that their decisions are passed at all meetings.

With a public limited company the situation is very different. There are often thousands of shareholders – even millions in the case of the largest companies. It is impossible for all these people to be involved in taking decisions – although they are all invited to attend the **Annual General Meeting** (AGM). The only decision that shareholders can have a real impact on at the AGM is the election of professional managers as company directors. They are given the responsibility of running the business and taking decisions. They will only meet with the other shareholders at the annual AGM. The directors cannot possibly control all of the business by themselves so they appoint other managers, who may not be shareholders at all, to take day-to-day decisions. The diagram below explains this situation.

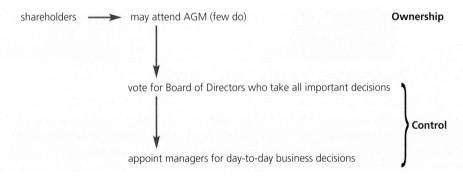

▲ Control and ownership in a public limited company

> **Definitions to learn**
>
> An **Annual General Meeting** is a legal requirement for all companies. Shareholders may attend and vote on who they want to be on the Board of Directors for the coming year.

> **Definitions to learn**
>
> **Dividends** are payments made to shareholders from the profits (after tax) of a company. They are the return to shareholders for investing in the company.

So, the shareholders own, but the directors and managers control. Sometimes, this is called the divorce between ownership and control.

Does this matter? It might be important for the shareholder. It means that the directors and managers may run the business to meet their own objectives. These could be increased status, growth of the business to justify higher management salaries, or reducing **dividends** to shareholders to pay for expansion plans. The shareholders are not able to influence these decisions – other than by replacing the directors at the next AGM. Doing this would give the company very bad publicity and cause the business to be unstable as the new directors may be inexperienced.

Key info

The largest company in the world is the American retail company Walmart, with 2.3 million employees and a revenue in 2016/17 of $485 873 million.

▲ Walmart is a public limited company

Case study

Mike and Gita had decided to convert the company into a public one – Express Taxi and Bus plc. By selling shares in their company, they had not only raised the capital they needed but they had also become very rich. They were elected as directors at the first AGM for the new plc. The expansion into buying the privatised bus companies was successful – at first. Profits rose and management salaries did too. However, new bus competitors were forcing bus fares down. Profits started to fall. The accounts published last year showed the lowest profits for three years. Mike and Gita were voted off the Board of Directors. They no longer had a majority of the shares – when it was a private limited company they owned 50 per cent of the shares each. Since 'going public', they owned only 20 per cent of the total shares issued. They had lost control of what had been their business. The new directors owned few shares. They reduced dividends to shareholders and announced a new expansion programme to increase profits.

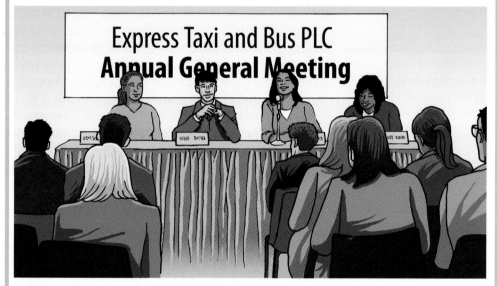

▲ Mike and Gita now have to explain the performance of the company to a large number of shareholders at the AGM

Mike and Gita were rich but they no longer controlled the business that had once belonged just to them. Mike missed being in control. He was thinking of setting up his own business by buying a luxury hotel. He planned to operate as a sole trader!

Public limited companies

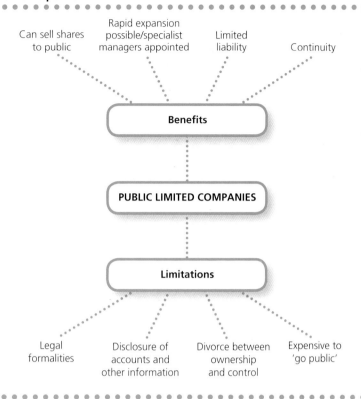

Activity 4.3

a How does the existence of limited liability benefit an individual shareholder?

b Does limited liability make it easier or more difficult for companies to attract new shareholders? Explain your answer.

c Explain why a sole trader might not want to convert their business into a partnership.

d It is possible to convert a public limited company back into a private limited company. This is done by individuals buying up a majority of the shares. Richard Branson did this several years ago with the Virgin Group. Why might Mike and Gita have wanted to do this with Express Taxi and Bus plc?

Risk, ownership and limited liability – summary

Business organisation	Risk	Ownership	Limited liability
Sole trader	Carried by sole owner	One person	No
Partnership	Carried by all partners	Several partners	No
Private limited company	Shareholders up to their original investment	Shareholders – may be few or many but shares cannot be sold to the public	Yes
Public limited company	Shareholders up to their original investment	Shareholders – many (may be millions!)	Yes

Other private sector business organisations

Two other types of private sector business organisation exist.

Franchising

This is now an extremely widespread form of business operation. The franchisor is a business with a product or service idea that it does not want to sell to consumers directly. Instead, it appoints franchisees to use the idea or product and to sell it to consumers. Two of the best known international examples of a **franchise** are McDonald's restaurants and The Body Shop.

	To the franchisor	To the franchisee
Advantages	• The franchisee buys a licence from the franchisor to use the brand name • Expansion of the franchised business is much faster than if the franchisor had to finance all new outlets • The management of the outlets is the responsibility of the franchisee • All products sold must be obtained from the franchisor	• The chances of business failure are much reduced because a well-known product is being sold • The franchisor pays for advertising • All supplies are obtained from a central source – the franchisor • There are fewer decisions to make than with an independent business – prices, store layout and range of products will have been decided by the franchisor • Training for staff and management is provided by the franchisor • Banks are often willing to lend to franchisees due to relatively low risk
Disadvantages	• Poor management of one franchised outlet could lead to a bad reputation for the whole business • The franchisee keeps profits from the outlet	• Less independence than with operating a non-franchised business • May be unable to make decisions that would suit the local area, for example, new products that are not part of the range offered by the franchisor • Licence fee must be paid to the franchisor and possibly a percentage of the annual turnover

Franchisee contributes:
- capital
- management
- enterprise

Franchisor contributes:
- use of brand name and products
- original idea
- advertising and training

▲ Franchised businesses give benefits to both the franchisor and the franchisee – but they must both contribute too

Joint ventures

Definitions to learn

A **joint venture** is where two or more businesses start a new project together, sharing capital, risks and profits.

A **joint venture** is when two or more businesses agree to start a new project together, sharing the capital, the risks and the profits. Many European companies have set up joint ventures in China with Chinese businesses, as the local managers will have good knowledge of market needs and consumer tastes.

Advantages of joint ventures	Disadvantages of joint ventures
Sharing of costs – very important for expensive projects such as new aircraft	If the new project is successful, then the profits have to be shared with the joint venture partner
Local knowledge when joint venture company is already based in the country	Disagreements over important decisions might occur
Risks are shared	The two joint venture partners might have different ways of running a business – different cultures

➡ Case study: Walmart's joint venture in India

Walmart is the world's largest retail business. The company wanted to enter the Indian market. Walmart did not set up its own stores initially as it had little knowledge of the Indian market or Indian consumers. Walmart set up a joint venture with Bharti Enterprises, one of India's largest business groups. The joint venture set up a business called BestPrice Modern Wholesale which sells vegetables to hotels, restaurants and shops. One day, Walmart might open its own named stores in India – as it has in many Asian countries.

▶ Activity 4.4

Read the case study above.

a Define 'joint venture'.
b Explain **two** benefits to Walmart of setting up a joint venture to enter the Indian market.
c Explain **two** problems that Walmart might have in the future if it opens its own stores in India.

Study tips

Many well-known international businesses (multinational corporations) use franchising as a way of expanding into new foreign markets. The combination of a large well-known business and the local knowledge of the franchisees can lead to very successful operations.

Business organisations in the public sector

The public sector is a very important part of the economy of all mixed economies. The term 'public sector' includes all businesses owned by the government/state and local government, and public services such as hospitals, schools, fire services and government departments.

Public corporations

These are wholly owned by the state or central government. They are usually businesses which have been nationalised. This means that they were once owned by private individuals, but were purchased by the government. Examples of these in many countries include water supply and rail services – but, as we saw in Chapter 2, even these businesses are now being privatised in many countries.

Public corporations are owned by the government but it does not directly operate the businesses. Government ministers appoint a Board of Directors, who will be given the responsibility of managing the business. The government will, however, make clear what the objectives of the business should be. The directors are expected to run the corporation according to these objectives.

Definitions to learn

A **public corporation** is a business in the public sector that is owned and controlled by the state (government).

Advantages of public corporations

» Some industries are considered so important that government ownership is thought to be essential. These include water supply and electricity generation in many countries.

» If industries are controlled by monopolies because it would be wasteful to have competitors – two sets of railway lines to a certain town, for example – then these natural monopolies are often owned by the government. It is argued that this will ensure consumers are not taken advantage of by privately owned monopolists.

» If an important business is failing and likely to collapse, the government can step in to nationalise it. This will keep the business open and secure jobs.

» Important public services, such as TV and radio broadcasting, are often in the public sector. Non-profitable but important programmes can still be made available to the public.

Disadvantages of public corporations

» There are no private shareholders to insist on high profits and efficiency. The profit motive might not be as powerful as in private sector industries.

» Government subsidies can lead to inefficiency as managers will always think that the government will help them if the business makes a loss. It may also be unfair if the public corporation receives a subsidy but private firms in the same industry do not.

» Often there is no close competition to the public corporations. There is therefore a lack of incentive to increase consumer choice, increase efficiency or even improve customer service.

» Governments can use these businesses for political reasons, for example, to create more jobs just before an election. This prevents the public corporations being operated like other profit-making businesses.

Other public sector enterprises

Local government authorities or municipalities usually operate some trading activities. Some of these services are free to the user and paid for out of local taxes, such as street lighting and schools. Other services are charged for and expected to break even at least. These might include street markets, swimming pools and theatres. If they do not cover their costs, a local government subsidy is usually provided. In order to cut costs and reduce the burden on local taxpayers, an increasing range of services is now being privatised, so reducing the role of local government in providing goods and services.

▲ Examples of other public sector enterprises

International business in focus

Private companies 'go public'

TD Power Systems was incorporated as a private limited company in India in 1999. It has slowly expanded its range of advanced electric generators. The company needed more capital to:

- pay back debt
- invest in a huge expansion of its factory in Dabaspct.

The private shareholders decided to sell at least 25 per cent of their shares and convert the business into a public limited company. This decision raised the capital needed.

Reva Medical makes medical equipment in San Diego, USA. The owners were keen to make the business 'public' to raise capital for new research into heart medicine equipment. There was little interest from shareholders in the USA – they were worried the profits from the new equipment would take several years to be earned. Reva's directors looked abroad – and decided on converting into a public company in Australia! The sale of shares on the Australian Stock Market allowed the company to raise the finance needed.

The owners of some young businesses have decided against 'going public' because of the cost involved, the loss of control and the need to make more information public.

Discussion points

- Do you think it would be better to keep a business such as TD Power Systems as a private limited company or to convert it into a public limited company?
- Why are some business owners reluctant to convert their companies into public limited companies?

▲ Share prices in public limited companies can fluctuate daily

Exam-style questions: Short answer and data response

1 When Jameel lost his job in a fruit and vegetable shop that closed down, he decided to open his own store. He had good contacts with suppliers. They said they would give him one month's credit before he paid for supplies. Jameel had $5000 in savings to invest in the shop. He thought this would be sufficient to start the business. He is an independent man – he never liked taking the manager's orders in the food shop! He wanted to operate his new business as a sole trader.

   a Define 'sole trader'.   [2]
   b Identify **two** other types of business organisation.   [2]
   c Outline **two** benefits to Jameel of operating his business as a sole trader. [4]
   d Explain **two** drawbacks to Jameel of operating his business as a sole trader. [6]
   e Do you think Jameel should open new branches of his business by selling franchises? Justify your answer. [6]

2 Aurelie and Nadine set up the A and N Partnership ten years ago. It specialises in handmade shoes and boots. The business now employs around 20 people. Demand for these products is increasing rapidly. The partners need to invest much more capital in the business but they need to avoid a lot of risk as they both have families dependent on the income made from the business. Their main competitor is ShoeWorks plc, which has a much larger market share than A and N and can afford extensive advertising.

   a Define 'partnership'.   [2]
   b Identify **two** benefits to Aurelie and Nadine of their partnership.   [2]
   c Outline **two** possible benefits to ShoeWorks plc of being a public limited company. [4]
   d Explain **two** drawbacks to Aurelie and Nadine of the partnership form of legal structure. [6]
   e If the A and N Partnership business continues, recommend whether a private limited company is a suitable form of legal structure for this business. Justify your answer by considering the advantages and disadvantages of a private limited company. [6]

Revision checklist

In this chapter you have learned:

✔ the differences between and advantages and disadvantages of: sole traders, partnerships, private and public limited companies, franchises and joint ventures

✔ the main features of unincorporated businesses and limited companies, and what makes them different

✔ what risk, ownership and limited liability are

✔ when each type of business organisation is most appropriate

✔ what public sector businesses are.

NOW – test your understanding with the revision questions in the Student etextbook and the Workbook.

5 Business objectives and stakeholder objectives

This chapter will explain:

★ the need for and importance of business objectives
★ about different business objectives
★ about the objectives of social enterprises
★ the main internal and external stakeholder groups
★ the objectives of different stakeholder groups
★ how these objectives might conflict with each other, with examples
★ the differences in the objectives of private and public sector enterprises.

Need for and importance of business objectives

An **objective** is an aim or a target to work towards. All businesses should have objectives. They help to make a business successful – although just setting an objective does not 'guarantee success'. There are many benefits of setting objectives:

» They give workers and managers a clear target to work towards and this helps motivate people.
» Taking decisions will be focused on: 'Will it help achieve our objectives?'
» Clear and measurable objectives help unite the whole business towards the same goal.
» Business managers can compare how the business has performed to their objectives – to see if they have been successful or not.

So setting objectives is very important for all businesses – small or large, newly formed or well established.

Different business objectives

Objectives are often different for different businesses. A business may have been formed by an entrepreneur to provide employment and security for the owner or his/her family. It could have been started to make as big a profit as possible for the owner. On the other hand, the business might have a more charitable aim in mind – many of the leading world charities are very large businesses indeed.

The most common objectives for businesses in the private sector are to achieve:

» business survival
» profit
» returns to shareholders
» growth of the business
» market share
» service to the community.

Survival

When a business has recently been set up, or when the economy is moving into recession, the objectives of the business will be more concerned with survival than anything else. New competitors can also make a business feel less secure. The managers of a business threatened in this way could decide to lower prices in order to survive, even though this would lower the profit on each item sold.

Profit

> **Definitions to learn**
>
> **Profit** is total income of a business (revenue) less total costs.

When a business is owned by private individuals rather than the government it is usually the case that the business is operated with the aim of making a **profit**. The owners will each take a share of these profits. Profits are needed to:

>> **pay a return** to the owners of the business for the capital invested and the risk taken
>> **provide finance** for further investment in the business.

Without any profit at all, the owners are likely to close the business.

Will a business try to make as much profit as possible? It is often assumed that this will be the case. But there are dangers to this aim. Suppose a business put up its prices to raise profits. It may find that consumers stop buying its goods. Other people will be encouraged to set up in competition, which will reduce profits in the long term for the original business.

It is often said that the owners of a business will aim for a satisfactory level of profits which will avoid them having to work too many hours or pay too much in tax to the government.

Returns to shareholders

Shareholders own limited companies (see Chapter 4). The managers of companies will often set the objective of 'increasing returns to shareholders'. This is to discourage shareholders from selling their shares and helps managers keep their jobs!

Returns to shareholders are increased in two ways:

>> **Increasing profit** and the share of profit paid to shareholders as dividends.
>> **Increasing share price** – managers can try to achieve this not just by making profits but by putting plans in place that give the business a good chance of growth and higher profits in the future.

Growth

The owners and managers of a business may aim for growth in the size of the business – usually measured by value of sales or output – in order to:

>> make jobs more secure if the business is larger
>> increase the salaries and status of managers as the business expands
>> open up new possibilities and help to spread the risks of the business by moving into new products and new markets
>> obtain a higher market share from growth in sales
>> obtain cost advantages, called economies of scale, from business expansion. These are considered in more detail in Chapter 19.

Growth will be achieved only if the business's customers are satisfied with the products or services being provided. For this reason it might be important to put meeting customers' needs as a very high priority.

Market share

If the total value of sales in a market is $100 million in one year and Company A sold $20 million, then Company A's **market share** is 20 per cent.

$$\text{Market share } \% = \frac{Company\ sales}{Total\ market\ sales} \times 100$$

Increased market share gives a business:

» good publicity, as it could claim that it is becoming 'the most popular'
» increased influence over suppliers, as they will be very keen to sell to a business that is becoming relatively larger than others in the industry
» increased influence over customers (for example, in setting prices).

Providing a service to the community – the objectives of social enterprises

Social enterprises are operated by private individuals – they are in the private sector – but they do not just have profit as an objective. The people operating the social enterprise often set three objectives for their business:

» **Social:** to provide jobs and support for disadvantaged groups in society, such as the disabled or homeless.
» **Environmental:** to protect the environment.
» **Financial:** to make a profit to invest back into the social enterprise to expand the social work that it performs.

An example of a social enterprise is RangSutra in India. This helps very poor village communities develop skills in craft work and clothing products and helps them market their products at a fair price.

▲ A display of RangSutra products. RangSutra's core value is 'respect for both the producer and the customer'. They ensure a fair price to the producer as well as quality products to the customer. Profits earned from sales go back to ensure a better life for their communities, as the producers are also the owners of RangSutra.

Why business objectives could change

It is most unusual for a business to have the same objective forever! Here are some examples of situations in which a business might change its objective.

1 A business set up recently has survived for three years and the owner now aims to work towards higher profit.
2 A business has achieved higher market share and now has the objective of earning higher returns for shareholders.
3 A profit-making business operates in a country facing a serious economic recession so now has the short-term objective of survival.

Activity 5.1: Which objective for which business?

Here are brief details of four businesses:

- A small firm of builders which has noticed new businesses being set up in the building industry.
- A recently established business in the rapidly expanding computer industry, which is owned by two young and ambitious entrepreneurs.
- A large book publisher which dominates the market in textbooks in your country.
- A group of people who are concerned about the lack of clean water provided to poor communities.

a Explain the most likely main objective of the managers of each of these businesses.
b In each example, explain the decisions that could help the business to achieve these objectives.

The main internal and external stakeholder groups and their objectives

The following groups of people are involved in business activity in one way or another, or are affected by it:

» owners
» workers
» managers
» consumers
» government
» the whole community
» banks.

These groups are sometimes called the **stakeholders** of the business as they have an interest in how the business is run. Some of these groups are internal to the business – they work for it or own it – and others are external – they are groups outside of the business.

Why are these groups of people important to business? How are they affected by business activity? Consider the table on page 55.

Stakeholder group	Main features	Most likely objectives for the stakeholder group
Owners (Internal)	• They put capital in to set up and expand the business. • They will take a share of the profits if the business succeeds. • If the business does not attract enough customers, they may lose the money they invested. • They are risk takers.	• share of the profits so that they gain a rate of return on the money put into the business • growth of the business so that the value of their investment increases
Workers (Internal)	• They are employed by the business. • They have to follow the instructions of managers and may need training to do their work effectively. • They may be employed on full- or part-time contracts and on a temporary or permanent basis. • If there is not enough work for all workers, some may be made redundant (retrenchment) and told to leave the business.	• regular payment for their work • contract of employment • job security – workers do not want to look for new jobs frequently • job that gives satisfaction and provides motivation
Managers (Internal)	• They are also employees of the business and control the work of other workers. • They take important decisions. • Their successful decisions could lead to the business expanding. • If they make poor decisions, the business could fail.	• high salaries because of the important work they do • job security – this depends on how successful they are • growth of the business so that managers can control a bigger and better known business. This gives them more status and power
Customers (External)	• They are important to every business. They buy the goods that the business produces or the services that the business provides. • Without enough customers, a business will make losses and will eventually fail. • The most successful businesses often find out what consumers want before making goods or providing services – this is called market research.	• safe and reliable products • value for money • well-designed products of good quality • reliability of service and maintenance
Government (External)	• It is responsible for the economy of the country. • It passes laws to protect workers and consumers.	• wants businesses to succeed in its country. Successful businesses will employ workers, pay taxes and increase the country's output • expects all firms to stay within the law – laws affect business activity
The whole community (External)	• The community is greatly affected by business activity. For example, dangerous products might harm the population. Factories can produce pollution that damages rivers, the sea and air quality. • Businesses also create jobs and allow workers to raise their living standards. Many products are beneficial to the community, such as medicines or public transport.	• jobs for the working population • production that does not damage the environment • safe products that are socially responsible
Banks (External)	• They provide finance for the business's operations.	• expect the business to be able to pay interest and repay capital lent – business must remain liquid

Study tips

You should not suggest that public sector businesses 'do not want to make a profit'. Most of them do have this aim – but they have other objectives set for them by governments too.

Objectives of public sector businesses

In Chapter 2 we explained that the government owns and controls many businesses and other activities in mixed economies. These were in the public sector. What are the likely objectives for public sector businesses and organisations?

>> *Financial*: Meet profit targets set by government – sometimes the profit is reinvested back in the business and on other occasions it is handed over to the government as the 'owner' of the organisation.

>> *Service*: Provide a service to the public and meet quality targets set by government. For example, health services and education services will be expected to achieve targets laid down for them, and state-owned train and postal services will have reliability and punctuality targets.

>> *Social*: Protect or create employment in certain areas – especially poor regions with few other business employers.

REVISION SUMMARY   **Business objectives (private sector)**

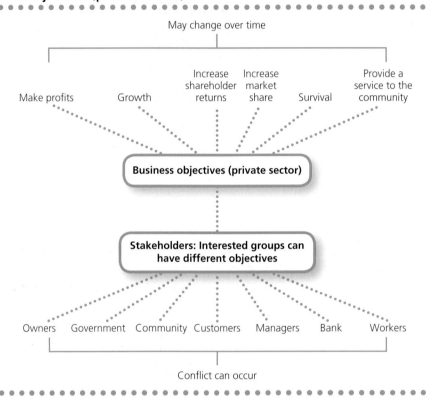

Activity 5.2: Coca-Cola's objectives

Coca-Cola's senior managers have set the objective of increasing returns to owners of the company – that is, its millions of shareholders. However, the managers believe that this can only be achieved if Coca-Cola meets three other objectives:

- Remain the world's largest soft drinks company by value of sales.
- Continue to satisfy consumers with a top-value and clearly branded product.
- Protect the environment of the local communities where Coca-Cola drinks are made.

a Why do you think the senior managers believe that 'increasing returns to owners' is important?

b Explain why Coca-Cola has set three other objectives as well as 'returns to owners'?

c By referring to the market in your own country, explain how you think Coca-Cola could achieve its aim of remaining the world's largest soft drinks company.

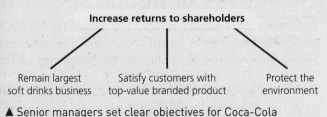

▲ Senior managers set clear objectives for Coca-Cola

Conflict of stakeholders' objectives

In the previous section we assumed that businesses could set one objective and aim for that. However, life is not that simple and most businesses are trying to satisfy the objectives of more than one group, as the diagram below shows.

Study tips

Be prepared to explain how a business objective might satisfy some stakeholders but not others.

Key info

Consumers throw plastic bottles away but they are not biodegradable and many end up in the oceans. This garbage is harming fish and spoiling the coastlines of many countries. Manufacturers want a cheap way to package their products but people also want an unpolluted place to live. Can these two objectives be reconciled?

→ Case study: Business stakeholders

Oilco is a large oil company operating in your country. The following stakeholder groups are interested in the work of this company:

- *Owners of the company.* They are likely to want the business to work towards as much profit as possible.
- *Directors* (senior managers of the company appointed by the owners). They will be interested in growth of the business as their salaries are likely to depend on this.
- *Workers.* They will want as high a wage as possible with security of employment.
- *Local community.* It will be concerned about jobs too, but it will also be worried about pollution from the oil refinery.
- *Consumers.* They will want reasonably priced products of appropriate quality – or they may buy goods from competitors.

In practice, these stakeholder objectives could conflict with each other. For example:

- it could be that a cheap method of production increases profits but causes more pollution
- a decision to expand the plant could lead to a dirtier, noisier local environment
- a decision to introduce new machines could reduce the jobs at the refinery but lead to higher profits
- expansion could be expensive, reducing payments to owners, and this could reduce short-term profits.

▶ Activity 5.3

Read the case study above.

a Define 'stakeholder group'.
b Explain **one** other possible conflict of objectives between Oilco's stakeholders.

Managers therefore have to compromise when they come to decide on the best objectives for the business they are running. They would be unwise to ignore the real worries or aims of other groups with an interest in the operation of the business. Managers will also have to be prepared to change the objectives over time. Growth could be the best option during a period of expansion in the economy, but survival by cost cutting might be better if the economy is in recession.

Business stakeholders and their aims

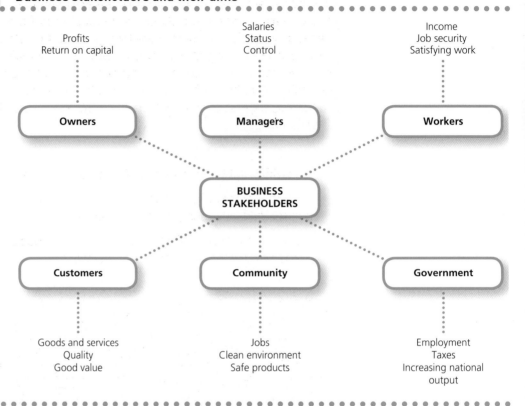

International business in focus

Toyota makes clear its business objectives

Toyota recently announced a set of objectives to be achieved over the next 35 years to reduce the negative impact of manufacturing and the driving of vehicles as much as possible. It has the following objectives:

- **Producing ever-better cars** Toyota is developing electric and hybrid cars that use reclaimed energy, which is the same technology used in Formula 1 cars. Hydrogen-powered vehicles, such as the Mirai, are also important to Toyota's strategy for promoting widespread use of fuel cell vehicles. Toyota's plan is to reduce global average new-vehicle carbon emissions by 90 per cent by 2050, compared to its 2010 global average.

- **Using ever-better manufacturing** Toyota wants to reduce all carbon emissions from its factories to zero by 2050. This will be achieved through use of low-carbon methods of production. It will also use renewable power, such as wind, biomass and hydroelectric to run its factories.

- **Enriching lives of communities** when driving their cars by establishing a 'recycling-based society and systems' through the promotion of a global rollout of end-of-life vehicle-recycling technologies developed in Japan.

Toyota's other main objective over the next few years is sales growth in the emerging markets of Asia, Africa and South America. Although profits are important, Toyota sets quite low earnings targets, preferring to focus on growth in a competitive market. However, China's emission and fuel economy rules have been making it harder for Toyota to achieve its objective of selling 2 million vehicles a year in China by around 2025. In order to meet these regulations, Toyota will need to sell a large number of smaller cars and hybrid cars.

Discussion points

- Why did Toyota set objectives for the next few years?

- Why do you think developing new models seems to be more important than making as much profit as possible?

- Which stakeholder groups will be affected – positively or negatively – by Toyota working towards these objectives?

- Do any of these objectives conflict with each other?

▲ One of Toyota's objectives is to produce and sell more hybrid cars

Exam-style questions: Short answer and data response

1 Sunita and her partner Sunil decided to start a business selling flowers called S and S Blooms. They agreed on the business objectives they would set. There are several other flower shops in their town and there is much competition. Sunita and Sunil had very little cash to start their shop. However, five years after being set up, it is still open. Business objectives have changed. There are plans to open two or three more shops – perhaps by taking over some of their competitors. The business now employs five workers and uses several local flower growers as suppliers.

   a Define 'business objective'. [2]

   b Identify **two** of S and S Blooms' stakeholder groups, other than workers and suppliers. [2]

   c Outline **two** likely business objectives for S and S Blooms when the business was first established. [4]

   d Explain **two** likely reasons why Sunita and Sunil have changed the business objectives of S and S Blooms. [6]

   e Do you think that setting business objectives for S and S Blooms will make sure that the business is successful? Justify your answer. [6]

2 The Big Pit Mining business (BPM) owns and operates coal and gold mines in several different countries. It employs thousands of workers. Most of them work in very dangerous conditions for low pay. Waste from the mines is often dumped in local rivers. 'Making higher profits and raising returns to our shareholders are our most important objectives,' said the Managing Director of BPM to his other senior managers recently. 'Shareholders are our most important stakeholder group,' he added.

   a Define 'stakeholders'. [2]

   b Identify **two** objectives that the managers could set for BPM, apart from profits and returns to shareholders. [2]

   c Outline **two** possible reasons why BPM has profit as an objective. [4]

   d Explain how a decision to open a new BPM mine might affect **two** stakeholder groups. [6]

   e Do you agree with the Managing Director when he said that shareholders are the most important stakeholder group? Justify your answer. [6]

Revision checklist

In this chapter you have learned:

✔ why a business needs objectives and the different objectives that can be set

✔ what objectives may be set by social enterprises

✔ what stakeholder groups are and their objectives and potential for conflicts between objectives

✔ how objectives of private and public sector enterprises differ.

NOW – test your understanding with the revision questions in the Student etextbook and the Workbook.

Understanding business activity: end-of-section case study

 A new business but which one?

Derek's job is to repair motorcycles. He works for a large motorcycle sales business that sells new and second-hand motorcycles. Derek's uncle died earlier this year and left him $10 000. He has always wanted to work for himself and now he has some money to start his own business. He could do this by opening his own business or buying a franchise.

Derek is going to choose between opening his own shop selling motorcycle clothes or buying a franchise from a big motorcycle clothes retail business. To open his own motorcycle clothes shop will take a lot of effort to find a suitable location with the shop fittings needed. Buying a franchise for a clothes shop will be expensive. However, the franchise company will help Derek with a lot of the start-up problems such as finding a suitable shop.

 Appendix 1: Letter to bank manager

```
Dear Sir/Madam

I want to set up my own business. I have $10000 to invest in my business but I need additional
funds. I have two possible business ideas.

The first one is to set up my own motorcycle clothes shop and for that I will need an additional
$15000 to buy clothes to sell in the shop.
I will rent my shop.

The second idea is to buy a franchise for a motorcycle clothes shop and for that I will need
an additional $100000. $50000 will be needed to buy the franchise and $50000 to buy clothes
inventories. I will rent my shop.

I would like to come to see you to discuss my two ideas.

Yours faithfully,

Derek
```

Exam-style questions: Case study

1 a Explain **four** personal characteristics that Derek needs to be a successful entrepreneur. [8]

  b Derek has to decide which type of business organisation to choose if he sets up his own business. Consider the advantages and disadvantages of the following types of business organisation. Recommend which one Derek should choose. Justify your choice.
   • Sole trader.
   • Partnership.
   • Private limited company. [12]

2 a Identify **two** stakeholders in Derek's new business. Explain why each stakeholder is interested in his business. [8]

  b Consider the advantages and disadvantages to Derek of buying a franchise from a big clothes retail business instead of setting up his own clothes shop. Which option do you think he should take? Justify your choice. [12]

SECTION 2

People in business

Chapters

6 Motivating employees
7 Organisation and management
8 Recruitment, selection and training of employees
9 Internal and external communication

6 Motivating employees

This chapter will explain:

★ why people work and what motivation means
★ the benefits of a well-motivated workforce: labour productivity, reduced absenteeism and labour turnover
★ the concept of human needs – Maslow's hierarchy
★ key motivational theories – Taylor and Herzberg
★ financial rewards as a method of motivation, for example, wage, salary, bonus, commission, profit sharing
★ non-financial methods of motivation, for example, job enrichment, job rotation, teamworking, training, opportunities for promotion
★ how to recommend and justify appropriate methods of motivation in given circumstances.

Why people work

Definitions to learn

Motivation is the reason why employees want to work hard and work effectively for the business.

People work for a variety of reasons. The main reason why most people work is because they need to earn money to buy food and the basic necessities for life. But some work is voluntary and does not yield any money. This chapter considers a wide range of **motivations** for work and how businesses can make use of this motivation to encourage their workers to work more effectively.

The reasons why people work are summarised in the diagram below.

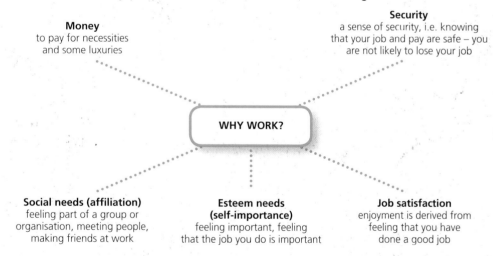

Money
to pay for necessities and some luxuries

Security
a sense of security, i.e. knowing that your job and pay are safe – you are not likely to lose your job

WHY WORK?

Social needs (affiliation)
feeling part of a group or organisation, meeting people, making friends at work

Esteem needs (self-importance)
feeling important, feeling that the job you do is important

Job satisfaction
enjoyment is derived from feeling that you have done a good job

Benefits of a well-motivated workforce

High productivity – high output per worker – in a business usually comes from a workforce that is motivated to work effectively and from this comes increased profits. A well-motivated workforce gives benefits to a business, including:

» high output per worker – which helps to keep costs low and increase profits
» willingness to accept change, for example, new methods of working
» two-way communication with management, for example, suggestions for improving quality

» low labour turnover – a loyal workforce – this reduces the cost of recruiting workers who leave
» low rates of absenteeism – reducing the disruption caused by absence from work
» low rates of strike action – avoiding damage to customer relations.

All businesses should recognise that the value of their employees' output, in terms of how much they produce and the quality of it, depends on how well motivated they are to work effectively. Employees are a business's greatest asset!

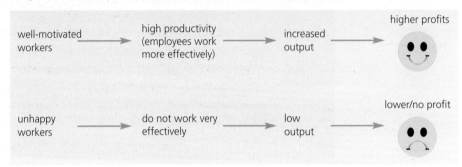

▲ Well-motivated and unhappy workers

Human needs – Maslow's hierarchy
Maslow

Abraham Maslow studied employee motivation. He proposed a hierarchy of needs, shown in this diagram.

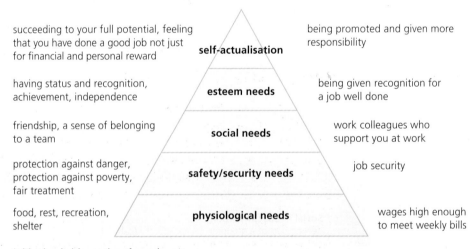

▲ Maslow's hierarchy of needs

» Most business managers now recognise that if employees are going to be motivated to work effectively then the higher levels in the hierarchy must be available to them – money alone will not be the single route to increased productivity as was thought by Taylor (see next section). Evidence for the hierarchy can be seen in people who are unemployed. They very often lose their self-respect and self-esteem and may not have the feeling of belonging to society, which often comes from working.
» Maslow also suggested that each level in the hierarchy must be achieved before an employee can be motivated by the next level. For example, once social needs are met, this will no longer motivate the employee, but the opportunity

to gain the respect of fellow workers and to gain esteem could motivate the
employee to work effectively. If this is true, then there are important messages
for management in the way employees are managed.

» There are problems in that some levels do not appear to exist for certain
individuals, while some rewards appear to fit into more than one level. For
example, money allows basic needs to be purchased, but high pay can also be a
status symbol or indicator of personal worth.

» Managers must identify the level of the hierarchy that a particular job provides
and then look for ways of allowing the employees to benefit from the next level
up the hierarchy. For example, workers in agriculture who work on a temporary
basis, when required, will probably have their physiological needs fulfilled, but
security needs may be lacking. If they were offered full-time jobs, they might
feel more committed to the business and work more effectively for it.

> **Activity 6.1**

- Miguel works as a farm labourer for a rich landlord. He has a small house on the
estate and is allowed to grow his own food on a piece of land next to his house. He
grows enough food to feed himself and his family and is paid a small wage, which
pays for the other needs of the family such as clothes, shoes and medicines.
- Pierre works in a car factory on the assembly line. He works in a team with other
workers welding the car body together. He is also a member of the company football
team. He is well paid and his family can afford quite a few luxuries.
- Anya has a degree in Business Management and professional qualifications in
human resources management. She is the Human Resources Manager of a large
company. She has her own office with her name on the door and is in charge of the
rest of the human resources staff. She works long hours but feels it is worth it if the
right employees are recruited to the company.

Identify which of Maslow's needs are being satisfied for each of these employees.
Explain the reasons for your choices.

Motivation theories

When people work for themselves, for example, entrepreneurs, they tend to work hard
and effectively as they see the direct benefits of their efforts. However, once people
work for someone else then they may not work as effectively. One of the tasks of
management is to encourage the workforce to contribute fully to the success of the
business. To this end, many studies have been carried out to discover what makes
employees work effectively. Two of the main theories are outlined below.

F.W. Taylor

Frederick Taylor started his working life as a labourer in a factory in America
in the 1880s. He rose to become chief engineer. During this time he conducted
experiments at the steel company where he worked, into how labour productivity
could be increased. Taylor based his ideas on the assumption that all individuals
are motivated by personal gain and therefore, if they are paid more, they will
work more effectively. He was looking at workers who worked in factories. He
broke down their jobs into simple processes and then calculated how much output
they should be able to do in a day. If they produced this target output, they
would be paid more money. Taylor saw employees rather like machines – when
they were working hard, their productivity would be high and therefore the
labour costs would be low for each unit produced.

Taylor's ideas resulted in big productivity gains at the company where he worked and many other businesses adopted his ideas. But there are several criticisms of Taylor's ideas:

» His ideas were too simplistic – employees are motivated by many things and not just money.

» You can pay an employee more money, but if they are unfulfilled by their work in some way, there will be no increase in their effectiveness at work and there will be no productivity gains.

» A practical problem arises if you cannot easily measure an employee's output.

Activity 6.2

a From the following list of jobs, say what you could measure to find out how effectively the employees are working:
- car production worker
- shop assistant
- waiter
- teacher
- police officer
- soldier
- baker.

b Are there any jobs on the list for which output is difficult to measure? If so, explain why it is difficult to measure the output in each case.

c If you cannot measure workers' output, how can you pay them more money if they work harder or more effectively?

d Does this present problems for modern economies today where the majority of the workforce work in service sector jobs?

Herzberg

Frederick Herzberg's motivation theories were based on his study of the work of engineers and accountants in the USA. According to Herzberg, humans have two sets of needs; one is for the basic needs, which he called 'hygiene' factors or needs, and the second is for a human being to be able to grow psychologically, which he called 'motivational' needs or 'motivators'.

Motivators
achievement
recognition
personal growth/development
advancement/promotion
work itself
'Hygiene' (or 'maintenance') factors
status
security
work conditions
company policies and administration
relationship with supervisor
relationship with subordinates
salary

Study tips

Make sure you can explain each of these theories and also explain how knowledge of them can help managers to improve the motivation of their employees.

According to Herzberg, the 'hygiene' factors must be satisfied; if they are not satisfied, they can act as demotivators to the worker. However, they do not act as motivators, as once satisfied the effects of them quickly wear off. True motivators are found in other factors, as shown in the table on page 66.

 Case study

Company A employs 100 workers taking telephone orders and making calls to potential customers. The company thinks it treats its workers well. The offices they work in are well lit, warm but not too hot, the salary is similar to the pay in other similar jobs, the supervisors are polite and keep checking the work of the employees. The workers are told what to do and have no opportunities for promotion. There is no recognition of workers who have done well in their jobs. The management is worried because the workers do not seem to be particularly happy and have not increased their productivity. There is high labour turnover.

Activity 6.3

Read the case study above.

a Why do you think the workers might not be happy in their jobs?
b Suggest ways the management might use to increase the motivation of their employees.

People often say that money is the main motivator. It may not be. Surveys show that the other factors discussed on page 71 may be much more important to people than money alone. The lack of these other motivators is often a reason why employees leave a job and seek employment elsewhere.

REVISION SUMMARY **Motivation theories**

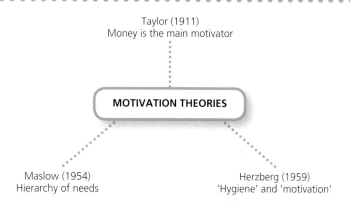

Taylor (1911)
Money is the main motivator

MOTIVATION THEORIES

Maslow (1954)
Hierarchy of needs

Herzberg (1959)
'Hygiene' and 'motivation'

Methods of motivation – financial rewards

There are many ways in which businesses can offer financial rewards to their employees. The methods of payment or financial reward are used to provide incentives to employees to encourage them to work hard and effectively. Five of the most frequently used methods are:

» wage
» salary
» bonus
» commission
» profit sharing.

Wages

Wages are often paid every week, sometimes in cash and sometimes directly into a bank account.

» The worker gets paid on a regular basis and does not have to wait long for some money. Wages tend to be paid to manual workers, such as those who work in a warehouse or factory.
» If the employee works longer than their normal hours, they can usually be paid overtime. This is their regular amount per hour plus an extra amount. This is an incentive to work additional hours when required by the business.

However, there are some drawbacks:

» As the wages are paid weekly, they have to be calculated every week, which takes time and money.
» Wages clerks are often employed to perform this task.

When calculating the wages to be paid, they can be worked out in a number of different ways. They can use time rate or piece rate.

Time rate

Time rate is payment by the hour (payment for a period of time). For example, if an employee is paid $10 per hour and they work for 40 hours, then they will be paid $400.

» This makes it easy to calculate the worker's wages and the worker knows exactly how much they will be paid for working a certain period of time.

Possible limitations

» The hours worked are often recorded on a time-sheet which must be filled in and used to calculate the wages by the Accounts department. This system takes time.
» Good and bad workers get paid the same amount of money.
» Often supervisors are needed to make sure the workers keep working and producing a good quality product. This is expensive because more supervisors are needed by the business.
» A clocking-in system is needed to determine the number of hours worked by the employees.

Time rate is often used where it is difficult to measure the output of the worker, for example, a bus driver or hotel receptionist.

Piece rate

Piece rate is where the workers are paid depending on the quantity of products made – the more they make, the more they get paid. A basic rate is usually paid, with additional money paid according to how many products have been produced. Piece rate can be applied to bonus systems where employees who produce more than a set target of output can be rewarded. Piece rates can only be used where it is possible to measure the performance of an individual or a team.

>> The advantage with this system is that it encourages workers to work faster and produce more goods.

Possible limitations

>> Workers may concentrate on making a large number of products and ignore quality, producing goods that may not sell very well because they are of a poor quality. This usually requires a quality control system and this is expensive. If poor quality goods are produced, this could damage the reputation of the business.

>> Workers who are careful in their work will not earn as much as those who rush, which may not be seen as fair. Friction between employees may be caused as some will earn more than others.

>> If the machinery breaks down, the employees will earn less money. Because of this, workers are often paid a guaranteed minimum amount of money.

Salaries

Salaries are paid monthly, normally straight into a bank account. They are not paid in cash. It is usual for office staff or management to be paid salaries.

>> A salary is calculated as an amount of money per year for the job performed by the worker. It is divided into 12 monthly amounts. This means it is easy to calculate salary costs for the business.

>> The employer has the money in their bank account for longer than if they were paying their workers' wages, as salaries are paid only once a month.

>> The payment has to be calculated only once a month instead of at least four times a month – as with wages.

Possible limitations

>> Workers may prefer to be paid weekly.

>> No payment for extra time worked – workers may be reluctant to work longer.

Bonuses

A **bonus** is a lump sum paid to workers when they have worked well. It can be paid at the end of the year or at intervals during the year.

Bonuses do not have to be paid – a business can decide to pay a bonus just to an individual worker who has performed well or to all of its employees if the business has exceeded certain targets. A bonus is paid in addition to the standard wage or salary. Being paid a bonus can have a positive motivating effect. Workers often consider themselves to be 'recognised' and 'special' if they are paid a bonus.

Possible limitations

>> Bonuses can become 'expected' every year and if they are not paid – perhaps because the business has had a poor year – then employee disappointment can be difficult to manage.

>> If only one or a small number of workers are paid a bonus, then bad feelings can be caused as other workers resent this and question why they did not receive one.

> **Definitions to learn**
>
> A **salary** is payment for work, usually paid monthly.

> **Definitions to learn**
>
> A **bonus** is an additional amount of payment above basic pay as a reward for good work.

Commission

These additional payments are often paid to sales staff. The more sales they make, the more money they are paid – similar to piece rate but applying only to sales staff. This encourages the sales staff to sell as many products as possible. This should be good for the business as sales may increase. **Commission** is paid in addition to the existing wage or salary.

Possible limitations

» If the sales staff are very persuasive and encourage people to buy goods they don't really want, then the business may see its sales increase only in the short term and then fall again as it gets a bad reputation.
» It can be very stressful for the sales staff because, if they have a bad month, their pay will fall.
» There might be too much competition between sales staff to 'get the next customer' who enters the shop!

Profit sharing

Employees receive a share of the profits in addition to their basic wage or salary. This additional payment should motivate the workers to work hard as they all receive a share of the profits earned by the business. The rest of the profits will be paid as dividends to the shareholders or retained by the business. **Profit sharing** is often used in the service sector where it is difficult to identify an individual employee's contribution to the increased profits, but they will all benefit from more productive work.

Possible limitations

» If a business makes very low profits or even a loss, then no 'profit share' will be possible, leading to employee disappointment.
» The profit share is usually calculated on the basis of an additional percentage of a worker's existing wage or salary – so higher paid workers will receive a higher profit share. This could cause bad feeling among lower paid workers who consider that they have worked just as hard!

REVISION SUMMARY   **Methods of financial reward**

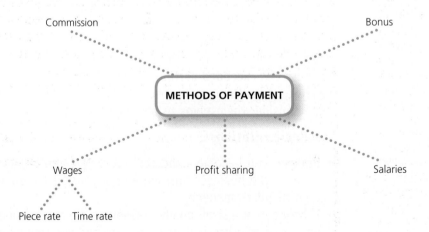

Fringe benefits

In addition to these financial rewards, businesses may give other employee benefits. These usually vary according to the seniority of the job. Factory workers may get discounts on the business's products, but they would not all have a company car, whereas a senior manager may have several non-financial rewards, such as a house, car and expense account. These are sometimes called 'perks' or 'fringe benefits' of a job.

Examples include:

» company vehicle (car)
» discounts on the business's products
» health care paid for
» children's education fees paid
» free accommodation
» share options (where company shares are given to employees)
» generous expense accounts (for food and clothing)
» pension paid for by the business
» free trips abroad/holidays.

> ## Activity 6.4
>
> For the following jobs, say which methods of motivation would be most suitable and why. (Remember to consider whether it is easy to measure their output – this may affect how you decide to reward their efforts.)
>
> **a** Car production worker **d** Shop assistant
> **b** Hotel receptionist **e** Managing director
> **c** Teacher **f** Taxi driver

Motivating factors – non-financial methods

There are ways other than pay that can be used to motivate workers and make them more committed to their job and work more effectively. Many non-financial methods of motivation are focused on increasing the level of **job satisfaction** – the enjoyment from doing a job. However, there are some factors that will make employees unhappy and these must be changed before the employees can be motivated in a positive way. For example, if the management of the business is not good and the employees are treated badly, giving them either fringe benefits or using non-financial motivation will probably not motivate them. If rates of pay are perceived by the employees as very low relative to those of similar workers, this will be a source of dissatisfaction to the employees. If these sources of dissatisfaction have been overcome, for example if reasonable wage rates are paid and employees are treated fairly at work, then other sources of job satisfaction can motivate employees.

> ## Activity 6.5
>
> Compare a nurse with a machine operator in a factory. What do you think makes their jobs satisfying? Copy out the table below and list your ideas for each.
>
> | Nurse | Machine operator |
> | --- | --- |
> | | |
> | | |
> | | |
> | | |

Some of the motivation theories (particularly Maslow and Herzberg) emphasise that the important aspects of jobs are that they should give recognition, responsibility and satisfaction to the people doing them and allow the employee to gain a sense of achievement from the work itself. Some jobs may seem dull and boring, but with a little thought and creativity they can be made more interesting and consequently increase motivation.

There are several ways in which a business can increase the job satisfaction of its employees.

Job rotation

Workers on a production line may carry out simple but different tasks. **Job rotation** involves the workers swapping round and doing each specific task for only a limited time (for example, for one hour) and then changing around again. This increases the variety in the work itself and also makes it easier for the managers to move workers around the factory if people are ill and their jobs need covering. However, it does not make the tasks themselves more interesting.

filling machine   labelling   putting product   packing boxes in larger
                                       into boxes   boxes for storage/transport

every hour, or every half day, each person moves along and changes jobs

Job enrichment

Job enrichment involves looking at jobs and adding tasks that require more skill and/or responsibility. Additional training may be necessary to enable the employee to take on extra tasks. For example, employees may be given responsibility for a whole area of the work. If managers can design jobs so that they provide scope for fulfilling higher human needs, workers will often become more committed because they get more satisfaction from their jobs, again raising productivity.

reception   now also   word-processes letters   takes
                                                                        orders
receptionist employed   deals with telephone enquiries
to greet customers   training will be needed – receptionist will need to
                                    know about products sold in order to deal with enquiries

Autonomous work groups or teamworking

Teamworking involves a group of workers being given responsibility for a particular process, product or development. They can decide as a group how to complete the tasks or organise the jobs. The workers can become more involved in the decision making and take responsibility for this process. This gives a feeling of control over the jobs/tasks and the employees feel more committed, therefore increasing job satisfaction. An example of this way of organising employees is on a car production line where particular parts of the assembly line are given over to teams of workers and they decide how to organise themselves. Often this leads to job rotation and job enrichment. Working as a group helps improve morale as well as giving a greater sense of belonging to the company.

A team of workers is responsible for a particular part of the assembly
The team decides how the processes will be completed
The tasks are allocated by the team themselves – they make the decisions

Training

Improving a worker's level of skills can have beneficial effects on motivation levels. First, workers can feel a great sense of achievement if they successfully gain and apply new work-based skills. Second, they could now be given more challenging and rewarding work to perform – and this is an important element of job enrichment.

Workers can also feel as if they have been selected by management for **training** courses and this can give them a feeling that their good work has been recognised.

Opportunities for promotion

Many businesses prefer to fill posts of responsibility, for example, supervisors, team leaders, junior and senior managers, from within the existing workforce. This internal recruitment offers opportunities for advancement to existing workers. Not only does the business benefit from promoting workers who already 'know how it operates' but it also gains from better motivated workers. Employees offered **promotion** will feel recognised, have a higher status and will be given more challenging work to perform. All of these benefits are closely linked to the views of both Maslow and Herzberg.

REVISION SUMMARY **Motivating factors at all levels**

Study tips

Make sure you are able to choose suitable ways of increasing job satisfaction for employees in different jobs.

Activity 6.6

- Duncan is a computer programmer. He has a degree in Computer Studies and enjoyed writing programs as part of his degree course. He thought computer programming would be his ideal job. However, all he does is write simple programs for businesses' Accounts departments which allow the processing of their paperwork. He is told what to do by his manager and is given little opportunity to visit the client to discuss its requirements and does not go to install the software at the business when it is finished. He is so fed up he is looking for another job.
- Sita works in a clothes shop. She spends her time looking after the changing room, where she checks customers into the changing rooms and takes the garments which are not going to be purchased from them when the customers have tried them on. There are several other shop employees, one works at the cash till, one puts out the clothes on the rails and does the shop displays, one person works in the stock room and there is a manager who does all the ordering and administration for the shop. The shop can be very quiet on some days and very busy on others. Sita does not care if customers find the right clothes – she gets paid whether they buy the clothes or not.
- Tim works in a clothing factory. He cuts out the collars for shirts. The rest of the processes for making shirts are carried out by other employees. He has done this job for two years now and gets very fed up with what he is doing. He does not worry too much if the collars are slightly uneven as he thinks customers will not notice. The other employees who work with him in the shirt department feel the same as he does.

These three employees are not happy in their work. Suggest how you would try to improve their job satisfaction. Explain the reasons for your suggestions. (You may suggest more than one way for each of the employees.) Which do you think would be the best one to use in each case and why?

International business in focus

Low levels of job satisfaction among Malaysian nurses

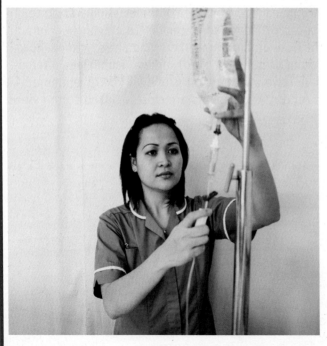

A recent study reported that shortages of nurses in Malaysia are resulting in a heavy workload

and job stress, which have also been linked to low job satisfaction. Financial rewards for the job include wages, benefits and bonuses. Hospital managers claim that the job of nursing offers personal rewards including status, recognition, and personal and professional development opportunities. Reasons for nurse dissatisfaction appear to include lack of involvement in decision making, a poor relationship with management, low salaries compared to other jobs with a similar level of qualifications, lack of job security and low levels of recognition. Job dissatisfaction is shown when nurses say they wish to leave their job.

Discussion points

- Why do the nurses seem to have a low level of job satisfaction?
- What could managers do to improve motivation?
- Which methods to improve motivation of nurses would be most effective and why?

Exam-style questions: Short answer and data response

1 Joe owns a business which produces wooden furniture. He employs 20 workers in the Production department and three workers in the offices. Joe pays all his workers wages which are calculated by time rate, but he is thinking of changing to piece rate. He has a high labour turnover from the factory as his workers are not well motivated.

   a Define 'piece rate'. [2]

   b Identify **two** examples of non-financial benefits Joe could give to his employees. [2]

   c Outline **two** reasons why many employees leave their job at the furniture company. [4]

   d Explain **two** ways Joe can improve the job satisfaction of his employees. [6]

   e Do you think a wage calculated by piece rate is a suitable method of payment for all Joe's employees? Justify your answer. [6]

2 Sasha is a hotel manager. She has 30 employees and they are divided into teams working in the following departments: kitchen; restaurant; hotel reception; housekeeping (room cleaning). Two of the hotel receptionists have been trained by Sasha in some aspects of hotel management. A modern hotel has recently opened two kilometres away. Sasha wants to improve the motivation of all the employees and is thinking of introducing a bonus. She thinks it will make the hotel more profitable.

   a Define 'bonus'. [2]

   b Identify **two** reasons why people work. [2]

   c Outline **two** levels in Maslow's hierarchy of needs experienced by the hotel workers. [4]

   d Explain **two** benefits to the hotel of having well-motivated employees. [6]

   e Do you think introducing a bonus is the best way to improve the motivation of the employees at the hotel? Justify your answer. [6]

Revision checklist

In this chapter you have learned:
- ✔ about the reasons people work and why well-motivated employees are important
- ✔ about Maslow's hierarchy: the concept of human needs
- ✔ about Taylor and Herzberg: the key motivation theories
- ✔ about using financial and non-financial rewards as methods of motivation
- ✔ to identify when and which motivational methods would be appropriate to use.

NOW – test your understanding with the revision questions in the Student etextbook and the Workbook.

Organisation and management

This chapter will explain:

★ how to draw, interpret and understand simple organisational charts
★ simple hierarchical structures: span of control, levels of hierarchy, chain of command
★ the roles and responsibilities of directors, managers, supervisors and other employees in an organisation, and inter-relationships between them
★ the role and functions of management – planning, organising, coordinating, commanding and controlling
★ the importance of delegation; trust versus control
★ features of the main leadership styles – autocratic, democratic and laissez-faire
★ how to recommend and justify an appropriate leadership style in a given circumstance
★ what a trade union is and the effects of employees being union members.

What is organisational structure?

Organisational structure refers to the levels of management and division of responsibilities within an organisation. This structure is often presented in the form of an **organisational chart** with several **levels of hierarchy.**

Definitions to learn

Organisational structure refers to the levels of management and division of responsibilities within an organisation.

Organisational chart refers to a diagram that outlines the internal management structure.

Hierarchy refers to the levels of management in any organisation, from the highest to the lowest. A **level of hierarchy** refers to managers/supervisors/other employees who are given a similar level of responsibility in an organisation.

➡ Case study

The Cosy Corner Convenience Store is owned and managed by Bill Murray. It is a sole trader business. Bill has no employees. He works a long day – 12 hours, usually. As he works alone in the business he has to do all the jobs which are involved in running a busy convenience store. Here is a list of just six of his tasks:

- Ordering new stock
- Serving customers
- Going to the bank to pay in cash – he does this on Wednesday afternoons when the shop is closed
- Arranging shelf displays
- Keeping all the paperwork up to date, for example, to make sure suppliers are paid on time
- Contacting the local newspaper to arrange an advertisement for the shop.

▶ Activity 7.1

Read the case study above. List **three** other tasks that you think Bill has to do in order to run Cosy Corner efficiently.

In Bill's business there is no need for an organisational structure because he works alone. There is no need to outline the responsibilities and duties of other employees or to indicate their links with other workers – because there aren't any! As he is the only manager, there can be no other management levels. This example shows the simplest form of business. What would happen to the organisation of Bill's business if it expanded?

Organisational structure changes as businesses expand

Case study

Bill was exhausted. It was the end of another long day. He had decided during the day that he could no longer do all the work of running the store by himself. He was going to advertise for a shop assistant. He thought carefully about what work he would want the assistant to perform. Bill remembered from his previous job, working for a large retail chain, that it was important to make clear the tasks and responsibilities of employees. If this was not done then two people might end up doing the same work – and some work might not get done at all.

He decided to write out a job description (see right) which he would give to all the people who applied for the job. This would make clear what the job would involve. Bill thought this would have two main advantages:

- People applying for the job could see if they were suitable for the work expected of them.
- Once in the job, the new employee would know exactly what their duties and responsibilities were. Their work should therefore help Bill, not just repeat what he was doing.

Bill wrote out the following job description.

```
Job description

Shop Assistant

Main tasks:

• To open the shop in the morning
• To be responsible for ordering all goods
  from suppliers
• To arrange all shelf displays
• To help serve customers
• To assist the manager in other ways
  directed by him

Working conditions:

• Five days a week
• Eight hours a day
• Four weeks' holiday – by negotiation, but
  not at same time as the manager
```

Activity 7.2

Read the case study above.

a Study the job description. Do you think Bill is looking to recruit an experienced shop assistant? What evidence is there to support your answer?
b Make a list of the important tasks and responsibilities Bill still has to perform himself.

Bill's business now has a very simple organisational structure. There are two people in the organisation and they are specialising in different jobs. Bill now manages the work of his shop assistant.

Organisation charts

Case study

Bill Murray's business had expanded rapidly. More employees had been appointed. Some of them managed the shop because Bill spent more time on office work. Shop opening hours were lengthened. Eventually, Bill decided to open four further stores in other towns. It became clear to Bill that his business needed the advantages of limited company status (see Chapter 4). A business friend agreed to buy shares and become one of the directors of the company. As the organisation was growing, Bill decided it needed a clear structure. After discussions with his directors and senior managers, he drew up the chart below.

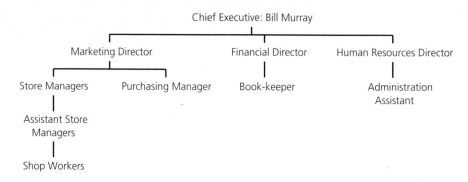

In fact, this is a typical type of organisation chart for many businesses. The most important features are as follows.

- It is a hierarchy. This means that there are different levels in the organisation. Each level has a different degree of authority. People on the same level of hierarchy have the same degree of authority. There are five levels of hierarchy from Chief Executive down to Shop Worker.
- It is organised into departments. Each of these departments has a particular job or function.
- As there are different levels of management, there is a **chain of command**. This is how power and authority are passed down from the top to the lower levels in the organisation. Because Cosy Corner Ltd is still quite a small business, the chain of command is quite short as there are not many levels of management. Bigger businesses are likely to have many more levels of hierarchy and therefore a longer chain of command.

Bill decided to give a copy of this chart to all members of staff. He considered that there were several advantages in both constructing the organisation chart as a hierarchy and informing everybody of it.

> **Definitions to learn**
>
> **Chain of command** is the structure in an organisation which allows instructions to be passed down from senior management to lower levels of management.

Advantages of an organisation chart

» The chart shows how everybody is linked together in the organisation. All employees are aware of which communication channel is used to reach them with messages and instructions.

- Every individual can see their own position in the organisation. They can identify who they are accountable to and who they have authority over. Employees can see who they should take orders from.
- It shows the links and relationship between different departments within the organisation.

» Everyone is in a department and this gives them a sense of belonging.

Chain of command and span of control

Look at the two organisation charts below. There are two essential differences between them.

» Business A has a tall structure and a long chain of command.
» Business B has a wide structure and a short chain of command.

As a result of these two different structures, the **span of control** (the number of subordinates working directly under a manager) is wider in Business B than in Business A – in Business A this number is two and in Business B it is five.

There is therefore an important link between the span of control and the chain of command. The longer the chain of command, the 'taller' will be the organisational structure and the 'narrower' the span of control.

When the chain of command is short, the organisation will have 'wider' spans of control.

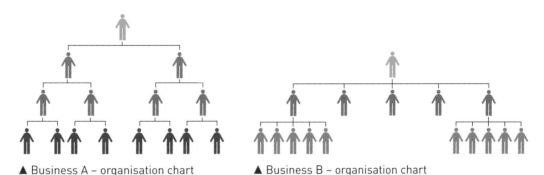

▲ Business A – organisation chart   ▲ Business B – organisation chart

There is no perfect organisational structure. In recent years many organisations have made their structure 'wider' and with a shorter chain of command. In some cases, this has been done by removing a whole level of management – called delayering. The claimed advantages of short chains of command are listed below.

Advantages of short chains of command

» Communication is quicker and more accurate. Each message has fewer levels to pass through before reaching the intended person.
» Top managers are less remote from the lower level of the hierarchy. These top managers should be more in touch with people below them as there are fewer management levels to get to know.
» Spans of control will be wider. This means that each manager is responsible for more subordinates. Why is this an advantage?
   • If superiors have more people to manage, it will encourage managers to delegate more. This is because, as their department is larger, they cannot possibly do all the important work by themselves.
   • There will be less direct control of each worker and they will feel more trusted. They will be able to take more decisions by themselves. They may obtain more job satisfaction.

However, wider spans of control, with more people to be directly responsible for, could mean that the managers lose control of what their subordinates are doing. The subordinates could make many mistakes if they are poorly trained.

Case study

Mustafa was bored with his work. He was a telephone operator in a large telephone banking firm. The business received calls from customers who wanted to use banking services but did not have time to go to a bank branch.

Mustafa worked in a team, called Team A, with other colleagues, Hammed and Asif. They were supervised by Aziz, who was under the authority of Mohammed. There were two other groups of telephone operators, Team B and Team C. These two teams were the same size as Team A. They also had their own supervisors who reported to Mohammed.

All calls were recorded and supervisors could listen in to make sure that all workers were polite and helpful to customers. Telephone operators were only allowed to do certain tasks for customers. Other jobs, such as transfers of large sums of money, had to be referred to a supervisor or manager. Telephone operators had to aim to answer 20 calls each hour. No wonder Mustafa was bored with his work!

Activity 7.3

Read the case study above.

a Draw the organisation chart for this telephone business.
b What is the span of control of the supervisors?
c What would be the advantages and disadvantages of removing the supervisors altogether? Your answer should include references to:
  • chain of command   • delegation   • span of control.

Roles, responsibilities and inter-relationships between people in organisations

 Case study

The newly opened branches of Cosy Corner plc proved to be just as popular as the first one. Profits increased and the business expanded in other ways. Bill and his fellow directors decided to open the first store in a foreign country, France. They had plans to open several more. The directors had also taken the step of opening a food processing factory to provide some of the goods sold by the Cosy Corner stores. It was found to be cheaper to produce these goods than to buy them from outside suppliers.

These expansion projects had required a great deal of capital. The business had converted to a public limited company several months ago. The sales of shares to the public raised the necessary finance. Bill was Chairman of the company as well as Chief Executive. He and his Board of Directors were answerable to the shareholders. The management structure below him was now more complicated than when the business was smaller. The current organisational chart is shown below.

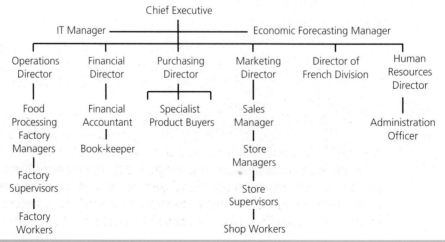

The key features of the current organisational chart, which is typical of many larger businesses, are as follows.

- It is still largely arranged into functional departments, such as Finance and Marketing. These departments are responsible for one important part of the work of the organisation. These departments are led by a **director** who has final responsibility for the work of everyone in the department. However, businesses organised in this way may find that workers feel more loyalty to their department than to the organisation as a whole. There could be conflict between departments. For example, Operations may wish to purchase new machinery, but Finance does not make the necessary money available. Managers working in these departments are called **line managers**. They have the authority to give orders to **supervisors** and other employees and to have their decisions put into effect in their department. They supervise subordinates in a clear line of authority.

- In addition to the functional departments, there is also a regional division responsible for the Cosy Corner stores in other countries. This department has the advantage of being able to use specialist knowledge to help it run the stores abroad, such as knowledge of local cultures and customs.
- There are other departments which do not have a typical function and which employ specialists in particular areas. Examples from Cosy Corner plc are the Economic Forecasting department and the Information Technology department. Some people include the Human Resources department in this group too. These departments report directly to the Board of Directors. (Meetings of the Board of Directors will be attended by the departmental directors and the Chief Executive.) The people in these departments are called **staff managers** because they provide specialist advice and support to the Board of Directors and to line managers of the functional departments. Staff managers tend to be very well-qualified experts.

Definitions to learn

Directors are senior managers who lead a particular department or division of a business.
Line managers have direct responsibility for people below them in the hierarchy of an organisation.
Supervisors are junior managers who have direct control over the employees below them in the organisational structure.
Staff managers are specialists who provide support, information and assistance to line managers.

▶ Activity 7.4

Read the case study above.

a What are the advantages and disadvantages of this tall organisational structure for Cosy Corner plc?
b Give **three** examples of conflicts which may arise from this structure.
c Do you think this organisational structure increases motivation for its employees?
d What are the benefits of having a regional division for the business?

The role and functions of management

All organisations, including businesses, have managers. They may not be called managers because different titles can be used – leader, director, headteacher, and so on. Whatever their title the tasks of all managers are very similar, no matter what the organisation. If you are a student in a school or college or if you are in full-time employment, the managers of your organisation will, at some time, have to fulfil the following functions.

Planning

Planning for the future of the organisation involves setting aims or targets, for example: 'The school will aim to increase its sixth form to over 200 students in two years' time' or 'We should plan to increase sales of our new fruit juice range by 50 per cent in three years.'

These aims or targets will give the organisation a sense of direction or purpose. There will be a common feeling in the organisation of having something to work towards. It is a poor manager who does not plan for the future at all.

In addition to these aims, a manager must also plan for the resources which will be needed. For example: 'To achieve our aim of increasing student numbers in the sixth form, we will need to build a new sixth form centre' or 'Increased advertising expenditure will be needed to increase sales of our fruit juices.' These are two examples of strategies which are designed to help the organisation achieve the aims set for it.

Organising

A manager cannot do everything. Tasks must be delegated to others in the organisation. These people must have the resources to be able to do these tasks successfully. It is therefore the manager's responsibility to organise people and resources effectively.

An organisational chart can help to show who has the authority to do different jobs. It also helps to make sure that specialisation occurs and that two people do not end up doing the same task. An effective manager will organise people and resources very carefully indeed.

Coordinating

Coordinating means 'bringing together'. A manager may be very good at planning and organising but may have failed to 'bring people in the organisation together'. This is a real danger with the functional form of organisation. Different departments can be working away in their own specialist area without making contact with people from other departments. For example, there is no point in the Marketing department planning the launch of a new product unless they have worked with (coordinated with) the Operations department. It is the Operations department that will have to produce the product at the right time, in the right quantities.

A good manager will therefore make sure that all departments in the organisation work together to achieve the plans originally set by the manager. In the example above, this could be done by regular meetings between people in the different departments. Alternatively, a project team could have been set up to develop and launch the new product. The team would be made up of people from different departments.

Commanding

Many people think that this is all managers do! In fact, the task of management is more concerned with guiding, leading and supervising people than just telling them what to do – although this may be important too. Managers have to make sure that all supervisors and workers are keeping to targets and deadlines. Instructions and guidance must be provided by managers and it is also their responsibility to make sure that the tasks are carried out by people below them in the organisation.

Controlling

This is a never-ending task of management. Managers must try to measure and evaluate the work of all individuals and groups to make sure that they are on target. There is little point in planning and organising if managers then fail to check that the original aims are being met. If it seems that certain groups are failing to do what is expected of them, then managers may have to take some corrective action. This is not necessarily disciplining staff – although that might be important. There might be reasons for poor performance other than inefficient workers – it is the manager's job to find out why targets are not being met and then to correct the problem.

Do you now have a clearer idea of what managers do? Management is not easy to define, but the list of tasks above helps to demonstrate the varied and important work that good managers should be doing.

From studying the list of points on pages 81–82, it should also become clear why management is necessary to any organisation. Without clear and effective management, a business is going to lack:

» a sense of control and direction
» coordination between departments, leading to wastage of effort
» control of employees
» organisation of resources, leading to low output and sales.

In short, without management to take the business forward, the business will drift and eventually fail.

▶ Activity 7.5

Naomi is a student at a sixth form college. She recently took part in a work shadowing exercise to find out what it is like to be a manager. Work shadowing means that a student follows a manager for a day or more to experience the work that they do. Naomi 'shadowed' Sabrina Choolun, who is the manager of the sportswear section in Suresave plc, a large department store. Naomi kept the following diary for one day.

08:30   Attended meeting with other departmental heads and Chief Executive to agree targets for the next two years. Departmental heads told to plan their own strategy to meet these goals.

09:15   Two staff members failed to turn up for work. Sabrina asked other staff to cover these absences by working longer shifts today.

10:00   Meeting with Sales Manager from big sports manufacturer. Sabrina discussed the range of goods she may purchase next year to meet the store's targets.

11:00   New member of staff did not cope well with awkward customer. When customer had gone, Sabrina reminded the shop assistant of the correct procedure that should be followed. Asked worker always follow company policy in these matters.

14:30   Computer printouts of individual staff sales figures were studied. One worker in particular has failed to meet sales targets and it was agreed with him that further product training was necessary.

16:00   Email received from Sabrina's line manager. There was a problem with another department selling clothing including sports clothes. It was now possible for customers to find the same goods in the store in two departments at different prices! Sabrina needed to meet with the other departmental manager to agree on a common policy.

For each of the tasks that Sabrina carried out, identify whether it was concerned with: planning, organising, coordinating, commanding or controlling.

Delegation

Even when Bill's business was still very small with just one employee it was possible to see a very important idea being used. This idea is called **delegation**. This means giving a subordinate the authority to perform particular tasks. It is very important to remember that it is the authority to perform a task which is being delegated – not the final responsibility. If the job is done badly by the subordinate then it is the manager who has to accept the responsibility for this.

Definitions to learn

Delegation means giving a subordinate the authority to perform particular tasks.

Advantages of delegation for the manager

» Managers cannot do every job themselves. As we have seen, it became very difficult for Bill to control all of the running of Cosy Corner by himself. By delegating, he was able to concentrate his time on other important management functions.
» Managers are less likely to make mistakes if some of the tasks are performed by their subordinates.
» Managers can measure the success of their staff more easily. They can see how well they have done in performing the tasks delegated to them.

Advantages of delegation for the subordinate

» The work becomes more interesting and rewarding.
» The employee feels more important and believes that trust is being put in them to perform a job well.
» Delegation helps to train workers and they can then make progress in the organisation. It gives them career opportunities.

Why might a manager not delegate?

Despite the advantages of delegation, there are some managers who are reluctant to delegate. Some may be afraid that the subordinates might fail and the manager wants to control everything by themselves. Also, there is a risk that the subordinates might do a better job than the manager! This could make the manager feel very insecure.

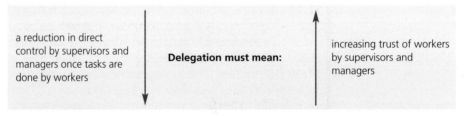

| a reduction in direct control by supervisors and managers once tasks are done by workers | **Delegation must mean:** | increasing trust of workers by supervisors and managers |

▲ There needs to be an increase in trust in order to reduce control over workers

REVISION SUMMARY **Delegation**

DELEGATION

Makes work more interesting

Gives authority to others to take decisions and perform tasks

Employee development increases job satisfaction

Subordinate feels trusted if no training given

Some managers are reluctant to delegate

Manager loses some control over subordinates

Allows managers to give time to other issues

Why is it important to have good managers?

A good manager should:

» motivate employees
» give guidance and advice to employees they manage
» inspire employees they manage to achieve more than they thought possible
» manage resources effectively and keep costs under control
» increase profitability of the business.

Effective managers

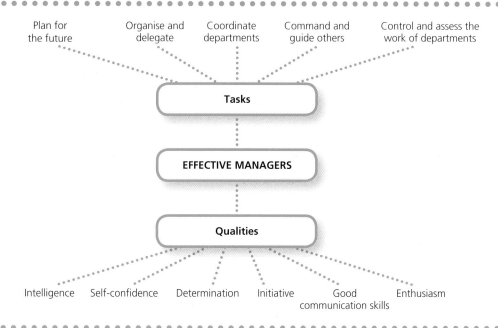

Plan for the future | Organise and delegate | Coordinate departments | Command and guide others | Control and assess the work of departments

Tasks

EFFECTIVE MANAGERS

Qualities

Intelligence | Self-confidence | Determination | Initiative | Good communication skills | Enthusiasm

Leadership

Studies on motivation have emphasised the importance of good management in business and the need for leadership. There are many leaders in society – from politicians, religious leaders and captains of sports teams, to leaders of large businesses. Many people take on the role of being a leader and some are more effective than others. A good leader in a large business is someone who can inspire and get the best out of the workforce, getting them to work towards a common goal.

Styles of leadership

There are different approaches to leadership that are adopted and these can be summarised into three main **leadership styles**:

» autocratic leadership
» democratic leadership
» laissez-faire leadership.

Autocratic leadership

Autocratic leadership is where the manager expects to be in charge of the business and to have their orders followed. They keep themselves separate from the rest of the employees. They make virtually all the decisions and keep

Definitions to learn

Leadership styles are the different approaches to dealing with people and making decisions when in a position of authority – autocratic, democratic or laissez-faire.

Autocratic leadership is where the manager expects to be in charge of the business and to have their orders followed.

85

information to themselves. They tell employees only what they need to know. Communication in the business is mainly one way, that is, downward or top-down, and the workers have little or no opportunity to comment on anything.

Potential advantage

» Quick decision making, for example, during a crisis.

Potential disadvantage

» No opportunity for employee input into key decisions, which can be demotivating.

Democratic leadership

Democratic leadership gets other employees involved in the decision-making process. Information about future plans is openly discussed before the final decision is made, often by the leader. Communication is both downward or top-down, and upward or bottom-up.

Possible advantage

» Better decisions could result from consulting with employees and using their experience and ideas – as well as being a motivating factor.

Possible disadvantage

» Unpopular decisions, such as making workers redundant, could not effectively be made using this style of leadership.

Laissez-faire leadership

Laissez-faire is French for 'leave to do'. **Laissez-faire leadership** tends to make the broad objectives of the business known to employees, but then they are left to make their own decisions and organise their own work. Communication can be difficult in this type of organisation as clear direction is not given. The leader has only a very limited role to play.

Possible advantage

» Encourages employees to show creativity and responsibility.

Possible disadvantage

» Unlikely to be appropriate in organisations where a consistent and clear decision-making structure is needed, for example, in providing customer service.

The style of leadership used by a manager can vary depending on the employees being dealt with and the problem to be solved. For example, managers may not be autocratic leaders all of the time – it may be appropriate for them to be democratic over some issues, whereas other issues will need a decision imposing on the workforce.

Different situations often require different styles of leadership. The way in which a manager deals with a situation can have a very important impact on people and how they react to the manager. It is important to remember here that a good manager will adopt the style of leadership that best suits each situation.

> **Definitions to learn**
>
> **Democratic leadership** gets other employees involved in the decision-making process.

> **Definitions to learn**
>
> **Laissez-faire leadership** makes the broad objectives of the business known to employees, but then they are left to make their own decisions and organise their own work.

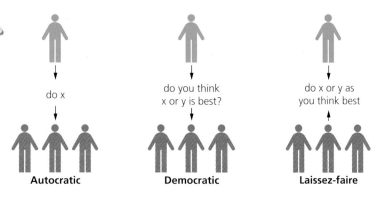

▲ Leadership styles

Activity 7.6

When Cosy Corner convenience store started it was small and Bill Murray, the sole owner, knew all the employees by name. He used a management style which involved asking the workers what they thought about his decisions and encouraged them to tell him their ideas about the business. The business has now grown into a large public limited company with many more employees.

Look back at the case study on pages 80–81 and consider the different leadership styles which might be suitable for Bill or his managers to use within this public limited company.

Which do you think will be the best leadership style for Bill and his managers to use? Explain your answer.

Study tips

Make sure you know the leadership styles and can apply them to different work situations.

Trade unions

Employees generally share many of the same interests, such as improving their pay, having a pleasant environment in which to work, being treated fairly by their employer, being given proper training and working in a safe environment. Forming a **trade union** is a way of helping employees to achieve improvements in these different aspects of their employment – a trade union is a type of pressure group.

Today, trade unions are found in many different countries around the world from the USA to Papua New Guinea.

Effects of employees being union members

When a person starts work they may be asked by someone who represents a trade union if they want to join. If the worker decides to join the trade union, they will pay an annual subscription (a yearly fee).

So what benefits does the employee receive in exchange for paying their subscription? It varies from union to union, but generally includes many of the following benefits:

» Strength in numbers when negotiating with employers.
» Improved conditions of employment, for example, rates of pay, holidays and hours of work.
» Improved environment where people work, for example, health and safety, noise, heating.
» Improved benefits for members who are not working because they are sick, retired or have been made redundant.

Definitions to learn

A **trade union** is a group of employees who have joined together to ensure their interests are protected.

»» Improved job satisfaction by encouraging training.

»» Advice and/or financial support if a member thinks that they have been unfairly dismissed or made redundant, have received unfair treatment, or have been asked to do something that is not part of their job.

»» Benefits that have been negotiated or provided for union members such as discounts in certain shops, provision of sporting facilities or clubs.

»» Trade unions often meet government officials to influence policies for the benefit of workers.

»» More secure employment where there is a **closed shop**.

However, there are disadvantages for an employee of trade union membership:

»» It costs money to be a member.

»» Workers may be required to take industrial action even if they don't agree.

Trade unions can have both advantages and disadvantages for employers too:

»» They can help improve communications between workers and management.

»» Wage agreements will be easier to negotiate with a trade union than with many individual workers.

However:

»» trade unions can organise strikes if they do not receive the pay levels and work conditions they demand

»» wages are likely to be higher – adding to business costs – when many employees are trade union members.

> **Definitions to learn**
>
> A **closed shop** is when all employees must be a member of the same trade union.

> **Key info**
>
> In 2017 the trade unions representing the employees of Air India, a state-owned airline, wrote to the Indian government opposing plans to privatise the company. The trade unions threatened 'large scale protests' if the airline was sold to the private sector as employees' jobs would be put at risk.

REVISION SUMMARY

Benefits of joining a trade union

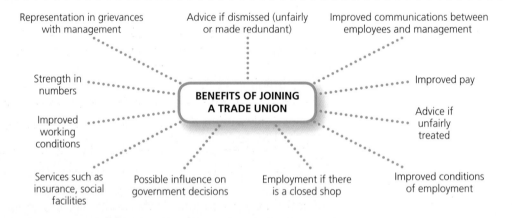

Representation in grievances with management

Advice if dismissed (unfairly or made redundant)

Improved communications between employees and management

Strength in numbers

Improved pay

BENEFITS OF JOINING A TRADE UNION

Improved working conditions

Advice if unfairly treated

Services such as insurance, social facilities

Possible influence on government decisions

Employment if there is a closed shop

Improved conditions of employment

> **Study tips**
>
> Make sure you can explain the advantages and disadvantages of trade union membership from both the employees' and employers' viewpoints.

> ▶ **Activity 7.7**
>
> Shona has just started work as an Administrative Assistant in a government department and has been asked if she wants to join the trade union that represents the workers in that department. She does not know what to do as she knows nothing about trade unions. Write her a letter outlining the advantages and disadvantages of joining a trade union. Include a recommendation to Shona as to whether to join the trade union or not.

International business in focus

Chelsea football club

Chelsea Football Club has had several managers in recent years. One manager was replaced because the club had not been winning many games and the club's owner decided to employ a new one. The manager who lost his job did not tell the players what to do, he would ask them for their opinions on the game and which players the captain thought should play in the next games.

'I am a professional footballer and I know what I am talking about,' said one of the players.

The owner thought it was time for a new approach to managing and leading the players. In 2017 the club won the English Premier League.

Discussion points

- What type of leadership style did the replaced manager use?
- Why did the owner want a new manager with a new leadership style?
- How might the players have reacted to the new manager?

Exam-style questions: Short answer and data response

1 Sasha owns a business which produces office furniture. She employs 100 workers in the Operations department and 15 workers in the offices. Sasha believes in a democratic leadership style. Sasha says that being a good manager is very important to the success of the business. Very few workers leave each year. She sees no need for any of her workers to join a trade union.

   a Define 'democratic leadership'. [2]

   b Identify **two** other leadership styles Sasha could use. [2]

   c Outline **two** roles/functions Sasha undertakes as the manager of this business. [4]

   d Explain **two** reasons why having good managers is important to this business. [6]

   e Do you think Sasha is right to say that her workers do not need to join a trade union? Justify your answer. [6]

2 The following organisation chart is for PPB Ltd. It is a private limited company which owns and operates a chain of supermarkets. The organisational chart shows the hierarchical structure of the business.

   a Define 'hierarchical structure'. [2]

   b Identify the span of control for the:
- Operations Director
- Finance Director. [2]

   c Outline **two** functions of the Managing Director. [4]

   d Explain **two** disadvantages to this business of having a tall organisational structure. [6]

   e Do you think more delegation would be a good idea for this business? Justify your answer. [6]

Revision checklist

In this chapter you have learned:

✔ about simple organisational charts: how to draw, interpret and understand them
✔ the meaning of hierarchical structures, span of control, chain of command and delegation
✔ the roles, responsibilities and inter-relationships between people in organisations
✔ the role and functions of management
✔ the different styles of leadership that management might use
✔ how to recommend and justify a leadership style in particular circumstances
✔ why employees join trade unions.

NOW – test your understanding with the revision questions in the Student etextbook and the Workbook.

Recruitment, selection and training of employees

This chapter will explain:

★ recruitment and selection methods
★ differences between internal recruitment and external recruitment
★ the main stages in recruitment and selection of employees
★ how to recommend and justify who to employ in given circumstances
★ the benefits and limitations of part-time employees and full-time employees
★ the importance of training to a business and employees
★ the benefits and limitations of induction training, on-the-job training and off-the-job training
★ the differences between dismissal and redundancy, with examples
★ how to understand situations in which downsizing the workforce might be necessary, for example, automation or reduced demand for products
★ how to recommend and justify which employees to make redundant in given circumstances
★ legal controls over employment contracts, unfair dismissal, discrimination, health and safety, legal minimum wage, and their impact on employers and employees.

Definitions to learn

Recruitment is the process from identifying that the business needs to employ someone up to the point at which applications have arrived at the business.
Employee selection is the process of evaluating candidates for a specific job and selecting an individual for employment based on the needs of the organisation.

The work of the Human Resources department

Recruitment and **employee selection** are the most familiar roles of the Human Resources department, but there are several others such as training, meeting legal requirements regarding employment, and being responsible for redundancy and dismissal. This chapter studies all these roles in detail.

Recruitment and selection
Involves attracting and selecting the best candidates for vacancies that arise

Wages and salaries
These must attract and retain the right people and be sufficiently high to motivate employees

Industrial relations
There must be effective communication between representatives of the management and of the workforce. This may be to resolve grievances and disputes but also to put forward ideas and suggestions for improvements

HUMAN RESOURCES DEPARTMENT

Training programmes
Involves assessing and fulfilling the training needs of employees. This should be linked to the future plans of the business

Health and safety
The business needs to make sure that it complies with all the laws on health and safety

Redundancy (retrenchment) and dismissal
This involves releasing employees either because the business changes in some way or because the employee is not satisfactory. The business must be sure to comply with all the laws on redundancy, dismissal and disciplinary matters

▲ The responsibilities of the Human Resources department

Recruitment and selection

Businesses need to start the process of recruitment and selection when:

- » an employee leaves their job and they need to be replaced
- » it is a new business starting up and needs employees
- » it is a successful business and wants to expand by employing more people.

The recruitment process gives the business an opportunity to assess the role of employees, the nature of their jobs and future workforce requirements.

In a large business this process of recruiting and selecting staff is usually undertaken by the Human Resources department. Small businesses do not recruit enough people to make it worthwhile having a separate Human Resources department – often the managers who will be supervising the employee will deal with recruitment for their department. For example, in a hotel a restaurant manager might recruit the employees who serve customers in the restaurant.

The more important the job is to the business – the more technical and senior the position – the more careful and time-consuming the recruitment and selection process will be.

The recruitment process is summarised in the diagram below.

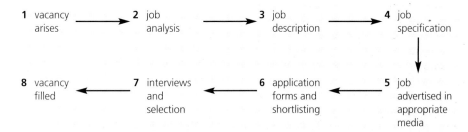

The recruitment process

Job analysis and description

The first stage of the recruitment process is to carry out a **job analysis** to study the tasks and activities to be carried out by the new employee. If the business is recruiting an employee to fill an existing position, an outline of the duties for the new employee will be easy to draw up, and may already exist. If the new employee is needed due to the business expanding or because the business has identified skills no one in the business has, more thought will have to go into the analysis of the job.

Once the job has been analysed, a **job description** will be produced. A job description has several functions:

- » It is given to the applicants for the job so they know exactly what the job entails.
- » It will allow a **job specification** to be drawn up, to see if the applicants 'match up to the job', so that people with the right skills will be employed.
- » Once someone has been employed, it can show whether they are carrying out the job effectively. If a dispute occurs about the employee's tasks, the job specification can be referred to in order to settle these questions.

The exact structure and content of a job description varies from business to business, but generally it will contain the headings outlined in the following case study.

> **Case study**
>
> Here is a job description for a housekeeper in a hotel.
>
> | Job title: | Housekeeper |
> |---|---|
> | Department: | Housekeeping |
> | Responsible to: | Hotel Manager |
> | Responsible for: | Cleaners, room attendants |
>
> **Main purpose of the job:**
> * Responsible for domestic services in the hotel, with an aim to keeping accommodation clean and maintained for the hotel guests.
> * Responsible for the cleaners and room attendants. To take a supervisory role.
>
> **Main duties:**
> * Allocation of duties, such as cleaning.
> * Advising staff when queries arise.
> * Sending soiled linen to the laundry.
> * Organising repairs and replacement of worn items from rooms.
> * Checking that belongings have not been left in rooms.
> * Checking that the rooms are ready to receive guests.
> * Informing reception when rooms are ready for occupancy.
>
> **Occasional duties:**
> * Appointment of new staff.
> * Training new staff in their duties.
> * Training new staff to use the equipment.
> * Disciplining staff as and when required.
> * Dismissing staff if necessary.

Job descriptions often also contain information about:

» the conditions of employment – salary, hours of work, pension scheme and staff welfare
» training that will be offered
» opportunities for promotion.

Job specification

Once a job description has been drawn up, the qualifications and qualities necessary to undertake the job can be specified. This list of desirable and essential requirements for the job is called a job, or person, specification. The requirements will usually include:

» the level of educational qualifications
» the amount of experience and type of experience
» special skills, knowledge or particular aptitude
» personal characteristics, such as type of personality.

> **Study tips**
>
> Make sure you know the difference between a job description and a job specification and what they are each used for.

Case study

Here is a job specification for a housekeeper in a hotel.

Job title:	Housekeeper
Department:	Housekeeping

Details of job:
- Responsible for domestic services in the hotel, with an aim to keeping accommodation clean and maintained for the hotel guests.
- Responsible for cleaners and room attendants. To take a supervisory role.

Qualifications:
Essential: 4 IGCSEs (A–C) including Maths and English.

Experience:
Desirable: Minimum 1 year's experience of working in hotels.

Skills:
- Communicates effectively with people.
- Ability to manage people.

Physical fitness:
- Fit, needs to be on feet all day.

Personal characteristics:
- Honest and responsible.
- Friendly, helpful, organised.

Activity 8.1

a Draw up a job description for **one** of the following:
- Accountant
- Shop assistant
- Hotel manager
- Teacher

Research information to help you by asking someone who does the job or from careers information.

b Now draw up a job specification for your chosen job. The same research should help you to complete this task. Show which are essential and which are desirable requirements for the job.

c How do a job description and a job specification help to ensure the most suitable person for the job is recruited?

Difference between internal recruitment and external recruitment

The next stage is to decide how the post will be filled.

Internal recruitment

The post could be filled from inside the organisation – **internal recruitment**. The vacancy may be advertised on a company noticeboard or, if the business is large, in a company newspaper which may be electronically available to all employees. This method of recruitment would be suitable for an employee who seeks promotion within the business and when a business is happy to recruit someone from its existing workforce.

Definitions to learn

Internal recruitment is when a vacancy is filled by someone who is an existing employee of the business.

Advantages of internal recruitment

» It is quicker and cheaper than external recruitment, which may involve expensive advertising.
» The person is already known to the business and their reliability, ability and potential are known.
» The person also knows how the organisation works, its structure and what is expected from its employees.
» It can be very motivating for employees to see their fellow workers being promoted – it makes them work harder if they consider that promotion is possible for them too.

Disadvantages of internal recruitment

» No new ideas or experience come into the business. Other companies may have different ways of working and these ways may be better in some respects, including making the business more efficient. Internal recruitment does not allow for these working practices to be brought into the business and this is a major limitation when the industry is changing rapidly.

» There may be rivalry among existing employees and jealousy towards the worker who gains promotion.

» The quality of internal candidates might be low.

External recruitment

Some businesses use mainly **external recruitment**. This involves advertising the vacancy beyond the business itself. When a business plans to recruit externally, it will need to advertise the vacancy. Advertising job vacancies can be done in several ways:

» *Local newspapers* – These are often used for advertising vacancies for jobs which do not require high skill levels, such as clerical (office) or manual (factory) positions. It is likely that many people locally could fill these vacancies.

» *National newspapers* – These are usually used for senior positions where there may be few, if any, local people who have the right experience, skills and qualifications to do the job. National newspapers are read by many people who live in different parts of the country and by people who live in other countries who can access the newspapers online. With senior positions, which are highly paid, people will be willing to move to another part of the country.

» *Specialist magazines* – These will usually be used for specialist technical employees such as scientists. These people will read the specialist magazines and see the advertisements.

» *Online recruitment sites*, such as LinkedIn – These offer the ability to create online job adverts for vacant positions in a business. These can be searched by job seekers through their networks. For example, the LinkedIn network has millions of members worldwide. Vacancies can be recommended to potential candidates through the 'Jobs You May Be Interested In' feature.

» *Recruitment agencies* – These are specialists in recruiting employees. They will advertise, usually by means of their website, and interview people for many types of jobs. They hold details of qualified people looking for another job and, when a suitable vacancy arises, they will put forward candidates to be interviewed for the job. Agencies are also approached by companies who need to employ a particular type of skilled worker. The agency will suggest applicants they think will be suitable. The use of recruitment agencies has increased in recent years. Some businesses 'outsource' the recruitment process to agencies to reduce the need for the employment of their own recruitment team. Agencies also have a wide range of candidates on their registers. However, the services of an agency are expensive – they charge a fee for recruiting an applicant which is based on a percentage of the salary for the vacancy, if the person is successfully appointed to the job.

» *Centres run by the government (Job Centres)* – These are places where job vacancies can be advertised. Details of vacancies are given to interested people. The vacancies are usually for unskilled and semi-skilled jobs.

Key info

An increasing proportion of leading global companies are recruiting new Chief Executive Officers (CEOs) externally. The trend is greatest among those businesses that face rapid and significant changes. In the four years to 2017, 38 per cent of new CEOs in telecommunications and energy businesses were recruited externally.

Study tips

Be prepared to analyse why a business might recruit a senior manager externally rather than from internal applicants.

Activity 8.2

On a large sheet of paper, copy out the table below and then fill in the gaps.

Advantages and disadvantages of the different methods of recruitment

Method of recruitment	Advantages	Disadvantages	Examples of jobs suitable for this method of recruitment
Internal: Noticeboard at the company (or company newspaper)			
External: Local newspapers			
National newspapers			
Specialist magazines			
Online recruitment sites			
Recruitment agencies			
Government-run Job Centres			

Study tips

You should be able to give examples of jobs which could be advertised using each of the different methods.

Job advertisements for external recruitment

When drawing up a job advertisement, the business will need to ask itself the following questions:

» What should be included in the advert?
» Where should the advertisement be placed?
» How much will the advertising cost and is it within the budget of the Human Resources department?

Answering the first question is straightforward – information about the job has to be included. This will usually be the duties involved, qualifications required, salary, conditions of employment, and information about the method of application (see below).

Answers to the other two questions will depend on the vacancy being filled and whether it is a senior position or one which does not require any qualifications.

Case study

Night Cashier for busy petrol station, 38 hours per week, Wed to Sat, 22:00–07:30, $10.50 per hour. Start immediately. Tel.1122 44551

Industrial Engineering Professional

Multi-site role throughout the country: based in New City. Competitive rate of pay with fringe benefits.

Qualityfoam Ltd is a leading manufacturer of polyurethane foam operating in 16 countries and a major supplier to the home country's furniture industry.

Appealing to a results-orientated professional, responsibilities will include performance improvement, business analysis, project management and capital expenditure appraisal.

You will be a graduate of calibre, numerate and PC literate, with at least three years' experience in manufacturing.

Please write with full CV to: Mr M. Ahmed, MD, Qualityfoam Ltd, New Road, New City, 3412 8769.

Administration Assistant required, $16.00 per hour

Good all-round administration skills needed to undertake a variety of duties within the organisation. Knowledge of Word or similar package essential. Immediate start.

Please write or telephone for an application form from:

Mr S. Singh, ZYT Ltd, 2341 Old Road, New City, 456723. Tel. 0892 557739

Activity 8.3

Read the case study on the previous page.

a Which advert would have appeared in a national newspaper and which would have been in a local newspaper? Explain your choice.

b Design your own advertisement for the job for which you drew up a job description and job specification (page 95). Where would you place this advertisement, and why?

c Compare your advert with that of the other students in your group. Which would be most likely to attract the best people to apply for the job and why?

Methods of application

A job advertisement will require the applicant to apply in writing. This can either be by filling in an application form, or by writing a letter of application and enclosing a curriculum vitae (CV) or résumé. A CV is a summary of a person's qualifications, experience and qualities, and is written in a standard format.

A business will use the application forms, or letters and CVs, to see which of the applicants best match the job specification. The applicants who are the closest match will be invited for an interview – the selection stage. A shortlist will be drawn up of the best applicants.

A curriculum vitae should be well laid out and clear. It should usually contain the following details:

» name
» address
» telephone number
» email address
» nationality
» education and qualifications

» work experience
» positions of responsibility
» interests
» names and addresses of referees (for references).

The letter of application should outline briefly:

» why the applicant wants the job
» why the applicant feels he/she would be suitable.

Application forms are sometimes completed in place of the CV and usually ask for the same information. They may sometimes ask for other information that is specifically relevant to the job. Many job application forms are completed online.

Activity 8.4: Who to employ?

a Study this job advertisement and the information from three application forms below. Which of the three people would be most suitable for the job? Give reasons for your choice of the successful applicant and why you would reject the other two applicants.

Personal Assistant (PA)

Salary in excess of $25 000 per year

The General Manager at our New City office requires an experienced and highly skilled Personal Assistant to provide a complete support service. In a typically busy day you will manage the General Manager's office, word process a variety of documents, maintain an accurate diary, and liaise with customers, clients and corporate contacts.

You will need to be able to demonstrate excellent IT skills, knowledge of Microsoft Office and associated programs, a good standard of numeracy and literacy, and have previous experience in a similar role.

If you enjoy working with a friendly team, please send your CV to Corinne Ogunbanjo, Human Resources, NYDB plc, 3286 New Street, New City, 467813

	Applicant 1	**Applicant 2**	**Applicant 3**
Name	Caroline Sharma	Pablo Gitano	Sara Gherman
Address	2144 Main Road, New City	4245 Long Row, New City	9876 New Road, New City
Age	19	29	38
Educational qualifications	5 IGCSEs, including English, Maths and Computer Studies. Administration qualifications – Level 1	6 IGCSEs, including English, Maths and Computer Studies. Administration qualifications – Levels 1 and 2	5 IGCSEs, including English and Maths. Administration qualifications – Levels 1, 2 and 3
Previous employment	6 months as a junior administration assistant with NYDB	1 year as office junior 3 years on reception 6 years as Personal Assistant to Senior Manager of DFG plc	Switchboard duties – 2 years Reception – 3 years Head of Administration section – 6 years Personal Assistant within RET Ltd - 6 years
Interests/ hobbies	Playing sports – member of several local teams, going to see friends, voluntary helper with a youth group	Reading, member of local football team, playing piano, rock climbing	Reading, going to the cinema, watching television

b What additional questions do you think should have been on the application form? Why should they have been asked?
c Design your own application form for the job for which you produced an advertisement in Activity 8.3.

Methods of selection

The applicants who are shortlisted and invited for interview will have provided the names and addresses of referees. These are people who will be asked to provide a reference (give their opinion on the applicant's character, honesty, reliability and suitability for the job). References are usually confidential, which means the applicant does not see what has been written about them.

If the applicant is a school leaver, it is normal to give the school as a referee. If the applicant is older, usually a former employer will be used.

Interviews are still the most widely used form of selection. However, interviews are not always the most reliable way of choosing the best person for the job. The main purposes of an interview are to assess, in the shortest possible time:

» the applicant's ability to do the job
» any personal qualities that are an advantage or disadvantage
» the general character and personality of the applicant – will they fit in?

Interviews can be one-to-one, two-to-one or a panel of people to interview the applicant. Panel interviews are usually used for more senior positions.

Some businesses include tests in their selection process, for example:

» *Skills tests* aim to show the ability of the candidate to carry out certain tasks.
» *Aptitude tests* aim to show the candidate's potential to gain additional skills. Either general intelligence tests or more specific tests are used to assess the candidate's ability to train for a particular job.
» *Personality tests* are used if a particular type of person is required for the job, if the job requires the ability to work under stress or if the person will need to fit in as part of a team of people.
» *Group situation tests* give tasks to applicants to complete in group situations and the group is observed. Each applicant will be assessed on the way they work as a member of the team and the way they tackle the tasks themselves.

> **Study tips**
>
> Make sure you can explain how the information from these tests might be helpful in choosing between applicants.

Key info

It is estimated that over 50 per cent of employers are prepared to check applicants' social media profiles before offering them a job. Increasingly, perhaps, people who are seeking employment will think carefully about the information and images they upload to sites such as Facebook and the comments they make on Twitter and similar social media sites.

Activity 8.5

Imagine that you are now going to interview candidates for the vacancy that you advertised in Activity 8.3. You have drawn up the following six questions to ask the interviewees:

1 What is it about the job that attracted you to apply for it?
2 What do you know about the company?
3 Tell me more about your hobbies and interests.
4 Why do you feel you are particularly suitable for the job?
5 Where do you see yourself in five years' time?
6 Do you have any questions?

- What is the purpose of each of these questions? What are you hoping to find out?
- What other questions ought to be asked?
- Get other students in your class to apply for the job you have advertised and then carry out a mock interview. Would you offer them the job?

Recommending which workers to employ

You should now understand the process of recruitment and selection. The final decision of which workers to employ depends on several factors:

» Work experience – how important is it that the worker has direct experience of the job?
» Educational and other qualifications – are these essential for filling the post, for example, doctor?
» Age – is youth or 'experience of life' more important? However, businesses must be careful not to break any 'age discrimination laws' that may exist in their country.
» Internal – how important is it that the applicant has a good understanding of how the business operates?
» External – how important is it that the new worker has experience and skills gained from outside the business?

The relative importance of these and other factors will depend on the circumstances – it is important to understand the type and size of business being considered and the nature of the job vacancy.

Rejecting unsuccessful applicants

When the suitable applicant has been offered the job and has accepted it, the unsuccessful applicants should be informed that they have not got the job and thanked for applying.

Activity 8.6

a An international construction company has just won a contract to build a dam in an African country. How might the Human Resources department recruit the following workers for the contract?
- Experienced engineers
- Labourers
b An international airline is expanding its operations in South America. It needs to recruit staff to be based only in this continent, as the flights will not go all around the world. What recruitment and selection methods would it use to appoint:
- airline pilots
- cabin crew (air stewardesses and stewards)?

REVISION SUMMARY	**The recruitment and selection process**

1 Analyse the exact nature of the job and duties to be undertaken	The requirements of the job need to be decided. Will the job be different to the old one? If the job is a new one, what will the person be required to do? Can other people do some of these duties?
2 Design **a job description**	Once the exact duties have been decided they will be put together to form a job description. This document outlines the duties that the job involves and states to whom the person will be responsible, i.e. who will be their boss.
3 Design a **job specification**	A job specification outlines in detail the type of person who is required to do the job. It includes the qualifications, experience and personal qualities of the person that are essential and those that are desirable.
4 Advertise the vacancy	Where to advertise has to be decided. If the job is a senior one which requires many qualifications, then the advert will need to be seen by people who live in different parts of the country or even in other countries. Online recruitment advertisements may be used or recruitment agencies or national newspaper or specialist magazine for the industry could be chosen. If the job is a basic one which does not require many qualifications or skills, then the advertisement could be placed in a local newspaper because many local people could have the necessary qualifications or skills to do the job.
5 Send out application forms to the applicants or read curriculum vitaes/résumés and letters of application	People will apply for the job by sending a letter of application and a CV/résumé, or they will request an application form from the business, fill it in and send it back.
6 Produce a **shortlist** from the replies of those to interview and take up references	From the applications for the job, a shortlist will be produced of those best matching the employer's requirements. References might be requested for those people to be interviewed. (If an applicant is to be offered the job subject to suitable references, these will be sought at Stage 8.)
7 Hold **interviews and selection tasks**	Interviews will be held. These can also include other selection tasks, for example, written tests, practical tests, delivering a presentation on a pre-determined topic.
8 Select suitable applicant and offer them the job. Reply to unsuccessful applicants	The most suitable person for the job is chosen. A letter is sent formally offering them the job. Letters are sent to the unsuccessful applicants telling them that they have not got the job but thanking them for their interest in the business.

The benefits and limitations of part-time and full-time employees

A **part-time** employee is someone who works fewer hours than a **full-time** employee. There is no specific number of hours that makes someone full- or part-time, but a full-time employee will usually work 35 hours or more a week. The number of full-time hours which employees usually work in a week will vary from one country to another. The contract of employment will show a different number of hours depending on whether it is a part-time or full-time job. Some employees prefer part-time contracts, for example, students who also have college work to do or parents with child care responsibilities.

Definitions to learn

Part-time employment is often considered to be between 1 and 30–35 hours a week.
Full-time employees will usually work 35 hours or more a week.

101

The benefits to a business of employing part-time employees are:

» more flexible in the hours of work
» easier to ask employees just to work at busy times
» easier to extend business opening/operating hours by working evenings or at weekends
» fits in with looking after children and therefore employee is willing to accept lower pay
» reduces business costs compared to employing and paying a full-time employee
» in some countries it is easier to make part-time workers redundant.

The limitations to a business of part-time employees are:

» less likely to seek training because the employees may see the job as temporary
» takes longer to recruit two part-time workers than one full-time employee
» part-time employees can be less committed to the business and may be more likely to leave to get another job
» less likely to be promoted because they will not have gained the same skills and experience as full-time employees
» more difficult to communicate with part-time employees when they are not in work.

The advantages and disadvantages of full-time employees are the opposite to part-time employees (that is, the advantages of part-time employees are the disadvantages of full-time employees).

The importance of training and the methods of training

There should be clear objectives for training employees. Training is important to a business as it may be used to:

» introduce a new process or new equipment
» improve the efficiency of the workforce
» provide training for unskilled workers to make them more valuable to the company
» decrease the supervision needed
» improve the opportunity for internal promotion
» decrease the chances of accidents.

Employees should be clear about the benefits of the training or they will not work hard or take the training seriously.

Training is usually trying to achieve one or more of the following:

» To increase skills.
» To increase knowledge.
» To improve employees' attitudes to encourage them to accept change and raise awareness, for example, a need to improve customer service.

There are three main types of training:

» **induction training**
» **on-the-job training**
» **off-the-job training.**

Key info

In many countries, the proportion of employees with a part-time contract is increasing. Over a recent 12-month period, 86 per cent of all new jobs created in Australia were part-time. In Switzerland and the Netherlands, over 25 per cent of all employees have a part-time contract.

Definitions to learn

Induction training is an introduction given to a new employee, explaining the business's activities, customs and procedures and introducing them to their fellow workers.
On-the-job training occurs by watching a more experienced worker doing the job.
Off-the-job training involves being trained away from the workplace, usually by specialist trainers.

Induction training

This is carried out when an employee is new to the job. When a new employee starts at a company, they will not know where anything is or who people are or what is expected of them. The induction programme will last sometimes for a day, sometimes for several days – it depends on the company and the particular job. When a person starts a new school, they are shown round, introduced to teachers and told about their lessons – this is the same type of information you would need to know if you had just joined a new company.

➡ Case study

The following is an induction programme for a shop assistant.

08:30	Introduction
08:45	Company history
09:00	Company structure
09:30	Administration details: • Company regulations • Health and safety in the workplace • Uniform
10:30	Break
10:45	Workplace: • Map of the premises – places of work • Staffroom • Staff canteen • First aid point • Fire exits • Human Resources Manager's office
11:45	Conditions of employment: • Rate of pay • Hours worked • Sickness and holiday pay • Pensions • Disciplinary procedures • Breaks • Staff purchase/discounts
12:45	Training opportunities
13:00	Lunch
13:30	Job training: • Customer service • Stacking shelves/presentation of shelves • Pricing goods • Using barcode reader • Using tills • How to deal with difficult customers • Security
17:00	Close

The advantages of induction training are that it:

»» helps new employees to settle into their job quickly
»» may be a legal requirement to give health and safety training at the start of a job
»» means workers are less likely to make mistakes.

The disadvantages of induction training are that it:

»» is time-consuming
»» means wages are paid but no work is being done by the worker
»» delays the start of the employee commencing their job.

On-the-job training

This is where a person is trained by watching a more experienced worker doing the job. They are shown what to do. This method of training is only suitable for unskilled and semi-skilled jobs.

The advantages of on-the-job training are that:

»» individual tuition is given and it is in the workplace so the employee does not need to be sent away (travel costs are expensive)
»» it ensures there is some production from the worker while they are training
»» it usually costs less than off-the-job training
»» it is training tailored to the specific needs of the business.

The disadvantages of on-the-job training are that:

»» the trainer will not be as productive as usual because they are showing the trainee what to do instead of getting on with their job
»» the trainer may have bad habits and they may pass these on to the trainee
»» it may not lead to training qualifications recognised outside the business.

Off-the-job training

This is where the worker goes away from the place where they work. This may be to a different part of the building or it may be at a different place altogether, such as a college or specialist training centre. The techniques used to train workers are more varied and can involve more complex tasks. Off-the-job training often involves classroom learning, using lecture, role play, case studies or computer simulations.

The advantages of off-the-job training are that:

»» a broad range of skills can be taught using these techniques
»» if these courses are taught in the evening after work, they are cheaper for the business because the employee will still carry out their normal duties during the day
»» the business will only need to pay for the course and it will not also lose the output of the employee
»» employees may be taught a variety of skills, becoming multi-skilled, and this makes them more versatile – they can be moved around the company when the need arises
»» it often uses expert trainers who have up-to-date knowledge of business practices.

The disadvantages of off-the-job training are that:

»» costs are high
»» it means wages are paid but no work is being done by the worker
»» the additional qualifications mean it is easier for the employee to leave and find another job.

Training is necessary for the success of most businesses. It is a form of investment, but in human capital not physical capital. Investment usually leads to greater output in the future and this is true of employees as well as machinery.

Activity 8.7

Copy out the table below and fill in the gaps.

Advantages and disadvantages of methods of training

Method of training	Description	Advantages	Disadvantages
Induction training			
On-the-job training			
Off-the-job training			

Study tips

Make sure you can explain and give examples of when on-the-job and off-the-job training are suitable for particular jobs.

REVISION SUMMARY   **Training (management/business)**

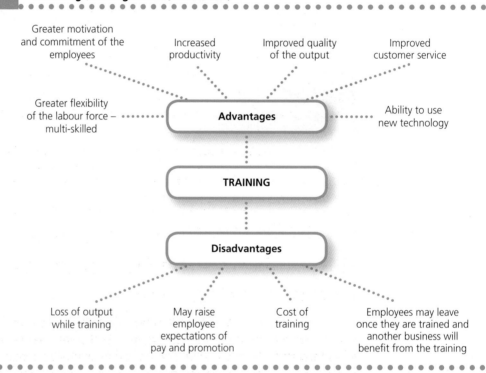

Greater motivation and commitment of the employees

Increased productivity

Improved quality of the output

Improved customer service

Greater flexibility of the labour force – multi-skilled

Advantages

Ability to use new technology

TRAINING

Disadvantages

Loss of output while training

May raise employee expectations of pay and promotion

Cost of training

Employees may leave once they are trained and another business will benefit from the training

REVISION SUMMARY | **Training (employee)**

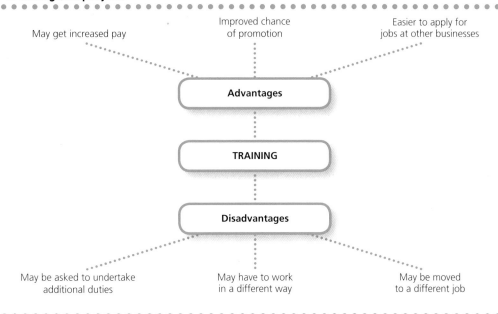

May get increased pay — Improved chance of promotion — Easier to apply for jobs at other businesses

Advantages

TRAINING

Disadvantages

May be asked to undertake additional duties — May have to work in a different way — May be moved to a different job

---

> ## Activity 8.8
>
> For each of the examples below, decide what type of training would be most appropriate and why.
>
> **a** S&S plc has just introduced a new computer program into the Accounts offices. All the Accounts employees will need to know how to use the new software.
> **b** Sandeep has been given a job as a trainee manager with a large retail company. The training will last for about two years.
> **c** James has just got a job as a hotel porter. He has never done this type of job before. He is starting work next week.

Why reducing the size of the workforce might be necessary

Workforce planning is where a business decides on the type and number of employees needed in the future. The number required will depend upon the business's sales forecasts, its future plans such as expansion or automation, and its objectives, for example, introducing new types of products. Often businesses will require additional employees when they are expanding, but sometimes they will need to downsize the workforce (reduce the number of employees). This can be because of:

» introduction of automation
» falling demand for their goods or services
» factory/shop/office closure
» relocating their factory abroad
» a business has merged or been taken over and some jobs have become surplus to requirements in the newly combined business.

When it has been decided how many employees will be required and what their skills need to be, the Human Resources department can plan how this will be achieved by:

» finding out the skills of all the present employees
» not including anyone who will be leaving soon, for example, due to retirement

Definitions to learn

Workforce planning is establishing the workforce needed by the business for the foreseeable future in terms of the number and skills of employees required.

»» consulting with existing staff as to who could and would want to retrain to fill the new jobs

»» preparing a recruitment plan to show how many new staff will be needed and how they should be recruited (internally or externally).

If a business needs to reduce the number of employees, this can be done in one of two ways:

»» **dismissal**
»» **redundancy**.

Workers may also leave their job because they:

»» retire (they are getting older and want to stop working)
»» resign (because they have found another job).

Dismissal

This is where a worker is told to leave their job because their work or behaviour is unsatisfactory. For example, an employee who was constantly late for work and who, despite being given warnings, continued to be late, would probably be dismissed. An employee who was caught stealing or who was unable to do the job to a satisfactory standard would be dismissed. In some countries, an employee can take the business to court if they feel they were unfairly dismissed. Therefore a business needs to make sure it has followed all the laws in its country before dismissing a worker.

Redundancy

There may be occasions when a number of employees will no longer be needed, through no fault of their own, for example, during a period of falling sales resulting from an economic recession.

When an employee is made redundant, they may be given some money to compensate them for losing their job. In some countries this is laid down in law, for example, one week's wages for every year that the employee has worked for the business.

Which workers to make redundant?

The following factors help a business to decide which workers to make redundant and which to retain:

»» Some workers may volunteer and be happy to be made redundant – because they may have another job they can go to, they want to retire early or they want to start their own business.
»» Length of time employed by the business – workers who have worked for the business for a long time are often retained. They will have the most experience and be the most expensive to make redundant, if redundancy payments are made.
»» Workers with essential skills that are needed by the business or whose skills could be transferable to other departments are often retained.
»» Employment history of the worker – whether they have a good/poor attendance, punctuality or appraisal record.
»» Which departments of the business need to lose workers and which need to retain workers.

Legal controls over employment issues

In many countries governments have passed laws that affect the relationship between employers and employees. The most important employment issues affected by legal controls are:

Definitions to learn

Dismissal is when employment is ended against the will of the employee, usually for not working in accordance with the employment contract.
Redundancy is when an employee is no longer needed and so loses their job. It is not due to any aspect of their work being unsatisfactory.

Study tips

Make sure you can explain the difference between redundancy and dismissal.

>> employment contracts
>> unfair dismissal
>> discrimination
>> health and safety
>> legal minimum wage.

The contract of employment

In many countries in the world it is a legal requirement for employers to provide a new employee with a **contract of employment** to sign. It will set out the terms of the relationship between the employee and the employer. It will usually be set out in writing and include:

>> name of the employer and name of the employee
>> job title
>> date when employment is to begin
>> hours to be worked
>> rate of pay and any other benefits such as bonus, sick pay, pension
>> when payment will be made
>> holiday entitlement
>> amount of notice that the employer or the employee must give to end the employment.

Impact of employment contracts on employers and employees

>> Both employers and employees know what is expected of them.
>> It provides some security of employment to the employee.
>> If the employee does not meet the conditions of the contract then legal dismissal is allowed.
>> If the employer fails to meet the conditions of the contract, for example, does not offer the holidays the worker is entitled to, then the employee can seek legally binding compensation.

Unfair dismissal

This occurs when an employer ends a worker's contract of employment for a reason that is not covered by that contract. This may be for reasons of discrimination (see below), or it might be that the employer wants to reduce worker numbers but does not want to pay 'redundancy compensation'. Unfair dismissal is illegal in many countries and the worker has the right either to compensation or to be offered their previous job back by taking the case to an **industrial tribunal**. An industrial tribunal is a type of law court that makes judgments on disagreements between companies and their employees.

Impact of unfair dismissal on employer and employee

>> Employer must keep very accurate records of a worker's performance if they want to claim that the employee has broken their contract of employment before dismissing them.
>> Employees have security of employment – as long as they fulfil their contract and are not made redundant.
>> Allows employees to take their employer to an industrial tribunal if they feel they have been treated unfairly and they may get compensation if this is found to be true.

Definitions to learn

A **contract of employment** is a legal agreement between an employer and employee, listing the rights and responsibilities of workers.

Definitions to learn

An **industrial tribunal** is a type of law court (or in some countries, a legal meeting) that makes judgments on disagreements between companies and their employees, for example, workers' complaints of unfair dismissal or discrimination at work.

>> Makes a business less likely to treat employees unfairly as they know they may be taken to an industrial tribunal and may have to pay compensation or give the employee their job back.

Protection against discrimination

Discrimination at work is when the employer makes decisions that are based on 'unfair' reasons. The main examples are when workers are treated differently because they:

>> are of a different race or colour
>> belong to a different religion
>> are of the opposite sex
>> are considered too old/young for the job
>> are disabled in some way.

In most countries many of these forms of discrimination are illegal. If they were not illegal, many sections of society would find it very difficult to gain jobs or to achieve promotion at work. Businesses can also lose out by practising unfair discrimination. They could fail to select a very good worker just because they used one of the reasons above not to select the person.

In addition to these laws, many employers have an equal opportunities policy. Employees who consider that they have been unfairly discriminated against can appeal to an equal opportunities committee.

Impact of discrimination on employers and employees

>> Employees should be treated equally in the workplace and when being recruited, and they should be paid equal amounts for similar work.
>> If a man and a woman are both equally well-qualified for a job they should be treated equally. It should not be the case that one rather than the other is given the job simply because of their sex.
>> Employees who have a disability, are from different races or of different religions should be treated in the same way as all other workers.
>> Employers have to be careful when wording an advertisement for a job, for example, they cannot advertise for a woman – they must say 'person'.
>> When selecting an employee for a job an employer must treat all applicants equally. If a business does not do this, then it could be prosecuted and fined.
>> By following these laws carefully, businesses should recruit and promote staff on merit alone and this should help to increase motivation at work.

Health and safety at work

Many years ago, most employers cared little for the safety of their workers. Machines did not have safety cages. Protective clothing was not issued. Conditions were often very hot or cold, noisy and unpleasant. The arguments often used by employers to explain such conditions were that: it would cost too much to make workplaces safe; if the existing workers did not like the conditions, then they could leave as there were many unemployed people who would do their work!

In our modern world such attitudes are no longer acceptable. Most employers now care for their workers' safety. One reason for this is that many laws have been passed that have forced them to improve health and safety at work. In most countries there are now laws which make sure that all employers:

>> protect workers from dangerous machinery
>> provide safety equipment and clothing

» maintain reasonable workplace temperatures
» provide hygienic conditions and washing facilities
» do not insist on excessively long shifts and provide breaks in the work timetable.

Impact of health and safety on employers and employees

» Cost to employer of meeting the health and safety regulations, for example, better fire-fighting equipment.
» Time needs to be found to train workers in health and safety precautions.
» Workers feel 'safer' and more motivated at work.
» Reduces accident rate and the cost of compensation for workers injured at work.

Are health and safety laws and controls over business a good idea? Most managers think so. Workers cost a great deal to recruit and train. It is worthwhile keeping them safe and healthy. Such workers are likely to be better motivated, work more efficiently and stay with the business for a longer period of time.

For these reasons, some employers in countries where there are weak health and safety laws will still provide working conditions of a very high safety standard. The managers of these firms have taken an **ethical decision**. Do these managers make better employers? Most workers would think so, and would be better motivated to work hard and stay with the business because of this.

Unfortunately, in some countries there are employers that still take advantage of workers. There may be no protection on the length of shifts and many millions of children can still be found working in industries that offer little protection from danger and ill health. In these countries workers are exploited and often paid low wages. Business costs are therefore very low. Should the rest of the world continue to buy products from these countries? What is your view?

Legal minimum wage

Workers have a right to be paid for work they do for employers. There should be a written agreement between worker and employer (contract of employment) which will contain details not only of the hours of work and the nature of the job but also of:

» the wage rate to be paid
» how frequently wages will be paid
» what deductions will be made from wages, for example, income tax.

In some countries employers can pay whatever wage rate they like. If there is high unemployment or if unemployment benefits are low, workers may be offered very low wages. Increasingly, governments are taking action against employers that pay low wages. This action often takes the form of a legal minimum wage. A minimum wage exists in parts of China and India and in the USA. A minimum wage makes it illegal for an employer to pay an hourly rate below the minimum wage set.

Impact of legal minimum wage on employers and employees

» It should prevent strong employers from exploiting unskilled workers who could not easily find other work.
» As many unskilled workers will now be receiving higher wages, it might encourage employers to train them to make sure that they are more productive.
» It will encourage more people to seek work. There should be fewer shortages of workers.
» Low-paid workers will earn more and will have higher living standards, meaning they will be able to afford to buy more.

» It increases business costs, which will force them to increase prices.
» Some employers will not be able to afford these wage rates. They may make workers redundant instead. Unemployment may rise.
» Other workers receiving just above the minimum wage level may ask for higher wages to keep the same differential between themselves and lower paid workers. Business costs will again increase.

Activity 8.9

Consider the way in which Gowri Kumaran was treated by her employer.

She applied for a job as machine operator in a television assembly factory. The employer offered her the job and said that her contract of employment would be sent to her after one month's trial. After one month, Gowri received her wages but was surprised to see that her wage rate was much less than expected. She was also earning much less than other workers doing the same work. There had been several deductions from her wages which she did not understand. She did not receive a contract of employment as had been promised.

Gowri had complained to her supervisor that there were some loose electrical wires on her machine but no action had been taken. She worked 10-hour shifts with only one break. Gowri decided to join a trade union but when the manager heard about this he called her into his office. He told her that her work was unsatisfactory and she was no longer required. Gowri was very upset about the way she had been treated. She asked for your advice, as her legal adviser, on what she should do.

a   Do you think that Gowri has been badly treated by her employer? Give reasons for your answer.
b   As Gowri's legal adviser, write a letter to the manager of the factory where she used to work. Explain to the manager all of the points of law which you think he has broken.
c   What might be the advantages to employers of treating their employees well?

International business in focus

Coca-Cola

Coca-Cola aims to help its employees (called 'associates') realise their full potential. It is committed to extending education and training programmes to all associates at all levels of the organisation and in all of the countries it operates in.

Coca-Cola University (CCU) is the company's education establishment, which provides a wide range of courses through classroom learning, e-learning and on-the-job training to help associates develop personally and professionally. CCU's learning and training programmes focus on leadership, marketing, human rights, ethics, diversity, sustainability and finance.

Discussion points

● Why do you think that Coca-Cola uses both off-the-job training ('classroom learning') and on-the-job training?

● Why do you think that effective training is important to both Coca-Cola and its employees?

● Suggest ways in which Coca-Cola could recruit and select appropriate people, such as Marketing Managers.

Exam-style questions: Short answer and data response

1 Sarah owns a business which manufactures musical instruments. There has been an increase in sales and profits over the last two years but there has been a fall in demand for some products. She employs 50 skilled production workers. She wants to recruit five more factory workers to make pianos but she needs fewer workers to make violins. She intends to carry out a job analysis for the factory workers who make pianos. Sarah uses on-the-job training for new workers joining the business.

   a Define 'job analysis'. [2]

   b Identify **two** examples of suitable ways in which Sarah could advertise the vacancies. [2]

   c Identify **two** questions which Sarah could ask the job applicants at interview. Outline why each question is asked. [4]

   d Explain **two** advantages of on-the-job training for this business. [6]

   e Sarah needs fewer skilled workers to make violins. What do you think Sarah should do? Justify your answer. [6]

2 Mr Patel owns an insurance company. He advises clients and arranges insurance policies for customers, who pay a fee for his services. He employs ten well-qualified workers who offer a high level of customer service. His business needs to recruit an extra five well-qualified workers and will need to draw up a job description and job specification. He also needs to recruit two supervisors. Mr Patel intends to use external recruitment to recruit the supervisors.

   a Define 'job description'. [2]

   b Identify **two** examples of requirements Mr Patel might put in a job (person) specification. [2]

   c Outline **two** reasons why Mr Patel wants to recruit well-qualified workers. [4]

   d Explain **two** features Mr Patel could include in an induction training programme. [6]

   e Do you think external recruitment is better than internal recruitment for the two supervisors? Justify your answer. [6]

Revision checklist

In this chapter you have learned:

✔ the role of the Human Resources department
✔ each stage of the recruitment and selection process
✔ how to draw up a job description and job specification
✔ how to choose suitable ways of advertising a vacancy – either internally or externally
✔ how to draw up questions for interviews
✔ benefits/limitations of part-time and full-time workers

✔ the importance of training and different types of training, including how to design an induction programme
✔ the difference between on-the-job and off-the-job training
✔ how to analyse and evaluate the relevance of training to both the management and the employee
✔ why reducing the size of the workforce might be necessary
✔ which workers to recruit/make redundant
✔ why governments pass laws to protect employees.

NOW – test your understanding with the revision questions in the Student etextbook and the Workbook.

9 Internal and external communication

This chapter will explain:

★ about effective communication and its importance to business
★ the benefits and limitations of different communication methods, including those based on information technology (IT)
★ how to recommend and justify which communication method to use in given circumstances
★ how communication barriers arise and problems of ineffective communication
★ how communication barriers can be reduced or removed.

Effective communication and its importance to business

Communication occurs when a **message** is transferred from one person to another, who understands the content of the message.

We all communicate with other people every day. We communicate with our families, at school or college, when we go shopping, when chatting with friends or when using social media. Communication with others is a natural part of life. Why do we need to study something which comes naturally to us? There is one important reason for this, and that is: communication must be effective. This means that the information or message being sent is received, understood and acted upon in the way intended. If it isn't, it can be annoying for us when, for example, we communicate with our friends. However, for businesses, communication which is ineffective, or which fails altogether, can result in serious consequences.

Internal communication

Why do people within a business need to communicate with each other?

In all organisations, it is necessary for people to communicate with each other in various ways. Without communication, we would all be working as individuals with no links with anybody else in the business we work in. The tasks of management in guiding, instructing, warning and encouraging workers would become impossible.

Here are some examples of common messages communicated within businesses (**internal communication**). The way in which each message is communicated is also shown.

» 'Please do not smoke in this area.' (notice on a table)
» 'How many hours did you work last week?' (manager asks a worker)
» 'There will be a Fire Drill at 11:00 today.' (notice on a board)
» 'The cutting machine has broken down. Can you call the engineer as soon as possible?' (telephone call)

>> 'Sales last week reached a record level. You will need to increase output so that we do not run out of inventories.' (emailed memorandum to Operations Manager)
>> 'Keep this door locked at all times.' (sign on a door)
>> 'You have been sacked because of frequent absences from work. Please acknowledge receipt of this letter.' (letter written to an employee)
>> 'Shoplifting is on the increase in our store – we all need to suggest ideas on how the problem can be reduced.' (meeting with all shop workers in a store)

The list could have been very long indeed, but these examples show the wide range of topics which need to be communicated within a business. Can you imagine the serious problems that could occur if these messages were not communicated effectively to the people who need the information they contain?

Activity 9.1

a Suggest three more examples of internal communication within a business or your school or college.
b For each example, give details of the message to be sent and the method you think should be used to send it.
c Justify why you have chosen these communication methods.

External communication

This occurs when messages are sent between one organisation and another, or between the organisation and people other than employees, for example, customers. Some of the main examples of **external communication** are:

>> orders for goods from suppliers
>> sending information to customers about prices and delivery times
>> advertising goods or services (this is covered in detail in Chapter 15)
>> asking customers to pay bills on time.

It is just as important for a business to have good external communication as good internal communication. The key features of both types are the same. The methods of communication which can be used are also similar, although the growth of the internet and social networking has transformed how a business can communicate with the 'outside world'. The main difference between internal and external communication is whom is being communicated with.

Why external communication has to work well

External communication is very important to the image and efficiency of a business. If a company communicates ineffectively with suppliers, it may be sent the wrong materials. If it sends inaccurate information to customers, they may buy a product from another company.

Here are some more examples of external communication. You can imagine how serious it would be if communication was not effective in all of these cases.

» A Finance Manager writes a letter to the tax office asking how much tax must be paid this year.
» A Sales Manager records a customer order taken over the internet for 330 items to be delivered by next Wednesday.
» A business must contact thousands of customers who have bought a product which turns out to be dangerous. An email is sent to all customers who bought the product to ask them to return the item for a refund.

> ### Activity 9.2
> **a** Suggest three more examples of external communication from a business or from your school or college.
> **b** Give details of the message to be sent and the method you think should be used to send it.
> **c** Justify why you have chosen these communication methods.

> **Definitions to learn**
>
> The **transmitter** or **sender** of the message is the person starting off the process by sending the message.
> The **medium of communication** is the method used to send a message, for example, a letter is a method of written communication and a meeting is a method of verbal communication.
> The **receiver** is the person who receives the message.
> **Feedback** is the reply from the receiver which shows whether the message has arrived, been understood and, if necessary, acted upon.

The process of effective communication

Effective communication involves the following four features:

» A **transmitter** or **sender** of the message – this is the person who wishes to pass on the information to others. This person has to choose the next two features carefully in order to make sure that communication occurs effectively.
» A **medium of communication** or a method for sending the message, for example, a letter or noticeboard.
» A **receiver** of the information – the person to whom the message should be sent.
» **Feedback**, where the receiver confirms that the message has been received and responds to it. This ensures that the information has been correctly received by the right person and, if necessary, acted upon.

▲ The features of effective communication

> ## Activity 9.3: Communicating with workers
>
> Sales were below target at the Co-operative Retail Store. The manager was very concerned about this. She decided to write to every worker, about 30 in all, to warn them of the problem of falling sales and how jobs were now at risk. In the letter she asked for ideas on how to increase sales. Workers were asked to confirm that they had received the letter and tell her if they had any good ideas.
>
> **a** In this case study, identify:
> - the sender of the message
> - the medium being used
> - the receiver of the message.
>
> **b** Did the communication involve feedback?
>
> **c** Do you think that the letter sent by the manager to workers was the best way to communicate with them? If not, which method would have been more effective? Explain your answer.

One-way and two-way communication

One-way communication occurs when the receiver of a message has no chance to reply or respond to the message. An example would be an instruction to 'take these goods to the customer'. One-way communication does not allow the receiver to contribute to communication or to provide any feedback.

Two-way communication is when there is a reply or a response from the receiver. This could be just simple confirmation of receipt of the message or it could be a discussion about the message. Both people are therefore involved in the communication process. This could lead to better and clearer information.

The advantages of two-way communication

When the receiver has to, or decides to, give feedback to the sender of the message there are two main benefits:

» It should become absolutely clear to the sender whether or not the person receiving the message has understood it and acted upon it. If they have not, then perhaps the message needs to be sent again or made clearer. Effective communication has not taken place until the message is understood by the receiver.

» Both people are now involved in the communication process. The receiver feels more a part of this process. He or she can make a real contribution to the topic being discussed or communicated. This may help to motivate the receiver.

> **Definitions to learn**
>
> **One-way communication** involves a message which does not call for or require a response.
>
> **Two-way communication** is when the receiver gives a response to the message and there is a discussion about it.

▲ The difference between one-way and two-way communication

> ### Activity 9.4
>
> Refer to the list of messages on pages 114–115. The method used to send or transmit each message is also given. Which messages are most likely to lead to:
>
> **a** two-way communication?
> **b** one-way communication?
>
> Give reasons for your answer in each case.

REVISION SUMMARY   **Effective communication**

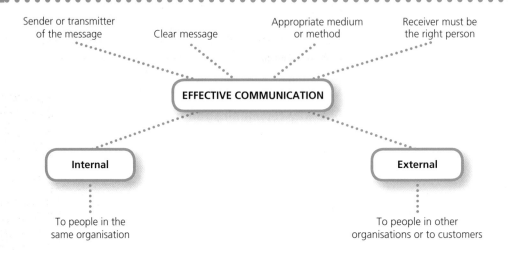

Sender or transmitter of the message

Clear message

Appropriate medium or method

Receiver must be the right person

EFFECTIVE COMMUNICATION

Internal

External

To people in the same organisation

To people in other organisations or to customers

Communication methods

Information can be sent or transmitted in a number of different ways – these are called the communication methods.

>> Verbal methods of communication involve the sender of the message speaking to the receiver.

» Written methods of communication include letters and notices/posters, but increasingly involve the use of information technology (IT).

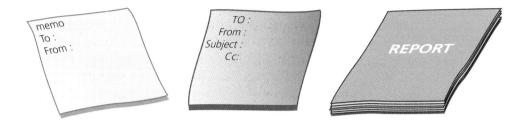

» Visual methods of communication include methods such as diagrams, charts and videos.

Which is the best way to communicate a message? There is no simple answer to this question. Sometimes it is better to use verbal communication, and on other occasions it is essential to use written communication. Different messages require different methods of communication, so there is no best method in all cases.

Choosing the appropriate communication method

There are several factors that the sender of a message should consider before choosing the most appropriate method to use to communicate with the receiver:

» *Speed* – is it important that the receiver gets the information really quickly? For example, a manager from a foreign division of a company must be told about a cancelled meeting before he catches his flight.
» *Cost* – is it important to keep costs down or is it more important to communicate effectively, regardless of cost? For example, customers need to be informed about a serious safety problem with a product.
» *Message details* – how detailed is the message? If it contains technical plans, figures and illustrations then, clearly, written and visual forms of communication are likely to be essential.
» *Leadership style* – is the leadership style a democratic one? If it is, then two-way verbal methods of communication with employees are much more likely to be used than they would be by an autocratic leader.

» *The receiver* – who is/are the 'target' receiver(s)? If just one person has to be communicated with, and they work in the next office, then one-to-one conversation is likely to be used. However, this would be inappropriate if hundreds of workers needed to receive a message.

» *Importance of a written record* – if it is essential that a written record can be referred to at some time in the future, then, clearly, verbal communication would be inappropriate. For example, legal contracts or receipt of new orders from customers must have written records.

» *Importance of feedback* – if it is essential that the sender receives feedback, perhaps very quickly, then a direct verbal method of communication might be most appropriate. For example, has the customer just leaving the shop paid for those goods yet?

REVISION SUMMARY   **How to choose communication methods**

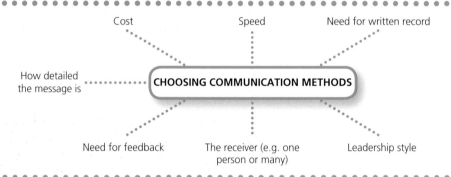

Verbal communication methods

Verbal, or oral, communication methods include:

» face-to-face/*one-to-one* talks/meetings between the sender and the receiver
» *telephone* conversations
» *video conferencing*, where groups of people in different locations are able to see and hear each other through a video/internet link
» *meetings and team briefings*, which could involve few or many people.

Advantages of verbal communication

» Information can be given out quickly. When this happens at big meetings, it is an efficient way of communicating with a large number of people.
» There is opportunity for immediate feedback and two-way communication.
» The message is often reinforced by seeing the speaker. The body language of the speaker, how they stand and their facial expressions, can help to put the message across effectively. This, of course, does not apply to telephone conversations.

Disadvantages of verbal communication

» In a big meeting, there is no way of telling whether everybody is listening or has understood the message.
» It can take longer to use verbal methods when feedback occurs than to use a written form of communication.
» When an accurate and permanent record of the message is needed, such as a warning to a worker, a verbal method is inappropriate.

Written communication methods including those based on information technology

Written methods of communication include the following:

» *Business letters* – used for either internal or external communication, they should follow a set structure.
» *Memos* (an abbreviation of memorandum) – written messages used only internally. Many businesses use computers to send these through the internal email system. An example of a memo sent by email is shown below.

MEMORANDUM

To: Sales Manager

From: Distribution Manager

Date: 3/3/2018

Subject: Delivery of damaged goods

The problem of damaged goods reaching our Newtown branch has been solved. It was discovered that the boxes were being loaded on to the truck without any rope attaching them.

I have met with the loading supervisor to tell them that this must not happen again.

» *Reports* – detailed documents about a particular issue or problem. These are often produced by experts working in the business. They can be sent to managers to read before a meeting to discuss the issue. Very often these reports are so detailed that they could not be understood by all employees.
» *Notices* pinned on boards – these are used to display information which is open to everyone. However, there is no certainty that they are read.
» *Text messages* – today, mobile (cell) phones are a major part of people's lives. They allow for quick and convenient communication with others. One of the most used functions on the mobile phone is not voice calls, but instant text (sms) messaging – such as when organising a business meeting at short notice: just take out your phone, type in a quick 'meet me @ 2 plz' and press send. Text messaging (sms) is an easy and discreet way of communicating with others. Text messaging allows the 'sender' to communicate with others in situations where a face-to-face or phone conversation is not possible or appropriate. Also, a record exists of the communication – until this is deleted. However, there is no way of assessing the tone of the message or the 'mood' of the sender and this can cause some failures in communication.
» *Email, social networking sites, tweeting* and other forms of electronic communication using information technology – these have revolutionised communications in recent years. Written messages can be sent between two or more people with computing facilities. Printouts of messages can be obtained if a 'hard copy' is required. Intranets provide easy messaging to all workers in a business with access to a computer. The internet allows easy and effective communication with customers and suppliers.

5 Days Left

Our tweets will be coming from a new home
@HodderSchools make sure you are following!

0	0	0
replies	retweets	likes

▲ An example of a tweet sent via Twitter®

Advantages of written communication

>> There is 'hard' evidence of the message which can be referred to in the future. This should help to reduce disagreements between the sender and the receiver about the contents of the message.
>> It is essential for certain messages involving complicated details which might be misunderstood if, for example, a telephone call was made. Also, the law in many countries requires certain safety messages to be written and displayed in offices and factories. It is not sufficient to tell people about safety measures – they could be forgotten.
>> A written message can be copied and sent to many people. This could be more efficient than telephoning all of those people to give them the same message verbally.
>> Electronic communication is a quick and cheap way to reach a large number of people.

Disadvantages of written communication

>> Direct feedback is not always possible, unless electronic communication is used. This can, however, lead to too many email messages being created and 'information overload', meaning people are unable to pick out the really important messages from the many that might be received. With written messages in other forms, two-way communication is difficult.
>> It is not so easy to check that the message has been received and acted upon as with verbal messages – although this can be done with email as a 'please acknowledge' function can be set up.
>> The language used can be difficult for some receivers to understand. If the written message is too long it may be confusing and lose the interest of the reader.
>> There is no opportunity for body language to be used to reinforce the message.

Visual communication methods

Visual methods of communication include the following:

>> *Films, videos* and *Microsoft PowerPoint* displays – often used by businesses to help train new staff or to inform sales people about new products.
>> *Posters* – can be used to explain a simple but important message by means of a picture or cartoon. For example, the dangers of operating an unguarded machine or the waste of energy from leaving lights switched on.

» *Charts* and *diagrams* – can be used in reports or letters to show numerical data or to simplify complicated ideas, such as how the business is organised. Examples of these appear in other chapters of this book. Computers and relevant IT packages can be used to present data in a wide variety of different tables, charts, graphs and diagrams. Printouts of these can then be obtained as a hard copy to add to reports and other documents.

» *Photographs* and *cartoons* – these can be used to add variety, colour and humour to a message – all of which may increase the chances of the communication being read and understood by the receiver.

Advantages of visual communication

» These methods can present information in an appealing and attractive way. People are often more prepared to look at films or posters than to read letters or notices because of the interesting way they communicate messages.

» They can be used to make a written message clearer by adding a chart or diagram to illustrate the point being made.

Disadvantages of visual communication

» There is no feedback and the sender of the message may need to use other forms of communication to check that the message has been understood. For example, training videos are often followed by a written test for the new staff to check their understanding.

» Charts and graphs are difficult for some people to interpret. The overall message might be misunderstood if the receiver is unsure how to read values from a graph or how to interpret a technical diagram.

> **Key info**
>
> In some cultures, non-verbal communication can be just as important as the words that make up a message. During a face-to-face conversation or during a meeting, the Chinese, for example, rely on facial expression, tone of voice and posture to tell them what someone feels.

> **Study tips**
>
> Remember that in some cases it might be essential to use written forms of communication (for example, with legal contracts). In other cases, for example, when advertising a new product, communication with potential customers could best be achieved with more visual methods.

▶ Activity 9.5: Methods of communication

Copy out this table of communication methods. Under the headings of Speed, Written record and Feedback, fill in the key advantages or disadvantages of each. The first one has been done for you.

	Speed	Written record	Feedback
Letter	Slow – takes time to write letter and postal service might be poor	Yes – receiver has the letter and the sender is likely to keep a copy	Likely to be slow – the receiver may not reply at all
Telephone call			
Meeting with employees			
Social network site			
Staff newspaper			
Website			
Email			
Notice			
Face-to-face conversation			
Advertising poster			
Text message (sms)			

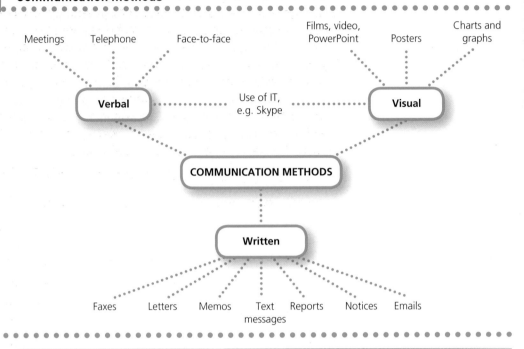

Activity 9.6

Which communication method might be most appropriate for the following messages? Justify your answer in each case.

a There should be no smoking in the staff canteen.
b The management want to instruct all employees on how the new computer system works.
c Details of the business's sales figures for the last four years are being sent to shareholders.
d The Finance Manager wants to remind the Operations Manager that they have arranged a meeting for next week.
e The Product Development Manager wants to inform directors of the market research into three new product ideas. He hopes that they will agree to launch one of these products.
f The Office Manager wants to obtain views from all office workers on how paper waste could be reduced.
g A supervisor plans to warn (for the last time) a worker who is always late for work.
h Next year's holiday dates need to be made available to all workers.
i The Human Resources Manager wants to invite an applicant for a job to an interview.
j The Operations Manager wants to send the plans for a new factory to the Managing Director, who is on a foreign business trip.
k Existing customers of a bank are to be informed about a new type of bank account.
l A new contract needs to be agreed and signed between a farmer and the cooperative he sells his milk to.
m The Marketing department of a cosmetics business wants to launch a new perfume aimed at women with above-average incomes.

Definitions to learn

Formal communication is when messages are sent through established channels using professional language.

Informal communication is when information is sent and received casually using everyday language.

Formal and informal communication

If you are a school student or in employment, how do you receive messages which are important to you? You may read notices on the noticeboard, receive reports, emails or memos, or attend official meetings. These are all examples of **formal communication**. Are they the only way you learn about what is going on in your organisation? Almost certainly not.

You are also likely to receive messages through **informal** channels, such as meetings with friends or contact with others in the canteen or at break times. These informal, or unrecognised, meetings are sometimes referred to as the 'grapevine'. Sometimes these informal channels can be used by managers to 'try out' the reaction to new ideas, such as a new shift system in the factory, before formally communicating details of the new system. If the reaction from the grapevine is negative, management may not introduce the new idea at all. At other times, the informal channels can spread gossip and rumour which is unhelpful to managers. Managers, however, cannot prevent the informal links existing between people in the organisation.

The direction of communications

A typical organisation chart for a business is shown below.

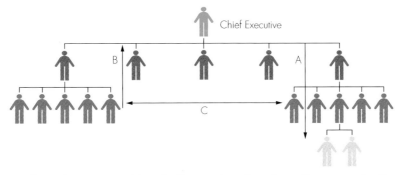

Look at the arrows. They indicate the direction of communication.

» Arrow A shows downward communication. This is when messages are sent from managers to subordinates. It can be used for instructions or statements on important business decisions. It does not allow for feedback. If these messages have to pass through many levels of hierarchy then the original meaning of the message could become distorted (see section on communication barriers below).

» Arrow B shows upward communication. This is when a message or feedback is passed from subordinates to managers. As we have seen, such feedback can be an essential part of effective communication. Workers in an organisation have much to offer by being involved in the communication process. They should not be afraid of contributing to discussions or meetings. The organisation has much to gain when the managers are prepared to listen to and act upon messages received from those lower down the organisation.

» Arrow C shows horizontal communication (sometimes referred to as lateral communication). This occurs when people at the same level in an organisation communicate with each other. Information and ideas can be exchanged at both formal and informal meetings. This can be a cause of conflict between departments, for example if Marketing informs Operations that the quality of output is so poor that consumers are returning goods as faulty!

How communication barriers arise and how to reduce or remove them

As we saw on page 116, there are four parts to any successful communication – sender, receiver, medium used and feedback. Communication can fail if any one of these four parts does not operate as it should. If one part fails, it would be called a **barrier** to effective **communication**. This would cause a breakdown in communications, which could lead to serious problems for the organisation.

Definitions to learn

Communication barriers are factors that stop effective communication of messages.

125

The most common barriers to effective communication and ways to overcome them are listed in the table below.

Communication barrier	Description	How the barrier can be reduced or removed
Problems with the sender	Language which is too difficult is used. 'Jargon' or technical terms may not be understood by the receiver.	The sender should ensure that the message uses language which is understandable. Use of jargon or terms which are too technical should be avoided.
	The sender uses verbal means of communication but speaks too quickly or not clearly enough.	The sender should make the message as clear as possible. Feedback should be asked for to ensure the message is being understood.
	The sender communicates the wrong message or passes it to the wrong receiver.	The sender must make sure that the right person is receiving the right message.
	The message is too long and too much detail prevents the main points being understood. This is again the fault of the sender.	The message should be as brief as possible to allow the main points to be understood.
Problems with the medium	The message may be lost so the receiver does not see it.	It is important to insist on feedback. If no feedback is received then the sender assumes the message was lost.
	The wrong channel has been used, for example, an important message was put on the noticeboard which most people did not read.	The sender must select the appropriate channel for each message sent.
	If the message is sent down a long chain of command, the original meaning of the message may be lost. It could become distorted.	The shortest possible channel should be used to avoid this problem.
	No feedback is received.	This could be because, for example, a letter was sent to workers asking for their opinions. A meeting would have been more useful.
	Breakdown of the medium, for example, computer failure or postal strike.	Other forms of communication should, where possible, be made available.
Problems with the receiver	They might not be listening or paying attention.	The importance of the message should be emphasised. The receivers should be asked for feedback to ensure understanding.
	The receiver may not like or trust the sender. They may be unwilling to act upon his or her message.	There should be trust between the sender and the receiver or effective communication is unlikely. Perhaps another sender should be used who is respected by the receiver.
Problems with feedback	There is no feedback.	Perhaps no feedback was asked for. Perhaps the method of communication used did not allow for feedback. An alternative method of communication might have been better that did allow feedback.
	It is received too slowly or is distorted. As with the original message, perhaps the feedback is passing through too many people before being received by the original sender of the message.	Direct lines of communication between subordinates and managers must be available. Direct communication is always more effective.

Activity 9.7: Reducing communication barriers

Sanchez is a successful business leader. He started his own business, STC, importing tea and coffee five years ago. He now employs 45 people – 30 in his country and 15 in countries that produce the tea and coffee. As he is very busy he holds few meetings with his workers. He emails his managers daily and expects them to pass on his instructions to the workers they are responsible for. In recent weeks, some supplies of tea and coffee have not been to the exact quality and taste that Sanchez demands and he is very angry. He wants to tell his managers and workers how they must improve. He wrote to them all several months ago for new ideas on how to improve the business but he did not get any replies!

a Identify **four** possible causes of communication barriers within STC.

b Explain to Sanchez how he could overcome the four communication barriers that you identified in **a**.

REVISION SUMMARY **Barriers to effective communication and how they can be overcome**

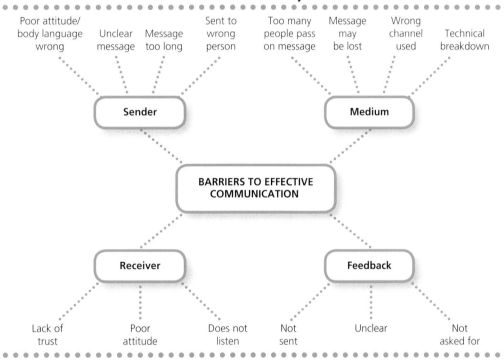

International business in focus

Coca-Cola blog for worldwide employee survey

The Coca-Cola corporation is using a blog as a communication channel through which the 55 000 employees of the global company can provide their views on Coca-Cola's vision, mission and values.

Orlando Ashford, head of Human Resources (HR) at Coca-Cola's US headquarters in Atlanta, Georgia, says that Coca-Cola can be one of the most respected companies in the world only when it's clear to employees what the company stands for. This will only be achieved by effective internal communication.

This blog method employee survey is not unique. IBM has recently used a similar method. Ashford says he wants to see Coca-Cola management everywhere in the world setting an example and participating in blogging.

Discussion points

- Explain why Coca-Cola's HR head believes that effective communication with workers is important.

- Do you think that blogging is the best way to obtain the views of a large number of workers?

Exam-style questions: Short answer and data response

1 Manuel is HR Manager for a large bank. His responsibilities include internal communication with individual workers and groups of workers. Sometimes he wants to send a message to all 15 000 workers employed by the bank. Some workers complain that unless they spend time reading notices or email messages they fail to receive important information.

   a Define 'internal communication'. [2]

   b Identify **two** benefits to the bank of effective internal communication. [2]

   c Outline **two** possible barriers to communication within the bank. [4]

   d Explain **two** ways in which Manuel could communicate with individual workers about their pay and working conditions. [6]

   e Do you think that electronic forms of communication are always the best ones to use when communicating with large numbers of workers? Justify your answer. [6]

2 SEP manufactures electrical appliances such as cookers and heaters. One of Phil's responsibilities as Marketing Manager at SEP is to communicate with thousands of customers in many countries. Some of these customers are wholesalers but many are individual consumers who have bought products directly from the business. Phil is worried that communication barriers sometimes prevent his messages being received effectively.

   a Define 'communication barriers'. [2]

   b Apart from customers, identify **two** external groups SEP might need to communicate with. [2]

   c Outline **two** types of written communication with customers that Phil could use. [4]

   d Explain **two** possible causes of communication barriers between Phil and SEP's customers. [6]

   e SEP has discovered a major safety problem with one of its products. It needs to communicate with customers quickly. Explain the advantages and disadvantages of i telephoning all customers and ii sending an email to them. Which method of communication is best in this case? Justify your answer. [6]

Revision checklist

In this chapter you have learned:

✔ why internal and external communication is important in different business situations

✔ how to select the best method of communication for different messages

✔ the most common reasons for communication failure – barriers to communication

✔ how businesses can overcome these barriers to communication.

NOW – test your understanding with the revision questions in the Student etextbook and the Workbook.

People in business: end-of-section case study

➡ The Lakeview Restaurant

The Lakeview Restaurant is owned by two brothers, Chris and Abdul. They set up the restaurant ten years ago as a private limited company. It is located on the edge of the city.

The business is split into two separate dining areas. One area is for families and the other area serves more expensive meals. The family dining area is large and is hired out for weddings and birthday parties. The other area is mainly for business customers.

Both sections of the restaurant are always busy and fully booked on weekdays. Chris and Abdul want to expand the business. The restaurant cannot be expanded on its existing site as it has buildings on one side and it is next to a lake on the other side. New workers for the kitchens and waiters will need to be recruited.

There are two options for the business to expand:

- Option 1: Buy a ship and convert it into a floating restaurant next to the main restaurant to hire out for weddings and birthday parties. The ship will cost $100 000 to buy and convert to a restaurant. The projected net profit is $20 000 per year. Unemployment in the area is high.
- Option 2: Close the existing restaurant and relocate to a new building which is much larger and in the centre of the city. The additional cost of buying a new restaurant is $250 000 and the projected net profit is $25 000 per year. Unemployment in the city centre is low.

➡ Appendix 1

Two job applications for the post of manager of the Lakeview Restaurant

Name	Mr J Patel	Mr N Guitano
Qualifications	10 IGCSEs, 3 A levels, BA Degree in Business Management	7 IGCSEs, 2 A levels
Management experience	3 years as General Manager of a small café	20 years as restaurant manager
Interests	Cricket, football, rugby, reading	Reading, watching television, helping to keep the accounts for a local children's charity
Personal status	Married, 4 children	Single, no children
Number of restaurants at which they have worked	4 restaurants for 4 weeks each as they were holiday jobs	10 different restaurants in 20 years
Preferred management style	Autocratic – believes the manager knows best	Democratic – believes employees should be asked their opinions

Appendix 2

```
5th June Meeting

From: Chris (c-smith@gotmail.co.uk)

Sent: 23 March 2018 23:41:47

To: Abdul (Abdul@gotmail.com)

Cc:

Hi Abdul

We need to employ a new restaurant manager. We had to dismiss the last
manager as he failed to motivate employees - we do not want someone like
him again.

I want someone who is careful with money and will give a good service to
the customers. They need to come up with ideas of how to increase the
number of customers to the restaurant on weekends.

What do you think?
```

Exam-style questions: Case study

1 a Explain **two** reasons why well-motivated employees are important for the restaurant. [8]

  b Chris and Abdul have advertised a job vacancy for a restaurant manager. Looking at Appendix 2, compare the two job applicants in Appendix 1 and decide whom you would choose to employ. Justify the reasons for your choice. [12]

2 a The Lakeview Restaurant is expanding. Explain **two** reasons why an organisation chart would be helpful to the management of the restaurant. [8]

  b The restaurant needs to communicate with its suppliers to order its weekly food ingredients. Consider the advantages and disadvantages of using email, letter or telephone. Recommend which is the best method for Chris and Abdul to use. Justify your answer. [12]

Optional question

3 a The Lakeview Restaurant is located near to several restaurants which are competitors. Explain **one** advantage and **one** disadvantage to the business of being located near to competitors. [8]

  b Consider the advantages and disadvantages of the **two** options for the restaurant business to expand. Recommend which option Chris and Abdul should choose. Justify your choice. [12]

SECTION 3

Marketing

Chapters

10 Marketing, competition and the customer
11 Market research
12 The marketing mix: product
13 The marketing mix: price
14 The marketing mix: place
15 The marketing mix: promotion
16 Technology and the marketing mix
17 Marketing strategy

Marketing, competition and the customer

The Marketing department

Definitions to learn

Marketing is identifying customer wants and satisfying them profitably. A **customer** is a person, business or other organisation which buys goods or services from a business.

Most businesses, unless they are very small, will have a **Marketing** department. In a large public limited company, the Marketing Director will have people responsible for market research of new products, promotion (including promotions and advertising), distribution, pricing and sales.

▲ The structure of a typical Marketing department

Large businesses will have different sections within their marketing departments:

» *The Sales team* is responsible for the sales of the product. It will usually have separate sections for each region to which the product is distributed. If the product is exported, there may also be an Export team.
» *The Market Research section* is responsible for finding out **customers'** needs, market changes and the impact of competitors' actions. It will report on these to the Marketing Director and this information will be used to help make decisions about research and development of new products, pricing levels, sales strategies and promotion strategies.
» *The Promotion section* deals with organising the advertising for products. It arranges for advertisements to be produced. For example, adverts are filmed if they are to be on television, or designed if they are to be in newspapers.

The department also decides on the types of promotion that will be included in campaigns. It will have a marketing budget – a fixed amount of money to spend. It has to decide which types of advertising media will be the most effective to use because there will only be a certain amount to spend; the department cannot spend what it likes!

>> *Distribution* transports the products to the market.

> ### Activity 10.1
>
> In which section of the Marketing department – Sales, Market Research, Promotion or Distribution – do each of the following people work?
>
> **a** Anya spends most of her time in other countries showing the product to people who buy inventory for large retail groups.
> **b** Mohamed spends his time arranging for adverts of the product to be placed in newspapers and magazines.
> **c** Paul spends much of his time carrying out questionnaires.
> **d** Mary organises the airline flights for the products to be sent to their markets abroad.

The role of marketing

Marketing is not just about advertising and selling a good or service, as can be seen by the different marketing activities found in a Marketing department. The central role of marketing undertakes the following:

>> **Identify customer needs** – finding out what kind of products or services customers want, the prices they are willing to pay, where and how they want to buy these goods or services, and what after-sales services they might want.
>> **Satisfy customer needs** – so that goods and services can be sold profitably. Customers want the right product, in the right place and at the right price. Failure to meet these needs, or doing it less well than competitors, will lead to the business facing the risk of closure.
>> **Maintain customer loyalty** – by building customer relationships. Keeping close links with customers and finding out if products or services are continuing to meet their needs will help to ensure the success of the business. If customers change their expectations of what they want from a good or service then the business should respond to meet these new needs. This will be identified by maintaining close **customer relationships**. It is very important to keep existing customers (customer loyalty) and not just concentrate on attracting new ones. It is much cheaper for a business to try to keep existing customers (for example, with loyalty cards) than trying to gain new customers.
>> Build customer relationships to **gain information about customers** – by building a long-term relationship with them so that their changing needs can be understood. This is one of the most important roles of the Marketing department in today's globally competitive world. Building a relationship with customers means that market research information can be used to understand why customers buy products and how they use them. This makes for more effective marketing.
>> **Anticipate changes in customer needs** – by identifying new trends in customer demand or gaps in the market so that businesses can produce goods or services which are not currently available.

If the Marketing department is successful in identifying customer requirements and predicting future customer needs, it should enable the business to:

» raise customer awareness of a product or service of the business
» increase revenue and profitability
» increase or maintain **market share**
» maintain or improve the image of products or a business
» target a new market or market segment
» enter new markets at home or abroad
» develop new products or improve existing products.

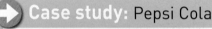

Case study: Pepsi Cola

At present, Pepsi Philippines, which manufactures Pepsi, Seven-Up, Mountain Dew, Gatorade, Tropicana and Lipton, accounts for 20 per cent of the total carbonated drinks market in the Philippines. It wants to expand its operation and increase its share of the market still further. The Marketing department will be vital in deciding how this can be achieved.

Activity 10.2

Read the case study above.

a Suggest ways Pepsi Philippines could increase its market share. Which way do you think will be most effective? Explain your answer.
b Do you think Pepsi Philippines should develop new varieties of drinks to sell in this market? Explain your answer.
c Identify who could be the new customers of these drinks.
d Explain what types of advertising and promotion might be effective in attracting these customers.

Understanding market changes

The world of markets and marketing is constantly changing. It is very unusual if a business does not have to change its goods and services over time to respond to important market changes. Things don't stay the same forever! Some markets are changing at a rapid pace, such as mobile (cell) phones, whereas other markets, such as breakfast cereals, don't change very quickly.

Why customer/consumer spending patterns change

» **Consumer tastes and fashions change** – fashions may change for clothes and so consumers may want different styles of clothes to those they wore last year.
» **Changes in technology** – with new products being developed, such as iPads, tablets and smartwatches, sales of desk computer/standalone computers have fallen in many countries. New products mean old versions/alternatives do not have high sales anymore.

>> **Change in incomes** – if an economy has high unemployment then many consumers will buy cheaper products. If the economy then grows and unemployment falls, the sales of more expensive products will increase.
>> **Ageing populations** – the age structure of the population in many countries is changing to a greater percentage of older people. This has changed the type of products which are increasing in demand, such as anti-ageing face creams for women.

The power and importance of changing customer needs

If businesses fail to respond to customer needs then they are likely to fail. The customer is 'king' because as their needs change, it is the businesses which research and know what these changes are, and respond to them, that will be successful (see the case study on page 136 and Activity 10.3).

Why have some markets become more competitive?

>> Globalisation of markets has meant that products are increasingly sold all over the world (see Chapter 29).
>> Transportation improvements have meant that it is easier and cheaper to transport products from one part of the world to another.
>> Internet/e-commerce has meant that consumers can search for products and buy from overseas markets. Even some services such as insurance can be bought from businesses based in another country. Increased consumer information about products and the different international businesses that produce them makes a market much more competitive.

How can businesses respond to changing spending patterns and increased competition?

A business will have to take action to maintain its level of sales and market share whenever there are changes to spending patterns or increasing competition.

In order to remain successful, a business may need to do the following:

>> **Maintain good customer relationships** – this has a key role in continuing to meet customer needs and it also provides market research information about customers. Marketing departments which become experts on customer needs will respond to these needs as and when they change and will maintain customer loyalty. It is often cheaper to keep existing customers than gain new ones.
>> **Keep improving its existing product** – this is especially true if its competitors improve their products. By making the goods or services it sells very different from those produced by competitors the business will become well known for differentiated products. Apple is a good example of a company that reacts to increased competition by making even more advanced products.
>> **Bring out new products to keep customers' interest** in the company rather than its competitors – this will help the business to maintain, or even increase, its market share. An example of this is Microsoft, which keeps on improving and developing its operating systems.
>> **Keep costs low to maintain competitiveness** – as this should help keep prices low.

Case study: What happens when change catches up with you?

'The world is changing very fast. Big will not beat small anymore. It will be the fast beating the slow.' (Rupert Murdoch)

One of the few things that is certain in this world is change. In a world where technology is advancing at such a rapid pace, change happens even more quickly. It is very important for companies to adapt to change as rapidly as they can.

Take the example of Kodak, which filed for bankruptcy in 2012 in a bid to survive a cash crisis, caused by years of falling sales of its photographic film for cameras (as digital cameras had taken over the market). Kodak, a pioneer in the photographic film business, has tried to restructure to become a seller of consumer products like cameras.

Consumers' preference for digital cameras is on the rise in India, with the market for digital cameras growing at 40 per cent in volume terms (according to industry estimates). Prices of digital cameras are falling, and with additional features that allow video recording it means camera manufacturers such as Sony, Canon and Samsung are enjoying rising sales.

Activity 10.3

Read the case study above.

a Why did Kodak get into financial difficulties? Explain your answer.
b Suggest how maintaining good customer relations might have helped Kodak avoid business failure.

What is meant by a market?

A market for a particular good or service is made up of the total number of customers and potential customers, as well as sellers, for that particular good or service. It can be measured by the total number of sales or by the value of the sales for that good or service by all suppliers of that particular good or service. These can be either mass markets or niche markets.

Mass marketing

Definitions to learn

Mass market is where there is a very large number of sales of a product.

If a product has a very high level of sales it is almost certainly being sold in a **mass market**. In these markets many people in the population will buy the product, for example, aspirin, washing powder or soap. Products are designed to appeal to the whole market and therefore advertising and promotions are intended to appeal to most customers. The advantages of selling to a mass market are:

» total sales in these markets are very high
» the business can benefit from economies of scale (see Chapter 19)
» risks can be spread, as often the business will sell several different variations of products to the mass market, and if one variety of the product fails then the other products may still sell well
» opportunities for growth of the business due to large potential sales.

However, there are disadvantages, which include:

» high levels of competition between businesses selling similar products
» high costs of advertising and promotion
» standardised products or services are produced and so may not meet the specific needs of all customers or potential customers, therefore leading to lost sales.

Niche marketing

However, some products are sold only to a very small number of customers who form a small segment of a much larger market. This is referred to as a **niche market.** These products are quite often specialised and sold by small businesses that would find it difficult to compete in a mass market. For example, there is a mass market for shops selling essential food products in any country. However, if there is a small group of migrant workers in that country then food shops selling specialised food for this group of people may be set up. Expensive products, such as Rolex watches or designer clothes, are aimed at a small section of much larger markets.

Being able to identify and supply a niche market has advantages:

>> Small businesses may be able to sell successfully in niche markets as larger businesses may not have identified them but concentrated on the mass markets instead. This will reduce competition from the larger businesses in niche markets.

>> The needs of consumers can be more closely focused on, and therefore targeted, by businesses in a niche market. This may lead to high levels of consumer loyalty and good customer relations.

However, there are disadvantages to operating in a niche market:

>> Niche markets are usually relatively small and therefore have limited sales potential. This means it is likely that only small businesses can operate profitably in these markets. If the business wants to grow it will need to look outside the niche market to develop products for mass markets.

>> Often businesses in a niche market will specialise in just one product. This means that if the product is no longer in demand the business will fail as the business has not spread its risks. Producing several products rather than just one product means that if one fails there are other products which are still in demand and the business carries on trading.

Market segments

The market for a particular good or service is made up of the total number of customers and potential customers for that particular good or service. Market segmentation recognises that potential users of a good or service are not all the same, and that what appeals to one set of consumers may not appeal to others.

Market segmentation is when a market is broken down into sub-groups which share similar characteristics. For example, chocolates are eaten by young children, teenagers and adults of both sexes. Different brands of chocolates will appeal to these different groups of people. A Marketing department will divide the whole market into different groups and categories; these are called market segments.

Each segment is researched in great detail. When it comes to advertising, the Marketing department knows the best places to advertise and the most likely place where the particular market segment will see the advertisement. It will also know how to design the advertisement to appeal to the target market segment. An example might be teenagers buying clothes. They might be asked questions about which social media they use, which television programmes they watch, which mobile phone they have and general questions about what they like. This will enable the Marketing department to select the best times to advertise, if television advertisements are to be used, and the type of adverts that will appeal to teenagers. They can advertise on the social media that are usually used by teenagers or design a new app for free download.

Segmenting a market can help a business to:

» make marketing expenditure cost effective by producing a product which closely meets the needs of these customers and targeting its marketing efforts only on this segment
» enjoy higher sales and profits for the business, because of cost-effective marketing
» identify a market segment which is not having its needs fully met, and therefore offers opportunities to increase sales.

Some of the most common ways a market can be segmented are shown in the table below.

Ways of segmenting a market

By socio-economic group	Income groups can be defined by grouping people's jobs according to how much they are paid. For example, managers are usually paid more than office workers. Office employees are usually paid more than production workers. Unemployed people will obviously be the lowest income group. This often means that products are priced differently to target certain income groups. For example, cars range in size, performance and price level. Only someone on a high income could afford a Ferrari, but a person on a much lower income might afford to buy a Tata Nano. Some perfumes are sold at low prices whereas other perfume brands are very expensive and are aimed at higher income groups.
By age	The products bought by people in different age groups will not be the same. Young people buy different clothes to elderly people. The toys bought for babies will vary from those bought for older children.
By region/location	In different regions of a country people might buy different products. For example, if there are dry and wet parts of the country then waterproof clothing would be sold in the rainy part of the country, but not in the dry part. If a product is exported, then it may need to be changed slightly (for example, a different name or different packaging) in order to appeal to the tastes of people in other countries.
By gender	Some products are bought only by women or only by men. For example, a shaving razor would normally be bought by a man, whereas a perfume would normally be bought by a woman.
By use of the product	For example, cars can be used by consumers for domestic use or for business use. The advertising media and promotion methods used will differ. Cars for business use may be advertised by sending brochures out to businesses, whereas cars for domestic use may be advertised on television. These cars may be the same models, but they will be marketed in a different way.
By lifestyle	For example, a single person earning the same income as a married person with three children will spend that income differently, buying different products. Businesses can 'aim' their products at people who enjoy different lifestyles.

Study tips

Remember that consumers can be part of more than one segment. You should be able to explain how and why businesses segment a market and use examples to illustrate this.

Potential benefits of segmentation to business

Businesses can use market segmentation to sell more products. They do this by making different brands of a product and then aiming each brand at a different market segment. As can be seen in the example of soap in the case study below, a business could produce various brands of soap to satisfy most of the market segments.

By finding out the different segments in a market, a business can sometimes identify a segment whose needs are not being met meaning there is a gap in the market. It can then produce a suitable product to meet these customers' needs and again increase sales.

A marketing manager would take all these factors into account when deciding which segments might buy new products or improved products. Therefore, once the segments have been identified, this will influence how the products are packaged and advertised. It will also affect the choice of shops the products are sold in, in order to get maximum sales.

 Case study

This is an example of how the market for soap may be segmented.

Type of soap	Characteristics of market segment
Beauty soap	People who buy beauty soap will be people who want to keep their skin soft. They will therefore buy soap which contains moisturisers. This will be bought mainly by women.
Baby soap	This is mild soap which will not harm a baby's skin. Bought mainly by mothers for their babies.
Medicated soap	Sometimes soap is sold to help fight acne. This tends to be bought mainly by teenagers, both male and female.
Non-branded soap	This is a low-price product which is plain soap with no extra perfume added. This will probably be bought by people on low incomes.

There may be other types of soap you can think of which are aimed at different groups. Sales of soap will be affected by income group, gender and also age.

▲ Which type of soap will each person use?

Activity 10.4

Read the case study above.

a List the different brands of soap sold in your local shops.
b Which segments of the market are each of these brands of soap aimed at?

Which method of segmentation should be used?

Different businesses will segment markets in different ways. A business that runs a number of gymnasiums is likely to use consumers' lifestyles as a way of segmenting the market. A health and beauty product business is more likely to use gender as the most important way of segmenting its market. In contrast, a jewellery maker will segment the market into designs affordable to consumers with different income levels. The factors a business will consider before choosing an appropriate method of segmentation include:

» detailed analysis of the market and the 'size' of each potential segment in terms of consumers and likely sales
» company image and brand image – a 'high-tech' business with an excellent reputation for innovation will not want to produce low-priced goods for low-income consumers
» cost of entering each segment, for example, with a specially designed product and advertising campaign.

> ### Activity 10.5
>
> Toyota produces a range of cars aimed at different market segments. It even owns a separate company called Lexus, whose cars are aimed at a particular market segment.
>
>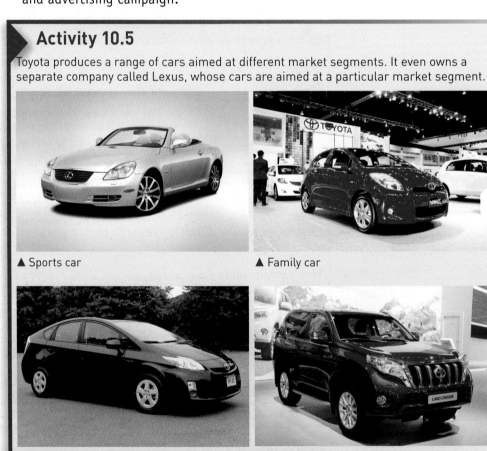
>
> ▲ Sports car   ▲ Family car
>
> ▲ Hybrid car   ▲ 4x4 SUV
>
> a Look at the photographs of the Toyota range of cars and identify what characteristics the consumers of these models are likely to have. The characteristics you identify might include income (socio-economic group), age, gender, use of the product, lifestyle.
> b Explain the benefits to Toyota of producing a large range of cars aimed at different market segments.

REVISION SUMMARY **Ways of segmenting markets**

Age   Region   Location   Use of product

MARKETS CAN BE SEGMENTED BY:

Gender   Lifestyle   Income/social group

International business in focus

Personal computers and technology

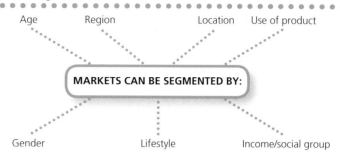

▲ Personal computer and mobile (cell) phone technology has seen many advances over the last twenty years

The personal computer market has seen many changes over the last few years. The standard desktop computer is becoming a thing of the past in many offices, where laptops have taken its place. In the home this is also true. However, the introduction of the netbook and then the Apple iPad changed the market again.

Predictions for the future of the personal computer market are that mobile devices will become market leaders in terms of global sales, followed by tablets and netbooks. Home computers are seen as becoming a smaller and smaller share of the global market.

Discussion points

- How has the market for personal computers changed?

- Why have these changes happened?

- How should businesses in the personal computer market respond to these changes?

Exam-style questions: Short answer and data response

1 D&F Limited owns several fruit farms. The fruit is sold to large supermarkets abroad. D&F also grows coffee which is sold to companies that process and brand the coffee. The branded coffee is also then sold to large supermarkets abroad. The world price of coffee has recently dropped by 20%. There has been a growing demand for fruit from consumers in developing countries with rising incomes. In developed countries there has been a growing trend towards 'healthy eating', encouraged by government policies to tackle the obesity problem. Fresh fruit is an important part of a healthy diet.

  a Define 'consumers'. [2]
  b Identify **two** reasons why the price of coffee might be falling. [2]
  c Outline **two** reasons why supermarkets are demanding more fruit. [4]
  d Explain **two** ways the Directors of D&F Limited could respond to increased competition from farms which are switching from growing vegetables to growing fruit. [6]
  e Do you think D&F Limited should stop producing coffee and grow more fruit instead? Justify your answer. [6]

2 TGH is a public limited company which makes sports shoes (trainers). It makes a variety of designs for the mass market. The mass market consumers are young people who want fashionable sports shoes as well as those who play sport. The Directors recently decided to target a niche market. This is a market segment of customers who have a medical problem with their feet and need specially designed shoes.

  a Define 'niche market'. [2]
  b Identify **two** examples of the different markets for TGH products. [2]
  c Outline **two** reasons why TGH sells to a niche market. [4]
  d Explain **two** advantages to TGH of segmenting the market for sports shoes. [6]
  e Do you think the Directors of TGH were right to target a niche market or should they just sell sports shoes to a mass market? [6]

Revision checklist

In this chapter you have learned:

✔ the role of marketing – identifying and satisfying customer needs as well as maintaining customer loyalty
✔ why market changes occur, such as when spending patterns change or there is increased competition, and how businesses can respond to these changes
✔ the difference between mass marketing and niche marketing
✔ what is meant by market segmentation and why market segmentation may be used
✔ to recommend and justify an appropriate method of market segmentation in given circumstances.

NOW – test your understanding with the revision questions in the Student etextbook and the Workbook.

Market research

This chapter will explain:

* ★ the role of market research and the methods used
* ★ market-orientated businesses (uses of market research information to a business)
* ★ primary research and secondary research (benefits and limitations of each)
* ★ methods of primary research, for example, postal questionnaires, online surveys, interviews, focus groups
* ★ the need for sampling
* ★ methods of secondary research, for example, online, accessing government sources, paying for commercial market research reports
* ★ factors influencing the accuracy of market research data
* ★ presentation and use of market research results: analyse market research data shown in the form of graphs, charts and diagrams; draw simple conclusions from such data.

The role of market research

A business needs to find out how many people would want to buy the product it is planning to offer for sale. If there is not a very big market for the product, a great deal of money could be wasted developing a product that not many people will buy. It could even cause the business to fail altogether. Therefore, it is very important that **market research** is carried out accurately.

The role of market research is to try to find out answers to these questions:

>> Would customers be willing to buy my product?
>> What price would they be prepared to pay?
>> Where would they be most likely to buy my product?
>> What feature of my product do customers most like or dislike?
>> What type of customer would buy my product?
>> What type of promotion would be effective with these types of customers?
>> How strong is the competition and who are the main competing businesses?

By carrying out market research, a business can identify customer needs in a changing and competitive international environment. This is essential if a business is to remain competitive in the future.

Product-orientated and market-orientated businesses

Some businesses produce the product first and then try to find a market for it. This is known as being **product-orientated**. This approach is not common today. Product-orientated businesses often produce basic necessities required for living, such as agricultural tools or fresh foods. These products may not have a brand name and are general products that consumers need to buy. The producer and retailer are mainly concerned with the price and quality of the product. Sometimes

Definitions to learn

Market research is the process of gathering, analysing and interpreting information about a market.

Key info

Market research is big business. According to ESOMAR, global business spending on market research reached US$68 billion in 2015. Obviously, businesses around the world know it is of great importance to 'find out more about the market and customer tastes'.

Definitions to learn

A **product-orientated** business is one whose main focus of activity is on the product itself.

when new technologies are being developed, new products, such as the original iPad, are launched on the market without first investigating possible demand for them. Consumers may not buy these products until they have been fully tried and tested and until advertising has persuaded them to purchase the products.

Businesses whose markets are national or international cannot usually afford to be product-orientated. It is risky to produce products and hope that they will sell, without first carrying out market research to find out if consumers will want the product. This approach of using market research is called being **market-orientated**. It requires businesses to have a **marketing budget**. Each business has to identify the wants and desires of customers, both now and in the future, in order to produce the right goods which will sell well and make a good profit for the business.

Market-orientated businesses are better able to survive in the market and be successful because they are usually more adaptable to changes in customer tastes. They are able to take advantage of new market opportunities which may arise. New products are launched with more confidence when customer needs have been identified before the product is introduced on to the market.

Case study

Joshua invents a new tool for planting seeds. It is much easier to use than existing tools. However, it has high manufacturing costs, twice as much as existing tools.

Activity 11.1

Read the case study above.

a Is Joshua's business product-orientated or market-orientated? Give reasons for your answer.
b What would you advise Joshua to do before he starts to manufacture the new tool? Explain your answer.

Market research methods

Market research can find out:

» *quantitative information*, which answers questions about the quantity of something, for example, 'How many sports shoes were sold in the month of December?' or 'What percentage of children drink sugar-free cola?'
» *qualitative information*, which answers questions where an opinion or judgement is necessary, for example, 'What do customers like about a particular product?' or 'Why do more women than men buy the company's products?'

Both types of information can be gathered as a result of:

» **primary research**, or field research
» **secondary research**, or desk research.

Primary research

Primary research, or field research, is the collection and collation of original data. It involves direct contact with potential or existing customers.

Advantages of primary research

» It is up to date and relevant to the business undertaking it.
» It is usually planned and carried out by the people who want to use the data; it is first-hand.

>> It is most effective when it is used to gather information which will help the business with a specific problem, for example, to test the market to see if a new product would be likely to succeed.

>> It is not available to other businesses (unless they undertake their own research).

Possible limitations

>> It can be expensive, for example, individually interviewing many people.

>> It is not available immediately – it takes time to collect.

There are various types of primary research methods, including:

>> **questionnaires**
>> **online surveys**
>> **interviews**
>> **focus groups.**

The process of primary research

To undertake primary research, a business will normally go through a number of stages, as summarised in the diagram below.

1 What is the purpose of the market research?

What does it want to find out? What information will be needed? What action will be taken as a result of the research? This will affect the type of market research undertaken.

2 Decide on the most suitable method of research

Will more than one method be necessary? Will just secondary research be sufficient or will primary research be needed as well? The cost of the research and the time required will need to be taken into account.

3 Decide on the size of sample needed and who is going to be asked

How big will the sample size need to be to keep costs down but get a sufficiently accurate result? Which different groups of people will need to be included in the survey? Different age groups? Different income groups?

4 Carry out the research

5 Collate the data and analyse the results

The information will need to be put together and the data analysed. What does it seem to show?

6 Produce a report of the findings

A report will need to be produced showing the findings. Included in the report will be a summary of the research findings and conclusions drawn based on these results. Recommendations should be made as to what actions are necessary as a result of the research; these should be based on the conclusions.

▲ The stages of primary research

Methods of primary research

Questionnaires

Questionnaires form the basis of most primary research. Questionnaires may be conducted face-to-face (for example, in the street), by telephone, by post or on the internet.

Deciding what questions to ask is difficult if you want to be sure of getting accurate results. Some questions may not be very clear, some questions may lead the respondents to answer in a certain way which may not be what they really think. 'Closed' questions often require a Yes/No answer but 'open' questions allow respondents to explain answers in their own words. The researcher also needs to decide whom to ask.

Advantages of questionnaires

» Detailed qualitative information can be gathered about the product or service.
» Customers' opinions about the product or service can be obtained.
» They can be carried out online – see section below.
» To encourage people to fill in the questionnaire, vouchers can be offered or participants entered into a 'prize draw'.

Disadvantages of questionnaires

» If questions are not well thought out, the answers to them will not be very accurate. It may be very misleading for the business if it is thought that a product is liked by consumers, when in fact the respondents were only saying they thought the product was quite attractive but they would not actually buy it.
» Carrying out questionnaires can take a lot of time and money.
» Collating and analysing the results is also time-consuming.

Online surveys

These can be carried out on specialised websites using any internet-connected device, including mobile phones. Researchers can design their own survey and post this on their website. The researcher will then email people to ask them to go to the website and complete the questionnaire.

Advantages of online surveys

» Fast, with quicker response times than other forms of survey.
» Cheaper than interviews or postal questionnaires.
» Easy to complete for the participant.
» Data collected can be quickly presented and analysed using IT tools.

Disadvantages of online surveys

» Absence of interviewer to explain open-ended questions or to ask follow-up question to gain more detailed information.
» Cannot reach potential respondents who do not have access to the internet.
» Scope for fraud – some people will just answer an online survey to gain any incentives being offered and not give honest answers, or they complete the survey carelessly.

Interviews

When interviews are used, the interviewer (the person asking the questions) will have ready-prepared questions for the interviewee (the person answering the questions).

Advantages of interviews

» The interviewer is able to explain any questions that the interviewee does not understand.
» Detailed information can be gathered about what the interviewees like and dislike about the product.

Disadvantages of interviews

» Whether consciously or unconsciously, the interviewer could lead the interviewee into answering in a certain way, resulting in inaccurate results due to interviewer bias.
» Interviews are very time-consuming to carry out and, therefore, they are often an expensive way of gathering information.

▲ Focus groups allow consumers to express their opinions

Focus groups

This is where groups of people (focus groups) agree to provide information through a group discussion with a researcher present. The group might discuss a specific product or their reaction to an advertising campaign, for example. This helps the business make future marketing decisions. Groups may also test new products and then discuss what they think of them, explaining what they like and what they dislike about them.

Advantages of focus groups

» They provide detailed information about consumers' tastes and preferences.
» Interaction between members of the group can help the business understand the reasons for people's opinions.
» Quicker and cheaper than individual interviews.

Disadvantages of focus groups

» They can be time-consuming and expensive if conducted by a specialist market research agency.
» Discussion could be biased if some people on the panel are influenced by the opinions of others.
» Can be dominated by just a few people so the researcher will need to be experienced to deal with this.

The need for sampling

When deciding whom to ask to fill in a questionnaire or survey or whom to interview, a **sample** has to be selected. This is because it would be too expensive and time-consuming to try to include all the relevant population in the research.

There are two common methods of sampling:

» A **random sample** – every member of the population has the same chance of being selected. People are selected at random (often by computer), for example, every hundredth name in a telephone directory. The advantage is that everyone has an even chance of being picked, but not everyone in the population may be a consumer of the particular product being investigated.
» A **quota sample** – people are selected on the basis of certain characteristics, for example, age, gender or income. Researchers are given a quota. If they are carrying out street interviews, the researchers can choose whom to interview, providing they ask a certain number of people with particular characteristics. For example, they may be required to interview 20 people from the age group 10–25, 30 people from the age group 26–45, and 20 people from the age group 46–60. The researchers can then find out the views of these specific groups.

Definitions to learn

A **sample** is the group of people who are selected to respond to a market research exercise, such as a questionnaire.
A **random sample** is when people are selected at random as a source of information for market research.
A **quota sample** is when people are selected on the basis of certain characteristics (such as age, gender or income) as a source of information for market research.

Study tips

Make sure you can select a suitable method of primary research for particular products and explain why it is suitable.

> ## Activity 11.2
>
> The following products require some primary research. Decide which type of research would be the most appropriate to use for each and why.
>
> a The possible success of a new chocolate bar.
> b Whether to introduce a new style of watch which uses fashionable bright colours.
> c Whether to extend an existing taxi service to cover a new town.
> d The feasibility of opening a new restaurant.
> e Why the sales of a sports shoe are falling.

Secondary research

Secondary research, or desk research, is the use of information that has already been collected and is available for use by others.

Advantages of secondary research

>> Often a much cheaper way of gathering information than primary research, as the data collection has already been done by others.
>> It can be used to help assess the total size of a market by finding out the size of the population and its age structure. This type of information could not be obtained by primary research.
>> Newspapers may carry vital economic forecasts if you are trying to assess when a recession is coming to an end and your sales are likely to increase again.
>> It is usually quicker to obtain secondary data than to undertake primary research.

Disadvantages of secondary research

>> Data may have been collected several years ago and be out of date.
>> Data is available to all businesses – not just collected for the sole use of one business.
>> Data may not be completely relevant as it was not collected with the needs of one business in mind.

Internal sources of secondary data

A lot of information may be readily and cheaply available from the business's own records. Relevant quantitative information will be available from the Sales department, which will hold detailed data on which brands of products have been selling well and in which area. The Finance department could give detailed information on the costs of manufacturing products or providing services.

Examples of internal sources of information include:

>> Sales department records, pricing data, customer records, sales reports
>> opinions of Distribution and Public Relations personnel
>> Finance department
>> Customer Service department.

External sources of secondary data

This is when information is obtained from outside the business. External sources are many and varied and tend to depend on the type of product that is being researched. Information from external sources is inevitably of a general nature as it has been gathered for some purpose other than the research that is being undertaken. The data can still be useful, as long as the limitations are taken into account.

>> **Government statistics** are a detailed source of general information about such things as the population and its age structure. This is available in most countries.
>> **Newspapers** may have useful articles, for example, information about the general state of the economy and whether customers are expected to increase or decrease their spending in the near future.

▲ Libraries are useful for secondary research

» If there is a **trade association** for the industry, it often provides information for the businesses in that industry. For example, there might be an agricultural association which helps farmers who grow particular crops.

» **Market research agencies** are specialist agencies that carry out research on behalf of companies or anyone who commissions them. They sometimes publish reports of their research into particular markets. However, while the reports contain very detailed information about the market, they are expensive to buy.

» **Online sources** provide an easily accessible source of a very wide range of information, including information on: companies from their own websites; government statistics; opinions about a product or brand on social media; newspaper websites. In fact any paper-based sources of information can often also be easily and quickly accessed through the internet. However, care must be taken to check the sources of online information as it is not always reliable or up to date.

▲ The internet provides access to a range of information for research

Activity 11.3

Which of the following sources of information gathered by a business are primary data and which are secondary?

Data	Primary or secondary?
The *Daily News* article on a competitor's new product	
Sales department's monthly sales figures	
A shop's daily inventory figures showing on which days sales are at their highest	
A traffic count to see how many vehicles pass your billboard advertisement in a week	
Online questionnaire results researching your new product	
A market research agency's report on what customers like and dislike about your product	
Annual government population statistics	
Data on customer complaints	

Case study

Pepsi manufactures fizzy drinks. It wants to start selling a new drink in your country. To help it assess the size of the market, you have been asked to find out:

- the size of the total population
- how many people there are in the age groups 1–10, 11–20 and 21–30 in your country
- how many different fizzy drinks are sold in your country (how many competitors there are)
- where these competitors come from – are they local companies or are the drinks imported?

> ### Activity 11.4
>
> Read the case study on page 149.
>
> What other research would you advise the company to undertake before starting to sell in your country? Explain your answer.

Who carries out market research?

Businesses can carry out their own research into different aspects of the market for their existing product or the possible market for a new product. Secondary research is often easier and cheaper to carry out, as primary research may be too expensive for the business to undertake itself.

The business may decide that it can afford to pay a specialist market research agency which will carry out whatever research it is asked to do. It will find out consumers' spending habits as well as what they think about an individual business's products and its competitors' products. However, these agencies are expensive to use.

Factors influencing the accuracy of market research data

The reliability or accuracy of the data that has been collected depends largely on:

» how carefully the sample was drawn up
» the way in which the questions in the questionnaire were phrased to ensure honest responses
» the sample selected – it is unlikely to be truly representative of the total population, but it needs to be as near as is possible. If a quota sample is used, rather than a random sample, it is easier to get more accurate data
» the size of the sample is also important. It is not possible to ask everyone in a population, which is why a sample is used. The larger the sample, the more accurate the results are likely to be, but the more expensive will be the research. If only a small sample is asked, the results are unlikely to be as accurate. Therefore, the researchers need to decide how many people will give them the accuracy they want and can afford
» the wording of the questions – trying out questionnaires on a small group of people before using them on a large sample can help to show if any of the questions could be misinterpreted. Any such questions can then be rephrased and the revised questionnaire carried out on the main sample
» who carried out the research – secondary research may not be as accurate as first thought because it was initially carried out for some other purpose and you would not know how the information was actually gathered
» bias – articles in newspapers sometimes have a bias and important information may be deliberately left out
» age of the information – statistics can quickly become out of date, no longer relating to current trends in consumers' buying habits, but reflecting what they used to be spending their money on.

These are just some of the reasons why information collected from all sources, both primary and secondary, should be used with care. It should never be assumed straightaway that information is correct.

Methods of market research

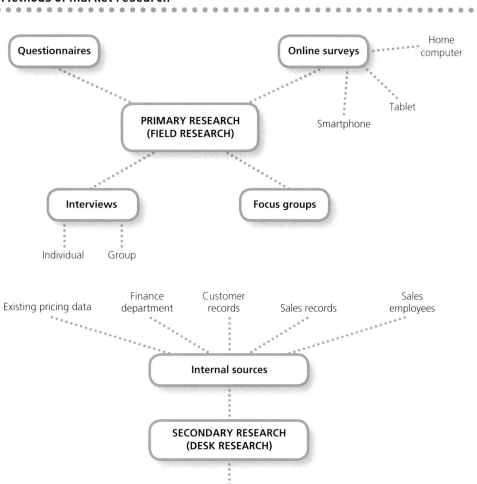

Activity 11.5

Copy out the table below and fill in the boxes.

Advantages and disadvantages of different types of market research

Method	Examples	Advantages	Disadvantages	Examples of appropriate use	Why the information might not be accurate
Primary research	Questionnaires				
	Interviews				
	Online surveys				
	Focus groups				
	Test markets				
Secondary research	Internal sources				
	External sources				

How to design and use a questionnaire

Ask yourself the following questions:

- ›› What do I want to find out?
- ›› Who do I need to ask? (age group, male/female, income level or occupation)
- ›› Where will I carry out my questionnaire?

Writing the questions

- ›› When deciding what questions to ask, it is advisable to ask no more than 12 questions.
- ›› Keep the questions short and clear. It is a good idea to keep the answers simple too, for example, ask for yes/no answers or provide a choice from which the respondents have to choose.
- ›› If you want to know the age of the interviewee, give a choice of age groups, for example 21–40.
- ›› Avoid open-ended questions unless people's opinions are sought.
- ›› Be careful not to lead the interviewee into an answer that may not be true by asking too direct a question.
- ›› Think about the order in which you ask the questions. Be logical!

Carrying out the questionnaire

Before going out and asking the questions, think about how you will ask the questions and how you are going to record the results. You may need to create a grid to put the respondents' replies on.

- ›› How many people are you going to ask?
- ›› At what time of the day are you going to carry out the questionnaire? Will this affect who will answer the questions?
- ›› Where are you going to carry out the questionnaire? Will this have an influence on whom you ask?

Case study

Below are some of the results of a questionnaire that was carried out to look into the feasibility of opening a fast-food restaurant in a city centre. One hundred people were asked at random to answer the questionnaire. The aim of the questionnaire was to identify the particular market segment to be targeted in any promotional campaign.

(i)	Responses to question 1:	Age group (years):	No. of persons:
	Age structure of persons in the sample	0–9	5
		10–19	40
		20–29	20
		30–39	20
		40–49	10
		50+	5
(ii)	Responses to question 2:	Response:	No. of persons:
	'How often do you eat out?'	Never	5
		Occasionally	20
		Once per month	30
		Once per week	20
		More than once per week	25
(iii)	Responses to question 3:	Response:	No. of persons:
	'Where do you purchase meals most often?'	Hotel	20
		Cafe	15
		Fast-food restaurant	35
		Food stalls (in street)	25
(iv)	Responses to question 4:	Response:	No. of persons:
	'How far do you usually travel when eating out?'	1 km	30
		2 km	40
		5 km	12
		5–10 km	8
		over 10 km	5

> ## Activity 11.6
>
> Analyse the results in the case study above and answer these questions.
>
> a Which age group would be most likely to eat in fast-food restaurants?
> b How could this information affect where the business would advertise its restaurant?
> c Why did the questionnaire contain the question 'How often do you eat out?'?
> d How will the responses to questions 2 and 3 be useful to the fast-food restaurant?
> e Suggest two additional questions that could have been included in the questionnaire. Explain why the information they provide would be useful to the business.
> f Explain why the questionnaire results might not be very accurate.

Presentation of data from market research

When information has been gathered as part of market research, it may be difficult to make sense of what it means. The raw data will need to be converted into a form which is easy to understand. The significant points need to be made clear. For example, after conducting a questionnaire, it may not be clear which answer has the greatest number of 'yes' responses.

The type of data that has been collected and what it is to be used for will affect the form of presentation which will be used. Information can be displayed in different forms:

» A table or tally chart – usually used to record the data in its original form; however, it is often better to convert the data into a chart or graph.

Time	Car	Lorry	Van	Bicycle	Person walking by
13:00–13:59	卌 卌	卌 卌 卌	|||	卌 |||	卌 卌 卌 卌
14:00–14:59	卌 卌 卌	卌 卌 卌 卌	卌 卌	卌	卌 卌 卌
15:00–15:59	卌 卌 卌 卌	卌 卌 卌	卌 卌 卌	卌	卌 卌 卌
16:00–16:59	卌 卌 卌 卌 卌 卌	卌 卌 卌	卌 卌 |||	卌 卌 卌	卌 卌 |||
17:00–17:59	卌 卌 卌 卌 卌 卌 卌 |||	卌 卌	卌 |||	卌 卌 卌 卌 卌	卌 卌 卌 卌 卌 卌 |||

▲ An example of a tally chart

» A chart – shows the total figures for each piece of data or the proportion of each piece of data in terms of the total number. For example, if a company sells its product in several countries, a pie chart can show at a glance which countries have the biggest percentage of sales and which have the lowest.

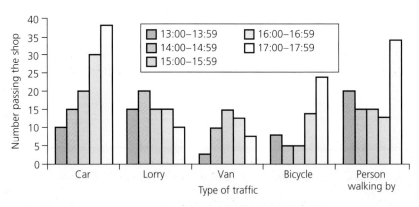

▲ A bar chart and a pie chart

» A graph – used to show the relationship between two sets of data. For example, how total cost changed over a number of years. The two variables are 'total cost' and 'time'.

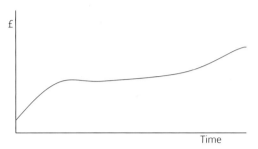

▲ A line graph

Presentation of data from market research

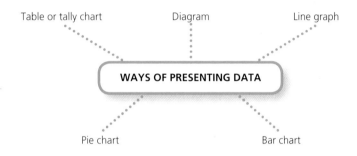

Activity 11.7

You have been asked to carry out some research into the feasibility of opening a new restaurant in your local area. Design your own questionnaire to carry out on friends and/or family.

Complete the following steps.

a Design the questionnaire.
b Decide who you are going to ask.
c Decide how many people you are going to ask (it is a good idea to carry out the questionnaire with friends and then put the results together so that you have a greater number of replies).
d Produce a summary sheet on which to collate the results.
e Collate the results.
f Present the results you have found.
g Evaluate your findings. What does the data tell you? Should a new restaurant be opened? If so, what type of restaurant would be successful?
h Evaluate your questionnaire. How accurate were your results? Would you redesign the questionnaire if you were carrying out the research again?

International business in focus

360-degree cameras – how will market research help?

Whether you're trying to capture a cityscape from a high viewpoint, recreate the experience of an amazing gig with footage that captures both the crowd and the band, or cover all angles while filming some extreme sport, a 360-degree camera is for you. There are now many businesses producing 360-degree cameras hoping to take a share of this booming market. A good example is Tesseract Imaging, which has developed India's first indigenous 360-degree 3D camera, called Methane. The camera is researched, designed and manufactured in India.

A recent report forecasts the global 360-degree camera market to grow at an annual rate of 35 per cent. It suggests that businesses producing 360-degree cameras need to do more market research to find out the following:

● Which type of consumers buy these cameras?

● What are they most used for?

According to the report, one of the main factors driving demand for 360-degree cameras is the increasing popularity of virtual reality (VR) headsets. The gaming market is among the fastest markets to incorporate advanced technologies in its products. The gaming market is the highest adopter of VR content. In 2015, VR games accounted for 5 per cent of the global gaming market, and this is expected to increase to 12 per cent by 2020. The share of VR content in the gaming segment is influenced by the increase in production and adoption of VR headsets. The increased penetration of VR headsets is going to greatly increase the potential market for 360-degree cameras.

Due to rapidly changing consumer trends and 'fads' in this market, up-to-date consumer research is essential. One of the latest trends is the creation of virtual theme parks. These give users a real-life experience of the virtual world, using a combination of the physical environment with 360-degree technology. The Walt Disney Company, one of the leading providers of outdoor entertainment, launched the *Star Wars*-themed park. The park gives fans an opportunity to experience the simulated world in 360 degrees.

Discussion points

● Why would secondary market research have been of little use to the first businesses developing 360-degree cameras?

● Do you think that market research would help a business planning to enter the 360-degree camera market in your country for the first time?

Exam-style questions: Short answer and data response

1 T&T is a small business which sells many different types of garden tools. It is well known for selling tools of high quality. Sales of its products are growing very quickly. Its Managing Director (MD) feels that market research isn't the most important factor contributing to the success of the business. However, the MD does want primary market research to be carried out before developing a new type of lightweight garden tool which is designed to be used by elderly gardeners.

  a Define 'primary research'. [2]

  b Identify **two** methods of primary market research. [2]

  c Outline **two** ways of presenting market research data on existing products that T&T could use. [4]

  d Explain **two** factors which should be taken into account by T&T when trying to ensure the research information is accurate. [6]

  e Do you think market research is necessary before T&T develops the new product? Justify your answer. [6]

2 H&H has recently designed a new app for the iPhone. It will allow people to control electronic devices in their home when they are not there. Phone users in many different countries will be likely to want to download this app. The Managing Director wants the Marketing department to carry out secondary research rather than primary research before launching this new app. There are very few competitors in the market for this type of app.

  a Define 'secondary market research'. [2]

  b Identify **two** sources of secondary market research data which could be used by H&H. [2]

  c Outline **two** advantages to H&H of using secondary market research. [4]

  d Explain **two** reasons why accurate market research information is important to H&H. [6]

  e Do you think the Managing Director is right to want to only carry out secondary research? Justify your answer. [6]

Revision checklist

In this chapter you have learned:

✔ about the role of market research and the methods used
✔ the differences between product-orientated and market-orientated businesses
✔ the methods of collecting primary market research data and their advantages and disadvantages
✔ the sources of secondary data and their advantages and disadvantages
✔ why sampling is often needed
✔ how to conduct your own market research
✔ to evaluate the factors that influence the accuracy of market research data
✔ how to present and use market research data.

NOW – test your understanding with the revision questions in the Student etextbook and the Workbook.

The marketing mix: product

This chapter will explain:

★ the four elements of the marketing mix
★ the role of product decisions in the marketing mix
★ the costs and benefits of developing new products
★ brand image – impact on sales and customer loyalty
★ the role of packaging
★ the product life cycle: main stages and extension strategies; draw and interpret a product life cycle diagram
★ how stages of the product life cycle can influence marketing decisions, e.g. promotion and pricing decisions.

The marketing mix

Definitions to learn

The **marketing mix** is a term which is used to describe all the activities which go into marketing a product or service. These activities are often summarised as the four Ps – product, price, place and promotion.

The **marketing mix** is a term which is used to describe all the activities which go into marketing products (remember that this includes both goods and services).

The producer might need to find out through market research what customers want from the product, then they may adapt the product to meet customers' wants. Once this is achieved, the producer will aim to convince the consumers that their product is the one that they want and that it meets their needs better than any of their competitors' products. Producers often do this by branding their product. This involves giving a product a unique name and packaging. It is then advertised to make consumers believe that it is different to any of the competitors' brands. The product also has to be sold in places that reinforce the brand image.

All of these activities are part of the marketing mix for a product. They are often summarised as the 'four Ps'.

The four Ps of the marketing mix

» *Product.* This applies to the good or service itself – its design, features and quality. How does the product compare with competitors' products? Does the packaging of the good help customers identify it? If it is a service being offered, do customers receive a clearly better service than rivals offer?
» *Price.* The price at which the product is sold to the customer is a key part of the marketing mix. A comparison must be made with the prices of competitors' products. Price should, in the long run, cover costs (see Chapter 13).
» *Place.* This refers to the channels of distribution that are selected. That is, what method of getting the product to the market and to the customer is to be used? Will the manufacturer sell its product to shops that sell to the public, or to wholesalers, or direct to the customers? (See Chapter 14.)
» *Promotion.* This is how the product is advertised and promoted. What types of advertising media will be used? It includes discounts that may be offered or any other types of sales promotion, such as money-off vouchers or free gifts (see Chapter 15).

Some people also talk about packaging as being a 'fifth P', but it can be included as part of both product and promotion.

Each part of the marketing mix has to be considered carefully to make sure that it all fits together and one part does not counteract another. For example, a high-priced perfume should be wrapped in expensive-looking packaging and advertised by glamorous people, but then it should not be sold in small food stores. If it were, the 'place' would not fit in with the other parts of the marketing mix.

REVISION SUMMARY   **The marketing mix**

The role of product decisions in the marketing mix

The product itself is probably the most important element in the marketing mix – without a product that meets customer needs, the rest of the marketing mix is unlikely to be able to achieve marketing success. As discussed in Chapter 11, some businesses are product-orientated, that is, they will develop a product and then try to decide who might buy it. Today most companies are market-orientated when developing new products. They spend a lot of money researching consumers' buying habits, their likes and dislikes, to see if they can design a product which people will want to buy. After deciding on the product and the appropriate market segment, the other parts of the marketing mix – price, place and promotion – will be determined.

Large companies often have a department which spends all its time developing new products. It will also look at competitors' products to see what they are successfully selling.

Types of product

There are several types of product. Some products are sold to consumers and some can be sold to other businesses (that is, to other producers). In addition to physical goods, services are also sold to consumers and to other producers. Products are usually grouped into the following types:

» *Consumer goods.* These are goods which are bought by consumers for their own use. They can be goods that do not last long, such as food and cleaning materials. Some goods last a relatively long time and give enjoyment over a long time, such as furniture and computers.
» *Consumer services.* These are services that are bought by consumers for their own use. Examples include repairing cars, hairdressing and education.
» *Producer goods.* These are goods that are produced for other businesses to use. They are bought to help with the production process. Examples include trucks, machinery and components.
» *Producer services.* These are services that are produced to help other businesses. Examples include accounting, insurance and advertising agencies.

Activity 12.1

Copy this table and tick the correct box for each product.

Product	Consumer good	Consumer service	Producer good	Producer service
Tube of toothpaste				
Bottle-filling machine				
Bank account				
Pair of sports shoes				
Chocolate bar				
Doctor's treatment of a patient				
Office cleaning				
Factory building				
Purchase of a hospital bed				
Television programme				

Defining the type of product the business is producing is important when deciding how the product will be developed and marketed.

Promotion of a producer good will be quite different to promotion of a consumer good – this is discussed in Chapter 15.

Producing the right product at the right price is an important part of the marketing mix.

» The product needs to satisfy consumer wants and needs. If it does not then it will not sell.
» The product also needs to be of the right quality so consumers are willing to pay the price for it.
» The product must not be so difficult to make that the costs of production are greater than the price charged for it – as this will mean the business makes a loss.
» Design of the product is very important. The quality needs to be appropriate for the brand image. For example, a high brand image means a high price, but quality must be high too. The product also has to last a reasonable length of time. If the product is not reliable and breaks down, or breaks soon after it is purchased, then it will get a bad reputation and is unlikely to sell well. The product also needs to perform to the standard expected by consumers and must meet legal controls, for example, food products must satisfy health regulations.

What makes a product successful?

Satisfies existing needs and wants of consumers

Design – performance, reliability, quality should all be consistent with the product's brand image

Capable of stimulating new wants from the consumer

SUCCESSFUL PRODUCT

Not too expensive to produce (relative to the price that could be charged)

The first business to produce the new product or introduce new changes to the original product before its competitors

Has something very distinctive that makes it appear different

> ### Activity 12.2
> **a** Choose three products that you have bought.
> **b** Do you think they have been successful? Why?
> **c** Try to analyse the success of each product using the criteria in the diagram above. For example, does it have a good design? Is it reliable? Is it very distinctive from other brands?

Product development

Large businesses are trying to develop new products all the time. Smaller businesses are also trying to stay competitive and therefore need to keep their products up to the standards of competitors. When developing a new product, most businesses go through the process outlined below.

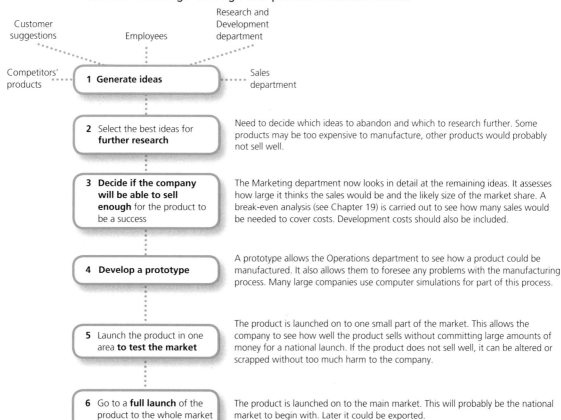

Customer suggestions

Employees

Research and Development department

Competitors' products

1 Generate ideas

Sales department

2 Select the best ideas for **further research**

Need to decide which ideas to abandon and which to research further. Some products may be too expensive to manufacture, other products would probably not sell well.

3 Decide if the company will be able to sell enough for the product to be a success

The Marketing department now looks in detail at the remaining ideas. It assesses how large it thinks the sales would be and the likely size of the market share. A break-even analysis (see Chapter 19) is carried out to see how many sales would be needed to cover costs. Development costs should also be included.

4 Develop a prototype

A prototype allows the Operations department to see how a product could be manufactured. It also allows them to foresee any problems with the manufacturing process. Many large companies use computer simulations for part of this process.

5 Launch the product in one area **to test the market**

The product is launched on to one small part of the market. This allows the company to see how well the product sells without committing large amounts of money for a national launch. If the product does not sell well, it can be altered or scrapped without too much harm to the company.

6 Go to a **full launch** of the product to the whole market

The product is launched on to the main market. This will probably be the national market to begin with. Later it could be exported.

> ### Activity 12.3
>
> You work for a company which manufactures ice cream. You have been given the task of designing a new ice cream on a stick (a lolly) suitable for small children. Describe in detail how you would do this.

The costs and benefits of developing new products

There are various benefits for the business when developing new products. These are as follows:

>> **Unique Selling Point (USP)** will mean the business will be first into the market with the new product.
>> Diversification for the business, giving it a broader range of products to sell.
>> It allows the business to expand into new markets.
>> It may allow the business to expand into existing markets.

However, there are also costs for the business when developing new products. These are as follows:

>> The costs of carrying out market research and analysing the findings.
>> The costs of producing trial products, including the costs of wasted materials.
>> The lack of sales if the target market is wrong.
>> The loss of company image if the new product fails to meet customer needs.

The importance of brand image

Selling a product directly to the customer makes it easy to inform the customer of the product's qualities and good points. The salesperson can persuade the customer to buy the product. If a small business produced handmade jewellery and sold it on a street stall, the business owner could explain to customers how the jewellery was made and why it was a good product to buy.

Today, the manufacturers of most products do not sell directly to the customer – products are sold to other businesses or retailers, who sell them on to the customer. This means that the product's unique features and the reasons for buying it must be conveyed in a different way. This is done by creating a brand for the product. It will have a unique name, a **brand name**. Advertising and other promotions will constantly refer to this brand name and will make consumers aware of the qualities of the product to try to persuade them to buy it. Branded products are normally sold as being of higher quality than unbranded products. It is the assurance of a standard quality that makes consumers confident in buying branded products.

Businesses use brands for their products to encourage consumers to keep buying their products and not those of their competitors. Consumers may have **brand loyalty**, which means they will keep buying the same brand of a product instead of trying other similar products.

Brand image is important. The brand is more than just an assurance of quality. By careful use of promotion and public relations, a business will try to create a complete image for the product based around the brand name. Coca-Cola, for example, is sold throughout the world and has an image of being a superior

Definitions to learn

The **USP** is the special feature of a product that differentiates it from the products of competitors.

Definitions to learn

The **brand name** is the unique name of a product that distinguishes it from other brands.
Brand loyalty is when consumers keep buying the same brand again and again instead of choosing a competitor's brand.
Brand image is an image or identity given to a product which gives it a personality of its own and distinguishes it from its competitors' brands.

quality cola drink which tastes better than its rivals' drinks. Advertising shows people having fun when they drink it and emphasises that it is a fashionable drink for young people.

➡ Case study

Nestlé manufactures chocolate bars. One of its best-selling bars is Milkybar, which appeals to young children. On the front of the packaging there is a picture of a smiling cowboy – called the Milkybar kid. The advertising will be on television and the adverts will feature the Milkybar kid – he will be a friendly, likeable character. The image of the chocolate bar will be embodied in the Milkybar kid as he has been created to appeal to young children.

Discussion points

- Which consumers are the target market for Milkybars?
- Explain how the packaging appeals to the target market.
- Describe the brand image for Milkybars and explain how the marketing of Milkybars develops this brand image.

REVISION SUMMARY   **Branding**

The role of packaging
===

Getting the **packaging** right is just as important as getting the other parts of the marketing mix right. The packaging has two functions to perform.

   It has to be suitable for the product to be put in. Packaging has to give protection to the product and not allow it to spoil. It also has to allow the product to be used easily. It is no good having hair shampoo in a tin which will not allow the liquid to pour out easily. It has to be suitable for transporting the product from the factory to the shops, so preferably the packaging should not be too delicate or the product could easily get damaged.

   Packaging is also used for promoting the product. It has to appeal to the consumer, therefore the colour and shape of the container is very important. It is the packaging that catches the customer's eye, not usually the product inside! The brand image will be reinforced by the packaging in which the product is sold. An expensive product will have a luxurious-looking container, often a gold colour. A low-cost product may have basic simple packaging with plain colours.

   The labels on some products must, as a legal requirement, carry vital information about the product. For example, most labels on food products sold in supermarkets must explain how to store it and for how long, and what ingredients it contains.

Activity 12.4

Select two products that have brand names. For each of the products identify:

a   who the customers of the product are
b   what it is that attracts them to the product
c   what brand image the manufacturer is trying to create
d   how the name and the packaging of the product help to reinforce the brand image
e   where it is sold.

Case study

Kellogg's manufactures breakfast cereals. The packaging used is bright and colourful and has the brand name clearly printed on the front of the packet in large letters. The outer packet is made of cardboard to keep its shape, so it will stand up on the shelves in shops and prevent the contents from being crushed. The side of the packet contains information about the nutritional qualities of the product. There is also sometimes a special offer printed on the outside of the packet to encourage consumers to buy the cereal. There are sometimes tokens on the packet to be cut out, collected and then sent off to receive a free gift. The cardboard packet has inner packaging to keep the product sealed in and fresh until it is purchased and consumed by the customer.

REVISION SUMMARY   Packaging

Protects the product   Easy to transport the product   Easy to open the container and use the product

PACKAGING

Suitable for the product to fit in   Eye-catching   Carries information about the product   Promotes the brand image

Case study

S&B Food Products plc has decided to produce a new fruit-flavoured milk drink especially for young children. The market segment that it expects to buy the product is parents, for their children. It is a healthy drink which contains vitamins and minerals.

> **Activity 12.5**
>
> Read the second case study on page 164.
>
> **a** Which of the possible containers drawn on page 164 would you use for the new fruit-flavoured milk drink? Explain your choice.
> **b** Suggest another container that might be more suitable for the new milk drink.
> **c** What colour(s) should the container be? Explain your choice.
> **d** Choose a brand name for the new milk drink. What image does the name give to the product?
> **e** Design a label for the container. Why do you think the design of the label will help the product to sell?
> **f** What information will need to be put on the label?

The product life cycle

Products do not last forever. A typical cycle for a product is as follows.

1 First, a product is **developed**. The prototype is tested and market research carried out before the product is launched on to the market. There are no sales at this time.

2 It is then **introduced** or launched on to the market. Sales grow slowly at first because most consumers are not aware of its existence. Informative advertising is used until the product becomes known. Price skimming (see Chapter 13) may be used if the product is a new development and there are no competitors. No profits are made at this point as development costs have not yet been covered.

3 Sales start to **grow** rapidly. The advertising is changed to persuasive advertising to encourage brand loyalty. Prices are reduced a little as new competitors enter the market and try to take some customers. Profits start to be made as the development costs are covered.

4 **Maturity**. Sales now increase only slowly. Competition becomes intense and pricing strategies are now competitive or promotional pricing (see Chapter 13). A lot of advertising is used to maintain sales growth. Profits are at their highest.

5 Sales reach **saturation** point and stabilise at their highest point. Competition is high but there are no new competitors. Competitive pricing is used. A high and stable level of advertising is used, but profits start to fall as sales are static and prices have to be reduced to be competitive.

6 Sales of the product **decline** as new products come along or because the product has lost its appeal. The product is usually withdrawn from the market when sales become so low and prices have been reduced so far that it becomes unprofitable to produce the product. Advertising is reduced and then stopped.

This process of what happens to a product is called the **product life cycle**. It is usually drawn as a graph like the one on page 166.

Definitions to learn

The **product life cycle** describes the stages a product will pass through from its introduction, through its growth until it is mature, and then finally its decline.

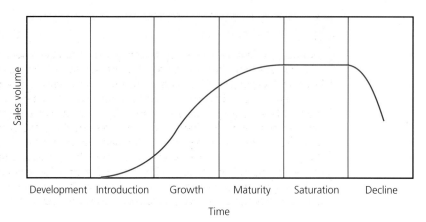

▲ A typical product life cycle

The exact length of the life cycle, in terms of time, varies a great deal from product to product. It is affected by the type of product, for example, fashionable items will go out of fashion quickly whereas food products may last a very long time. The life cycle of some very popular brands, such as Coca-Cola, is many years, whereas the life cycle of fashionable clothes is often less than a year. New developments in technology will make original products obsolete and their life cycle will come to a quick end as new products are purchased in preference to old technology.

How stages of the product life cycle influence marketing decisions

Knowing the stage of the life cycle that a product is in can help a business with pricing and promotion decisions.

Pricing

» A branded product is likely to be sold at a high price when it is first introduced to the market – as a low price could give the wrong message about quality.
» Prices are likely to be relatively higher than those of competitors in the growth stage as the product may still be 'newer' than those of rivals.
» In the saturation or maturity stage, when the business will want to try to stop sales declining, the price is likely to be reduced as competitors may have launched newer versions of their own products.
» Some substantial price discounts might be offered during the decline stage – especially if the business does not plan to 'extend its life'.

Promotion

» Spending on promotion will be higher at the introduction stage than in other stages as the business has to inform consumers of the product. Also, if it is a completely new brand, a clear identity will need to be established for it.
» Advertising would probably be reduced in later stages, either because the product is already well known or because the business wants to use its marketing budget on other, newer, products.
» Promotion spending might be increased again if the business decides to adopt an **extension strategy** – customers will need to be informed about this and 'convinced' that the product is worth buying once more.

Case study

Compute plc invented a new computer game. It had been developed over several months before it was finally launched on to the market. Initially it was expensive, being bought by only a few people who wanted to be the first to play the new game. It quickly became successful – a lot of advertising was used to promote the game and sales grew rapidly. Over the next few months, more and more shops ordered copies of the game and competition between the shops was fierce. The shops offered the game at cheaper and cheaper prices to attract customers and prices for the game started to fall. Sales grew steadily now, not at the fast rates of increase that were first seen. Once most computer users had purchased the game, the market was saturated and sales began to fall, even though prices by now were low. The game was making little or no profit for the company and so it decided to withdraw the game from sale and concentrate on the new games that it had introduced.

Study tips

Make sure you can identify the stages of the product life cycle for a particular product.

▶ **Activity 12.6**

Read the case study above.

Draw the product life cycle for the game invented by Compute plc. Label the diagram with the different stages that the game went through.

Extending the product life cycle

When a product reaches the maturity or saturation stage of its product life cycle, a business may stop sales starting to fall by adopting extension strategies. These are ways that sales may be given a boost. Some possible ways businesses might extend the life cycle of their products are shown in the diagram below.

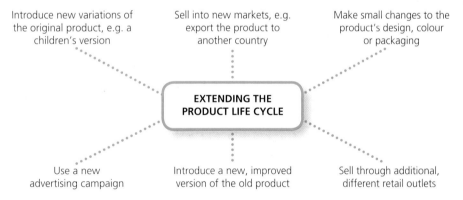

▶ Product life cycle extension strategies

If the extension strategies are effective, the maturity phase of the product life cycle will be prolonged. An example of what might happen is shown in the diagram below.

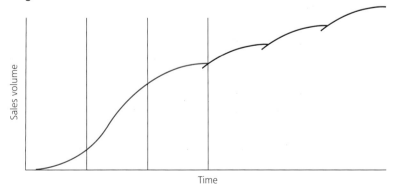

▶ The effect of extension strategies

Businesses will not usually manufacture just one product. They will have a range of products at different stages of the product life cycle. For example, a business will need to have products coming up into the growth phase to counteract those that are in decline.

International business in focus

Smartphones

The Apple iPhone, a smartphone, was first launched by Apple in January 2007 in North America and when it went on sale it quickly sold out. The production and sales of the iPhone continued to have increasing growth each year, and it is now marketed and sold all around the world. In 2017 it reached its sixth generation with the iPhone X. Each version has a better performance and offers more features than the previous version. There is fierce competition from other smartphones based around the Microsoft and Android operating systems. After growing rapidly for two years, sales of the iPhone 7 fell by 20 million units in 2016 compared to 2015.

Discussion points

- What stage of the product life cycle do you think the iPhone has reached?
- Why does Apple keep bringing out new versions of the iPhone?

Study tips

Make sure you can select suitable extension strategies for particular products.

Activity 12.7

Suggest possible ways to extend the product life cycle of the following products. State which extension strategy you would use for each product, and explain why you think it would be successful in boosting sales.

a A chocolate bar which has been sold for many years in the same packaging and has had the same brand image. There are several competitors' brands of chocolate bars also sold in the market and sales have stabilised.

b A sports shoe that is worn when playing a particular sport. This sport is no longer very popular with young people.

c The sales of a new model of a car have stagnated. The car is only sold in the home country where it is manufactured.

d A children's toy which is only sold in toy shops and saw steady growth in its sales, but now the sales are stable and not increasing any further.

Exam-style questions: Short answer and data response

1 ABC is a private limited company. It makes nuts and bolts, which are producer products, and they are sold to large car manufacturers. The sales of its products are at a high and steady level. The products are made to the exact specifications of the car companies and they are not sold to any other customers. Some other makers of nuts and bolts have developed new products which are made using new technology and lighter materials.

   a Define 'producer product'. [2]

   b ABC makes nuts and bolts. Identify **two** other examples of producer goods. [2]

   c Outline **two** characteristics of the packaging of ABC's products. [4]

   d Explain **two** decisions ABC's managers might take as one of the company's products reaches the saturation stage of the product life cycle. [6]

   e Do you think ABC should consider developing new products? Justify your answer. [6]

2 XYZ produces popular chocolate bars and sells them to supermarkets. Its best-selling brand is ChocDelight. It is wrapped in expensive packaging and is sold as a luxury chocolate product. This best-selling chocolate bar has had high and steady sales for the last five years. However, recently sales have started to fall as it has now reached the decline stage of the product life cycle.

   a Define 'brand'. [2]

   b Identify **two** elements of XYZ's marketing mix other than product. [2]

   c Outline **two** characteristics of the packaging of the chocolate bars. [4]

   d Explain **two** possible reasons why XYZ's chocolate bars are successful. [6]

   e Recommend to XYZ's managers how to respond to the falling sales of ChocDelight. Justify your answer. [6]

Revision checklist

In this chapter you have learned:

✔ to identify the four elements of the marketing mix
✔ about the role of product decisions in the marketing mix
✔ what makes a product successful
✔ what the costs and benefits of developing a new product are
✔ what is meant by brand image and how this can influence sales and customer loyalty
✔ about the role of packaging
✔ to draw and interpret a product life cycle
✔ about the different stages of the product life cycle and how they can influence marketing decisions
✔ to suggest different ways to extend the product life cycle.

NOW – test your understanding with the revision questions in the Student etextbook and the Workbook.

The marketing mix: price

The role of pricing decisions in the marketing mix

When deciding a price for either an existing product or a new product, the business must be very careful to choose a price which will fit in with the rest of the marketing mix for the product. For example, if a new product is of high quality, is to be aimed at consumers who have high incomes, is wrapped in luxurious packaging, but has a low price, consumers will not think it is a good quality product and will not buy it. Some products are sold in very competitive markets and prices have to be set near to their competitors' prices. Other products are the only ones available in their market and so consumers may be willing to pay a high price for one of these products.

▲ Example of a high-priced product and a low-priced product

Pricing strategies

If the product that is manufactured can easily be distinguished from other products in the market then it is probably a branded product. If the product is branded, it will have a distinctive name and packaging, and be aimed at a particular segment of the market. It will be important to select an appropriate price to complement the brand image; a value-for-money brand should have a low price. Today many products have developed a strong brand image. The producers of these products may therefore have a lot of influence over the price to be paid by customers.

If a product has many competitors in its market, the price it charges will be very important. The business must constantly monitor what its competitors are charging for their products to make sure its own prices remain competitive.

A business can adopt new pricing strategies for several reasons, including:

» to try to break into a new market
» to try to increase its market share
» to try to increase its profits
» to make sure all its costs are covered and a target profit is earned.

The business objective being aimed for will affect which of the pricing strategies the business decides to use. The price the business chooses to charge may not be related to the cost of manufacturing the product. Sometimes it might charge what it thinks the consumer will pay and this may be well above what it has cost to manufacture the product.

The main methods of pricing

Cost-plus pricing

Cost-plus pricing involves:

» estimating how many units of the product will be produced
» calculating the total cost of producing this output
» adding a percentage mark-up for profit.

Benefits

» The method is easy to apply.
» Different profit mark-ups could be used in different markets.
» Each product earns a profit for the business.

Limitations

» Businesses could lose sales if the selling price is higher than competitors' prices.
» A total profit will only be made if sufficient units of the product are sold.
» There is no incentive to reduce costs – any increase in costs is just passed on to the customer as a higher price.

> **Definitions to learn**
>
> **Cost-plus pricing** is the cost of manufacturing the product plus a profit mark-up.

➡ Worked example

For example, the total cost of making 2000 chocolate bars is $2000. The business wants to make 50 per cent profit on each bar. The calculation is as follows:

$$\left(\frac{\$2000}{2000}\right) + 50\% = \$1.50 \text{ per bar is the selling price}$$

$$(1 + 0.50 = \$1.50)$$

The calculation to find 50% of the selling price is as follows:

$$\frac{\$2000}{2000} \times \frac{50}{100} = 1 \times \frac{50}{100} = 0.50$$

$$\frac{\text{total cost}}{\text{output}} \times \% \text{ mark-up} = \text{profit on each unit}$$

> ### Activity 13.1
>
> Using the example on page 171, calculate the cost-plus price for the following:
>
> **a** The business now wants to make a 70 per cent profit mark-up on each unit.
> **b** Total costs of making 2000 chocolate bars rise to $3000 but the business wants to make a 50 per cent profit mark-up.
> **c** Total costs of making 2000 chocolate bars fall to $1800 and the business wants to make a 60 per cent profit mark-up.

Competitive pricing

Competitive pricing involves setting prices in line with your competitors' prices or just below their prices.

For example, a company wants to sell a brand of soap powder. It needs to sell it at a similar price to all the other brands available or consumers will buy the competitors' brands.

Benefits

» Sales are likely to be high as the price is at a realistic level and the product is not under- or over-priced.
» Avoids price competition, which can reduce profits for all businesses in the industry.
» Often used when it is difficult for consumers to tell the difference between the products of different businesses.

Limitations

» If the costs of production for a business are higher than those of competitors – perhaps because the product is of a higher quality – then a competitive price could lead to losses being made.
» A higher quality product might need to be sold at a price above competitors' prices to give it a higher quality image.
» In order to decide what this price should be, detailed research would be needed into what prices competitors are charging, and this research costs time and money.

Penetration pricing

Penetration pricing means the price would be set lower than the competitors' prices.

For example, a company launches a new chocolate bar at a price several cents below the prices of similar chocolate bars that are already on the market. If this is successful, consumers will try the new bar and become regular customers.

Benefits

» Often used for newly launched products to create an impact with customers.
» It should ensure that sales are made and the new product enters the market successfully.
» Market share should build up quickly.

Limitations

» The product is sold at a low price and therefore the profit per unit may be low.
» Customers might 'get used' to low prices and reject the product if the business starts to raise the price after the product's early success.
» Might not be appropriate for a branded product with a reputation for quality.

Price skimming

With **price skimming**, the product is usually a new invention, or a new development of an old product. Therefore it can be sold on the market at a high price and people will pay this high price because of the novelty factor. The product will often have cost a lot in research and development, and these costs need to be recouped. Sometimes the high price can be used to help indicate the high quality of the product.

For example, a new computer games system is developed. It will be sold in the shops at a very high price, much higher than the existing computer games systems. Because it is new and has better graphics than the old systems, consumers will be willing to pay the high price. This way, the business will earn high profits which will make the research and development costs worthwhile.

Benefits

» Skimming can help to establish the product as being of good quality.
» High research and development costs can be rapidly recouped from the profit made on the product at the high price.
» If the product is unique, a high price will lead to profits being made before competitors launch similar products – then the price will have to be reduced.

Limitations

» The high price may discourage some potential customers from buying it.
» The high price and high profitability may encourage more competitors to enter the market.

Promotional pricing

Promotional pricing would be used when a business wants to price a product at a low price for a set amount of time to increase short-term sales.

For example, at the end of summer, a shop might have a lot of summer clothes left unsold. It might have a sale offering 'Buy one, get one free'. This will encourage customers to buy one item in order to get a second one free and it will clear the end-of-season stock. However, the shop will not make much, if any, profit on the clothes. But at least it will get some money for clothes that it might not otherwise have been able to sell at all.

Benefits

» It is useful for getting rid of unwanted inventory that will not sell.
» It can help to renew interest in a product if sales are falling, for example during an economic recession.

Limitations

» The revenue will be lower because the price of each item will be reduced.
» It might lead to a price competition with competitors – so the business might have to reduce prices again.

Definitions to learn

Dynamic pricing is when businesses change product prices, usually when selling online, depending on the level of demand.

Study tips

Make sure you can select suitable pricing methods for particular products and explain why each is suitable.

Activity 13.2

Read the case study below.

Identify the different pricing strategies that Coca-Cola uses and explain when it uses them.

The impact of psychology on price decisions

The price of a product can have a significant psychological impact upon consumers' perceptions of the product.

» A very high price for a high-quality product may mean that high-income customers wish to purchase it as a status symbol.
» If a price for a product is set just below a whole number, for example, 99¢ is just below $1, this creates the impression of it being much cheaper.
» Supermarkets may charge low prices for products purchased on a regular basis, which will give customers the impression of being given good value for money.
» Repeat sales are often made when the price reinforces consumers' perceptions of the product – this may be its brand image when the price is set high.

Using different pricing methods for the same product

Many businesses sell their products using different pricing methods for different segments of the market or at different times. This is often called **dynamic pricing** – when customers are charged prices according to their ability to pay or the available supply of a product. Often customers can be split into two or more groups and are then charged different prices for basically the same product or service because they have different abilities or willingness to pay these prices. Businesses do this because the price sensitivity of these groups is different. Airlines regularly use dynamic pricing and charge different prices for flights to the same airport at different times of the day or different times of the year. For example, the price of flights to holiday resorts is much higher during school holidays than during term time.

Dynamic pricing can also be used, often when products are sold 'online', to reflect rapid changes in the level of demand. If demand increases then the price will be raised, and at times of low demand the price will be reduced. For example, at American football games ticket prices often change to reflect the increased demand for tickets at popular games and when a game is less popular the price is reduced to encourage sales and fill the stadium seats.

There are ethical issues with some examples of dynamic pricing because thanks to new technology firms can track the buying history of customers and then charge higher prices for products when they buy them online. This is compared to other customers who appear to have lower income from their past buying history; these customers are charged lower prices for the same product.

Case study: Coca-Cola

Coca-Cola is a large company that produces soft drinks. It has developed a new drink which contains an ingredient that gives people energy when they drink it. The company decided to target young people who like to go out dancing. They put the drink in a new shaped bottle which had bright colours on the outside so that it would be easily identified. The drink was advertised regularly on TV and was shown as a fashionable drink for young people. Teenagers were shown as happy, lively and enjoying life. The drink had a clearly identified brand name and was sold at a higher price than the other soft drinks that young people drink.

The company had developed a clear brand image for the product and spent a lot of money advertising the drink. As the product was new, fashionable and different, it could charge a high price for it.

Coca-Cola also manufactures a traditional soft drink that is consumed mainly by children. Sales have been falling due to more varieties of soft drinks becoming available. The company decides to reduce the price for a few months to try to attract the lost customers back.

The company uses pricing strategies to help it fulfil different aims at different times. The same product could have a very low price when entering a new market, until it is established, and then it might put prices similar to competitors' prices for a while.

REVISION SUMMARY   **Pricing strategies**

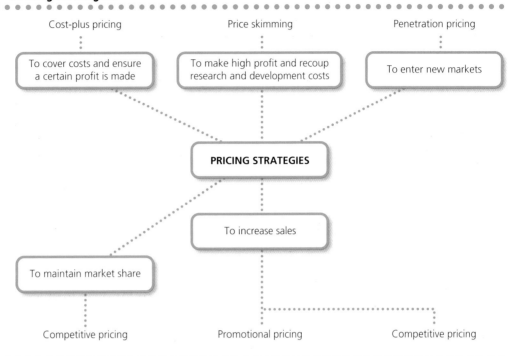

Activity 13.3

What pricing strategy would most probably be used for the following products? Explain your choice in each case.

a A watch that is very similar to other watches sold in the shops.
b A new type of mobile (cell) phone that has been developed and is a lot higher quality than existing mobile phones.
c A chocolate bar which has been on the market for several years and new brands are being brought out which are competing with it.
d A shop, which sells food, wants to get its money back on buying the inventory and make an extra 75 per cent as well.
e A new brand of soap powder is launched (there are already many similar brands available).
f A tour operator sells holidays during the school holidays as well as other times of the year.

Activity 13.4

Copy out the table and fill in the blank boxes.

Pricing strategy	Examples and when they might be used	Advantages	Disadvantages
Cost-plus pricing			
Competitive pricing			
Penetration pricing			
Price skimming			
Promotional pricing			

Price elasticity of demand

How responsive the demand for a product is to changes in price is affected by how many close substitutes there are. If there are many close substitutes for the product then, even if its price rises only a small percentage, consumers will respond by buying the substitute product. This means that demand for the original product will fall by a larger percentage. For example, if the price of a chocolate bar rose by 5 per cent, some customers would buy alternative chocolate bars and sales might fall by 15 per cent. This product would be said to have **price-elastic demand** – the percentage change in quantity demanded is greater than the percentage change in price. Consumers are very sensitive to changes in price.

»» Prices increase by 5% then sales decrease by 15% = falling revenue for the business.

If, however, there are not really any close substitutes for a product, for example, electricity, then an increase in price of 15 per cent will not cause much of a fall in sales – perhaps 5 per cent – as most consumers will carry on buying the product at the higher price. Such products are said to have a **price-inelastic demand** – the percentage change in quantity demanded is less than the percentage change in price. Consumers are not sensitive to changes in price.

»» Prices increase by 15% then sales decrease by 5% = increasing revenue for the business.

Therefore if the demand for the products of a business is price elastic then it is not a good idea to raise prices unless there has been rising costs. If the price elasticity of demand is inelastic then businesses can increase revenue by increasing prices.

International business in focus

Big Mac prices

McDonald's is a multinational company with restaurants all around the world – in 121 countries to be exact. Every country has its own customs and cultures that McDonald's recognises and respects. Menu items vary from country to country, but the company's most famous product – the Big Mac – is available in most of its restaurants (but is called Maharaja Mac in India and is not made from beef).

When the prices it charges for the Big Mac in all of these countries are converted into US dollars there are some surprising results. Instead of charging the same price in all countries (US$ Big Mac price converted into local currencies) there are some very wide variations in prices. The most expensive country is Switzerland with a price of US$6.59, followed by Norway with a price of US$5.51. In the USA the price is US$5.04 but in Egypt it is US$2.59 and in Ukraine (the lowest price) it is US$1.59.

Discussion points

● Why does McDonald's charge different prices in different countries for the same Big Mac product?

● Is the price of the Big Mac (or Maharaja Mac) in your own country higher or lower than the US price? Why do you think there is a difference? (You will have to find out your currency's US$ exchange rate!)

Exam-style questions: Short answer and data response

1 A&B is a private limited company. It produces a well-known branded breakfast cereal called Oatz which has a reputation for good quality. The cost of producing each box of Oatz is $1.

   The cereal is sold in shops at a price of $2 per box. The prices of competitors' cereals range from $1.20 to $2.10 a box. The Marketing Manager says 'We should change to a more competitive pricing strategy' to increase sales. She thinks the demand for Oatz is price elastic. A large supermarket has just launched its 'own brand' of breakfast cereal and this is currently sold using penetration pricing.

   a Define 'penetration pricing'. [2]
   b Define 'price-elastic demand'? [2]
   c Outline **two** reasons why demand for one brand of breakfast cereals might be price elastic. [4]
   d Explain **two** factors A&B should take into account when deciding which pricing method to use. [6]
   e Do you think changing to a more competitive pricing strategy for Oatz is a good idea? Justify your answer. [6]

2 X&Z has recently designed a new game for the Microsoft Xbox, a games console. People in many different countries have been waiting for this new game and they are willing to pay a high price to be some of the first people to play the game. 'The business can get back some of the development costs of the new game by using price skimming,' says the Marketing Manager. X&Z has a product range of 20 games, some of which were developed several years ago.

   a Define 'price skimming'. [2]
   b Identify **two** factors that affect the price of the new game for the Xbox. [2]
   c Outline **two** reasons why X&Z might use price skimming for its new game. [4]
   d Explain **two** other pricing methods X&Z could use for the new game. [6]
   e Do you think that just using the price skimming method for all the games produced by X&Z is the best decision to take? Justify your answer. [6]

Revision checklist

In this chapter you have learned:

✔ the role of pricing decisions in the marketing mix
✔ about the different methods of pricing that a business can use and their benefits and limitations
✔ how to select a suitable pricing strategy for a particular business situation/objective
✔ the difference between price-elastic demand and price-inelastic demand
✔ about the importance of price elasticity of demand in pricing decisions.

NOW – test your understanding with the revision questions in the Student etextbook and the Workbook.

The marketing mix: place

The role of place decisions in the marketing mix

After deciding on the product, its price and the best ways to promote it, the business has to actually sell the product to the consumer. The product or service must be available where and when customers want to buy it. How and where consumers can buy the product will affect how well it will sell. Think of your local shop where you buy food. Would expensive luxury chocolates sell well? If many of the customers who use the shop are on low incomes then not many highly priced chocolates will be sold. If the product is not available to customers in convenient locations and they have to go searching in different shops, then they may give up and buy a competitor's product. It is very easy for a business to get the place wrong and therefore lose sales.

Distribution channels

> **Definitions to learn**
>
> A **distribution channel** is the means by which a product is passed from the place of production to the customer.

Businesses have to decide where to sell their products. They also have to decide whether to sell directly to consumers or use other businesses to do this. This means deciding on the best **distribution channel** to use.

There are several different distribution channels that businesses can use – from selling directly to the consumer, to using intermediary channels. The diagram below summarises the main distribution channels that are used.

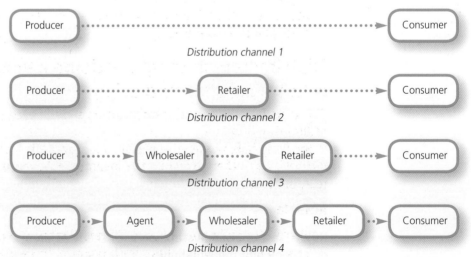

| Producer | ·····················➤ | Consumer |

Distribution channel 1

| Producer | ·······➤ | Retailer | ·······➤ | Consumer |

Distribution channel 2

| Producer | ···➤ | Wholesaler | ···➤ | Retailer | ···➤ | Consumer |

Distribution channel 3

| Producer | ··➤ | Agent | ··➤ | Wholesaler | ··➤ | Retailer | ··➤ | Consumer |

Distribution channel 4

▲ The main distribution channels

Distribution channel 1 – Direct to consumers

Advantages

>> This distribution channel is very simple. It involves manufacturers selling their products directly to the consumer.
>> It is suitable for products, such as certain types of food products, which are sometimes sold straight from the farm.
>> There is a lower price if sold direct to customers – cuts out wholesaler/retailer.
>> Products can be sold by mail order catalogue or via the internet.

Disadvantages

>> This is usually impractical for most products because the consumers probably do not live near to the factory and could not go there to buy the products.
>> This method may not be suitable for products which cannot easily be sent by post.
>> It can be very expensive to send products by post or courier and therefore it may not be cost effective.

This channel is also common when selling directly from one manufacturer to another manufacturer. For example, car components are sold directly to the car producer.

Distribution channel 2 – Using a retailer as the only intermediary

The second distribution channel is where the producer sells directly to retail outlets and then they sell the product to the consumer. This is most common where the retailer is large, such as a large supermarket, or when the products are expensive, such as furniture or jewellery.

Advantages

>> Producer sells large quantities to retailers.
>> Reduced distribution costs compared to selling directly to consumers (distribution channel 1).

Disadvantages

>> No direct contact with customers.
>> The price is often higher than 'direct selling' as the retailer has to cover its costs and make a profit.

Distribution channel 3 – Using a wholesaler and retailer as intermediaries

This distribution channel involves using a wholesaler, who performs the function of breaking bulk.
   Breaking bulk is where wholesalers buy products from manufacturers in large quantities and then divide up the inventory into much smaller quantities for retailers to buy.

Advantages

>> Wholesaler saves storage space for small retailer and reduces storage costs.
>> Small retailers can purchase fresh products in small quantities from wholesaler because they have a relatively short 'shelf life' before they deteriorate.

> **Key info**
>
> There are over 14 million small retailers in India with only 4 per cent of them having premises over 46 square metres.

» Wholesaler may give credit to retail customers so they can take the goods straightaway and pay at a later date.
» Wholesaler may deliver to the small retailer thus saving on transport costs.
» Wholesaler can give advice to small retailers about what is selling well. They can also advise the manufacturer what is selling well.

Disadvantages

» May be more expensive for the small shop to buy from a wholesaler than if it bought straight from the manufacturer.
» Wholesaler may not have the full range of products to sell.
» Takes longer for fresh produce to reach the shops, so may not be as good quality.
» Wholesaler may be a long way from the small shops.
» The consumer price is often higher than 'direct selling' as both the wholesaler and retailer have to cover costs and make a profit.

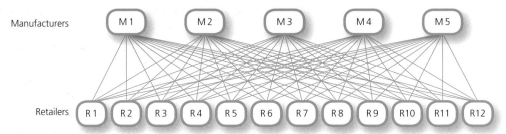

▲ Without a wholesaler, a manufacturer has to process many orders from retailers

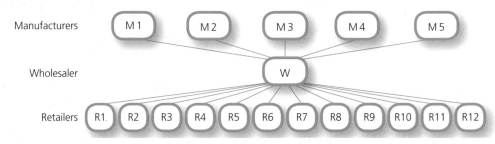

▲ With a wholesaler, a manufacturer has less paperwork

Distribution channel 4 – Using an additional intermediary such as an agent

When products are exported, the manufacturer sometimes uses an **agent** in the other country. The agent sells the products on behalf of the manufacturer. This can allow the manufacturer to have some control over the way the product is sold to consumers. The agent will either put an additional amount on the price to cover their expenses or will receive a commission on sales. The agent may also act as the wholesaler.

Advantages

» Manufacturer may not know the best way to sell the product in other markets.
» Agents will be aware of local conditions and will be in the best position to select the most effective places in which to sell.

Disadvantage

» The producer has less control over the way the product is sold to customers.

Case study

Unilever (M) Holdings Snd Bhd manufactures ice cream and sorbets. It is located in Malaysia.

It is famous for its quality ice cream and sorbets. The company sells ice cream and sorbets directly to local shops because they sell to tourists. Unilever (M) Holdings Snd Bhd also sells its ice cream to wholesalers that sell to small shops in other towns and cities. Very large retailers, for example, supermarkets, buy the ice cream and sorbets in bulk and purchase it directly from Unilever (M) Holdings Snd Bhd. A variety of channels of distribution are used by the company, depending on the customer and the quantity of ice cream and sorbets purchased.

Methods of distribution

The methods of distribution used can include the following:

Method of distribution	Description
Department stores	Large stores, usually in the centre of towns or cities, which sell a wide variety of products from a wide range of suppliers.
Chain stores	Two or more stores which have the same name and the same characteristics.
Discount stores	Retail stores offering a wide range of products, many branded products, at discount prices. Often the product ranges are of similar types of products, for example, electrical goods.
Superstores	Very large out-of-town stores which sell a wide range of food and non-food products.
Supermarkets	Retail grocery stores with dairy produce, fresh meat, packaged food and non-food departments.
Independent retailers	Single shops, often small, that offer a local, personalised service. Prices are often high.
Direct sales	Products are sold directly from the manufacturer to the customer – who may be a consumer or another business (distribution channel 1).
Mail order	Customers look through a catalogue or magazine and order by post. Orders can also often be placed by telephone or internet.
Internet/e-commerce	Instead of looking at a catalogue, consumers view the goods on the business's website and then order on the internet or possibly by telephone or mail. Business can sell through other specialist websites such as eBay and Alibaba.com.

Key info

With total global sales of US$482 billion in 2016, Walmart is the world's biggest retailer. A typical Walmart superstore has 142 000 different product ranges. Compare that with your local convenience store!

▲ The range of goods in this store far exceeds that of independent shops and most other supermarkets

Study tips

Make sure you can select and justify suitable distribution channels for a particular business or its products.

Activity 14.1

Choose six different products that you or your family buy and find out which distribution channels are used to get the products from the manufacturer to you, the customer.

Are the distribution channels used the ones you would expect? Explain your answer.

Case study

You have been asked by a manufacturer of children's toys whether it should use a wholesaler to sell its products. It originally manufactured just a few different types of toys and sold them to a small number of large retailers. It has expanded and is now selling many different types of toys to a large number of small retailers.

Activity 14.2

Read the case study above.

Write to the company advising it why you think it might be advantageous to use a wholesaler. It needs persuading that a wholesaler will be beneficial, so give detailed explanation and examples to support your point of view.

Selecting the distribution channel to use

When deciding which distribution channel to use, manufacturers have to ask themselves a number of questions. This will help them to decide which channel will be the most successful for their products. These are the types of question that need to be answered:

» **What type of product is it?** Is it sold to other businesses (business-to-business) or to consumers (business-to-consumer)? If it is sold to other businesses, for example, large printing machines, then direct selling is much more likely to be used than for most consumer products.

» **Is the product very technical?** If it is, it should be sold to the customer by someone with technical knowledge who can explain how it works and what it will do. Direct selling from the manufacturer will probably be selected in this case. An example might be an aircraft engine.

» **How often is the product purchased?** If it is bought every day, it will need to be sold in many retail outlets. An example would be a product like newspapers which are purchased daily and are sold in many outlets. If they were not readily available, customers might not bother to buy them at all.

» **How expensive is the product?** Does it have an image of being expensive? If the product is marketed as being expensive and of high quality, it will probably be sold through only a limited number of outlets. These shops will be in expensive shopping areas. For example, if the product is an expensive watch, it is no good selling it in discount jewellery shops.

» **How perishable is the product?** If the product goes rotten quickly, such as fruit or bread, then it will need to be widely available in many shops so that it can be sold quickly.

» **Where are the customers located?** If most of the customers are located in cities, it is no good selling the product only in rural areas. If the customers are located in another country, then different retail routes might be appropriate. The internet might be used for online trading.

» **Where do the competitors sell their products?** The retail outlets that competitors use will need to be considered. Each manufacturer will probably sell their products in the same outlets as their competitors so that they can compete directly for customers.

Activity 14.3

Choose an appropriate distribution channel for each of the following products. Explain your choice in each case.

a Farm tractor

b Children's clothes for export

c Tins of peas

d Made-to-measure suits.

Factors affecting distribution channels

Technical product? Expensive product? Purchased often? Perishable product?

FACTORS AFFECTING DISTRIBUTION CHANNEL

Sold to producer or consumer? Selling abroad? Location of customers? Where are competitors' products sold?

Exam-style questions: Short answer and data response

1 D&D manufactures footballs. The footballs are sold in sports shops around the world. The distribution channels D&D uses are to sell its footballs direct to retailers in some countries and through an agent in other countries. The Managing Director of D&D wants the company to start selling footballs online but the Marketing Director thinks there are too many problems with this distribution channel.

   a Define 'distribution channel'. [2]

   b Identify **two** other examples of products which might be sold directly to retailers rather than using a wholesaler. [2]

   c Outline **two** reasons why 'place' is an important part of the marketing mix for D&D. [4]

   d Explain **two** possible benefits to D&D of selling footballs through agents in other countries. [6]

   e Do you think D&D would be better selling through a wholesaler and not directly to retailers? Justify your answer. [6]

2 Pinkor is a retail chain selling children's clothes on the market stalls and small shops that it owns. It buys most of its products from wholesalers. Rakesh, the owner, says, 'I think we should start to sell by mail order and on the internet and close some of our shops to save money.'

   a Define 'wholesaler'. [2]

   b Identify **two** disadvantages to Pinkor of buying supplies from wholesalers. [2]

   c Outline **two** benefits to Rakesh of selling through several small shops rather than by mail order and online. [4]

   d Explain **two** factors which affect Pinkor's choice of distribution channel. [6]

   e Do you think Rakesh is right to want to change the channel of distribution the business uses? Justify your answer. [6]

Revision checklist

In this chapter you have learned:

✔ about the role place decisions play in the marketing mix
✔ about the different distribution channels and the advantages and disadvantages of each distribution channel
✔ how to recommend the most suitable distribution channel for a given product.

NOW – test your understanding with the revision questions in the Student etextbook and the Workbook.

The marketing mix: promotion

This chapter will explain:

★ the aims of promotion
★ different forms of promotion and how they influence sales, for example, advertising, sales promotion
★ the need for cost effectiveness in spending the marketing budget on promotion.

The role of promotion decisions in the marketing mix

Definitions to learn

Promotion is where marketing activities aim to raise customer awareness of a product or brand, generating sales and helping to create brand loyalty.

Promotion gives the consumer information about the rest of the marketing mix – without it, consumers would not know about the product, the price it sells for or the place where the product is sold. It is often thought that promotion is just about advertising the product, but it includes several different types of sales promotion as well as advertising.

Commodities such as oil and iron are not advertised or promoted, but nearly all processed and manufactured goods and most services are. Most products are sold in competitive markets so advertising and promotion have an important role to play in making them successful. Producer goods are often sold directly by sales representatives visiting businesses, but even these products are advertised in trade magazines, or leaflets are sent out to businesses informing them about the product.

Promotion is essential when a brand image, especially for consumer goods, is being created for a product.

Promotion as part of the marketing mix includes the following:

» *Advertisements* – this involves 'above-the-line' promotions. These can take different forms, such as advertising on television, via the internet including social media, in newspapers and magazines, and other forms of advertising media.
» *Sales promotion* – this involves 'below-the-line' promotions. These are often used for short periods of time in order to reinforce the above-the-line promotions. Examples include giving money-off coupons or free gifts, or product placements in television programmes or in newly released films.

The aims of promotion

As you can see, promotion includes many activities that are undertaken by businesses. All these activities have one thing in common – their objective – which is to raise awareness of a business's products and encourage consumers to make a purchase. The specific aims of promotion are summarised in the diagram on the next page.

To inform people about particular issues, often used by government

To introduce new products on to the market

To compete with competitors' products

AIMS OF PROMOTION

To create a brand image

To increase sales

To improve the company image

Advertising

Advertising communicates to potential customers to encourage them to buy a product. This is sometimes known as 'above-the-line' promotion.

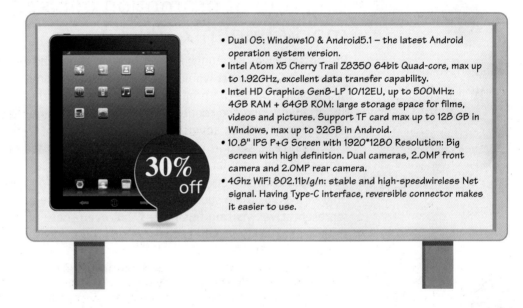

- Dual OS: Windows10 & Android5.1 – the latest Android operation system version.
- Intel Atom X5 Cherry Trail Z8350 64bit Quad-core, max up to 1.92GHz, excellent data transfer capability.
- Intel HD Graphics Gen8-LP 10/12EU, up to 500MHz: 4GB RAM + 64GB ROM: large storage space for films, videos and pictures. Support TF card max up to 128 GB in Windows, max up to 32GB in Android.
- 10.8" IPS P+G Screen with 1920*1280 Resolution: Big screen with high definition. Dual cameras, 2.0MP front camera and 2.0MP rear camera.
- 4Ghz WiFi 802.11b/g/n: stable and high-speedwireless Net signal. Having Type-C interface, reversible connector makes it easier to use.

30% off

Definitions to learn

Advertising paid for communication with potential customers about a product to encourage them to buy it.

Informative advertising is where the emphasis of advertising or sales promotion is to give full information about the product.

Persuasive advertising is advertising or promotion which is trying to persuade the consumer that they really need the product and should buy it.

Different types of advertising

Advertising can be either **informative** or **persuasive**. '1 million' by Paco Rabanne is an expensive aftershave. It is not sold by telling people all about what it will do for the skin. The advertising is meant to make consumers think that when wearing the aftershave they will smell nice to the opposite sex and look more attractive. The adverts for the aftershave used in magazines show a picture of an attractive man, which is meant to persuade the readers to buy the aftershave so that they will be attractive like the man in the advert.

Would consumers buy a laptop that was shown in adverts as being used by an attractive person, but with no technical information provided? Probably not. When buying a laptop or tablet, consumers want to know what speed it will run at and what memory it has. They want information about the product and its price.

The advertising process

When planning an advertising campaign the business will need to go through the steps shown in the diagram on page 187.

1 Set objectives	The business will have to decide the purpose of the advertising. Is it to capture a new market? Is it to increase market share? Is it to improve the image of the company? Is it to create or improve a brand image?
2 Decide the advertising budget	The business will need to decide how much to spend on advertising. This is a difficult task – too much and money is wasted, too little and the advertising will not be effective. One way, used most often, is to predict how much sales will be in the future and then spend a certain percentage of the predicted sales on advertising the product. This way the expense of advertising is related to the revenue brought in by sales of the product. The percentage used is usually between 2 and 10 per cent of sales revenue. Sometimes the budget will be set by how much competitors are spending on their advertising. Or sometimes it is simply what the business can afford to spend. This is particularly true of small businesses.
3 Create an advertising campaign	The business will need to decide what sort of advertising campaign to run. For example, will the adverts need to attract young people? The target audience (the people who the advertisers think might buy the product) and the purpose of the advertising must be kept in mind when creating the campaign.
4 Select the media to use	The business will need to decide which is the best type of advertising media to use. The target audience will determine the most suitable forms of media to use to make sure that the adverts are seen by the people intended. The business will also need to decide how often the adverts will appear in order to make sure the target audience sees them and is encouraged to buy the product. The type of media selected has to be *cost effective*. It is pointless spending a lot of money on television advertising when the business is not trying to reach a mass audience, but only wants to target bicycle riders. It would be more cost effective to advertise in bicycle magazines which would be cheaper and seen by the people who are the potential customers and no one else.
5 Evaluate the effectiveness of the campaign	The business needs to see if sales have increased as a result of the advertising campaign or see if the product's brand image has improved, i.e. has the advertising campaign met its objective?

> **Definitions to learn**
>
> The **target audience** refers to people who are potential buyers of a product or service.

The following table shows types of advertising media that businesses can use, together with the advantages and disadvantages of each and some examples of when they may be used.

Advertising media	Advantages	Disadvantages	Examples of suitable products/services to advertise using this method
Television	• The advert will go out to millions of people • The product can be shown in a very favourable way, making it look attractive • It reaches the biggest number of consumers and can reach a **target audience** by advertising at times when the programmes the potential buyers are likely to watch are being shown	• Very expensive form of advertising • Young consumers often download films/music and may not watch many television programmes	• Food products and drinks that are bought by most people • Cars that are bought by a large number of customers • Household products, for example, soap powder, that are bought by most of the population
Radio	• Cheaper than television • Usually reaches a large audience • Often uses a memorable song or tune so that the advert will be remembered	• Cannot put across a visual message • Quite expensive relative to other methods of advertising • The advert needs to be remembered, the customer cannot look back at a hard copy of the advert • Not as wide an audience as television	• Local services or events are often advertised on the radio on local channels, for example, local shops, car showrooms

Advertising media	Advantages	Disadvantages	Examples of suitable products/services to advertise using this method
Newspapers (national or local)	• National newspapers are often bought by particular customers and therefore the newspaper in which the advertisement is placed can be selected to target a particular group of people • A large number of people purchase and read national newspapers • Local newspapers are relatively cheap to place adverts in and are a cost-effective way to advertise • Adverts are permanent and can be cut out and kept • A lot of information can be put in the advert	• Newspaper adverts are often only in black and white and are therefore not very eye-catching. Not as attention grabbing as television adverts and may not be noticed by the reader, especially if the advert is small • Many young people do not purchase/read traditional newspapers	• Local products, local events in local newspapers • Cars, banks in national newspapers
Magazines	• Magazines are read by a specific type of person or business, for example, bicycle enthusiasts read bicycle magazines – very effective way to reach the target population if there are specialist magazines which cover a particular activity • Magazine adverts are in colour and therefore can look more attractive	• Magazines are often only published once a month or once a week • Advertising in magazines is relatively more expensive than newspapers	• Perfume in specialist magazines for women • Golf equipment in golf magazines • Medical equipment in professional journals
Posters/billboards	• They are permanent. • Relatively cheap • They are potentially seen by everyone who passes them	• Can easily be missed as people go past them • No detailed information can be included in the advert	• Local events • Products purchased by a large section of the population as posters are seen by everyone passing the advertisement
Cinema, DVD and Blu-ray discs	• Can give visual image of the product and show the product in a positive way • Relatively low cost • Can be very effective if the target audience goes to see particular films	• Seen by only a limited number of people who go to watch the film or buy the DVD or Blu-ray disc	• Coca-Cola when a film for teenagers is showing

Advertising media	Advantages	Disadvantages	Examples of suitable products/services to advertise using this method
Leaflets	• Cheap method of advertising • Given out in the street to a wide range of people • Direct mail – could be delivered door to door or mailed to a large number of people • Sometimes contain a money-off voucher to encourage the reader to keep the advert • The adverts are permanent and can be kept for future reference	• May not be read • Direct mail, also called 'junk mail', can be annoying and put customers off buying the product	• Leaflets are often used to advertise local events • Could be given out to promote retail outlets and may contain a money-off voucher on the leaflet
Internet (see Chapter 16 on technology and advertising)	• A large amount of information can be placed on a website, which can be seen by a vast number of people at home and abroad • Orders can be made instantly via the website • Direct mail sent via email is cheap	• Internet searches may not highlight the website and it could be missed • In some countries internet access is limited • There is a lot of competition from other websites • Security issues may discourage customers from buying online	• Products that customers are already familiar with, for example, electrical goods, books, fashion clothes • Services such as train information and ticketing, and insurance, are also suitable
Other forms of publicity	• Very cheap form of advertising, e.g. on delivery vehicles, T-shirts and on the sides of bags from shops	• May not be seen by customers in the target market	• Shops use the bags given out with purchases to advertise their name • Coca-Cola uses neon signs to advertise its name

Key info

It is estimated that total global expenditure by businesses on promotion in 2017 was US$1 trillion, of which US$552 billion was spent just on advertising.

Case study

ING is a global institution of Dutch origin, offering banking, investments, life insurance and retirement services. As it is a large international business, it can afford a large marketing budget. It uses advertising on the internet, television, magazines and billboards.

Activity 15.1

Read the case study above.

Do you think ING's current methods of advertising are the best methods to use or should it change them? Explain your answer.

Types of advertising media

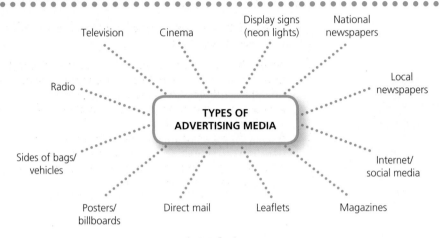

Activity 15.2

a Choose ten products which you and your friends buy regularly. Collect examples of the advertising for them and write down where the products are advertised. Copy out the table below and fill in the blanks when you have all your examples.

Product	TV	Radio	Newspapers	Magazines	Cinema	Posters/ billboards	Leaflets	Internet	Other

After you have filled it in:

b What can you observe from your completed table?
c Do the places where the adverts are found suggest a particular target audience for the products?
d Is the target population a very large number of people or a relatively small number of people?
e Do the places suggest the product is only sold locally or also nationally?
f Are these findings what you expected? Explain your answer.

Study tips

Make sure you can select suitable types of advertising for particular products and explain why they are suitable.

> ### Activity 15.3
>
> For each of the following products, decide on the best advertising media to use. Explain your choice in each case.
>
> **a** Nike, which produces an established brand of sports shoes that is sold to teenagers as a leisure shoe, wants to become more competitive with rival companies. This product is sold in many areas of the country.
> **b** A new bicycle has been produced which is suitable for using over rough ground and for cycling up mountains.
> **c** A new computer game has been developed.
> **d** A new restaurant in a small town has opened.
> **e** A famous brand of carbonated soft drink wants to expand its sales.
> **f** A local town is holding a festival.

Sales promotion

Different types of sales promotion

> **Definitions to learn**
>
> **Sales promotions** are incentives such as special offers or special deals aimed at consumers to achieve short-term increases in sales.

Promotion is used to support advertising and encourage new or existing consumers to buy the product. This is sometimes known as 'below-the-line' promotion.

Sales promotion is used in the short term to give a boost to sales, but it is not used over long periods of time. An example of this might be when a new chocolate bar has been introduced on to the market and is being advertised on television. In the shops where the chocolate bars are to be sold, free samples may be given out to encourage the customers to try the new chocolate bar and, if they like it, to become regular buyers.

There are several different types of sales promotion that can be used by businesses.

After-sales service

With expensive products, like cars or computers, providing an after-sales service can be a way of encouraging the customer to buy. They can be reassured that, if the product goes wrong in the first few weeks or months after they have bought it, they will be able to take it back and get it repaired with no additional charge to themselves. This may make the customer buy from a shop that offers an after-sales service rather than from somewhere that does not.

Gifts

Sometimes small gifts are placed in the packaging of a product to encourage the consumer to buy it. This is often used with products like breakfast cereals and the gifts are usually aimed at children. Sometimes coupons are put on the back of packets and have to be cut out and collected. When a specific number have been gathered they can be exchanged for a gift, such as a book. If the item on offer is more expensive, the coupons may be exchanged for the item but a small additional charge may also have to be paid. Collecting coupons requires several packets of the product to be purchased before the gift can be claimed and so several packets of the product will be sold. The aim is that the customer may continue buying the product even after the promotion has ended.

BOGOF

This is where multiple purchases are encouraged (for example, 'Buy one, get one free').

Price reductions

Examples include reduced prices in shops at specific times of the year and money-off coupons to be used when a product is next purchased. These can be linked to loyalty cards and customers sent money-off coupons after they have spent a certain amount of money at the shop. Money-off coupons are sometimes found on the bottom of leaflets, in newspapers or on the packet of the product itself, for example, '$1.00 off your next packet'. This encourages the consumer to try the product and hopefully they will become a regular customer. 'Flash sales' are big discounts on certain products for a very limited time period – sometimes just an hour or two. These can be advertised on the internet or 'in-store' as customers are browsing in the shop or emailed directly to potential customers.

Competitions

The packaging of a product may include an entry form which allows the customer to enter a competition. The prize is often an expensive item, such as a car. This again obviously encourages the consumer to buy the product.

Point-of-sale displays and demonstrations

Point-of-sale is the place where the product is being sold – usually a shop.
In the shop, there may be a special display of the product. With some products it can be an advantage to show how they should be used and therefore a demonstration in the shop can be a good way of encouraging customers to buy.

Free samples

This is most commonly used with products like food, shampoo and cleaning products. A free sample can be handed out in the shop to encourage the customer to try the product and hopefully buy it. Free samples can be delivered to people's houses – although this would not be to every person's house, just the neighbourhoods where the business thinks people will buy the product. Free samples can also be given away with other products. For example, new washing machines often contain a free sample of washing powder.

Product placement

This is when branded goods and services are featured in television programmes, movies or music videos. Products are associated with the image in the programme or movie. A specific audience who view the programme, movie or music video can be targeted. However, it can be expensive to pay for the placement of the product in the programme and it may have negative effects on the consumer if the image is not attractive to them. Expensive, high-powered cars used in James Bond films that portray excitement and speed are a good example of successful product placement.

> **Study tips**
>
> Make sure you can select a suitable sales promotion for particular products and explain why it is suitable.

REVISION SUMMARY

Types of sales promotion

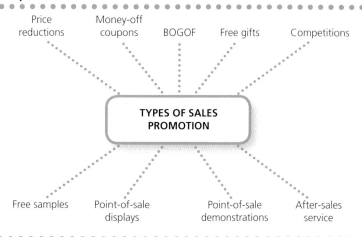

Price reductions · Money-off coupons · BOGOF · Free gifts · Competitions

TYPES OF SALES PROMOTION

Free samples · Point-of-sale displays · Point-of-sale demonstrations · After-sales service

The advantages of sales promotion

» It can promote sales at times in the year when sales are traditionally low (off-season purchases).
» It encourages new customers to try an existing product.
» It encourages consumers to try a new product.
» It encourages existing customers to buy a product more often or in greater quantities, increasing consumer loyalty.
» It encourages customers to buy your product instead of a competing brand.

Key info

The use by McDonald's restaurants of the 'Monopoly' game as a form of promotion, turning peeling stickers into a high-stakes game, has been one of the most successful sales promotions of all time. Over US$1 billion in cash and prizes have been given away in the last ten years. During this period McDonald's sales have increased by 25 per cent and some analysts believe that much of this growth has been due to Monopoly.

Activity 15.4

Choose ten products which you and your friends buy regularly. Collect examples of sales promotions that have been used for these products and explain why these methods of promotion were used.

Activity 15.5

For each of the following five products decide the best method of sales promotion to use. Explain your choice in each case.

a A new magazine aimed at teenage boys.
b A new type of pen which is very comfortable to use and does not smudge.
c A company making a famous brand of football boots wants to expand sales.
d A new fast-food takeaway opens in a small town.
e A soft toy has been invented that changes colour when hugged and can be dressed in different clothes which also change colour when warmed.

⮕ Case study

Mattel sells a range of Barbie dolls for young children. They are sold through toy shops, where a special stand is provided for the shop to display the dolls so that they are easily seen by customers. A new Chinese Barbie doll in the range has just been introduced. To show children the new doll and its range of clothes, a representative of the company is visiting toy shops to demonstrate the doll and its accessories. Also, with each purchase of the new doll there is a chance to enter a prize draw – the first prize is a trip to Disneyland.

> ### Activity 15.6
>
> Read the case study on page 193.
>
> Do you think all these ways to promote this range of Barbie dolls will be effective? Explain your answer.

The importance of the marketing budget

When deciding which type of promotion (advertising and sales promotion methods) will be most suitable to use for a particular product, the marketing budget is perhaps the most important factor.

So, the size of the **marketing budget** is crucial. It specifies how much money is available to market the product or range, so that the Marketing department knows how much it may spend. If the business cannot afford a very large budget, this will limit the places where the business can advertise. For instance, if the budget is small then television advertising will not be possible, and the number of times adverts appear in a magazine could be higher if the budget was larger.

The need for cost effectiveness in spending the marketing budget is very important. A business will need to compare the cost of advertising with the increase in expected sales. It is not good to spend large amounts of money on an advertising campaign if there is only a small increase in sales.

Small businesses will find it very difficult to compete with larger ones because of the large marketing budget available to them.

Which type of promotion should be used?

The following points also need to be considered when deciding on the type of promotion to use:

>> *The stage of the product life cycle that has been reached*. Read Chapter 12, page 165, to see which stages of the life cycle require different methods of promotion. If the product is new and has just been launched the advertising may be more informative, but if the product is well established and is at maturity then the advertising may be persuasive.
>> *The nature of the product itself*. If the product is a producer good, the type of promotion that would be used when promoting the product to other producers would be quite different to the methods used with consumer goods. For example, money-off coupons would not be suitable, but discounts when goods are purchased in bulk would be appropriate. Businesses would not be influenced by collecting money-off coupons, but they will buy in large quantities and will be influenced by a discount. A product sold to other businesses, for example, a machine to wrap perfume, will not be advertised in the same way as the perfume itself, which will be bought by consumers. The advertising for the machine will be informative, while the advertising for the perfume will be persuasive.
>> *The cultural issues involved in international marketing*. If the product is to be sold abroad then different types of promotion may be appropriate. The advertising media used will be dependent on factors such as the number of televisions owned, literacy of the population, availability of radio and cinema. It is no use advertising in a national newspaper if most of the population do not read or cannot afford a newspaper. Free samples, competitions, special offers, and so on, will also have to be suitable for the culture of the population. In some countries it might not be usual to enter competitions and therefore this promotional route would not act as an attraction to buy the

product. The business might need to consider the types of promotion in terms of what is acceptable to people in the countries where the product is being sold. For instance, the use of women in adverts or the promotion of alcohol would not be allowed in some parts of the world.

» *The nature of the target market* – whether it is local, national or international and its size – a local market will require different media to a national or international one. Is the product a specialist product, such as water skis, or is it one that is sold to the majority of the population, such as cola? If the target market is mainly formed of young people then social media could be the most effective form of promotion to use.

Public relations/sponsorship

This is concerned with promoting a good image for the business and/or its products. Public relations can take many forms, from sponsoring events such as football matches, to publicity stunts where employees, or owners of the company, take part in a sponsored activity for a good cause or to raise awareness.

Another example is where companies donate some of their products to charity – for relief when there has been a natural disaster, or food for victims of a famine.

All these types of activity raise the public's awareness of the company and its products, and increase the likelihood of their choosing its products over its competitors'.

🔍 International business in focus

Justin Bieber

Justin Bieber is a Canadian pop/R&B singer, songwriter and actor. He was discovered in 2008 by Scooter Braun, who came across Bieber's videos on YouTube and later became his manager. Justin is very popular, particularly among younger age groups. He is preparing to go on a world tour. The tour will involve concerts in many countries around the world and it is predicted that tickets for his concerts will be sold out very quickly.

Discussion points

- Discuss the best way for the tour dates of the concerts to be advertised.

- Choose another singer and consider what other promotions could be used to promote them and their music.

Exam-style questions: Short answer and data response

1 TP manufactures expensive shoes for women. It sells its range of shoes through shops which also sell made-to-measure designer clothes for women. 'We need to be clear who our target market is,' says the Marketing Manager. TP's Directors want to reduce costs to try to improve profitability. One Director thinks that as TP is a well-known business, advertising is a waste of money.

  a Define 'target market'. [2]

  b Identify **two** examples of advertising TP could use. [2]

  c Outline **two** reasons why it is important for TP to know the target market when deciding how to advertise the shoes. [4]

  d Explain **two** possible aims for TP's promotion. [6]

  e Do you think advertising is needed for TP's range of shoes? Justify your answer. [6]

2 FK is a partnership and it manufactures drinking glasses. Customers pay FK to put their own designs or messages on the outside of the glass. These are often given as gifts at weddings, births or other special celebrations. FK is planning to also manufacture plain glasses for everyday use. These glasses would be sold in supermarkets, but the specially designed glasses can only be ordered on the internet. FK only has a small marketing budget so the owners will have to think carefully about where will be the best place to advertise the plain glasses.

  a Define 'marketing budget'. [2]

  b Identify **two** places, other than the internet, where FK could advertise its glasses. [2]

  c Outline **two** reasons for promoting the plain glasses. [4]

  d Explain **two** methods of sales promotion FK could use to promote the plain glasses sold in supermarkets. [6]

  e Do you think the promotion of the plain glasses should be different to the promotion used for the specially designed glasses? Justify your answer. [6]

Revision checklist

In this chapter you have learned:

✔ about the role of promotion decisions in the marketing mix
✔ about the aims of promotion
✔ differences between advertising and sales promotion
✔ how to select appropriate types of advertising and sales promotion for different products/business objectives
✔ how to spend the marketing budget effectively
✔ the importance of the marketing budget in making promotion decisions.

NOW – test your understanding with the revision questions in the Student etextbook and the Workbook.

Technology and the marketing mix

How technology influences the marketing mix

Definitions to learn

Social media marketing is a form of internet marketing that involves creating and sharing content on social media networks in order to achieve marketing and branding goals. It includes activities such as posting text and image updates, videos, and other content that achieves audience engagement, as well as paid social media advertising.

Viral marketing is when consumers are encouraged to share information online about the products of a business.

e-commerce is the 'online' buying and selling of goods and services using computer systems linked to the internet and apps on mobile (cell) phones.

New technology is becoming integrated into marketing decisions. It presents new opportunities for businesses to market their products and services and it means there are frequent changes to all four elements of the marketing mix.

The **product** part of the marketing mix may be changed to respond to new technology. For example, new features added to mobile (cell) phones. Social media networking sites such as Facebook are changing the way businesses reach their potential customers. Twitter, pop-ups, sponsored links, paying search engines to put your websites at the top of searches, posting reviews on own websites, blogs, to name but a few, are all new ways businesses are using to **promote** their business or its products on the internet using **social media marketing** and **viral marketing**. The internet allows businesses to gather information about customer purchasing habits which means dynamic **pricing** can be used to increase revenue by changing prices frequently depending on the level of demand for a product on the internet. Finally, the internet has facilitated the widespread use of online purchasing, e-commerce, and created new opportunities for the **place** part of the marketing mix.

Use of the internet and social media networks for promotion

Activity 16.1

Research the internet to find different ways businesses advertise online, including social media advertising.

Write down a list of at least ten different businesses or products and how they are being advertised. (Try to include a variety of methods they are using.)

Include screenshots of the adverts if possible.

There are a number of benefits to a business of advertising on social media networking sites such as Facebook, including:

» targets specific demographic groups who will share product information through viral marketing
» target customers will see the advert when they go on Facebook
» speed in response to market changes – information can be updated regularly
» cheap to use – it has low costs if just placing advertisements
» reaches groups that are difficult to reach any other way.

However, there are disadvantages too:

» It can alienate customers if they find the adverts annoying.
» Businesses have to pay for advertising if using pop-ups.
» Potential customers may not use social media networks.
» There is a lack of control of advertising if used by others.
» Messages may be altered or used in a bad way and forwarded on to other users, giving the business bad publicity.

If a business advertises on its own website it will enjoy the following benefits:

» No extra cost if own website is already set up.
» Control of advertising as it is on your own site.
» Can change adverts quickly and update pictures/prices, and so on.
» Interactive adverts can be more attractive than those in other forms of advertising media such as magazines and posters.
» Can provide more information in adverts and link to other pages with further information and pictures.
» Attracts funds/payments from companies that want to advertise or be associated or linked with your website.

However, there are disadvantages too:

» Potential customers may not see the website as the page may come up in a long list of results when using a search engine such as Google.
» Relies on customers finding the website.
» Design costs of the website may be high.

Activity 16.2

Look at the lists above and produce a similar list of advantages and disadvantages for a business that is using the following to promote its products or services:

- tweets
- blogs
- specialised apps to be downloaded for the business/brand of products
- text (sms) messages.

Activity 16.3

For each of the following products, choose three different ways to advertise it using the internet. Explain the advantages and disadvantages for each way. Then choose which you think is the best way. Justify your choice and explain why it is better than the other two ways.

a Reebok, which produces an established brand of sports shoes that is sold to teenagers as a leisure shoe, wants to increase its market share.
b RAOUL makes smart casual outfits and business shirts and jackets which are sold in boutiques in fashionable malls throughout Singapore.
c A new restaurant has opened in your nearby city centre.
d Your school is holding a charity fundraising event.

e-commerce

When was the last time you purchased a product by computer or mobile phone linked to the internet? Some people will answer 'I never have' to this question but others will say 'Five minutes ago!' The growth of internet selling has been incredible in recent years. Online retailing only started in the USA in 1992 – yet by 2017 internet sales in the USA alone were US$459 billion!

Consider these two statements by different marketing managers:

» Manager A: 'Since my company introduced a new website which allows e-commerce, sales have increased by 55 per cent. This includes sales to countries we have never sold to before. We are now thinking about closing some of our retail shops.'

» Manager B: 'My company sells handmade suits for men and women. We offer a personal service and customers visit us several times during the making of their suit to check for size and style. We use the internet only for gaining market research and dealing with suppliers.'

How can both managers be so convinced their company has the correct approach to e-commerce? The answer is ... they could both be right! Not every product or every service will be successfully sold by e-commerce. This means that we need to consider the different impacts that the internet and e-commerce can have on businesses and consumers.

Opportunities of e-commerce to business	Opportunities of e-commerce to consumers
Websites can be used to promote the company and its products worldwide much more cheaply than other forms of marketing, for example, setting up shops in many countries.	No need to leave the house to 'go shopping' and this convenience is a major factor explaining the growth of e-commerce.
Orders can be taken over the internet and sent directly to the company warehouse for dispatch.	Comparisons between prices and products or services offered can be easily made by surfing from one website to another – or using 'price comparison' websites.
Consumers might be encouraged to purchase more products than they intended by attractive and easy-to-follow websites, for example, giving links to other products that could be bought with the original purchase.	Payment by credit or debit card is very easy.
Businesses can also easily make online purchases of supplies and materials from other businesses – this is called business-to-business (or B2B) e-commerce.	Consumers can now easily access products and services from businesses located abroad – this would be very difficult or expensive without e-commerce.
Selling online makes **dynamic pricing** much easier for businesses. This is when they vary the price of a product being sold online depending on the numbers of customers 'hitting' the product's web page at a particular time of day or day of the week. It gives great price flexibility and usually leads to higher revenue for the business.	Consumers can buy some products for prices much lower than they would be without the competition of e-commerce, for example, books, music and insurance policies.
	Customers can buy parts or components from manufacturers without the addition of retailers' profit margin.
	Packaging and transport costs have fallen due to competition on the internet so it is cheaper to buy from abroad now.

Definitions to learn

Dynamic pricing is when businesses change product prices, usually when selling online, depending on the level of demand.

Threats of e-commerce to business	Threats of e-commerce to consumers
With so many businesses now offering e-commerce websites, competition between businesses is very high. If a business is charging higher prices, consumers can easily find an alternative supplier.	Consumers need access to the internet! It is still the case that in many countries internet access, especially for low-income consumers, is not good.
Website design must be very clear, attractive and easy to operate. Website designs can be expensive – and will often need to be updated which will lead to further costs.	Computer systems failures or weak internet connections can result in frustrated consumers who cannot access websites or make their purchases.
Transport costs per product sold are likely to be higher than selling through traditional shops. Each item must be packaged and delivered separately. Should consumers be asked to pay these costs? Or will this make the business uncompetitive?	Products cannot be seen, touched or tried on (clothing, for example) and sending products back because they are unsuitable ('returns') is often inconvenient.
There is no face-to-face contact with consumers, so the business does not gain this useful market research feedback.	There is no face-to-face contact with sales staff so it is difficult to find out more information about the goods and services being sold other than that which is provided on the website.
Consumers in most countries have the legal right to reject goods bought through e-commerce because they have not seen, touched or worn the actual good. 'Returns' can add to business costs.	Many consumers are concerned about identity theft or fraudulent use of credit cards if they buy goods online. Security systems are improving but there are still some risks.
Although fewer shops may be needed, a large warehouse and efficient inventory control system are essential to fulfil consumers' orders accurately and efficiently.	
e-commerce is not suitable for businesses that sell personal services such as hairdressing or products for which consumers expect personal face-to-face service.	

Study tips

Make sure you can explain the threats and opportunities of e-commerce to a particular business.

REVISION SUMMARY   **e-commerce – impact on businesses**

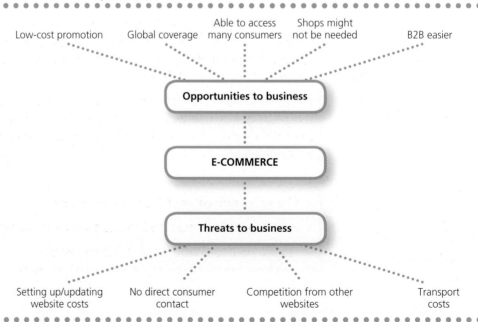

REVISION SUMMARY   **e-commerce – impact on consumers**

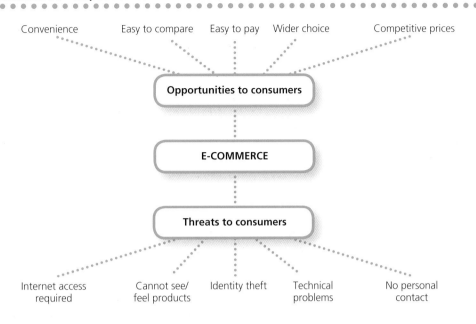

| Convenience | Easy to compare | Easy to pay | Wider choice | Competitive prices |

Opportunities to consumers

E-COMMERCE

Threats to consumers

| Internet access required | Cannot see/ feel products | Identity theft | Technical problems | No personal contact |

International business in focus

Airbnb

Airbnb allows people to lease or rent short-term accommodation including holiday apartments, rooms or hotel rooms. Airbnb does not own any of the accommodation. It acts as an intermediary and receives a percentage of the fee charged from both guests and owners of the accommodation for every booking. Airbnb has over 3 million types of accommodation listed in 65 000 cities and 191 countries. The price is set by the owner of the accommodation.

Airbnb can be accessed via either the Airbnb websites or mobile apps. On each booking Airbnb charges a guest services fee of between 6 and 12 per cent and charges the owner of the accommodation a host service fee of between 3 and 5 per cent.

People can search online for different types of accommodation including lodging type, dates, location and price. Before booking, customers must provide a valid name, email address, telephone number, photo and payment information.

Discussion points

- Could Airbnb exist without the internet?
- How has Airbnb changed the market for accommodation across the world?
- How is Airbnb a threat to local businesses?

Exam-style questions: Short answer and data response

1 JJ sells expensive handmade jewellery. The jewellery items are designed and made to the exact requirements of the customer. JJ is successfully promoted on social media networks. Jonathan, the owner of JJ, only sells through JJ's own shop. However, he is thinking of selling directly to customers through JJ's own website.

   a Define 'social media networks'. [2]

   b Identify **two** other examples of how products might be promoted directly to customers using the internet. [2]

   c Outline **two** reasons why 'social media marketing' is an important part of the marketing mix for JJ. [4]

   d Explain **two** possible limitations to JJ of using the internet for promotion. [6]

   e Do you think JJ would be better selling through its own shop or its own website? Justify your answer. [6]

2 PP provides house cleaning products. PP sells its products only through its own website. PP does not sell any of its products to wholesalers or retailers. The owner believes that e-commerce is the future for selling all products and that in time all shops will close.

   a Define 'e-commerce'. [2]

   b Identify **two** disadvantages to customers of buying on the internet. [2]

   c Outline **two** drawbacks to PP of selling only through its own website. [4]

   d Explain **two** factors that affect PP's choice to distribute its products only through the internet. [6]

   e Do you think PP is right to sell to customers only using its website? Justify your answer. [6]

Revision checklist

In this chapter you have learned:

✔ how businesses can use the internet and social media sites for promotion
✔ about e-commerce and its advantages and disadvantages
✔ about the threats and opportunities e-commerce offers to businesses and consumers.

NOW – test your understanding with the revision questions in the Student etextbook and the Workbook.

Marketing strategy

This chapter will explain:

★ the importance of different elements of the marketing mix in influencing consumer decisions in given circumstances
★ how to recommend and justify an appropriate marketing strategy in given circumstances
★ the impact of legal controls on marketing strategy, for example, misleading promotion, faulty and dangerous goods
★ growth potential of new markets in other countries
★ problems of entering foreign markets, for example, cultural differences and lack of knowledge
★ the benefits and limitations of methods to overcome such problems, for example, joint ventures, licensing.

Marketing strategy

A **marketing strategy** is a plan to combine the right combination of the four elements of the marketing mix for a product or service to achieve a particular marketing objective(s).

The marketing strategy developed by a business will depend on the size of the market and the number and size of competitors. It will need to identify the marketing objectives of the business, the target market and the finance available – this is called the marketing budget.

The marketing objective could include:

» increasing sales of an existing product/service by selling to new markets or selling more to the existing market
» increasing sales of a product or service by improving it (extension strategy – see Chapter 12)
» achieving a target market share with a newly launched product
» increasing market share
» maintaining market share if competition is increasing
» increasing sales in a niche market.

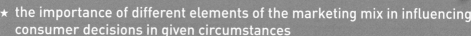 **Case study:** Marketing strategies cannot stand still

For 14 years, Nokia was the world's biggest seller of mobile (cell) phones. In 2007 it had almost 50 per cent of the market. By 2013, this had fallen to just 3 per cent, with substantial sales decline not just in the USA but also India, China and Africa. What went wrong?

'Nokia left the door wide open for Apple and Samsung and others by not delivering a full-touch feature phone. Apple and Samsung figured it out years ago, yet by 2013 Nokia still did not have a competitive product,' said Ben Wood, head of research at CCS Insight.

So even though Nokia had a good reputation, its phones were priced competitively, they were well promoted and sold in appropriate places for consumers, buyers still switched to other handsets with more modern operating systems. Nokia mobile (cell)

phones had failed to keep up with the latest technology and customer preferences. The 'product' part of the marketing strategy wasn't right and so sales were falling even when the other three elements of the marketing mix were right.

Are Samsung and Apple now suffering from the same problem? In the first half of 2017, both companies experienced a fall in global market share. The Chinese mobile phone suppliers Huawei, Oppo and Vivo now present a real challenge to Apple and Samsung, the market leaders since 2012. How should these two famous companies change their marketing strategy to respond to increased competition? Reduce prices? – but will this damage brand image and reduce profits needed for new investment. Increase promotion spending? – but are consumers more interested in new features than sales promotions? Add new distribution channels? – these phones are already available from thousands of retailers worldwide. Perhaps the answer lies in product development as a key feature of a marketing strategy to stay ahead of the competition, a fact ignored by Nokia several years ago.

Study tips

Make sure you can develop a marketing strategy for a given product/service. The four elements of the marketing mix should all link together in order to be effective in attracting the target market to buy the product/service.

Activity 17.1

Choose a product which you think will sell very well in your country (this could be a new product or an existing product such as bottled water). Create a marketing strategy for this product by including answers to the following questions.

a Who is your target market? What are the characteristics of the consumers you think will buy your product? What is their market segment? Justify your answers.
b How does your product meet their needs? Why will consumers buy your product rather than a competitor's product? What is your product's unique selling point (USP) that makes it different to your competitors' products? Justify your answers.
c What price will the target market be willing to pay? What pricing strategy will you use? Justify your answers.
d Which methods of distribution (place) will you use and will these be suitable for your target market? Which methods of distribution do your competitors use? Justify your answers.
e What methods of promotion will you use? Remember you may have a limited budget/amount of money to spend. Decide both where you will advertise and what promotional offers you might use. Justify your answers.
f Summarise by explaining why you think your new product will be successful.

Importance of the marketing mix in influencing consumer decisions

The four elements of the marketing mix are important in influencing consumer decisions when developing a marketing strategy aimed at a specific target market. If the marketing strategy does not combine the elements of the marketing mix correctly then the marketing objectives will not be achieved. For example:

» A product which meets customer needs and is priced at a suitable price which the target market is prepared to pay but potential consumers are not informed about it – promotion is ineffective.
» A product which does not meet the needs of the target market will not sell at any price, even if it is heavily advertised.

The marketing strategy – the combination of the four elements of the marketing mix – will need adapting throughout a product's life cycle to ensure that consumer decisions are being influenced positively.

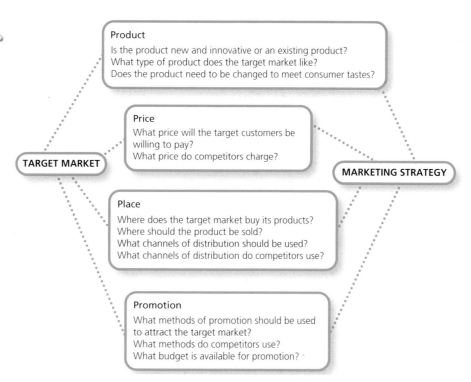

Product
Is the product new and innovative or an existing product?
What type of product does the target market like?
Does the product need to be changed to meet consumer tastes?

Price
What price will the target customers be willing to pay?
What price do competitors charge?

TARGET MARKET

MARKETING STRATEGY

Place
Where does the target market buy its products?
Where should the product be sold?
What channels of distribution should be used?
What channels of distribution do competitors use?

Promotion
What methods of promotion should be used to attract the target market?
What methods do competitors use?
What budget is available for promotion?

Recommending and justifying a marketing strategy in given circumstances

If you are asked to recommend and justify a marketing strategy for a business, consider and develop these points in your answer:

» Marketing objective, for example, is it to increase sales or to launch new products?
» Marketing budget, for example, can TV advertising be afforded or would social media be more cost effective?
» Target market, for example, high-income consumers or families with young children?
» Balanced marketing mix, for example, do all four elements of the mix 'fit together' and 'tell the same story' about the product?

Activity 17.2

Copy out the table below on a large sheet of paper. Then select the correct answer from the list on page 206 to fit each stage of the product life cycle.

The choices for Sales have already been filled in to get you started.

Note: You will need to study Chapters 12, 13 and 15 before completing this activity.

	Introduction	Growth	Maturity	Saturation	Decline
Sales	Low sales because the product is new	Sales rise rapidly	Sales increase more slowly	Sales level off as market saturation is reached	Sales fall as new products become available or the product goes out of fashion
Pricing policy					
Promotion/ advertising					
Likely profits/losses					

Pricing policy
- Price skimming as few/no competitors.
- Penetration pricing by competitors as a few competing products are introduced, small reduction in your prices to compete with these products.
- Competitive pricing/promotional pricing as competition becomes intense.
- Price reductions to encourage sales as sales are falling; some competitors stop making the product.
- Competitive pricing/prices are reduced to compete with existing competitors; no new competitors enter the market.

Promotion/advertising
- Advertising reduced or may stop altogether as sales fall.
- Informative advertising as the product is new; free samples may be given out to get customers to try it.
- A lot of image-creating advertising to encourage brand loyalty and to compete with other very competitive products.
- A high, stable level of advertising may be promoting new improved versions of the original product.
- Informative advertising changed to persuasive advertising to encourage brand loyalty as sales start to rise rapidly.

Likely profits/losses
- Loss made due to high development costs.
- Profits fall as sales fall.
- Profits fall as sales are static and prices have been reduced.
- Profits start to be made after development costs have been covered.
- Profits at their highest as sales growth is high.

Legal controls on marketing

Consumers can be easily misled. It is quite easy to sell consumers goods that are either unsuitable for the purpose intended or that fail to perform as the manufacturer claimed. This is not because consumers are stupid! It is because products are now so complicated and technical that it is very difficult for a consumer to know how good they are or how they are likely to work. Also, modern advertising can be so persuasive that nearly all of us could be sold products, even if they were later discovered to be of poor quality or not as good as the advert claimed. Consumers need protection against businesses which could, unfortunately, take advantage of the consumers' lack of knowledge and lack of accurate product information.

In the UK, the laws on consumer protection are typical of those existing in most countries and include some of the following forms of consumer protection:

» *Weights and Measures*. Retailers and producers commit an offence if they sell underweight goods or if the weighing equipment they use is inaccurate.
» *Trade Descriptions*. It is illegal to give the consumer a deliberately misleading impression about a product. For example, it is illegal to state that a pair of trousers is made of wool, when it is made of cotton. Advertisements must therefore be truthful.
» *Sale of Goods*. It is illegal to sell: products which have serious flaws or problems, that is they are not of a satisfactory quality; products which are not fit for the purpose intended by the consumer, for example, if the consumer asks for a drill to make holes in walls and is sold one which is only suitable for wood; products which do not perform as described on the label or by the retailer, for example, if the label states 'These shoes are completely waterproof' and they leak the first time they are used!

'These shoes are completely waterproof!'

My feet are soaked

▲ It is illegal in many countries to sell items that do not live up to the claims made for them

» *Supply of Goods and Services Act.* This Act does the same for services as the Sale of Goods Act does for products. A service must be provided with reasonable skill and care.
» It is illegal to make misleading pricing claims, such as '£40 off for this week only' when the product was being sold for the same price the previous week. Most importantly, the law makes retailers and manufacturers liable – that is, responsible – for any damage which their faulty goods might cause. Anyone injured by faulty goods can take the supplier to court and ask for compensation.
» *The Consumer Contracts Regulations* (formerly Distance Selling Regulations) allow customers a cooling-off period of 14 working days when products are not bought in a face-to-face situation such as with internet shopping. This means they can change their mind about purchasing the good or service. For goods this starts from the day after the goods are delivered, and for services it's 14 working days from the contract being agreed. These regulations apply to all transactions carried out over at a distance from the retailer, such as online shopping.

Here are some examples of consumer protection laws from Pakistan and South Africa:

» Under the Consumer Protection Act 2005, councils were set up in different regions in Pakistan, for example, the Punjab Consumer Protection Council (PCPC). If consumers are not satisfied with a product or service they have purchased and the business has not dealt with the complaint in a satisfactory way then the consumer can register a complaint with the council. It will hear the case and then decide who is at fault. These councils have resolved hundreds of cases, for example, overcharging above normal rates, misleading statements by a shopkeeper, warranty issues and misleading advertising.
» Consumer Protection Act 2011, South Africa – here, consumers have up to six months to return faulty or unsafe goods and they have a choice between the supplier repairing or replacing these, or refunding you in full. This only applies to general wear and tear of your appliances and not gross negligence on your part. Also, if you order online then the goods will have to be delivered at an agreed date, time and place. If not, you will be free to accept or cancel the agreement – it's your choice. Companies are also obliged to deliver goods that match the sample or description of the product. You have the right to examine your purchases before accepting them, and to reject them if you're not happy.

Study tips

Make sure you can explain why governments pass laws to protect consumers and what the laws mean for businesses when selling their goods or services.

Is all consumer protection a good idea? Most people would say that the consumer needs to be protected as much as possible. They believe that goods should be as safe and as suitable for the purpose intended as possible. However, some business managers believe that these laws add to the costs of making and selling products and this increases the prices in the shops. What is your view?

> ### Activity 17.3
>
> Here are three situations in which consumers might need some protection:
>
> **a** 'These shoes are made of the finest leather.' In fact they are made of plastic.
> **b** A consumer buys one kilogram of potatoes and re-weighs them at home. In fact, he has only 800 grams.
> **c** A motorist asks for a tow rope 'strong enough for my trailer'. It breaks the first time he tries to use it.
>
> Do you think the consumer needs some legal protection in these cases? For each example, identify which consumer protection laws may have been broken by the business selling the goods.

> ### Activity 17.4
>
> Research the consumer protection laws in your country.
>
> * What can a customer do if a product is faulty?
> * What can a customer do if a product does not do what it is advertised to do?
> * What other protection do the laws give customers?

Growth potential of new markets in other countries

Opportunities

These days a large number of businesses market their products in many different countries. Why has there been this trend towards more globalisation of business?

» Markets in other countries might have much greater growth potential than existing markets. Countries in different parts of the world are now developing and seeing their populations enjoying rising incomes. This provides opportunities for entering new markets abroad.

» Home markets might be saturated and these new markets give the chance for higher sales.

» There is a wider choice of location to produce products and this encourages businesses to sell as well as produce in these countries. The business will have more information about these markets and be better placed to sell to them as well.

» Trade barriers have been lowered in many parts of the world, making it easier and more profitable now to enter these markets.

Problems of entering foreign markets

» *Lack of knowledge* – the business may not be aware of competitors or the habits of consumers in these markets. For example, where do most people do their shopping?

» *Cultural differences* – religion or culture may mean that some products won't sell in another market. For example, alcohol products will not be sold in most Middle Eastern countries.

>> *Exchange rate changes* (see Chapter 29) – if the exchange rate is not very stable then exchange rate changes can mean the prices of imported goods change and the products can become too expensive to sell in the new market.
>> *Import restrictions* (see Chapter 27) – if there are tariffs or quotas on imported products then the prices of these products may be higher than domestically produced goods – reducing sales or profits or both.
>> *Increased risk of non-payment* – methods of payment may be different in these new markets and it may be more difficult to be certain that payment for imported goods will be made.
>> *Increased transport costs* – as products have to be transported over long distances the costs of getting products to market will increase. However, there have been benefits from using containers to transport products and the container ships are getting larger and all this has led to reductions in transport costs.

Methods to overcome the problems of entering new markets abroad

>> *Joint ventures* (see Chapter 4), for example, McDonald's has a 50–50 joint venture with two Indian restaurant chains, Hardcastle restaurants and Connaught Plaza restaurants. This allows the business to gain important local knowledge so that culture and customs can be adapted to enable a more successful entry into the new market. The risks of entering markets abroad are therefore reduced – but also shared between the partner businesses.

Main limitations:
- Management conflict between the two businesses
- Profits shared.

>> *Licensing* – this is where the business gives permission for another company in the new market being entered to produce the branded or 'patented' products under licence. This means the products do not have to be physically transported to the new market which saves time and transport costs and can get round trade restrictions.

Main limitations:
- Quality problems caused by an inexperienced licensee could damage brand reputation.
- Licensee now has access to information about how the product is made – could develop a better version and become a competitor.

>> *International franchising* – this means that foreign franchises are used to operate a business's franchise abroad. For example, Dunkin' Donuts, which is a US-based baked goods and coffee franchise, sold the franchise in the United Arab Emirates so franchisees operate all the outlets. This means that again local knowledge is used to choose the best place to locate the Dunkin' Donuts outlets.

Main limitations:
- Quality problems or poor service offered by franchisees could damage brand image.
- Training and support will need to be provided by franchisor.

>> *Localising existing brands* – there is a phrase 'thinking global – acting local' which is being used by several global businesses. It means that there is still a common brand image for the business but it has adapted to local tastes and culture, therefore increasing sales.

Main limitations:
- May be less successful than a new product made to meet local cultures and market conditions.

* Expensive to change packaging, promotion, and so on for each market the product is sold in.

 Case study: McDonald's enters foreign markets

McDonald's has developed a special menu for its restaurants in India. The menu does not have beef burgers, but does have chicken burgers known as Chicken Maharaja-Macs and cheeseburgers called Big Spicy Paneer on its menu. These products are suitable for the culture of this market as the majority of Indians are Hindus so do not eat beef for religious reasons, but many do eat chicken, fish and cheese.

Activity 17.5

Read the case study above.

a Why did McDonald's change its menu in Indian restaurants?
b Should it have a different menu for all of the countries it operates in?

International business in focus

Yeo's

Yeo's is a food business which was set up in 1900 in China, originally as a small shop making soy sauce. It moved to Singapore in the 1930s and started expanding. The business now makes a variety of food and cooking products including curry sauces, pastes, noodles and drinks. Today the company sells across the world including Singapore, Malaysia, Indonesia, Hong Kong, China, Canada and the USA.

The Directors of Yeo's want to expand sales in the European market. It conducted 'sampling tours' throughout major UK, French and German Chinese supermarkets to raise awareness of its products. The company did not introduce the full range of its products into the European market.

Discussion points

* Why do you think Yeo's conducted 'sampling tours' across European countries?
* Why did Yeo's not introduce the full range of its products into the European market?
* What possible problems do you think Yeo's might have had in entering the European market?

Exam-style questions: Short answer and data response

1 YeyYo owns a chain of cafés selling cakes, biscuits and coffee. The company wants to change its marketing strategy to increase its market share. Its traditional cafés are in small towns and its target market is local people who shop in these towns. The company does not advertise or use any sales promotions. The prices are kept low because in these towns consumer incomes are low. YeyYo wants to open modern cafés in city centres but the Marketing Director thinks it will need to change its marketing strategy to appeal to the higher income people in the city centres.

   a Define 'marketing strategy'. [2]
   b Identify **two** questions the Marketing Director will ask before deciding on prices in the new cafés. [2]
   c Outline **two** reasons why YeyYo might need a new marketing strategy to increase market share. [4]
   d Explain **two** reasons why it is important for YeyYo to have a clear marketing objective. [6]
   e Recommend a marketing strategy for the new city centre cafés. Justify your answer. [6]

2 KKosmetics manufactures make-up for women. The company sells its products across Europe but wants to start selling to African countries. The Marketing Director says, 'There are a lot of opportunities in these markets but also several problems. We are reaching saturation in the European markets and we need to increase sales in new markets.' The Managing Director would prefer to expand in Africa by forming a joint venture.

   a Define 'joint venture'. [2]
   b Identify **two** ways a new market abroad for KKosmetics might be different to the home market. [2]
   c Outline **two** possible reasons why KKosmetics wants to enter new markets abroad. [4]
   d Explain **two** possible problems for KKosmetics of entering new markets abroad. [6]
   e Do you think these problems can be easily overcome by KKosmetics? Justify your answer. [6]

Revision checklist

In this chapter you have learned:

✔ the importance of different elements of the marketing mix in influencing consumer decisions
✔ how to develop an appropriate marketing strategy in given circumstances
✔ to explain the nature and impact of legal controls related to marketing
✔ to explain the growth potential of new markets abroad
✔ about the problems of entering new markets abroad
✔ the benefits and limitations of ways to overcome these problems.

NOW – test your understanding with the revision questions in the Student etextbook and the Workbook.

Marketing: end-of-section case study

ChocoCrocs

ChocoCrocs was set up ten years ago as a private limited company. The business grew slowly as the owners used reinvested profits as the only source of finance for expansion. The company has share capital of $10 million which is owned by six members of the Patel family.
   ChocoCrocs has three main types of products, which are:

- large chocolate bars mainly sold to men
- chocolates with praline-filled centres mainly sold to women
- small chocolate bars shaped like a crocodile mainly sold to children.

ChocoCrocs employs skilled workers in the Marketing department. This department carries out market research and it also develops new products for the company to market. The Managing Director says this is one of the most important departments in the company.
   The Directors of ChocoCrocs want to expand the business.

Appendix 1: Sales for the products of ChocoCrocs

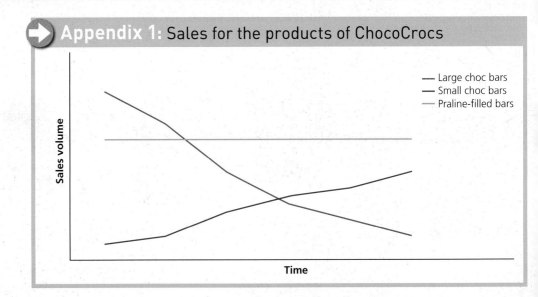

Exam-style questions: Case study

1 a Appendix 1 shows large chocolate bars are in the decline stage of the product life cycle. Explain four other stages of the product life cycle. [8]
  b ChocoCrocs is considering what pricing strategy to use for the crocodile-shaped children's chocolate bars. Consider **three** suitable pricing strategies it could use and recommend which one it should choose. Justify your answer. [12]
2 a ChocoCrocs has a website which gives customers information about the products it sells. Explain **two** other ways that ChocoCrocs could find the internet useful to the business in the marketing of its products. [8]
  b The Marketing department is one of ChocoCrocs' most important departments. Consider why market research is important to the success of ChocoCrocs. Is this section of the Marketing department the most important? Justify your answer. [12]

Optional question

3 a Explain **two** ways the size of the ChocoCrocs company could be measured. [8]
  b Consider the alternative ways the directors could expand ChocoCrocs. Recommend which way it should choose. Justify your answer. [12]

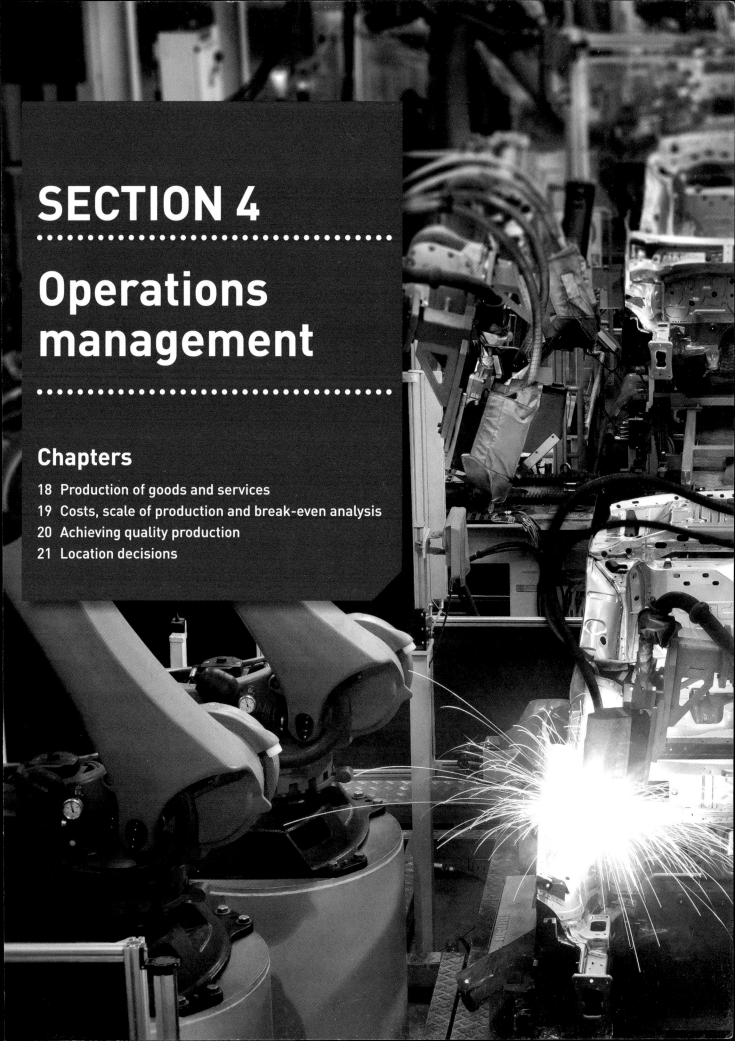

SECTION 4

Operations management

Chapters

18 Production of goods and services
19 Costs, scale of production and break-even analysis
20 Achieving quality production
21 Location decisions

Production of goods and services

This chapter will explain:

★ the meaning of production – managing resources effectively to produce goods and services
★ the difference between production and productivity
★ the benefits of increasing efficiency and how to increase it, for example, increasing productivity by automation and technology, improved labour skills
★ why businesses hold inventories
★ the concept of lean production; how to achieve it, for example, just-in-time inventory control and Kaizen; benefits of lean production
★ the main methods of production: the features, benefits and limitations of job, batch and flow production
★ how to recommend and justify an appropriate production method for a given situation
★ how technology is changing production methods, e.g. using computers in design and manufacturing.

Managing resources effectively to produce goods and services

Production is the provision of a product or a service to satisfy consumer wants and needs. The process of production adds value to the raw materials and bought-in components. As you learned in Chapter 1, value added is the difference between the cost of inputs (raw materials or components) and the final selling price of the product or service.

The production process applies to manufacturing as well as service industries. In adding value, businesses combine the 'inputs' of a business (factors of production, such as land, labour, capital and enterprise) to produce more valuable 'outputs' (the final good or service) to satisfy consumer wants or needs. However, these factors of production, also called economic resources, can be combined in different proportions – as inputs – to the production process, as shown in the diagram below.

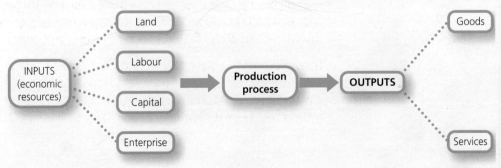

For a business to be competitive it should combine these inputs of resources efficiently so that it makes the best use of resources at its disposal to keep costs low and increase profits. In a developing country, where wages are low, it may be more efficient to use many workers and few machines to produce goods – this production process is called 'labour-intensive'. However, in developed countries where labour costs are high, production is often 'capital-intensive', where businesses use machines/robots and employ few workers.

➡ Case study

A restaurant combines the four factors of production to produce a meal for customers.

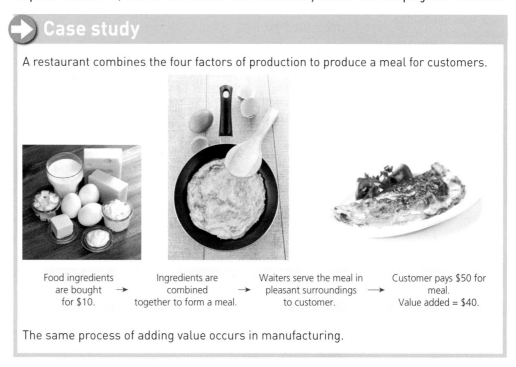

| Food ingredients are bought for $10. | → | Ingredients are combined together to form a meal. | → | Waiters serve the meal in pleasant surroundings to customer. | → | Customer pays $50 for meal. Value added = $40. |

The same process of adding value occurs in manufacturing.

Operations department

The role of the Operations department in a business is to take inputs and change them into outputs for customer use. Inputs can be physical goods or services.

The Operations Manager is responsible for making sure that raw materials are provided and made into finished goods or services. The different sections of this department will vary depending on what the business produces. A typical manufacturing business will have:

» a Factory Manager who will be responsible for the quantity and quality of products coming off a production line; this will include the maintenance of the production line and other necessary repairs
» a Purchasing Manager who will be responsible for providing the materials, components and equipment required for the production
» a Research and Development Manager who will be responsible for the design and testing of new production processes and products.

In a retailing business this department will be similar but the Factory Manager will be replaced by the managers for the shops. In a service business such as a restaurant the Operations department will include managers for each of the restaurants (see the organisation charts in Chapter 7).

Productivity

The level of production is the total output of a business in a given time period, for example, one year. This is different to productivity. **Productivity** is how a business can measure its efficiency. The productivity of a business can be measured by:

$$\text{Productivity} = \frac{\text{Output}}{\text{Quantity of input}}$$

Businesses often want to measure the productivity of one of the factors of production or inputs, usually labour. This is measured by dividing the output over a given period of time by the number of employees:

$$\text{Labour productivity} = \frac{\text{Output (over a given period of time)}}{\text{Number of employees}}$$

Productivity can be raised by either using fewer inputs to produce the same output or using the same inputs to produce a higher level of output.

If employees become more efficient, the amount of output produced per employee will rise and therefore the costs of producing each product will fall. This will make the business more competitive and is the main reason why businesses are usually very focused on increasing productivity.

Activity 18.1

Better Bakers produces cakes for local supermarkets. It has steadily increased the number of workers it employs. The owner, Benson, thinks this has been good for the business as output has increased.

a Do you agree with the owner? Use the information below to justify your answer.

Year	Output = number of cakes produced	Number of workers	Output per worker
2016	10 000	30	
2017	20 000	40	
2018	25 000	50	

b Suggest how the owner, Benson, could increase the productivity of Better Bakers.
c Can Benson measure the output of his workers? If so, how?

There are a number of ways to increase productivity and efficiency. These include:

» Improve quality of the product and inventory control to reduce waste.
» Replace employees with machines – automation.
» Improve training to increase employee efficiency.
» Motivate employees more effectively.
» Introduce new technology.
» Use more automation.

Chapter 8 — lost section 6

Ways to increase productivity

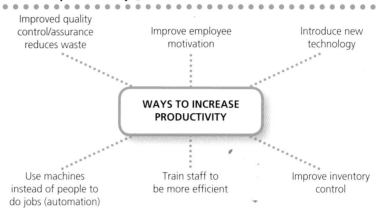

Improved quality control/assurance reduces waste

Improve employee motivation

Introduce new technology

WAYS TO INCREASE PRODUCTIVITY

Use machines instead of people to do jobs (automation)

Train staff to be more efficient

Improve inventory control

Benefits of increasing efficiency/productivity

» Reduced inputs needed for the same output level.
» Lower costs per unit (average cost).
» Fewer workers may be needed, possibly leading to lower wage costs.
» Higher wages might now be paid to workers, which increases motivation.

Why businesses hold inventories (stock)

Have you ever gone into a shop and found it has run out of what you wanted? If so, then the shop might have had higher sales than usual or else its delivery of supplies might have been late. To ensure that there is always enough inventory to satisfy demand, inventory levels must be carefully controlled.

Inventories can take various forms, including raw materials, components, partly finished goods, or finished products ready for delivery. It can even include inventory of spare parts for machinery in case of breakdowns. Holding inventories allows a business to maintain production and satisfy customer demand quickly.

When inventories get to a certain point (reorder point), they will be reordered so that when a delivery is made it will bring inventories back up to the maximum level again. The business must reorder before inventories get too low to allow time for the goods to be delivered. If inventory levels get too low they might actually run out if there is an unexpectedly high demand for the goods. If too high a level of inventory is held then this costs a lot of money; the business has bought the goods but they are not being used and the money could be put to better use. The following graph demonstrates how inventory levels can be managed.

> **Definitions to learn**
>
> The **buffer inventory** level is the inventory held to deal with uncertainty in customer demand and deliveries of supplies.

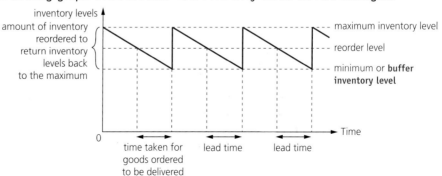

Effectively managing inventory levels is very important to all types of businesses, especially manufacturing and retail businesses.

Lean production

Lean production covers a variety of techniques used by businesses to cut down on waste of resources, including time, and therefore increase efficiency. It aims to reduce the time it takes for a product to be developed and become available in the shops for sale. Lean production cuts out any activities which do not add value for the customer and this can apply to services as well.

There are seven types of waste that can occur in production:

» Overproduction – producing goods before they have been ordered by customers. This results in high storage costs and possible damage to goods while in storage.
» Waiting – when goods are not moving or being processed in any way, waste is occurring.
» Transportation – moving goods around unnecessarily causes waste and is not adding value to the product. Goods may also be damaged when they are being moved around.
» Unnecessary inventory – if there is too much inventory then this takes up space, may get in the way of production and costs money.
» Motion – any actions, including bending or stretching movements of the body of the employee, wastes time. It may also be a health and safety risk for the employees. This also applies to the movement of machines which may not be necessary.
» Over-processing – if complex machinery is being used to perform simple tasks then this is wasteful. Some activities in producing the goods may not be necessary and may be because the design of the product is poor.
» Defects – any faults require the goods being fixed and time can be wasted inspecting the products.

> ### Activity 18.2
> Choose a business activity with which you are familiar, for example a restaurant, café or hairdresser, and identify examples of the seven types of waste which might occur.
> How could these types of waste be eliminated?

Benefits of lean production

Costs are saved through:

» less storage of raw materials or components
» quicker production of goods or services
» no need to repair defects or provide a replacement service for a dissatisfied customer
» better use of equipment
» cutting out some processes, which speeds up production
» less money tied up in inventories
» improved health and safety, leading to less time off work due to injury.

Reduced costs can lead to lower prices for customers, businesses being more competitive and possibly also increased profits.

Lean production can be achieved by using the following methods:

» Kaizen
» just-in-time inventory control
» cell production.

Kaizen

Kaizen means 'continuous improvement' in Japanese and its focus is on the elimination of waste. The improvement does not come from investing in new technology or equipment but through the ideas of the workers themselves. Small groups of workers meet regularly to discuss problems and possible solutions. This has proved effective because no one knows the problems that exist better than the workers who work with them all the time, so they are often the best ones to think of ways to overcome them.

Kaizen eliminates waste, for example, by getting rid of large amounts of inventory or reducing the amount of time taken for workers to walk between jobs so that they eliminate unnecessary movements. When Kaizen is introduced, the factory floor is reorganised by repositioning machines tightly together in cells, in order to improve the flow of production through the factory. The floor will be open and marked with colour-coded lines which map out the flow of materials through the production process.

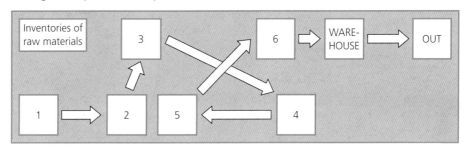

▲ The Kaizen effect: before

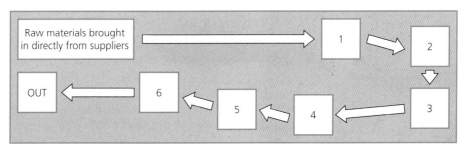

▲ The Kaizen effect: after

Activity 18.3

Identify the changes that have taken place in the reorganisation of the factory floor using Kaizen principles.

The advantages of Kaizen might be:

» increased productivity
» reduced amount of space needed for the production process
» work-in-progress is reduced
» improved layout of the factory floor may allow some jobs to be combined, thereby freeing up employees to carry out some other job in the factory.

Just-in-time inventory control

Just-in-time or **JIT** is a production method which focuses on reducing or virtually eliminating the need to hold inventories of raw materials or components and on reducing work-in-progress and inventories of the finished product. The raw materials or components are delivered just in time to be used in the production process, the making of any parts is undertaken just in time to be used in the next stage of production and the finished product is made just in time to be delivered to the customer.

» All this reduces the costs of holding inventory, as no raw materials and components are ordered to keep in the warehouse just in case they are needed.
» Warehouse space is not needed, again reducing costs.
» The finished product is sold quickly and so money will come back to the business more quickly, helping its cash flow.

To operate just-in-time, inventories of raw materials, work-in-progress and finished products are run down and no extra inventory is kept. The business therefore needs very reliable suppliers and an efficient system of ordering raw materials or components.

Cell production

Cell production is where the production line is divided into separate, self-contained units (cells), each making an identifiable part of the finished product, instead of having a flow or mass production line. This method of production improves the morale of the employees and makes them work harder so they become more efficient. The employees feel more valued and are less likely to strike or cause disruption.

Definitions to learn

Just-in-time (JIT) is a production method that involves reducing or virtually eliminating the need to hold inventories of raw materials or unsold inventories of the finished product.

Key info

JIT is not just used by manufacturing businesses. Service providers such as hotels and fast-food restaurants can reduce waste and lower costs by only ordering food and other supplies as and when needed – as long as they arrive 'just in time' to provide a good customer service.

➡ Case study

Tara wanted to start her own business. She knew that Thai food restaurants were very popular and she was an excellent cook of Thai food. She decided to start cooking dishes of Thai food and selling them to local people for dinner parties. She advertised in the local newspaper and used her own kitchen to prepare the food. Customers would ask her to cook a particular dish of their choice and she would cook it especially for them just how they wanted it. The food was extremely popular and soon she had many more orders for dinner parties than she could cope with and had to turn down customers.

So Tara decided to rent a small factory unit in which she could put large cookers. She expanded and took on several employees to help her. The number of orders received continued to grow as her reputation for producing excellent food spread. Shops started to order large quantities of a particular dish and they would sell it to customers in smaller containers as a takeaway dinner which they could heat up at home. In the new premises Tara did things slightly differently. Now, instead of making one pan of a particular dish, she would make a large quantity in one go and then divide it into large containers ready to be sent out for sale. She would then make a large quantity of another dish, and so on. Still the popularity of the food grew!

After about two years of expanding at the small factory unit, Tara decided she could afford to buy much larger premises and invest in new automated machinery to cook the food. The demand was there, the food sold to airlines, hotels and supermarkets, as well as the original shops. The new automated process would produce particular dishes in very large quantities, and would produce the same dish continually.

> ### Activity 18.4
>
> Read the case study on page 220.
>
> **a** What are the different methods of production that Tara used as her business expanded?
>
> **b** Why do you think she changed production methods as her businesses expanded?

Methods of production

Tara used three main methods of production during the growth of her company:

» **job production**
» **batch production**
» **flow production**.

Job production

This is where products are made specifically to order, for example, a customer would order a particular dish and Tara would make it. Each order is different, and may or may not be repeated. Other examples include: specialist machinery manufacturers that will produce a machine for another business to meet a particular specification, bridges, ships, made-to-measure suits, cinema films, or individual computer programs that perform specialised tasks.

Advantages of job production

» It is most suitable for personal services or 'one-off' products.
» The product meets the exact requirements of the customer.
» The workers often have more varied jobs (they don't carry out just one task).
» More varied work increases employee motivation – giving them greater job satisfaction.
» It is flexible and often used for high-quality goods and services, meaning that a higher price can be charged.

Disadvantages of job production

» Skilled labour is often used and this raises costs.
» The costs are higher because it is often labour intensive.
» Production often takes a long time.
» Products are specially made to order and so any errors can be expensive to correct.
» Materials may have to be specially purchased, leading to higher costs.

Batch production

This is where similar products are made in blocks or batches. A certain number of one product is made, then a certain number of another product is made, and so on. Tara made a batch of one type of dish and then made a batch of another type of dish, and so on. Other examples include: a small bakery making batches of bread, several houses built together using the same design, furniture production (a certain number of tables are made, then a certain number of chairs), or clothing (a batch of a particular size of jeans is produced and then a batch of another size).

Advantages of batch production

» It is a flexible way of working and production can easily be changed from one product to another.
» It still gives some variety to workers' jobs.
» It allows more variety to products which would otherwise be identical. This gives more consumer choice (for example, different flavours of ready-meals).
» Production may not be affected to any great extent if machinery breaks down.

Disadvantages of batch production

» It can be expensive as semi-finished products will need moving about to the next production stage.
» Machines have to be reset between production batches which means there is a delay in production and output is lost.
» Warehouse space will be needed for inventories of raw materials, components and finished batches of goods. This is costly.

Flow production

This is when large quantities of a product are produced in a continuous process. It is sometimes referred to as mass production because of the large quantity of a standardised product that is produced.

It is called flow production because products look as if they are flowing down the production line (they move continuously along a production line). The basic ingredients are put together at one end of the production line and then the product moves down and more parts are added, and so on, until the product is finished and packaged ready for sale. Large numbers of identical products are made and the costs of production are low (the business will gain from economies of scale). Examples of products produced in this way include: cars, cameras, televisions, packaged foods and drinks; in fact any mass produced, standardised product which is sold to a mass market will be produced in this way.

Advantages of flow production

» There is a high output of a standardised product.
» Costs of making each item are kept low and therefore prices are also lower.
» It is easy for capital-intensive production methods to be used – reducing labour costs and increasing efficiency.
» Capital-intensive methods allow workers to specialise in specific, repeated tasks and therefore the business may require only relatively unskilled workers – little training may be needed.
» It may benefit from economies of scale in purchasing.
» Low average costs and therefore low prices usually mean high sales.
» Automated production lines can operate 24 hours a day.
» There is no need to move goods from one part of the factory to another as with batch production, so time is saved.

Disadvantages of flow production

» It is a very boring system for the workers, so there is little job satisfaction, leading to a lack of motivation for employees.
» There are significant storage requirements – costs of inventories of raw materials/components and finished products can be very high unless just-in-time systems are used.

» The capital costs of setting up the production line can be very high.

» If one machine breaks down the whole production line will have to be halted.

Factors affecting which method of production to use

The factors which determine which method of production to use are as follows:

» *The nature of the product.* If a fairly unique product or an individual service is required (in fact many services are individual to the customer and will be specifically tailored to their requirements), job production will be used. If the product can be mass produced using an automated production line then flow production will be used.

» *The size of the market.* If demand is higher and more products can be sold but not in very large quantities, batch production will be used. The product will be produced in a certain quantity to meet the particular order. Small local markets or niche markets will be served by businesses using job or batch production. International markets are served by businesses using flow production.

» *The nature of demand.* If there is a large and fairly steady demand for the product, such as soap powder, it becomes economical to set up a production line and continuously produce the product (flow production). If demand is less frequent, such as for furniture, then production may be more likely to be job or batch production.

» *The size of the business.* If the business is small and does not have the access to large amounts of capital then it will not produce on a large scale using automated production lines. Only large businesses can operate on this scale. Small businesses are more likely to use job or batch production methods.

Activity 18.5

a What method of production is used by each of the following businesses? Explain the reasons for your choice.
   • Walls manufactures well-known brands of ice cream. The ice creams are sold in many different shops and other outlets, and millions are sold a year.
   • Alexander is a hairdresser. He styles men's hair and has a number of regular customers.

b Hudson Limited has been in business for ten years manufacturing components for cars. It sells to several large car producers. Hudson Limited wants to expand and manufacture components for aircraft engines. It has decided to build a new factory abroad, near to where aircraft engines are manufactured. Some of the new components it plans to produce will be designed for only one type of engine, whereas most of the other components will be standardised and used in several different models of engine. Hudson Limited has chosen the new site for the factory but has not decided on the method of production to use. You have been asked to advise it on what to use. Explain your choice of the method(s) of production it should use.

How technology has changed production methods

Technological advances have allowed the mechanisation and automation of production methods in many industries. For example, the car industry is almost entirely automated. The use of automation, robotics and CAD/CAM keeps businesses ahead of the competition, keeps costs falling, reduces prices and improves the products manufactured.

>> *Automation* is where the equipment used in the factory is controlled by a computer to carry out mechanical processes, such as paint-spraying on a car assembly line. The production line will consist mainly of machines and only a few people will be needed to ensure that everything proceeds smoothly.

>> *Mechanisation* is where the production is done by machines but operated by people, for example, a printing press. Robots are machines that are programmed to do tasks, and are particularly useful for unpleasant, dangerous and difficult jobs. They are quick, very accurate and work non-stop, 24 hours a day.

>> *CAD (computer-aided design)* is computer software that draws items being designed more quickly and allows them to be rotated to see the item from all sides instead of having to draw it several times. It is used to design new products or to re-style existing products. It is particularly useful for detailed technical drawings.

>> *CAM (computer-aided manufacture)* is where computers monitor the production process and control machines or robots on the factory floor. For example, on the production line of a car plant computers will control the robots that spot-weld the car body together or the robots that spray paint the car.

>> *CIM (computer-integrated manufacturing)* is the total integration of computer-aided design (CAD) and computer-aided manufacturing (CAM). The computers that design the products are linked directly to the computers that aid the manufacturing process.

Technology has also improved productivity in shops with electronic payment methods and scanners at the tills.

>> *EPOS (electronic point of sale)*. This is used at checkouts where the operator scans the barcode of each item individually. The price and description of the item is displayed on the checkout monitor and printed on the till receipt. The inventory record is automatically changed to show one item has been sold and if inventory is low (at the reorder point) then more inventory can be automatically ordered.

>> *EFTPOS (electronic funds transfer at point of sale)*. This is where the electronic cash register is connected to the retailer's main computer and also to banks over a wide area computer network. The shopper's card will be swiped at the till and the bank information will automatically be read from the card. The money will be directly debited from the customer's account after they have signed for the debit to be made or have entered their PIN (personal identification number). A receipt will be printed as confirmation that the payment has gone out of the customer's account.

>> *Contactless payment* is increasingly being used in many countries. It is a fast, easy and secure way to pay for purchases that are less than a small amount, for example, in the UK this is £30 or less. Sometimes larger transactions can be made but then a passcode, fingerprint or some other way is used to ensure this is a correct transaction. Pre-paid, debit, charge and credit cards, key fobs, wearable devices such as watches and wristbands, and mobile devices, such as smartphones and tablets, can be used to make contactless payments.

It works by the contactless device having an antenna. When it is touched against a contactless terminal, it securely transmits information about the purchase.

> ## Activity 18.6
> Using the internet, research contactless payment methods and when they can be used. What are the advantages and disadvantages of using this method of payment both for the customer and the business?

The advantages of new technology

» Productivity is greater as new, more efficient production methods are used, reducing average costs.
» Greater job satisfaction stimulates workers, as routine and boring jobs are now done by machines.
» More skilled workers may be needed to use and maintain the new technology. Businesses must offer training to existing workers in the use of new technology. The workers may become more motivated and therefore improve the quality of their work.
» Better quality products are produced owing to more accurate production methods.
» Quicker communication and reduced paperwork, owing to computers, lead to increased profitability.
» The information that is available to managers through the use of IT is much greater and this should result in better and quicker decision making.
» New 'high tech' products are introduced as new technology makes completely new products available.

The disadvantages of new technology

» Unemployment could rise as machines/computers replace people on the factory floor and in offices.
» It is expensive to invest in new technology products and machinery. This increases the risks as large quantities of products need to be sold to cover the cost of purchasing the equipment.
» Employees may be unhappy with the changes in their work practices when new technology is introduced.
» New technology is changing all the time and will often become outdated quite quickly and need to be replaced if the business is to remain competitive.

Key info

In the United States of America it has been estimated by the NBER (National Bureau of Economic Research) that hundreds of thousands of jobs will be replaced by automation. The NBER recently stated that roughly three workers have been eliminated for each new individual industrial robot.

Study tips

Make sure you can discuss the effects of new technology on employers and employees. How are the effects different?

> ## Activity 18.7
> a Choose a business that manufactures a product and find out what new technology/equipment has been installed in the Operations department over the last five years.
> b What are the advantages and disadvantages of these changes?
> c How have these changes affected the business (for example, employment, profits, sales, quality of the products)?

> ## Activity 18.8
> a Choose a business that produces a service and find out what new technology/equipment has been installed in the business over the last five years. (This will probably be computers or specialised computer software.)
> b What are the advantages and disadvantages of these changes?
> c How have these changes affected the business (for example, employment, profits, sales, quality of service)?

International business in focus

Technology in banking

Nigerian banks, for example, GT Bank, Oceanic Bank, Zenith Bank and Intercontinental Bank, have found that most Nigerians are gradually losing the desire to carry cash around and most customers prefer banks with efficient online banking facilities as they do not like to queue in branch banks. Increasing profits and increasing the number of customers is a major incentive to change the way they provide banking services.

The impact of technology in banking is leading to fewer branch banks with face-to-face services and to new channels of accessing banking services such as automated teller machines (ATMs), internet banking, point of sale terminals (POS) and mobile (cell) phone banking. Using these technologies allows banks to achieve economies of scale as well as responding to customers' preferences.

Discussion points

- Why are Nigerian banks changing the way they provide bank services?

- How is technology changing the way banks provide their services to customers?

- What benefits do the banks gain from introducing more technology into their business?

Exam-style questions: Short answer and data response

1 Carlos owns a private limited company called BettaBakers Limited. It produces bread loaves and a variety of cakes which are sold in local shops. The method of production used by BettaBakers is batch production. Carlos says, 'I have been told that lean production techniques in the bakery would help me to increase productivity and profits.'

   a Define 'lean production'. [2]

   b Identify **two** ways lean production might be achieved. [2]

   c Outline **two** ways, other than lean production, that Carlos could increase productivity. [4]

   d Explain **two** advantages to Carlos of using batch production. [6]

   e Do you think Carlos should change his production method to flow production in the bakery? Justify your answer. [6]

2 Mr Patel owns a business which manufactures wooden furniture. He uses traditional labour-intensive methods of production in the factory. Workers measure, cut and shape the wood needed for each piece of furniture. The furniture is made using job production to the exact requirements of each customer. Mr Patel is worried about the level of efficiency in his factory and wants to improve productivity. He is thinking of introducing new technology into his factory.

   a Define 'productivity'. [2]

   b Identify **two** benefits to Mr Patel of increasing productivity. [2]

   c Outline **two** ways technology could change production methods for Mr Patel. [4]

   d Explain **two** disadvantages of using job production for Mr Patel. [6]

   e Do you think Mr Patel should introduce new technology into his factory? Justify your answer. [6]

Revision checklist

In this chapter you have learned:

✔ what 'production' means
✔ the difference between production and productivity
✔ about how businesses can increase efficiency and the benefits of achieving this
✔ the reasons why businesses hold inventories
✔ what lean production is and how it can be achieved
✔ the advantages and disadvantages of different production methods and how to recommend a suitable production method
✔ how technology is bringing about change in production methods.

NOW – test your understanding with the revision questions in the Student etextbook and the Workbook.

Costs, scale of production and break-even analysis

This chapter will explain:

- ★ how to classify costs – fixed, variable, average, total; use examples to illustrate these
- ★ how to use cost data to help make simple cost-based decisions, e.g. to stop production or continue
- ★ the concept of economies of scale with examples, e.g. purchasing, marketing, financial, managerial, technical
- ★ the concept of diseconomies of scale with examples, e.g. poor communication, lack of commitment from employees, weak coordination
- ★ the concept of break-even
- ★ how to construct, complete or amend a simple break-even chart
- ★ how to interpret a given chart and use it to analyse a situation
- ★ how to calculate break-even output from given data
- ★ the definition, calculation and interpretation of the margin of safety
- ★ how to use break-even analysis to help make simple decisions, for example, impact of higher price
- ★ the limitations of break-even analysis.

Business costs

All business activities involve costs of some sort. These costs cannot be ignored. For example, the manager of a business is planning to open a new factory making sports shoes. Why does the manager need to think about costs? Some of the reasons are explained below.

» The costs of operating the factory can be **compared** with the revenue from the sale of the sports shoes to calculate whether or not the business will make a profit or loss. This calculation is one of the most important made in any business.
» The costs of **two different locations** for the new factory can be **compared**. This would help the owner make the best decision.
» To help the manager decide **what price** should be charged for a pair of sports shoes.

Accurate cost information is therefore very important for managers.

Definitions to learn

Fixed costs are costs which do not vary in the short run with the number of items sold or produced. They have to be paid whether the business is making any sales or not. They are also known as overhead costs.
Variable costs are costs which vary directly with the number of items sold or produced.

> ### Activity 19.1
>
> These are some of the costs involved in opening and operating a new sports shoe factory:
>
> - rent of the factory
> - insurance of the factory
> - bank fees
> - raw materials used
> - management salaries.
>
> Add six other costs to this list that the owner would have to pay.

Fixed costs and variable costs

In calculating the costs of the business it is important to understand the difference between different types of costs. The main types of costs are **fixed costs** and **variable costs**. Examples of fixed costs include management salaries and rent paid for property. Even if output was zero, these costs would still have to be paid. Examples of variable costs include material costs and piece-rate labour costs. The more units that are produced, the higher these variable costs will be.

Business costs

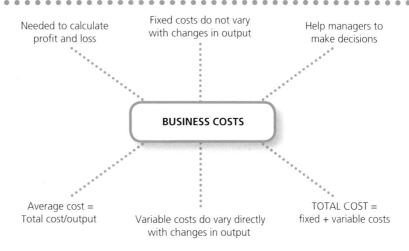

Total cost and average cost

Study tips

Avoid making this mistake: 'Fixed costs do not vary over time'. This is not true because a business might expand by building a new shop, factory or offices. Fixed costs are those that do not vary with the output of the business, given the existing factory, shop or office buildings.

Definitions to learn

Total costs are fixed and variable costs combined.
Average cost per unit is the total cost of production divided by total output (sometimes referred to as 'unit cost').

> ## Activity 19.2
>
> Separate the costs listed in Activity 19.1 on page 228 and the six additional costs on your list into two lists: fixed costs and variable costs. Explain why you have put each cost under either 'fixed costs' or 'variable costs'.

The **total costs** of a business, during a period of time, are all fixed costs added to all variable costs of production. This total figure can then be compared with the sales revenue for the period to calculate the profit or loss made.

An **average cost per unit** can be calculated from the total cost figure. Average cost is the total cost of production divided by total output. For a sports shoe manufacturer producing 30 000 pairs of shoes each year, this could be calculated as follows:

Stage 1

Total costs of production ($150 000) = fixed costs ($50 000) + total variable costs ($100 000)

Stage 2

$$\text{Average cost of production} = \frac{\text{Total costs of production (in a time period)}}{\text{Total output (in a time period)}}$$

$$= \frac{\$150\,000}{30\,000} = \$5 \text{ per pair}$$

If both the average cost of production and the level of output is known, then total cost can be calculated by multiplying average cost per unit by output.

Total cost = average cost per unit × output

Activity 19.3: Calculating total cost and average cost

A car manufacturer produces three models of vehicle, X, Y and Z. It has calculated the costs of these three products to be as follows:

	X	Y	Z
Variable material costs ($ m)	5	10	8
Variable labour costs ($ m)	10	14	6
Allocated fixed costs ($ m)	9	12	6
Annual output of vehicles	4000	12 000	5000

The total variable cost of manufacturing Model X = $15 million

Total cost of manufacturing Model X = $15 million + $9 million = $24 million

The average cost per unit of X = $\dfrac{\$24\,000\,000}{4000\ units}$ = $6000 *per vehicle*

a Calculate the total variable cost of manufacturing vehicle Models Y and Z.
b Calculate the total cost of manufacturing Models Y and Z.
c Calculate the average cost of manufacturing Models Y and Z.
d Identify and explain two possible uses of these results to managers of the car manufacturer.

Using cost data

Once a business has classified all costs into either fixed or variable, this information can be used to help make business decisions. Here are three examples.

Use of cost data	Example	Explanation
Setting prices	Average cost of making a pizza = $3. If the business wants to make $1 profit on each pizza sold, it will charge a price of $4. See Chapter 13 for more examples of cost-based pricing.	If the average cost per unit is not known, the business could charge a price that leads to a loss being made on each item sold.
Deciding whether to stop production or continue	If the total annual cost of producing a product is $25 000 **but** the total revenue is only $23 000, then the business is making a loss and could decide to stop making the product.	No business wants to continue to make a loss, but the decision to stop making a product will also depend on whether: • the product has just been launched on the market – sales revenue might increase in future • the fixed costs will still have to be paid, e.g. if the factory being used for the product is not sold.
Deciding on the best location	Location A for a new shop has total annual costs of $34 000. Location B for a new shop has total annual costs of $50 000. On this data alone, Location A should be chosen.	Costs are not the only factor to consider – there might not be any point in choosing a low-cost location for a new shop if it is in the worst part of town!

Economies of scale and diseconomies of scale

Look again at the definition of average cost on page 229. It is the cost of producing one unit of output. Would you expect all businesses in the same industry to have the same average costs? This would be rather unlikely.

> ### ➡ Case study: Cost of making bricks
>
> Consider the average cost and total output of the following two businesses, which both make bricks.
>
> | | Brick Co. A | Brick Co. B |
> |---|---|---|
> | Total output per year | 10 million | 1 million |
> | Average cost per brick | 50 cents | 75 cents |
>
> The bigger company has much lower average costs than the smaller one. This cost advantage results from the economies of being a large business. These are called the **economies of scale**.

Definitions to learn

Economies of scale are the factors that lead to a reduction in average costs as a business increases in size.

▶ Activity 19.4

Read the case study above.

Explain **three** possible reasons why the unit cost of making bricks is lower for Brick Co. A than for Brick Co. B.

Economies of scale

There are five economies of scale.

Purchasing economies

When businesses buy large numbers of components, for example, materials or spare parts, they are able to gain discounts for buying in bulk. This reduces the unit cost of each item bought and gives the firm an advantage over smaller businesses which buy in small quantities.

Marketing economies

There are several advantages for a large business when marketing its products. It might be able to afford to purchase its own vehicles to distribute goods rather than depending on other firms. Transport costs will be reduced by using larger vehicles. Advertising rates in papers and on television do not go up in the same proportion as the size of an advertisement ordered by the business. The business will not need twice as many sales staff to sell ten product lines as a smaller firm needs to sell five.

Financial economies

Larger businesses are often able to raise capital more cheaply than smaller ones. Bank managers often consider that lending to large organisations is less risky than lending to small ones. A lower rate of interest is therefore often charged.

Managerial economies

Small businesses cannot usually afford to pay for specialist managers, for example, marketing managers and qualified accountants. This tends to reduce their efficiency. Larger companies can afford specialists and this increases their efficiency and helps to reduce their average costs.

Study tips

Economies of scale can result in lower average (or unit) costs, not lower total costs. A large business is likely to have higher total costs than a small one – but lower average costs. Make sure you can explain this.

Definitions to learn

Diseconomies of scale are the factors that lead to an increase in average costs as a business grows beyond a certain size.

Technical economies

There are many of these, but a few examples will help to show how important they can be. Transport costs can be cut by a large amount when using larger ships and vehicles. Large manufacturing firms often use flow production methods (see Chapter 18). These apply the principle of the division of labour. Specialist machines are used to produce items in a continuous flow with workers responsible for just one stage of production. Small businesses cannot usually afford this expensive equipment. It could also be that they sell their products in small quantities and flow production could not be justified. The use of flow production and the latest equipment will reduce the average costs for the large manufacturing businesses.

In addition, some machinery is only made with a certain high output capacity. For example, an automatic welding machine can do 100 welds a minute. A small firm, if it bought such a machine, could not keep the machine working all day and the average cost of using it would be high. This is because the machinery is not 'divisible' into smaller capacity machines.

Diseconomies of scale

Is it possible for a business to become so large that it becomes less and less efficient? Is there a limit to economies of scale? Some research suggests that very large businesses may become less efficient than the smaller ones and this could lead to higher average costs for big firms.

How is this possible? It could occur because of certain **diseconomies of scale**.

Poor communication

The larger the organisation the more difficult it becomes to send and receive accurate messages. If there is slow or inaccurate communication then serious mistakes can occur which lead to lower efficiency and higher average costs. Poor communication in a large business with many managers is considered in Chapter 9.

Lack of commitment from employees

Large businesses can employ thousands of workers. It is possible that one worker will never see the top managers of the business. Workers may feel that they are unimportant and not valued by the management. In small firms it is possible to establish close relationships between workers and top managers. The lack of these relationships in a large business can lead to a lack of commitment and low efficiency among the workers. This will tend to push up average costs.

Weak coordination

It often takes longer for decisions made by managers to reach all parts of a large business and different groups of workers. This could make it difficult to coordinate the work and decisions of all parts of the business and ensure that they are working towards the same objectives. Employees could also take a long time to react to a managerial decision once it has been taken. The top managers will be so busy directing the affairs of the business that they may have no contact at all with the customers of the business. They could become too removed from the products and markets the business operates in.

It is very difficult to 'prove' that these diseconomies exist in practice. However, many very large businesses are now breaking themselves up into smaller units which can control themselves and communicate more effectively. This trend is aimed at preventing diseconomies of scale that reduce efficiency and raise average costs.

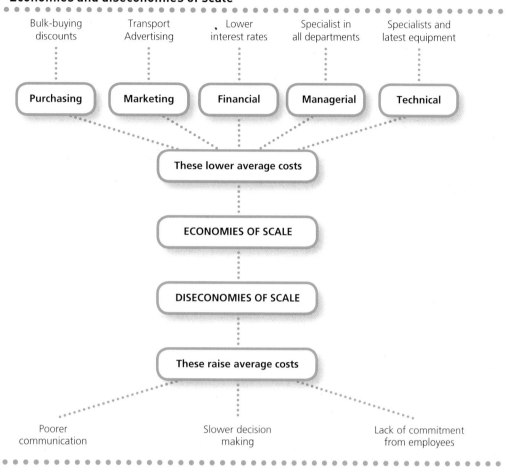

REVISION SUMMARY

Economies and diseconomies of scale

Bulk-buying discounts → **Purchasing**

Transport Advertising → **Marketing**

Lower interest rates → **Financial**

Specialist in all departments → **Managerial**

Specialists and latest equipment → **Technical**

These lower average costs

ECONOMIES OF SCALE

DISECONOMIES OF SCALE

These raise average costs

Poorer communication

Slower decision making

Lack of commitment from employees

> ## Activity 19.5: Comparing costs between two businesses
>
> The following cost data has been collected from two shoe manufacturing companies.
>
> | | Company A | Company B |
> |---|---|---|
> | Annual output – pairs of shoes | 20 000 | 700 000 |
> | Variable cost per shoe | $4 | $2.50 |
> | Annual fixed costs | $120 000 | $2.1m |
>
> **a** Calculate the total annual cost of manufacturing shoes for both businesses.
> **b** Calculate the average cost per unit (pair of shoes).
> **c** Explain **three** reasons why the average total cost (per unit) for Company B is lower than for Company A.
> **d** Explain **two** benefits gained by Company B as a result of lower average cost (cost per unit).

Break-even charts: comparing costs with revenue

The concept of break-even

'Break-even' is a very important idea for any business – especially a newly set up business. The **break-even level of output** or sales indicates to the owner or manager of a business the minimum level of output that must be sold so that total costs are covered. At this break-even level of output it is important to note that a profit is **not** being made – **but** neither is a loss! The 'quicker' a newly set up business can reach break-even point the more likely it is to survive – and go on to make a profit. If a business never reaches break-even point then it will always make a loss.

The break-even level of output can be worked out in two ways – by drawing a break-even chart or graph and by calculation.

Drawing a break-even chart

In order to draw a **break-even chart** we need information about the fixed costs, variable costs and **revenue** of a business. For example, in a sports shoe business we will assume that:

» fixed costs are $5000 per year
» the variable costs of each pair of shoes are $3
» each pair of shoes is sold for a price of $8
» the factory can produce a maximum output of 2000 pairs of shoes per year.

To draw a break-even chart it will help if a table, such as the one below, is completed. Take note of variable costs and revenue when no output is being produced. Clearly, there will be no variable costs as no shoes are being made and, as no shoes are being sold, there will be no revenue.

	Sales ($) = 0 units	Sales ($) = 500 units	Sales ($) = 2000 units
Fixed costs	5000	5000	5000
Variable costs	0	1500	6000
Total costs	5000	6500	11 000
Revenue	0	4000	16 000

When output is 2000 units, variable costs will be: 2000 × $3 = $6000.

Assuming all output is sold, total revenue will be: 2000 × $8 = $16 000.

Make sure you understand how the other figures were arrived at before looking at how the data is used to construct a break-even graph.

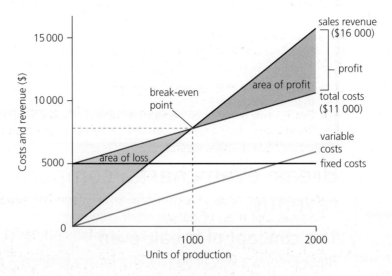

Now we can plot the information on the graph. Note the following points:

» The *y*-axis (the vertical axis) measures money amounts – costs and revenue.
» The *x*-axis (the horizontal axis) shows the number of units produced and sold.
» The fixed costs do not change at any level of output.
» The total cost line is the addition of variable costs and fixed costs.

What does the graph show?

The **break-even point** of production is where total costs and total revenue cross. The business must therefore sell 1000 pairs of shoes in order to avoid making a loss.

At production below the break-even point, the business is making a loss. At production above the break-even point, it makes a profit. Maximum profit is made when maximum output is reached and this is a profit level of $5000.

➡ Case study: Is Namib Tyres breaking even?

Namib Tyres Ltd produces motorcycle tyres. The following information about the business has been obtained:

- Fixed costs are $30 000 per year.
- Variable costs are $5 per unit.
- Each tyre is sold for $10.
- Maximum output is 10 000 tyres per year.

▶ Activity 19.6

Read the case study above.

a   Copy this table and fill in the missing figures.

	Output = 0	Output = 10 000
Fixed costs	x	$30 000
Variable costs	0	a
Total costs	y	b
Revenue	z	$100 000

b   Draw a break-even chart from the information in the table.
c   From your break-even chart identify:
   • the break-even level of output
   • the level of profit at maximum output.

Uses of break-even charts

Apart from the use we have already made of these graphs – identifying the break-even point of production and calculating maximum profit – there are other benefits of break-even charts.

Advantages of break-even charts

» Managers are able to read off from the graph the **expected profit or loss** to be made at any level of output.
» The impact on profit or loss of certain business decisions can also be shown by **redrawing the graph**. Consider again the sports shoe business. What would happen to the break-even point and the maximum output level if the manager decided to increase the selling price to $9 per pair? This new situation can be shown on another break-even chart.

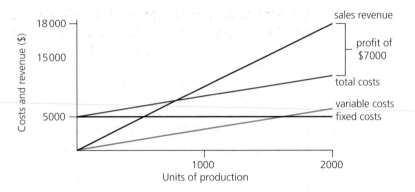

Definitions to learn

Margin of safety is the amount by which sales exceed the break-even point.

» Maximum revenue now rises to $18 000. The break-even point of production falls to 833 units and maximum profit rises to $7000. Seems like a wise decision! However, the manager needs to consider competitors' prices too and he may not be able to sell all 2000 pairs at $9 each. This point is explained below.

» The break-even chart can also be used to **show the margin of safety** – the amount by which sales exceed the break-even point. In the graph above, if the firm is producing 1000 units, the safety margin is 167 units (1000 – 833). However, if it sells 2000 units then the margin of safety is 1167 units. The higher the margin of safety, the better. It means that if sales were to fall for any reason then it is likely that the business will still be making a profit because sales have to fall much further before the break-even point is reached or even a loss made.

Activity 19.7

Refer to the data about sports shoes on page 234.

a Draw a new break-even chart to show a reduction in variable costs to $2 per pair of shoes as a result of the manager buying cheaper materials.
[Assume that the manager keeps the price at $8 per pair of shoes.]

b Compare your break-even chart with the one showing the increase in selling price. Would you advise the manager to raise the price of shoes or to use cheaper raw materials? Justify your answer

Limitations of break-even charts

The break-even chart is therefore useful to managers, but the technique does have some limitations, as listed below. These must be remembered by managers whenever they use these charts to help them take decisions.

» Break-even charts are constructed assuming that all goods produced by the firm **are actually sold** – the graph does not show the possibility that inventories may build up if not all goods are sold.

» Fixed costs only remain constant if the **scale of production does not change**. For example, a decision to double output is almost certainly going to increase fixed costs. In the case of the sports shoe business, an increase in output above 2000 will need a larger factory and more machinery.

» Break-even charts concentrate on the break-even point of production, but there are **many other aspects of the operations of a business** which need to be analysed by managers, for example, how to reduce wastage or how to increase sales.

» The simple charts used in this section have **assumed that costs and revenues can be drawn with straight lines**. This will not often be the case; for example, increasing output to the capacity of a factory may involve paying overtime wage rates to production workers. This will make the variable cost line slope more steeply upwards as output expands. Also, in order to increase sales a business may need to offer discounts for large orders and this will cause the slope of the revenue line to be less steep.

Activity 19.8: Using break-even analysis

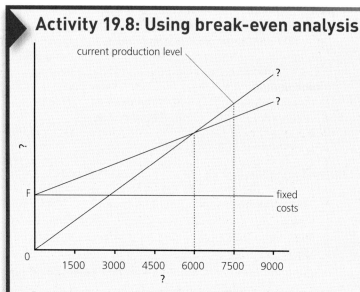

a Draw out this break-even graph and complete it with the following information:
  * Fixed costs = $6000.
  * Variable costs per unit = $1.
  * Selling price = $2.
  * Label all of the lines/axes.
b Identify from your graph: the break-even level of output; the current safety margin; the level of profit at an output level of 9000.
c Explain what would happen to profit at an output of 9000 units, and the break-even point of production if the selling price was increased to $3.
d Explain why the business might decide **not** to increase the price to $3.

REVISION SUMMARY

Uses and limitations of break-even charts

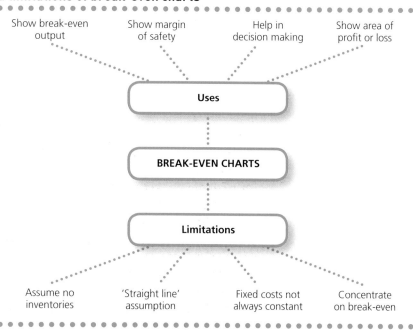

Break-even point: the calculation method

It is not always necessary to draw a break-even chart in order to show the break-even point of production. It is possible to calculate this. Study the following example.

> ## Case study
>
> Cape Designs Ltd makes wooden desks. The selling price of each desk is $50. The variable costs of materials and production labour are $20. The weekly fixed costs are $6000. What is the break-even level of production? It is necessary to calculate the **contribution** of each desk. This is the selling price less the variable cost per unit.
>
> The calculation for the contribution of each desk is:
>
> Selling price – Variable cost = Contribution
>
> $50 – $20 = $30
>
> Each desk gives a contribution to fixed costs and gross profit of $30. In order to break even each week, the business must make sufficient desks, contributing $30 each, to cover the fixed costs of $6000.
>
> The following formula should be used:
>
> $$\text{Break-even level of production} = \frac{\text{Total fixed costs}}{\text{Contribution per unit}}$$
> $$= \frac{\$6000}{\$30} = 200 \text{ units per week}$$

Activity 19.9: Is the restaurant breaking even?

A fast-food restaurant sells meals for $6 each. The variable costs of preparing and serving each meal are $2. The monthly fixed costs of the restaurant amount to $3600.

a How many meals must be sold each month for the restaurant to break even?
b If the restaurant sold 1500 meals in one month, what was the profit made in that month?
c If the cost of the food ingredients rose by $1 per meal, what would be the new break-even level of production?

(This question could be answered by using a break-even graph.)

International business in focus

Tesla Motors – economies of scale and break-even

Tesla Motors began construction of the Gigafactory in June 2014. The 1.36 million square metre factory should be completed in 2020. When the Gigafactory is finished, it will produce more lithium ion batteries than were produced by the entire world in 2014. According to Tesla's website, 'The Gigafactory will produce batteries for significantly lower average cost using economies of scale, reduction of waste, and the simple process of locating the manufacturing process under one roof.' By producing the batteries in this volume, Tesla estimates that it can reduce the cost by over 30 per cent. This will help the company achieve the annual break-even target output of 400 000 units of its new Model 3 at a retail price of US$41 000.

Discussion points

- Discuss why it is expected that the new Tesla Gigafactory will have lower average costs for making batteries than existing factories.

- Assess ways in which a car manufacturer such as Tesla could try to reduce the break-even point of production in order to increase profits.

Exam-style questions: Short answer and data response

1 Sasha rents a market stall selling jewellery. She makes most of the jewellery herself but she also buys in items from large manufacturers. Her only other variable cost is the pay of her sales assistant, who receives a small payment for each item she sells. Sasha wants to expand her business and she has found out that there is an empty shop near her home. The fixed costs of the shop are three times greater than those of the market stall.

   a Define 'variable costs'. [2]

   b Identify **two** fixed costs that Sasha has. [2]

   c Outline **two** ways in which Sasha could reduce the break-even level of sales from her market stall. [4]

   d Explain **two** reasons why large jewellery manufacturers can produce jewellery at a lower average cost than Sasha can. [6]

   e Would you advise Sasha to close her market stall and open a shop instead? Justify your answer. [6]

2 Popsquash plc is one of the world's largest makers of soft drinks. Sales have increased in recent years but profits have not. Rising fixed and variable costs have meant that higher sales revenue has not led to higher profits. The Chief Executive recently said: 'Perhaps the company is just too big to manage efficiently.' A new factory is planned for Country Z. An incomplete break-even chart is shown.

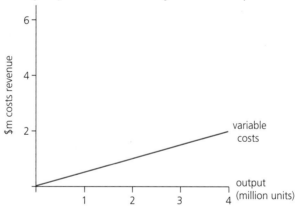

   a Define 'fixed costs'. [2]

   b Identify **two** variable costs that Popsquash plc has. [2]

   c Outline **two** reasons why a business being 'too big' can lead to higher average costs. [4]

   d Copy out and complete the break-even chart by adding:
     • fixed costs of $2 million [1]
     • total costs [2]
     • sales revenue assuming 4 million drinks are sold at $1.50 [1]
     • the break-even point of production [1]
     • profit made at 4 million drinks. [1]

   e Explain **two** ways in which Popsquash plc could try to reduce the break-even level of output in the new factory. Recommend to the Chief Executive which one the company should use. Justify your answer. [6]

Revision checklist

In this chapter you have learned:

✔ the differences between fixed costs and variable costs
✔ why cost data is useful to business managers
✔ to understand the main causes of economies of scale and diseconomies of scale
✔ to understand what the break-even level of output means
✔ how to use break-even charts to find the break-even level of output and draw simple break-even charts
✔ how to explain the uses and disadvantages of break-even analysis.

NOW – test your understanding with the revision questions in the Student etextbook and the Workbook.

Achieving quality production

This chapter will explain:

★ what quality means and why it is important for all businesses
★ the concept of quality control and how businesses implement quality control
★ the concept of quality assurance and how this can be implemented.

What quality means and why it is important for all businesses

Imagine you went shopping and bought a pair of jeans, took them home and found that they had a hole in them – you would not be a very happy customer! The business would get a bad reputation if this happened very often and would lose sales. You would probably take the jeans back to the shop and expect a replacement. If the shop refused to replace the jeans you would feel this was unfair. This is why in some countries there are laws to protect consumers so that shops have to replace faulty products or refund the price. A business needs to try to ensure that all the products or services it sells are free of faults or defects.

Quality products help businesses:

» establish a brand image
» build brand loyalty
» maintain a good reputation
» increase sales
» attract new customers.

But if quality is not maintained then businesses will:

» lose customers to other brands
» have to replace faulty products or offer to repeat a service that was poor, which raises costs
» have customers who tell other people about their experiences and this will create a bad reputation, leading to lower sales and profits.

What does **quality** mean? Quality does not necessarily mean producing an excellent product or service. Ask yourself this question – if you buy a low-priced remote-controlled toy car would you expect it to work as well as an expensive toy car? The answer will probably be no. Consumers' expectations of quality will be much higher for an expensive product than for one sold at a lower price. But you do expect the low-priced product to be 'fit for purpose', to work effectively and not have any faults.

> **Definitions to learn**
>
> **Quality** means to produce a good or a service which meets customer expectations.

Study tips

Remember that 'quality' does not necessarily mean producing a high-priced, excellent product.

Activity 20.1

What do you, as a customer, expect from the following products or services?

- A meal at McDonald's
- A meal at a restaurant at the Sail hotel in Dubai
- A Ferrari car
- Tata's Nano car
- Football lessons from a coach at a local football club
- Football lessons from the coach at Barcelona FC

A manufacturing business needs a product with a good design, that is manufactured without any faults and that satisfies the expectations of customers. A business providing services, such as hotels or banks, needs to match customer expectations with its level of customer service, customer waiting times and convenience.

Therefore, quality is a very important part of any business in both the manufacturing and service sectors. There are several ways businesses can try to ensure that they produce a good quality product or provide a good service.

Quality control

Definitions to learn

Quality control is the checking for quality at the end of the production process, whether it is the production of a product or a service. It uses quality inspectors as a way of finding any faults.

A traditional way to try to make sure that products were delivered from factories with no defects was to have **Quality Control** departments with quality inspectors whose job it was to take samples at regular intervals to check for errors. If errors or faults were found then a whole batch of production might have to be scrapped or reworked. The inspectors from the Quality Control department would check that quality was being maintained during the production of goods, try to eliminate errors before they occurred, and find any defective products before they went out of the factory to customers. A business may also use a 'mystery customer' to test out the service to check if the quality is as expected.

Definitions to learn

Quality assurance is the checking for quality standards throughout the production process by employees, whether it is the production of a product or a service.

Advantages of quality control

>> Tries to eliminate faults or errors before the customer receives the product or service.
>> Less training is required for the workers as inspectors are employed to check quality.

Drawbacks of quality control

>> Expensive as inspectors need to be paid to check the product or service.
>> Identifies faulty products but doesn't find why the fault has occurred and therefore is difficult to solve the problem.
>> High costs if products have to be scrapped or reworked or service repeated.

Quality assurance

This takes a slightly different approach to quality. The business will make sure quality standards are set and applied at all stages of production. The purpose of quality assurance is to make sure that the customer is satisfied, with the aim of achieving greater sales, increased added value and increased profits. To implement a **quality assurance** system, all aspects of production must be considered. Attention must be paid to the design of the product, the components and materials used, delivery schedules, after-sales service and quality-checking procedures. The workforce must support the use of quality standards at all stages of production or this system will not be effective.

Advantages of quality assurance

>> Tries to eliminate faults or errors at all stages of production before passing on to the next stage.
>> There are fewer customer complaints.
>> Reduced costs if products do not have to be scrapped or reworked or service repeated.

Drawbacks of quality assurance

>> Expensive to train employees to check the quality of their own work at each stage of production.
>> Relies on employees being committed to maintaining the standards set.

Total Quality Management (TQM) is one approach to implementing a quality assurance system.

Total Quality Management

The influence of Japanese management has changed the way quality is ensured in many businesses today. The idea of **Total Quality Management (TQM)** is at the heart of many practices. TQM is the continuous improvement of products and processes by focusing on quality at each and every stage of production. It tries to get it right first time and not have any defects – 'zero faults' is the TQM aim. There is an emphasis on ensuring that the customer is always satisfied, and the customer can be other people/departments in the same business that you are completing tasks for, not just the final customer. This should mean that quality is maintained throughout the business and no faults should occur, as all employees

Definitions to learn

Total Quality Management (TQM) is the continuous improvement of products and processes by focusing on quality at each and every stage of production.

are involved in accepting responsibility for a quality good or service being delivered. TQM should mean that production costs will fall. It is closely linked with Kaizen and the use of quality circles. Quality circles are where groups of workers meet regularly and discuss problems and possible solutions. Workers are encouraged to suggest new ideas to reduce waste and ensure zero defects.

Advantages of TQM

» Quality is built into every part of the production of a product or service and becomes central to the ethos of all employees.
» It eliminates all faults or errors before the customer receives the product or service as it has a 'right first time' approach.
» No customer complaints and so brand image is improved – leading to higher sales.
» Reduced costs as products do not have to be scrapped or reworked or service repeated.
» Waste is removed and efficiency increases.

Drawbacks of TQM

» It is expensive to train all employees to check the product or service.
» Relies on all employees following TQM ideology and accepting responsibility for quality.

| TOTAL QUALITY MANAGEMENT | Encourages everyone to think about quality
Quality is the aim for all staff
Customers' needs are paramount |

| QUALITY ASSURANCE | Inspection during and after production
Aim is to stop faults from happening
Aim is to ensure products attain a pre-set standard
Team working and responsibility |

| QUALITY CONTROL | Inspectors checking finished goods
Detection of components or products that are faulty
Considerable waste |

Case study

Rolls-Royce manufactures aircraft engines for international airlines, such as Emirates and Cathay Pacific. The engines are produced individually using quality assurance methods. New engines are checked at every part of the production process and also additional inspections are carried out at various stages in the process. Rolls-Royce uses a form of TQM where every employee is responsible for ensuring quality, but in addition to this it also has specially trained employees to carry out further checks on the engines to be certain of zero defects.

Study tips

Make sure you can discuss the difference between quality control and quality assurance and select an appropriate method in a given situation.

> ### Activity 20.2
>
> Read the case study on page 244.
>
> **a** Why is producing a high-quality product important to Rolls-Royce?
> **b** Do you think quality control would be a suitable method for ensuring quality at Rolls-Royce? Justify your answer.

How can a customer be assured of a quality product or service?

▲ Example **of** a quality mark

If a customer wants to be sure that a product or service will meet particular standards then they can look for a quality mark associated with the product or service. The business can apply to have this quality mark on its goods or services and it will have to follow certain rules – and be inspected to make sure that it is following them – to be able to keep this quality mark. An example is the ISO (International Organization for Standardization) which grants a business the right to use an ISO number in its literature and advertising. Some customers only purchase products from businesses that have these 'quality marks' issued to them.

Ensuring good customer service is also important to service sector businesses. They may not usually use a quality mark to show they provide a good service, but by having a good reputation and recommendations from satisfied customers they will keep repeat customers as well as gain new ones. Internet sites, such as TripAdvisor, are useful ways for businesses to gain a good reputation if satisfied customers put positive reviews on the site. Of course bad reviews will have the opposite effect and the business will lose many potential customers as well as the dissatisfied customer who posted the review.

Key info

Due to advancements in quality assurance standards and sustainable practices, Hilton Hotels has earned ISO 9001 certification for Quality Management Systems and ISO 14001 certification for Environmental Management Systems. With these certifications, Hilton Hotels can promote itself as being a quality and sustainable supplier of hotel services.

> ### Activity 20.3
>
> **a** Look at products or services that are sold in your country. Do any of them have any marks on them to show that they are a quality product?
> **b** Use the internet to find out what the International Organization for Standardization (ISO) is.
> **c** What does a business have to do to get ISO approval?
> **d** Can you find any other similar standard bodies in your country or region?
> **e** Why do you think a business would want to obtain one of these quality marks?

International business in focus

Quality at McDonald's

McDonald's restaurants have a checklist for employees to follow when serving customers. This is to ensure that a customer is always served to the standard expected by the business. McDonald's has found that ensuring the same quality standard is achieved by training employees to follow the set of rules in preparation of food as well as the service of customers.

Discussion points

- Identify which type of quality checking system McDonald's is using.

- Discuss whether this is the best method for McDonald's to use.

- Consider why McDonald's wants to ensure a quality service in its restaurants.

Exam-style questions: Short answer and data response

1 DR manufactures low-priced flip-flop shoes. It sells its flip-flop shoes through supermarkets across the country in towns and cities. 'We need to employ inspectors who use quality control when we manufacture the flip-flops to make sure they are good quality or our customers will not be happy,' said the Operations Manager.

   a Define 'quality control'. [2]
   b Identify **two** disadvantages to DR if quality is poor. [2]
   c Outline **two** benefits of using quality control to DR. [4]
   d Explain **two** possible disadvantages of using quality control to DR. [6]
   e Do you think the owners of DR should gain a quality mark, such as the ISO quality mark, for its flip-flop shoes? Justify your answer. [6]

2 LK is a private limited company and it owns and operates three cafés in a city centre. Customers expect the cafés to provide a quality service and also to be 'value for money'. There has been an increasing number of customer complaints about service waiting times and food quality. The owners of LK are planning to introduce quality assurance into their business. The city centre also has cafés which have a brand image of high-quality service but these charge high prices.

   a Define 'quality service'. [2]
   b Identify **two** possible problems for LK of an increasing number of customer complaints at its cafés. [2]
   c Outline **two** difficulties in introducing quality assurance into cafés. [4]
   d Explain **two** reasons why the owners of LK want to introduce quality assurance. [6]
   e Do you think the owners of LK should charge higher prices in the café if quality assurance is introduced? Justify your answer. [6]

Revision checklist

In this chapter you have learned:

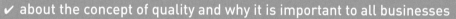

✔ about the concept of quality and why it is important to all businesses
✔ what is meant by quality control and how businesses can implement quality control
✔ about how businesses implement the concept of quality assurance.

NOW – test your understanding with the revision questions in the Student etextbook and the Workbook.

Location decisions

Location of industry

The geographical location of a business is usually considered either when the business is first setting up or when its present location proves unsatisfactory for some reason. The business environment is constantly changing and a business's objectives, for example, expansion or increasing profits, may result in a location no longer being suitable. The business may decide to look for an alternative site or may decide to set up additional factories/shops either in the home country or abroad.

Many businesses operate on a large scale and consider location globally, not just on a national or continental level. This is a feature of globalisation because businesses plan many aspects of their operations, such as location decisions, marketing and sales, on a global scale.

Factors affecting where a manufacturing business chooses to locate may be different to those factors affecting where a service sector business will set up, and so these are discussed separately even though some issues are common to both.

Factors affecting the location of a manufacturing business

Production methods and location decisions

The type of production methods used in a manufacturing business is going to have a significant influence on the location of that business.

» If job production is used, the business is likely to be on a small scale and so the influence of the nearness of components, for example, will be of less importance to the business than if flow production is used.
» If flow production is used on a large scale, the location of component suppliers might be of greater importance because a large number of components will need to be transported and the cost will be high. It also depends if JIT is used.

▲ An example of flow production

Market

Locating a factory near to the market for its products used to be thought important when the product gained weight – when it became heavier and more expensive to transport than the raw materials/components. An example might be a drinks manufacturer, where the bottles and ingredients are lighter than the filled bottles and so the factory may have to be located near to the main markets for the product.

Today, because transport links are much improved in most countries, being near to markets is of less importance, even for weight-gaining or bulk-increasing products. If the product perishes quickly and needs to be fresh when delivered to the market, such as milk, bread or cakes, the factory might be located close to its retail outlets. However, ways of preserving food for longer have reduced the importance of this factor.

Raw materials/components

The raw materials may be considerably heavier or more expensive to transport than the finished product. Where a mineral is processed from the ore, there will usually be considerable waste produced in this process. It is often cheaper to locate the ore-processing factory near to the mining site than to transport it long distances. If a particular process uses many different components, a business might look very carefully at its location. If many of these component suppliers are located near to one another, it might be preferable to locate near to these suppliers. This was often a factor in car manufacturing, where many different components are used to assemble a car, but again improved transport has lessened this influence.

If the raw material needs to be processed quickly while still fresh, locating near to the raw material source is still important. An example is frozen vegetables or tinned fruits, which need to be processed quickly. There will also be a lot of waste generated which does not go into the packaging.

External economies of scale

In addition to component suppliers, firms which support the business in other ways might need to be located nearby. Support businesses which install and maintain equipment may be better if nearby so that they can respond quickly to breakdowns. The local education establishments, such as universities, might have research departments that work with the business on developing new products – being in close contact may help the business to be more effective.

Availability of labour

To be able to manufacture products at least some labour will be necessary, even if it is not a great number. If particular skilled labour is needed, it may be easier and cheaper to recruit these employees if the business sets up in an area where people with the relevant skills live. If the manufacturing process requires a large number of unskilled workers, an area where there is high unemployment may be more suitable. Also, the wage rates paid to employees might vary and an area where wages are lower might be preferable.

Government influence

When a government wants to encourage businesses to locate in a particular area it will offer state-funded grants to encourage firms to move there. If an area has high unemployment, the government might give money to businesses which locate in that area. However, the government influence might be negative in that there might be regulations or restrictions on what businesses can do. In fact, a government can refuse to allow a business to set up altogether. An example might be where the business produces a harmful waste product during the manufacturing process and the government will not want the waste product, for example, nuclear waste, to poison the surrounding area.

Transport and communications

Businesses usually need to be near to a transport system, be it road, rail, inland waterway, port or airport. Where the product is for export, the ability to easily get to a port will be important. A nearby motorway can reduce costs by speeding up the time spent delivering the products to market even when the market is quite a distance away.

Power and water supply

Today electricity is available in most places and therefore the availability of power is not so important. But to some industries having a reliable source of power, and therefore no regular power cuts, may be essential.

The same could be said of water – a reliable supply will be needed. If large supplies of water are needed as part of the manufacturing process, for example, for cooling purposes in a power station, then being near to a water supply, such as the sea or a river, will be important.

Climate

This will not influence most manufacturing businesses but occasionally climate might be important. For instance, Silicon Valley in the USA has a very dry climate which aids the production of silicon chips.

> **Key info**
>
> The TVR sports car company is locating its new factory in Wales, close to both many specialist suppliers of car parts and the new Circuit of Wales race track which TVR will be able to use to test its cars.

> **Study tips**
>
> Make sure you can choose which location factors are the most important for a particular manufacturing business.

Factors affecting the location of manufacturing businesses

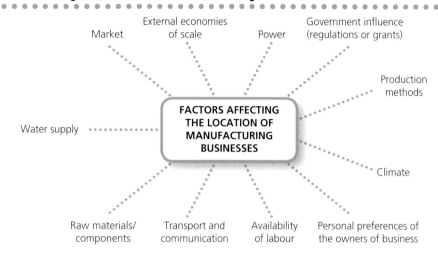

Case study

B&B plc manufactures food products. It wants to set up a factory to make a new ice cream. The new ice cream uses fresh ingredients – mainly freshly picked fruit – to maintain the fruit's flavour. The fruit used comes from one particular region of the country. This region is quite a long way away from the main cities where most of the country's population lives.

The production process is mainly automated and requires only a few skilled workers to supervise the equipment. It uses a lot of water in the mixture and also a lot of water to wash out the machinery every day to keep it clean.

The new ice cream is sold to domestic customers through supermarkets and other food stores. It is not sold abroad.

Activity 21.1

Read the case study above.

a Which factors affecting the location of manufacturing plants will be most important to this business when deciding where to locate? Explain why you think they will be important.
b Which do you think will be the most important factor and why?

Factors affecting the location of a service sector business

Customers

Locating a service sector business near its customers will be very important for certain types of services. These are usually services where direct contact between the business and the customer is required. If a quick response time is needed to serve the customers then the business needs to be located nearby. This would be true for plumbers and electricians who serve the local area in which they live. Other examples of personal services that need to be convenient for customers to use are hairdressers, beauticians, caterers, restaurants, cafés, gardeners, builders and post offices.

Some services do not need to be near to customers. Direct personal contact is not necessary as these services can be contacted by telephone, post or the internet. These businesses can therefore be located in different parts of the country or in different countries to where their customers live. With the increasing use of IT and the internet, more and more firms are becoming free from the need to locate near to their customers.

Personal preference of the owners

Business owners can influence where to locate the service centre. They often locate their business near to where they live.

Technology

Technology has allowed some services to locate away from their customers. Some services are now conducted by telephone or via the internet and therefore the business itself does not need to be near to customers, for example, website designers. These service businesses can locate anywhere and can therefore choose to locate on the outskirts of cities or even in remote areas (dependent on how many employees are required), so that they can take advantage of cheaper rent. They may even locate abroad.

Availability of labour

If a service business requires a large number of employees then it cannot locate in remote areas. It will need to locate near to a large town or city. If a particular type of skilled labour is required then it may also have to locate near to where this labour is found. However, it is more likely that the particular skilled labour will move near to the business for work rather than the other way round.

Climate

Climate will affect some businesses, particularly if they are linked to tourism in some way. Hotels often need to locate themselves where the climate is good and near to a beach.

Near to other businesses

Some services serve the needs of large businesses, such as firms that service equipment found in large companies. They will need to be nearby to respond quickly to a call to repair equipment. Services such as banks need to be near busy areas for the convenience of customers. However, internet and mobile banking has made this less important today.

Rent/taxes

If the service does not need to be on the main streets in a town or city centre, for example, doctors, dentists or lawyers, then the business will locate on the outskirts of town to benefit from lower rents and taxes.

REVISION SUMMARY

Factors affecting the location of a service sector business

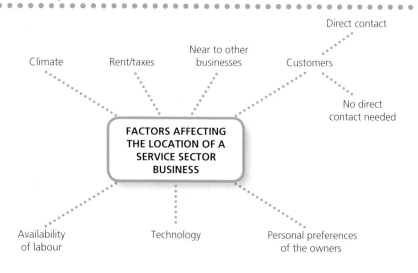

Factors affecting the location of a retailing business

Retail businesses are in the service sector but some special location factors often apply to these types of business. The following factors affect businesses that want a physical shop for their business; they want customers to be able to come into the shop and see the products. If the sales are only made online then these factors are no longer important.

Shoppers

Most retailers will want an area which is popular, such as a shopping mall/centre. The type of shopper an area attracts will also influence the attractiveness of the area to particular types of retailers. If a retailer sells expensive goods, it needs to be in an area where people on high incomes might visit; if the goods are small gift-type products, the retailer might want to be in an area visited by tourists.

Nearby shops

Being able to locate near to shops/businesses which are visited regularly, such as a post office or popular fast-food outlet, will mean that a lot of potential consumers pass the shop on the way to other shops and businesses. They might go in to make a purchase. There may be many competitors nearby. This could be bad for business, but it can also be a positive situation. If the business sells clothes, then being located near to many other clothes shops encourages people to visit the area as there is a lot of choice, therefore increasing business. If the clothes shop is in a position where there are no other similar shops nearby, it may not attract people to visit the shop as there will be limited choice.

Customer parking

Where parking is convenient and near to the shops, it will encourage shoppers to visit that area and therefore possibly increase sales. A lack of parking may put people off visiting the area and sales will be lower.

Availability of suitable vacant premises

If a suitable vacant shop or premises is not available for purchase or rent, the business may not be able to locate in the area it wishes.

Rent/taxes

The more central the site of the premises, the higher the rent and taxes will usually be. If a retail area is popular, there will be a high demand for sites in this area and therefore the cost of renting these sites will be higher. If the area is less popular, such as on the edge of town, the demand and therefore the rents will be lower.

Access for delivery vehicles

Access for delivery vehicles might be a consideration if it is very difficult for them to gain access to the premises.

Study tips

Make sure you can choose which location factors are the most important for a particular retailing business.

Security

High rates of crimes such as theft and vandalism may deter a business from locating in a particular area. Insurance companies may not want to insure the business if it is in an area of high crime. A shopping area which is patrolled by guards, even though it will be more expensive to rent the premises, might prove preferable.

Legislation

In some countries there may be laws restricting the trading or marketing of goods in particular areas.

REVISION SUMMARY   **Factors affecting the location of retailing businesses**

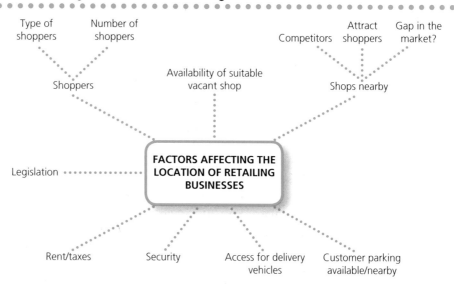

Case study

B&C Limited is going to open a new shop selling fashion shoes. The shoes are good quality and are aimed at young women. B&C Limited has narrowed down the choice of where to locate the new shop to two nearby towns.

	Town Y	Town Z
Population	30 000	10 000
% in age group: 0–9	15	20
10–25	30	35
26–40	30	30
41–65	20	10
66+	5	5
Unemployment	low	high
Crime rate	low	low
Shopping centre	large – about 100 shops	small – about 40 shops
Parking facilities	large car parks but queues build up at busy times	plenty of parking available – no problems at busy times
Types of shops in the shopping centre	clothes shops, shoe shops, banks, household goods, food shops	food shops, household goods, clothes shops, post office, banks

Activity 21.3

Read the case study above.

a Read the information on the two towns and then select which one will be the best location for the new shop. Justify your choice.
b What other information is needed to help make the final decision? Explain why the information is needed.

Factors that a business could consider when deciding in which country to locate operations

Multinational (transnational) companies have offices, factories, service operations or shops in many different countries. However, the rapid growth of newly industrialising countries, increasing international trade, improved global communications and improvements in transport have meant that many businesses can now consider where in the world to operate rather than just considering a single country; this is often called globalisation. Therefore, this means that many more businesses, other than multinationals, are considering moving to another country, either to expand their operations or sometimes to relocate entirely, many from developed countries to rapidly growing economies.

A number of factors will affect whether a business decides to relocate to another country and which country to choose.

New markets overseas

When a business sees a steady increase in its sales overseas it may decide to relocate nearer to these markets rather than transport its products from the existing manufacturing base, as it may be more cost effective. An example is JCB construction equipment, which has built additional factories in Brazil and China as well as keeping its existing factory in the UK.

If the business is in the service sector, then locating near to its customers may be essential (for example, Starbucks or Hilton Hotels). The better the forecasts for growth in these markets, the more attractive the location for business.

Cheaper or new sources of materials

If the raw material source runs out, a business must either bring in alternative supplies from elsewhere or move to a new site in a country where it can more easily obtain these supplies. This is particularly true of mineral sources such as oil wells – these need to be in the country where the oil is found. Also, it might be cheaper to use the raw materials at their source rather than transport them to another country to process.

Difficulties with the labour force and wage costs

If the business is located in a country where wage costs keep on rising, there may come a point when the business, particularly labour-intensive businesses, decides it is more profitable to relocate overseas to reduce wage costs. This has been true of many Western businesses moving their manufacturing plants to developing countries where the wages paid are much lower, e.g. Vietnam for textile products.

If particular types of skilled labour are needed by the business, it might need to relocate to a different country where it can recruit the right type of labour. This has been true for businesses which employ staff with IT skills being attracted to locate in India as it has a large number of university graduates with IT-related degrees.

Rents/taxes considerations

If other costs such as rent or taxes (on profits or personal incomes) keep increasing this might cause the business to relocate to countries where these rents or taxes are lower.

Availability of government grants and other incentives

Governments may want to encourage foreign businesses to locate in their country to bring in investment and job opportunities. They may be willing to give grants, lower taxes or other incentives to businesses to induce them to come to their country rather than go elsewhere. Governments do this because the businesses will provide jobs and possibly teach new skills and import their technology into the economy.

Trade and tariff barriers

If there are trade barriers, such as tariffs (tax on imported goods) or quotas (where a limit is placed on the quantity of imports of a particular good), then by locating in that country there will be no restrictions. An example of this is the investment by Japanese car companies in Europe to avoid the European Union's import tariffs on some imported cars.

Key info

British tea maker Twinings and automotive company Valeo are just two businesses located in Western European countries which received European Union subsidies. These helped with the establishment of new factories in Eastern European states, the extension of existing ones and the training of workers.

Study tips

Make sure you can choose which location factors are the most important for a particular business deciding which country to locate operations in.

Factors that influence a decision to locate in a different country

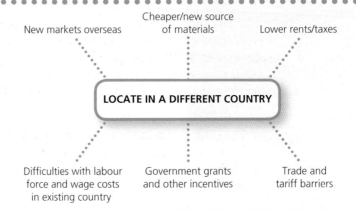

Case study

MT Furniture Limited wants to expand. Presently it is located in a small factory in the old part of the city. New markets are opening up abroad and MT has experienced a steady increase in its sales for the last five years. There is no room to build in to the existing factory and none of the adjacent factories are for sale. The business has been forced to look for another site if it wants to grow.

Because more and more of its sales are exported, it is considering whether to build a factory abroad or whether to build a larger factory in its home country. The following information has been gathered about two sites, one near MT's existing factory and one abroad in the country where most of MT's products are exported.

	Site A – on the outskirts of the city near to existing factory in home country	Site B – in the main export market overseas
Market	Large local market	Large export market and growing
Communications	Good communications – main roads connect to all parts of the country and the main port, which is several miles away	Good communications – main roads connect to all parts of the country and ports are very close to the site
Raw materials/components	Raw materials and components are close to the site – easily available	Raw materials and components are not close to the site – not easily available – some will need to be imported
Wage rates	High	Low – labour is very cheap
Skilled labour	Skilled workers employed at the present site – not too far from this site. Also additional skilled workers are available in the area	Very few skilled workers are available
Unemployment	Low	High
Rents/land taxes	High	Low
Government grants	No grants available	Grants paid towards capital investment when a new company is setting up in their country

Activity 21.4

Read the case study above.

Study the information provided and then write a report to the Board of Directors of MT Furniture Limited advising them of the advantages and disadvantages of each of the sites. Include a recommendation of which you think is the best site to choose. Remember to give reasons for your choice.

The role of legal controls on location decisions

The decisions by a firm about where to locate its business can have a very important effect on the firm's profitability. Managers will want to locate their businesses in the best possible area, taking into account factors such as cost of land, proximity to transport links and customers, availability of workers, and so on. Why do governments try to influence these location decisions? Usually for two main reasons:

» To encourage businesses to set up and expand in areas of high unemployment – in some countries these are called development areas.
» To discourage firms from locating in overcrowded areas or on sites which are noted for their natural beauty.

Two types of measures are often used by governments to influence where firms locate:

» *Planning regulations* legally restrict the business activities that can be undertaken in certain areas. For example, a business planning to open a factory in an area of residential housing might be refused planning permission. It would then be against the law for the firm to build the factory on this site. In certain parts of many countries, especially in particularly beautiful areas, it is not possible to establish any kind of business other than farming.
» *Government grants or subsidies* to businesses to encourage them to locate in undeveloped parts of the country. This assistance could be in the form of financial grants, such as a non-repayable amount of money paid to the business to locate in a particular area or subsidies paid to businesses (for example, low-rental factories). These development areas which receive government assistance usually have a very high unemployment rate and there is a great need for new jobs.

> **Study tips**
>
> Make sure you can explain why governments might intervene in the location decisions of businesses.

Case study: DEF Chemicals announces plans to build a new factory

Workers' leaders were delighted to hear today of plans by DEF Chemicals to build a huge new paint and chemicals plant in the Southern province. Many of these products will be sold abroad. The factory will create 1000 new jobs in an area badly affected by other factory closures. The new factory will require materials, components and supplies from many local firms. It is claimed that the government is planning to offer substantial grants to DEF for locating in this area of high unemployment.

However, it has insisted that it should not be too close to housing estates and schools. The grants being offered have angered other firms in the same industry as being unfair competition for them.

Local residents have mixed feelings about the plans. One elderly resident claimed: 'It will only bring more road traffic and risk of pollution. Don't forget that one DEF plant in the north was destroyed by an explosion a few years ago, killing several workers.' However, other local people welcomed the news as it will bring more businesses and wealth to the area.

> ## Activity 21.5
>
> Read the case study above.
>
> a Make a list of the stakeholders likely to be affected by DEF's plan to build a new chemical factory.
> b For each of the groups that you identified in **a**, explain why they are likely to be in support of, or are likely to oppose, these new plans.
> c Explain **three** reasons why, in your opinion, the government ought to be involved in this decision.

International business in focus

Chesapeake Bay Candle company

Chesapeake Bay Candle, a US company with its factories based in China, decided to open a new factory in the USA to supply its growing American market for candles. Rising wage costs of up to 40 per cent in China and a 6 per cent increase in shipping costs led to this decision. 'In addition to cost considerations, to be successful in the American market the business needs to be able to produce and ship the products the next day to meet the quickly changing fashions in the market,' says Ms Xu, the co-founder of the company. Import tariffs are high for Chinese-made candles being imported into the USA.

Discussion points

- Why has Ms Xu decided to build a new factory in America?

- How do you think Chesapeake Bay Candle might benefit from this location?

Exam-style questions: Short answer and data response

1 ABC Limited produces fruit juice drinks. The fruit to produce the drinks is grown locally on nearby farms. The fruit can also be imported at a cheaper price, but the quality is not as good. When producing the fruit drink there is a lot of waste from the parts of the fruit which are not used to make the drinks. Land near to the farm is available at a low price and the company wants to buy this land to expand rather than relocate the factory to another country. There is a big market for fruit drinks both at home and overseas.

   a What is meant by 'relocation of the factory'? [2]

   b Identify **two** reasons why ABC Limited buys its fruit from nearby farms. [2]

   c Outline **two** factors which influenced the location decision of ABC Limited when choosing its original site. [4]

   d Explain **two** reasons why ABC might want to buy land nearby to its existing factory to expand rather than relocate to another country. [6]

   e The government is offering grants to relocate to an area of the country with high unemployment. Do you think the managers of ABC Limited should take advantage of these grants? Justify your answer. [6]

2 SalesRUs is a chain of clothes shops. The owners are looking for a location in the city centre for a big new shop. The existing shops sell a range of clothes for men and women at low prices and are all located in busy shopping malls. There is a lot of competition from similar shops and the Managing Director thinks the new shop should not be located near to competitors.

   a Define 'competitors'. [2]

   b Identify **two** advantages of a shop being located in a small town rather than the city centre. [2]

   c Outline **two** ways the government might influence the decision of where to locate the new shop. [4]

   d Explain **two** ways in which the location chosen for the new shop might affect its profitability. [6]

   e Do you think the Managing Director is right in not wanting to locate the new shop near to its competitors' shops? Justify your answer. [6]

Revision checklist

In this chapter you have learned:

✔ to identify the relevant factors that affect the location of a manufacturing business
✔ to identify the relevant factors that affect the location of a service sector business
✔ to identify the relevant factors that affect the location of a retailing business
✔ to identify the relevant factors that a business considers when deciding which country to locate operations in
✔ about the role of legal controls on location decisions.

NOW – test your understanding with the revision questions in the Student etextbook and the Workbook.

Operations management: end-of-section case study

➡ Premium Suits

Sally owns a business called Premium Suits. It is a private limited company. The business makes suits for men using batch production and the production workers are paid an hourly wage. Sally employs 100 people who work on the production of suits. She has five employees who help her in the office but she only has one manager, who is responsible for finance. Sally carries out all the other functions for the business.

The business has grown quickly and profits have also grown rapidly over the last two years. Sally wants to continue to expand the business and increase the sales of different suits to add to her current range of medium-priced suits. There is a lot of competition for medium-priced suits and the market is not growing. She has identified two other markets for suits, both of which have increasing demand. However, she is unsure which option to choose.

- Option 1: She can start selling expensive suits that are handmade and of high-quality material. These suits would be made to measure for each customer and individually designed. The market for these suits is a niche market. She would need to employ more skilled workers.
- Option 2: She can start selling low-priced suits to the mass market. However, to enter this market Sally will need to invest in machinery to produce suits on a large scale. She could gain from economies of scale which would be an advantage.

Sally currently uses batch production. However, if she decides to follow Option 1 she will use job production and if she follows Option 2 she will use flow production.

➡ Appendix 1: Added value for Premium Suits

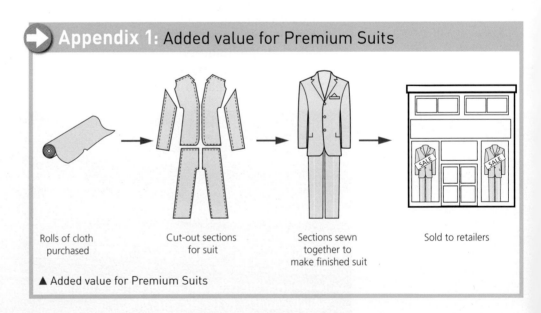

| Rolls of cloth purchased | Cut-out sections for suit | Sections sewn together to make finished suit | Sold to retailers |

▲ Added value for Premium Suits

Exam-style questions: Case study

1 a As Premium Suits grows larger it could gain from economies of scale. Explain **two** economies of scale the business might benefit from as it grows. [8]

b Quality is important to Sally. Consider the advantages and disadvantages of quality control and quality assurance. Recommend which method Sally should use to ensure quality suits are produced. Justify your answer. [12]

2 a Explain the main features of job production for Option 1 and the main features of flow production for Option 2. [8]

b Sally believes that new machinery will have advantages for the business but no disadvantages. Do you agree with Sally? Justify your answer. [12]

Optional question

3 a Appendix 1 shows added value for Sally's business. Explain **two** ways Sally could increase the added value for her suits. [8]

b Sally says that Option 1 would require a different marketing mix to Option 2. How do you think each of the elements of the marketing mix will be different for the two products in Option 1 and Option 2? Justify your answer. [12]
  - Product
  - Price
  - Promotion
  - Place

SECTION 5

Financial information and financial decisions

Chapters

22 Business finance: needs and sources
23 Cash flow forecasting and working capital
24 Income statements
25 Statement of financial position
26 Analysis of accounts

22 Business finance: needs and sources

This chapter will explain:

★ the main reasons why businesses need finance, for example, start-up capital, capital for expansion and additional working capital
★ how to understand the differences between short-term and long-term finance needs
★ the main sources of capital: internal sources and external sources with examples
★ short-term and long-term sources with examples, for example, overdraft for short-term finance and debt or equity for long-term finance
★ importance of alternative sources of capital, e.g. micro-finance, crowd-funding
★ the main factors considered in making the financial choice, e.g. size and legal form of business, amount required, length of time, existing loans
★ how to recommend and justify appropriate source(s) of finance in given circumstances.

What do Finance departments do?

Finance departments fulfil a very important role in business. They have the following responsibilities:

» Recording all financial transactions, such as payments to suppliers and revenue from customers.
» Preparing final accounts.
» Producing accounting information for managers.
» Forecasting cash flows.
» Making important financial decisions, for example, which source of finance to use for different purposes within the business.

The main reasons why businesses need finance

Finance is money. We all need money to purchase the goods and services we require – everyday goods, like food, but also more expensive items such as a house or car. Businesses need finance too – and this is often called 'capital'. Without finance, businesses could not pay wages, buy materials or pay for assets. Here are three examples of why finance or capital is needed:

» Starting up a business.
» Expansion of an existing business.
» Additional working capital.

Starting up a business

When an entrepreneur plans to start their own business, they should think about all of the buildings, land and equipment they will need to buy in order to start trading. These are usually called non-current (fixed) assets (see Chapter 25).

Definitions to learn

Start-up capital is the finance needed by a new business to pay for essential non-current (fixed) and current assets before it can begin trading.

Key info

One of the most common reasons for new business start-ups failing is not a lack of finance for buildings or equipment but a lack of finance for meeting regular expenses – especially before cash starts to flow in to the business from sales to customers. This is a shortage of working capital.

Definitions to learn

Working capital is the finance needed by a business to pay its day-to-day costs.
Capital expenditure is money spent on non-current (fixed) assets which will last for more than one year.
Revenue expenditure is money spent on day-to-day expenses which do not involve the purchase of a long-term asset, for example, wages or rent.

Nearly all new businesses will need to purchase some of these. In addition, the owner of the firm will need to obtain finance to purchase other assets such as inventories before goods can be sold to the first customers. The finance needed to launch a new business is often called **start-up capital**.

Expanding an existing business

The owners of a successful business will often take a decision to expand it in order to increase profits.

Additional non-current (fixed) assets could be purchased – such as larger buildings and more machinery.

Another business could be purchased through a takeover.

Other types of expansion include developing new products to reach new markets. This form of growth could require substantial amounts of finance for research and development.

Additional working capital

Working capital is often described as the 'life blood' of a business. It is finance that is constantly needed by firms to pay for all their day-to-day activities. They have to pay wages, pay for raw materials, pay electricity bills and so on. The money available to them to do this is known as the firm's working capital. It is vital to a business to have sufficient working capital to meet all its requirements. Many businesses have stopped trading, not because they were unprofitable, but because they suffered from shortages of working capital.

So, the third major business need for finance is often to raise additional working capital.

In all three cases above, businesses may need finance to pay for either **capital expenditure** or **revenue expenditure**. It is important to understand the difference.

» Capital expenditure is money spent on non-current assets, such as buildings, which will last for more than one year. These assets are needed at the start of a business and as it expands.
» Revenue expenditure is money spent on day-to-day expenses, for example, wages or rent.

REVISION SUMMARY   **Financial needs of business**

Activity 22.1

Look at the list below of expenses for a sports centre. Copy out the table and tick whether you consider each to be revenue expenditure or capital expenditure.

	Revenue expenditure	Capital expenditure
Purchase of building		
Water bills		
Employee wages		
Office computer		
Gym equipment		
Maintenance of equipment		

Activity 22.2: Paul's taxi business

Paul has decided to leave his job to set up his own taxi business.

a Explain to Paul why he will need finance for his new business.
b Make a list of the likely set-up costs of this business for its first month of operation.
c Indicate which of these costs are revenue expenditure and which are capital expenditure. Explain your answer.

Sources of finance

There are many different sources of finance available. It is common to split them up, or classify them, into different groups. The two most common ways of doing this are:

>> **internal** or **external** sources of finance
>> short-term or long-term sources of finance.

Internal finance

The most common examples of internal finance are as follows.

Retained profit

This is profit kept in the business after the owners have taken their share of the profits. It has the following advantages:

>> Retained profit does not have to be repaid, unlike, for example, a loan.
>> There is no interest to pay – the capital is raised from within the business.

There are disadvantages too:

>> A new business will not have any retained profits.
>> Many small firms' profits might be too low to finance the expansion needed.
>> Keeping more profits in the business reduces payments to owners, for example, dividends to shareholders who might invest in other businesses instead.

Sale of existing assets

Existing assets that could be sold are those items of value which are no longer required by the business, for example, redundant buildings or surplus equipment.

Definitions to learn

Internal finance is obtained from within the business itself.
External finance is obtained from sources outside of and separate from the business.

» This makes better use of the capital tied up in the business.
» It does not increase the debts of the business.

However:

» It may take some time to sell these assets and the amount raised is never certain until the asset is sold.
» This source of finance is not available for new businesses as they have no surplus assets to sell.

Sale of inventories to reduce inventory levels

» This reduces the opportunity cost and storage cost of high inventory levels.

However:

» It must be done carefully to avoid disappointing customers if not enough goods are kept as inventory.

Owners' savings

A sole trader or members of a partnership can put more of their savings into their unincorporated businesses. As we saw in Chapter 4, the owners of these firms are not separate from their businesses and therefore such finance is called internal.
    Advantages include the following:

» It should be available to the firm quickly.
» No interest is paid.

However:

» Savings may be too low.
» It increases the risk taken by the owners as they have unlimited liability.

REVISION SUMMARY   **Internal sources of finance**

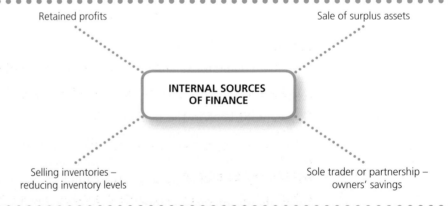

Retained profits

Sale of surplus assets

INTERNAL SOURCES
OF FINANCE

Selling inventories –
reducing inventory levels

Sole trader or partnership –
owners' savings

▶ Activity 22.3: Paul asks for your help

Paul needs advice on sources of finance before going ahead with his business plan (see Activity 22.2). Explain to him why:

a Retained profits are not, to start with, a possible source of finance.
b His savings will be likely to be an important source of funds.
c Selling off inventories is never likely to be an available source of finance to his taxi business.

External finance

The most common forms of external finance are as follows.

Issue of shares

This source of finance is only possible for limited companies.

» This is a permanent source of capital which would not have to be repaid to shareholders.
» No interest has to be paid.

However:

» Dividends are paid after tax, whereas interest on loans is paid before tax is deducted.
» Dividends will be expected by the shareholders.
» The ownership of the company could change hands if many shares are sold, which the original owners might object to.

Bank loans

A bank loan is a sum of money obtained from a bank which must be repaid and on which interest is payable.

» These are usually quick to arrange.
» They can be for varying lengths of time.
» Large companies are often offered low rates of interest by banks if they borrow large sums.

However:

» A bank loan will have to be repaid eventually and interest must be paid.
» Security or collateral is usually required. This means the bank may insist that it has the right to sell some of the property of the business if it fails to pay the interest or does not repay the loan. A sole trader may have to put his or her own house up as security on a bank loan.

Selling debentures

These are long-term loan certificates issued by limited companies.

» Debentures can be used to raise very long-term finance, for example, 25 years.

However:

» As with loans, these must be repaid and interest must be paid.

Factoring of debts

A debtor is a customer who owes a business money for goods bought. Debt factors are specialist agencies that 'buy' the claims on debtors of businesses for immediate cash. For example, a debt factor may offer 90 per cent of an existing debt. The debtor will then pay the factor and the 10 per cent represents the factor's profit – when the factor collects payment from the debtor.

» Immediate cash is made available to the business.
» The risk of collecting the debt becomes the factor's and not the business's.

However:

» The business does not receive 100 per cent of the value of its debts.

Grants and subsidies from outside agencies

Outside agencies include, for example, the government.

» These grants and subsidies usually do not have to be repaid.

However:

» They are often given with 'strings attached', for example, the firm must locate in a particular area.

Alternative sources of capital

The sources of finance that have been explained so far are very widely used by existing businesses or start-up businesses with a detailed business plan supported by owners' capital. In recent years, other sources of capital have become available to very small business start-ups, especially in developing economies, and to start-ups that carry significant risk, which can make sources of capital difficult to obtain.

Micro-finance

In many low-income developing countries, traditional commercial banks have been very unwilling to lend to poor people – even if they wanted the finance to set up an enterprise. Banks did not lend because:

» the size of the loans required by poor customers – perhaps a few dollars – meant that the bank could not make a profit from the loans
» the poorer groups in society often have no asset to act as 'security' for loans – banks are usually not prepared to take risks by lending without some form of security (assets they can sell if the borrower cannot repay).

Specialist institutions have been set up in most developing countries to meet the financial needs of poor people – especially poor entrepreneurs. The most famous of these is the Grameen Bank in Bangladesh. These institutions, including postal savings banks, finance cooperatives, credit unions and development banks, focus on lending small sums of money to people – hence the term **micro-finance** or micro-credit.

▲ Kaneez Fatima used a micro-finance loan to set up her textiles business – now she employs 20 workers

▲ This Mexican business used crowdfunding

Case study: 'Micro-finance has changed my life'

Parveen Baji lives in Pakistan. She has nine children and she used to ask neighbours for food to help feed them all. All it took to turn Parveen's life round was a $70 loan from the Kashf Foundation. The loan allowed her to start a jewellery-making business which quickly took off. Now she also owns a restaurant and a catering business that employs eight people. She has repaid the original loan and interest on it. She is able to pay for her children to go to high school and college. 'Micro-finance has changed my life,' Parveen says.

Activity 22.4

Read the case study above.

a Why do you think that traditional banks would not lend Parveen money for her business?
b Explain the benefits that this example of micro-finance has given to Parveen, her family and her country.

> **Definitions to learn**
>
> **Crowdfunding** is funding a project or venture by raising money from a large number of people who each contribute a relatively small amount, typically via the internet.

> **Key info**
>
> Crowdfunding is now the fastest-growing source of finance for business start-ups. Globally, US$34.3 billion was raised in this way in 2015. The World Bank forecasts this could reach US$90 billion by 2020 – some analysts think this is too pessimistic and this total might be reached in 2018! One of the biggest crowdfunded projects was for a video game called Star Citizen which raised US$148 million.

Crowdfunding

This idea of raising finance for new business start-ups by encouraging a large number of people to each invest small amounts has been used for many years. However, it has only become very popular since the widespread use of the internet. This allows entrepreneurs to contact millions of potential investors around the globe, usually by using 'crowdfunding platforms' such as Kickstarter, Rocket Hub and FundAnything. It is a source which is not suitable for raising very small sums – an invitation to global investors is not worthwhile if only $1000 is required! Crowdfunding is claimed to have these benefits:

» No initial fees are payable to the crowdfunding platform. Instead, if the finance required is raised, the platform will charge a percentage fee of this amount.
» Allows the public's reaction to the new business venture to be tested. If people are not prepared to invest, it probably is not a very good business idea.
» Can be a fast way to raise substantial sums.
» Often used by entrepreneurs when other 'traditional' sources are not available.

However:

» Crowdfunding platforms may reject an entrepreneur's proposal if it is not well thought out.
» If the total amount required is not raised, the finance that has been promised will have to be repaid.
» Media interest and publicity need to be generated to increase the chance of success.
» Publicising the new business idea or product on the crowdfunding platform could allow competitors to 'steal' the idea and reach the market first with a similar product.

External sources of finance

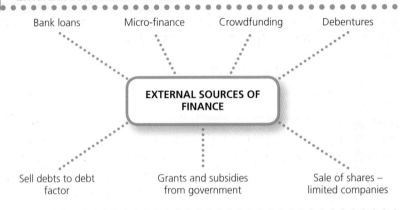

Bank loans   Micro-finance   Crowdfunding   Debentures

EXTERNAL SOURCES OF FINANCE

Sell debts to debt factor   Grants and subsidies from government   Sale of shares – limited companies

> ## Activity 22.5: Paul's business expands
>
> Paul's taxi business has now been operating for two years. He wants to expand by buying another taxi and employing two drivers on a shift system.
>
> **a** Explain to Paul the benefits of using the business profits to buy the taxi rather than taking out a bank loan.
> **b** When would you advise Paul to take out a bank loan to expand his business?

Short-term and long-term finance

Short-term finance

This provides the working capital needed by businesses for day-to-day operations. Shortages of cash in the short term can be overcome in three main ways.

Overdrafts

These are arranged by a bank.

» The bank gives the business the right to 'overdraw' its bank account (that is, spend more money than is currently in the account).
» The business could use this finance to pay wages or suppliers but, obviously, it cannot do this indefinitely.
» The overdraft will vary each month with the needs of the business – it is said to be a 'flexible' form of borrowing.
» Interest will be paid only on the amount overdrawn.
» Overdrafts can be cheaper than short-term loans.

However:

» Interest rates are variable, unlike most loans which have fixed interest rates.
» The bank can ask for the overdraft to be repaid at very short notice.

Trade credit

This is when a business delays paying its suppliers, which leaves the business in a better cash position.

» It is almost an interest-free loan to the business for the length of time that payment is delayed for.

However:

>> The supplier may refuse to give discounts or even refuse to supply any more goods if payment is not made quickly.

Factoring of debts

See page 269 under 'External finance'.

Long-term finance

This is finance which is available for more than a year – and sometimes for very many years. Usually this money would be used to purchase long-term fixed assets, to update or expand the business, or to finance a takeover of another business. The main sources of long-term finance are as follows.

Bank loans

These are payable over a fixed period of time. The advantages and disadvantages of these have already been considered under 'External finance'.

Hire purchase

This allows a business to buy a non-current (fixed) asset over a long period of time with monthly payments which include an interest charge.

>> The business does not have to find a large cash sum to purchase the asset.

However:

>> A cash deposit is paid at the start of the period.
>> Interest payments can be quite high.

Leasing

Leasing an asset allows the business to use the asset without having to purchase it. Monthly leasing payments are made. The business could decide to purchase the asset at the end of the leasing period. Some businesses decide to sell off some non-current (fixed) assets for cash and lease them back from a leasing company. This is called sale and leaseback.

>> The business does not have to find a large cash sum to purchase the asset to start with.
>> The care and maintenance of the asset are carried out by the leasing company.

However:

>> The total cost of the leasing charges will be higher than purchasing the asset.

Issue of shares

As we have seen already, this option is available only to limited companies. (See Chapter 4 for details of how sole traders and partnerships can convert to limited company status.) Shares are often referred to as equities – therefore the sale of shares is sometimes called equity finance.

Public limited companies have the ability to sell a large number of shares to the general public. These new issues, as they are called, can raise very large sums of money but can be expensive to organise and advertise. A rights issue of new shares is a very common way for public limited companies to raise additional capital. This gives existing shareholders the right to buy new shares in proportion to their current holding. This avoids the problem of new shareholders changing the balance of ownership. See pages 42–43 for the advantages and disadvantages of selling shares to raise finance.

Long-term loans or debt finance

Loans differ from share capital in the following ways:

» Loan interest is paid before tax and is an expense.
» Loan interest must be paid every year but dividends do not have to be paid if, for example, the business has made a loss.
» Loans must be repaid, as they are not permanent capital.
» Loans are often 'secured' against particular assets.

The advantages and disadvantages of loans have already been mentioned under 'External finance'.

Debentures

See page 269 under 'External finance'.

REVISION SUMMARY   **Over what period of time is the finance required?**

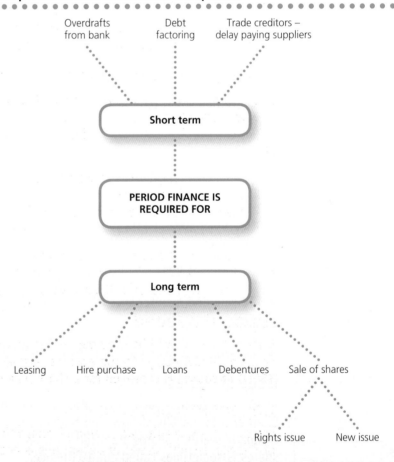

> ### ▶ Activity 22.6
>
> Consider all of the following sources of finance. Are they short-term or long-term sources of finance? Copy out the table and tick the relevant column for each source.
>
> | Source of finance | Short term | Long term |
> | --- | --- | --- |
> | Overdraft | | |
> | Debentures | | |
> | Issue of shares | | |
> | Four-year bank loan | | |
> | Trade credit | | |
> | Hire purchase | | |

Sources of finance: how businesses make the choice

We now know the main sources of finance available to businesses. What factors do managers consider before deciding where to obtain finance from?

Purpose and time period

What is the finance to be spent on? Is it to be used to pay for non-current assets or is it needed to pay for a short-term cash flow crisis?

The general rule is to match the source of finance to the use that will be made of it.

>> If the use is long term, for example, the purchase of a non-current asset, the source should be long term.
>> If the use is short term, for example, the purchase of additional inventories to cover a busy period, the source should be short term.

Think about the disadvantages of buying additional inventories that will only be needed for a few months with a long-term bank loan. Can you see why this would be unwise? What source of finance would be suitable for this?

Amount needed

Different sources will be used depending on the amount of money needed. A company would not go to the expense of arranging a new share issue if only $5000 of capital was needed for a short time period.

Legal form and size

Companies, especially public limited companies, have a greater choice of sources of finance. Issuing shares or debentures is not an option for sole traders and partnerships. These businesses, if they have plans to expand, may have to depend on the savings of their owners – personal capital. They also often have the disadvantage of having to pay higher interest rates to banks for loans than large and well-established companies.

Control

Owners of a business may lose control of that business if they ask other people to invest in their firm. Owners may have to decide: what is more important – expanding the business or keeping control of it?

Risk and gearing – does the business already have loans?

An important point about loan capital is that it will raise the gearing of the business – and this is a common measure of risk that the managers are taking. The gearing of a business measures the proportion of total capital raised from long-term loans. If this proportion is very high – say more than 50 per cent – the business is said to be highly geared. This is said to be a risky way of financing a business.

This is risky because interest must be paid on the loans, whether the business is making profits or not. When interest rates are high and company profits are low, the firm may not be able to pay all of the interest. The future of the business will be at risk. Therefore, banks are usually reluctant to lend to highly geared businesses, which may have to use other sources of finance.

Study tips

'Which is the best source of finance for this business?' is a very common question. Be prepared to analyse the advantages and disadvantages of the main sources of capital – and give a justified recommendation.

Case study: Choosing the right source of finance

Company A sells fashion clothing. It needs $15 000 to decorate its shop. A new issue of shares would be the wrong choice. This is because the issue of shares is complicated, expensive to arrange and would take a long time – the firm wants the shop decorated now!

Company B owns three restaurants. It plans to take over another restaurant company and offers $5 million. Company B already has a large bank loan.

Activity 22.7

Read the case study above.

a Advise Company A on the sources of finance that would be suitable.
b Advise Company B on the sources of finance that would be suitable.
c In each case, which source of finance would be the most suitable to use? Explain why you would choose this source rather than the other sources.
d In each case, explain what other information would have been useful before giving your advice.

Case study: Important decisions about source of finance

- A sole trader could take on a partner to bring in extra capital – but could that partner start to take important decisions without the original owner's permission?
- The directors of a private limited company could decide to 'go public' and sell shares to the public. This could raise very large sums of money for the business, but would the new shareholders own a controlling interest in the business?
- An existing plc could arrange a new issue of shares, but could these be bought by just one or two other companies who may put in a takeover bid?

These problems could all be overcome by using loan finance instead.

Activity 22.8

Read the first case study on page 276.

a Would you advise each of these three businesses to use loan capital instead of using the sources of finance outlined above? Explain your answer.

b Consider all of these following reasons for a private limited company needing finance. Copy out the table below and, for each type of need, fill in the gaps with:
  i what you consider could be the most suitable source of finance
  ii the reason for your choice.

Need for finance	Most suitable source	Reason for choice
Planned takeover of another business		
Temporary increase in inventories over the summer		
Purchase of new car for the Chief Executive		
Research and development of new product – to come on the market in four years' time		
Cost of building modern factory requiring much less land than the present one		

REVISION SUMMARY

Choosing sources of finance – factors involved in the decision

Purpose and period of time required

Amount required

CHOOSING SOURCES OF FINANCE

Risk and gearing

Status and size of business

Control over the business

Activity 22.9: Joe's dilemma

Joe Dagglio has $15 000 in savings. He wants to buy shares in public limited companies because he has heard that he could earn dividends and make a capital gain if the shares rise in price. He has received details of a plc that is arranging a new issue of shares. The company wishes to expand. He makes a note of the following information:

- The current share price is $5 but it has been as high as $7.
- The average value of shares on the stock exchange has risen over the last year.
- The gearing ratio of the company is 55 per cent.
- Interest rates are likely to rise in the next month or so.
- The company is offering high dividends to its existing shareholders.

a Considering all of the risks and possible gains, advise Joe whether he should buy these shares or not.

b What other information would you find helpful in advising Joe?

Will banks lend and shareholders invest?

A business can never be sure of being able to raise finance. Banks often refuse to lend to businesses – and shareholders may be reluctant to buy more shares. A business owner, especially of a new start-up business, will increase the chances of obtaining loan finance if the following is available:

» A cash flow forecast which shows why the finance is needed and how it will be used.
» An income statement for the last time period – and a forecast one for the next. These should show the chances of the business making a profit in future.
» Details of existing loans and sources of finance being used.
» Evidence that 'security' (or collateral) is available to reduce the bank's risk if it lends.
» A business plan to explain clearly what the business hopes to achieve in the future and why the finance is important to these plans.

Shareholders are most likely to buy additional shares when:

» the company's share price has been increasing
» dividends are high – or profits are rising so dividends might increase in the future
» other companies do not seem such a good investment
» the company has a good reputation and has plans for future growth.

Key info

The most common reasons why banks refuse loans to small businesses are:

→ weak cash flow
→ lack of security or collateral (for example, no assets that can be sold if the business fails)
→ poor preparation by the business owner when applying for the loan.

REVISION SUMMARY **Finance from banks and shareholders**

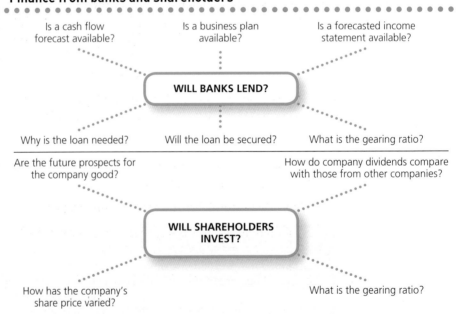

Is a cash flow forecast available?

Is a business plan available?

Is a forecasted income statement available?

WILL BANKS LEND?

Why is the loan needed?   Will the loan be secured?   What is the gearing ratio?

Are the future prospects for the company good?

How do company dividends compare with those from other companies?

WILL SHAREHOLDERS INVEST?

How has the company's share price varied?

What is the gearing ratio?

🔍 International business in focus

Godrej Properties

Indian property developing company Godrej Properties successfully raised over US$90 million from the sale of new shares. The founders of this Mumbai-based company owned near 84 per cent of the company before the share sale – but only 73 per cent once the shares had been sold. The Indian stock market has seen rising share prices this year and this helped to encourage investors to buy these new shares in Godrej Properties.

The company is expected to use the finance raised to reduce its bank loans and to buy more land for the long-term development of further properties.

Discussion points

- Explain whether Godrej Properties raised internal finance or external finance from the sale of shares.

- Why do you think shareholders were so keen to buy these new shares?

- Explain why the company wanted to reduce its bank loans.

Exam-style questions: Short answer and data response

1 Michelle lost her job when the sugar factory closed. She wanted to start her own business designing and making clothes. She has prepared several dress designs which she thinks are better than anything else on the market. All the main banks refused Michelle's request for a $100 loan, even though she had a business plan. Michelle did not want to use a crowdfunding platform. Finally, a development bank specialising in micro-finance agreed to lend her the capital she needed. That was three years ago – she now employs three other people and is planning further expansion of her business.

   a Define 'micro-finance'. [2]

   b Identify **two** reasons why Michelle needed $100 to start her business. [2]

   c Outline **two** likely reasons why Michelle decided not to try to raise the capital she needed by using crowdfunding. [4]

   d Michelle now wants to expand her business further. Explain **two** benefits of using internal sources of finance to pay for this. [6]

   e Ten years after setting up her business, Michelle converted it into a private limited company to raise finance for business expansion. Do you think she was right to do this? Justify your answer. [6]

2 Akram owns a small farm. The income of the business varies greatly during the year. The farm makes a small profit but Akram is ambitious. He wants to take over a neighbour's farm and increase the range of crops he sells. He thinks that he needs long-term finance and plans to take out a bank loan to pay for the takeover. He has already borrowed money to buy a new tractor. A friend has advised him to form a company and sell shares.

   a Define 'long-term finance'. [2]

   b Identify **two** types of short-term finance Akram could use when farm income is low. [2]

   c Outline **two** forms of internal finance Akram could have used to buy the tractor. [4]

   d Explain **two** pieces of information a bank would look at before granting a loan to Akram. [6]

   e Explain two sources of finance which could be used for the takeover. Justify which source should be used. [6]

Revision checklist

In this chapter you have learned to:

✔ recognise the different reasons why businesses need finance
✔ identify sources of finance as being either internal or external and whether they are short term or long term
✔ analyse and compare the advantages and disadvantages of different sources of finance
✔ analyse a firm's need for funds and make a reasoned choice between the different sources of finance available
✔ make decisions on whether finance should be provided to a business from the viewpoint of banks and other institutions.

NOW – test your understanding with the revision questions in the Student etextbook and the Workbook.

Cash flow forecasting and working capital

Why cash is important to a business

Cash is a liquid asset. This means that it is immediately available for spending on goods and services.

Do you ever run out of cash? Have you ever been unable to pay for goods which you need at one particular time because you did not have enough cash? Have you ever borrowed money or incurred bills which you cannot immediately pay? If you answered 'yes' to any of these questions, you have already experienced a **cash flow** problem! In business terms, cash flow means the flow of money into and out of a business over a certain time period.

If a business has too little cash – or even runs out of it completely – it will face major problems, such as:

>> being unable to pay workers, suppliers, landlord, government
>> production of goods and services will stop – workers will not work for no pay and suppliers will not supply goods if they are not paid
>> the business may be forced into 'liquidation' – selling up everything it owns to pay its debts.

> **Definitions to learn**
>
> The **cash flow** of a business is the cash inflows and outflows over a period of time.

What is meant by cash flows?

How can cash flow into a business (**cash inflow**)? Here are five of the most common ways:

>> The sale of products for cash.
>> Payments made by debtors – debtors are customers who have already purchased products from the business but did not pay for them at the time.
>> Borrowing money from an external source – this will lead to cash flowing into the business (it will have to be repaid eventually).
>> The sale of assets of the business, for example, unwanted property.
>> Investors, for example, shareholders in the case of companies, putting more money into the business.

How can cash flow out of a business (**cash outflow**)? Here are five of the most common ways:

>> Purchasing goods or materials for cash.
>> Paying wages, salaries and other expenses in cash.

> **Definitions to learn**
>
> **Cash inflows** are the sums of money received by a business during a period of time.
> **Cash outflows** are the sums of money paid out by a business during a period of time.

» Purchasing non-current (fixed) assets.
» Repaying loans.
» By paying creditors of the business – other firms which supplied items to the business but were not paid immediately.

Activity 23.1: Cash inflows or outflows?

Copy the table below. For each of the transactions, tick the correct column to indicate whether it represents a cash inflow or a cash outflow for Good Hope Enterprises Ltd.

Transaction	Cash inflow	Cash outflow
Purchase of new computer for cash		
Sale of goods to customers – no credit given		
Interest paid on bank loan		
Wages paid to employees		
Debtors pay their bills		
Additional shares sold to shareholders		
Creditors/suppliers paid		
Bank overdraft paid off		

Cash flow cycle

The following diagram will help to explain the link between some of the inflows and outflows mentioned above – the **cash flow cycle**. It explains why cash paid out is not returned immediately to the business.

Definitions to learn

A **cash flow cycle** shows the stages between paying out cash for labour, materials, and so on, and receiving cash from the sale of goods.

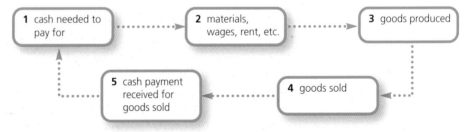

▲ The cash flow cycle

The diagram shows how cash is needed (1) to pay for essential materials and other costs (2) required to produce the product. Time is needed to produce the products (3) before they can be sold to customers (4). If these customers receive credit, they will not have to pay straightaway. When they do pay for the goods in cash (5), this money will be needed (1) to pay for buying further materials, etc. (2), and so the cycle continues.

The longer the time taken to complete these stages, the greater will be the firm's need for working capital (see page 289) and cash.

The diagram also helps us to understand the importance of planning for cash flows. What would happen in the following situations?

» If a business did not have enough cash at stage 1? Not enough materials and other requirements could be purchased and so output and sales would fall.
» If a business insisted on its customer paying cash at stage 4 because the business was short of money? It might lose the customer to a competitor who could offer credit.

» If a business had insufficient cash to pay its bills such as rent and electricity? It would be in a liquidity crisis and it might be forced out of business by its creditors.

These three examples illustrate the need for managers to plan ahead for their cash needs so that the business is not put at risk in these ways.

What cash flow is not!

Cash flow is not the same as **profit**. This is an important distinction.

➡ Case study: Cash flow is not the same as profit!

Good Hope Enterprises Ltd records the following transactions over the month of June:

Goods sold to customers	$40 000	(50% cash; 50% on one month's credit)
Costs of goods sold	$15 000	(paid for in cash)

• What was the gross profit in June?
  Revenue – cost of goods sold = $25 000
• Assuming the business started the month with no cash, how much cash did it have at the end of June? (Ignore any other transactions.)
  Net cash flow = cash inflow – cash outflow
  $20 000 (cash sales) – $15 000 = $5000

There is a clear difference between the profit made by Good Hope Enterprises Ltd in the case study above and the cash flow over the same period.

Q: Why is the cash figure lower than the gross profit?

A: Because, although all goods have been sold, cash payment has been received for only half of them. The customers buying the goods on credit will pay in later months.

This important example leads to further questions:

» Can profitable businesses run out of cash? Yes – and this is a major reason for businesses failing. It is called *insolvency*.
» How is this possible? By:
  • allowing customers too long a credit period, perhaps to encourage sales
  • purchasing too many non-current (fixed) assets at once
  • expanding too quickly and keeping a high inventory level. This means that cash is used to pay for higher inventory levels. This is often called overtrading.

➡ Case study

A business records the following transactions for one month:

Sales of goods	$45 000 (50% for cash; 50% on one month's credit)
Materials purchased and used	$12 000 (all paid in cash during the month)
Assume no other transactions.	

▶ Activity 23.2

Read the case study above.

a Calculate the gross profit made by the business in this month.
b Calculate the cash held by the business at the end of this month (assume it had no cash at the start of the month).
c Explain why the answers to **a** and **b** are different.

REVISION SUMMARY **Cash flow**

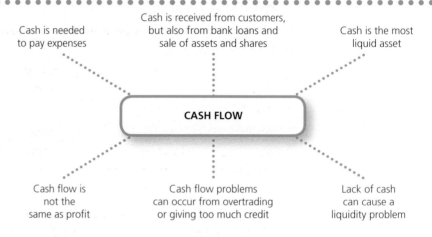

Cash is needed to pay expenses

Cash is received from customers, but also from bank loans and sale of assets and shares

Cash is the most liquid asset

CASH FLOW

Cash flow is not the same as profit

Cash flow problems can occur from overtrading or giving too much credit

Lack of cash can cause a liquidity problem

Definitions to learn

A **cash flow forecast** is an estimate of future cash inflows and outflows of a business, usually on a month-by-month basis. This then shows the expected cash balance at the end of each month.

Key info

An estimated 3967 companies entered insolvency (they ran out of cash) in the first three months of 2017 in the UK. Keeping control of cash flow is very important for a business to continue to trade.

Study tips

There can be slight variations in the way businesses lay out their cash flow forecasts. The examples used in this chapter cover what you need to know.

The importance of cash flow forecasts

We have seen how important cash is to any business. Without sufficient cash to pay bills and repay loans, a business may be forced to stop trading by its creditors and banks. It is therefore very important indeed for the manager of a business to know what cash will be available month-by-month. A **cash flow forecast** can be used to tell the manager:

» how much cash is available for paying bills, repaying loans or for buying fixed assets
» how much cash the bank might need to lend to the business in order to avoid insolvency
» whether the business is holding too much cash which could be put to a more profitable use.

Managers use cash flow forecasts to help them find out the future cash position of their business.

Uses of cash flow forecasts

Cash flow forecasts are useful in the following situations:

» starting up a business
» running an existing business
» keeping the bank manager informed
» managing cash flow.

Case study

Cash flow forecast – Good Hope Enterprises Ltd. January to March 2019 ($). Figures in brackets are negative.

	January	February	March
Cash inflows (A)	35 000	45 000	50 000
Cash outflows (B)	30 000	65 000	40 000
Opening bank balance (C)	10 000	15 000	(5000)
NET CASH FLOW (D) (A-B)	5000	(20 000)	10 000
CLOSING BANK BALANCE (C+D)	15 000	(5000)	5000

Note:

- A positive **net cash flow** will increase the closing bank balance.
- A negative net cash flow (as in February) will reduce the bank balance.
- Each **closing bank balance** becomes the **opening bank balance** for the next month.
- The bank account will become overdrawn in February.

Definitions to learn

Net cash flow is the difference, each month, between inflows and outflows.
Closing cash (or **bank**) **balance** is the amount of cash held by the business at the end of each month. This becomes next month's opening cash balance.
Opening cash (or **bank**) **balance** is the amount of cash held by the business at the start of the month.

Starting up a business

When planning to start a business, the owner needs to know how much cash will be needed in the first few months of operation. This is a very expensive time for new businesses as premises have to be purchased or rented, machinery must be purchased or hired, inventory must be built up, and advertising and promotion costs will be necessary to make consumers aware of the product or service. Many new businesses fail because owners do not realise how much cash is needed in the first few crucial months. A cash flow forecast should help to avoid these problems.

Keeping the bank manager informed

Banks provide loans to businesses. However, before bank managers will lend any money, they need to see the firm's cash flow forecast. This is particularly true of a new business, but also for existing ones. The bank manager will need to see how big a loan or overdraft is needed, when it is needed, how long the finance is needed for and when it might be repaid.

It is very rare for a bank to lend to a business unless a cash flow forecast is produced which shows these factors.

Managing an existing business

As seen from earlier examples, it is not just newly formed businesses which need to forecast cash flows. Any business can run out of cash and require an overdraft, perhaps because of an expensive non-current (fixed) asset being bought or a fall in sales. Borrowing money needs to be planned in advance so that the lowest rates of interest can be arranged. Telling the bank today that a loan is needed tomorrow could lead to the bank either refusing the loan – because of poor business planning – or charging high rates of interest. The bank will know that the business has little alternative but to pay these interest rates. If the business exceeds the overdraft limit from the bank without informing the bank manager first, the bank could insist that the overdraft is repaid immediately and this could force the business to close.

Managing cash flow

Too much cash held in the bank account of a business means that this capital could be better used in other areas of the business. If it seems that the business is likely to have a very high bank balance, the accountant could decide to pay off loans to help reduce interest charges. Another option would be to pay creditors quickly to take advantage of possible discounts. These are examples of actively managing the cash flow of a business.

Activity 23.3: Using a cash flow forecast

Cash flow forecast for Sierra Promotions Co. January to April 2018 ($). Figures in brackets are negative.

	January	February	March	April
Cash inflows:				
Cash sales	15 000	15 000	20 000	25 000
Payments from debtors	5000	5000	7000	8000
Total cash inflows	20 000	20 000	27 000	33 000
Cash outflows:				
Materials and wages	3000	3000	5000	7000
Rent and other expenses	15 000	15 000	25 000	15 000
Total cash outflows	18 000	18 000	30 000	z
Opening bank balance	3000	5000	7000	4000
Net cash flow	2000	x	(3000)	11 000
Closing bank balance	5000	7000	y	15 000

a Calculate values for x, y and z.
b Suggest one reason why 'materials and wages' are forecast to be so much higher in March and April than in the previous months.
c In April, cash sales are now expected to be 10 per cent higher than shown. Materials and wages are expected to be 20 per cent higher than forecast. Amend the cash flow forecast for April and calculate the new closing cash balance.

Case study

The manager of Capri Motors Ltd wants to plan the cash flows of the business over the next four months. She asks for your help in making a cash flow forecast. She provides you with the following information:

- Forecasted sales are: January $22 000; February $25 000; March $20 000; April $22 000.
- Customers always pay cash.
- Materials are purchased each month and are paid for in cash. The materials used each month are 50 per cent of revenue for that month.
- Other cash expenses (wages, rent, insurance, and so on) are forecast to be: January $4000; February $13 000; March $15 000; April $15 000.
- The opening cash balance in January is $2000.

Activity 23.4: Creating a cash flow forecast

Read the case study above.

a Explain to the manager the importance of a cash flow forecast.
b Using the same structure as in the examples above, draw up a cash flow forecast for this business over the four months from January to April.
c What do you notice about the closing bank balance in April? What action could the manager of Capri Motors Ltd take now that she is aware of this problem?

REVISION SUMMARY **Cash flow forecasts**

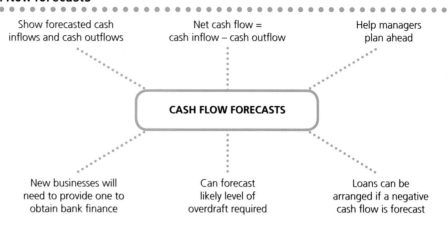

Show forecasted cash inflows and cash outflows

Net cash flow = cash inflow – cash outflow

Help managers plan ahead

CASH FLOW FORECASTS

New businesses will need to provide one to obtain bank finance

Can forecast likely level of overdraft required

Loans can be arranged if a negative cash flow is forecast

How a short-term cash flow problem might be overcome

There are several ways in which a short-term cash flow problem could be overcome. These are explained below – and the limitations of each method are outlined too.

Method of overcoming cash flow problem	How it works	Limitations
Increasing bank loans	Bank loans will inject more cash into the business	Interest must be paid – this will reduce profits The loans will have to be repaid eventually – a cash outflow
Delaying payments to suppliers	Cash outflows will decrease in the short term	Suppliers could refuse to supply Suppliers could offer lower discounts for late payments
Asking debtors to pay more quickly – or insisting on only 'cash sales'	Cash inflows will increase in the short term	Customers may purchase from another business that still offers them time to pay (trade credit)
Delay or cancel purchases of capital equipment	Cash outflows for purchase of equipment will decrease	The long-term efficiency of the business could decrease without up-to-date equipment

In the longer term, a business with cash flow difficulties will have to take other decisions to solve the problem. These could include the following:

» Attracting new investors, for example, by selling more company shares – but will this affect ownership of the business?
» Cutting costs and increasing efficiency – but will this be popular with employees and could product quality be affected?
» Developing new products that will attract more customers – this could take a long time and needs cash in the short term to pay for development.

Case study: Gardener's Green

Manuel Guitano set up in business as a sole trader nine years ago. He called his business Gardener's Green. Manuel designs and looks after the gardens of hotels, offices and large private houses. The business is very busy in the spring, summer and autumn but not very busy in winter. Manuel has six full-time employees. These employees have been with him for the past four years. Experienced gardeners are not always easy to find. Gardener's Green has a small amount of land with six

greenhouses although there is space for more. Gardener's Green grows about 50 per cent of the plants that it supplies to customers. The revenue of the business varies throughout the year, but expenses occur every month.

Look at the cash flow forecast for the next financial year below. There is a cash flow problem. You have been asked by Manuel to consider this problem and make recommendations as to what he can do to solve it.

Cash flow forecast for Gardener's Green (next 12 months). All figures in brackets are negative

	Aug. $	Sept. $	Oct. $	Nov. $	Dec. $	Jan. $	Feb. $	Mar. $	Apr. $	May $	Jun. $	Jul. $
Cash inflows												
Cash sales	70000	80000	1000	1400	200	200	1000	50000	80000	80000	60000	60000
Cash outflows												
Wages	20000	20000	20000	20000	20000	20000	20000	20000	20000	20000	20000	20000
Plants & trees purchased	20000	0	0	0	0	0	0	30000	30000	30000	30000	30000
Seeds & compost	0	6000	6000	0	0	6000	8000	8000	7000	0	0	0
Heating & water	1000	1000	1000	1000	1000	1000	1000	1000	1000	1000	1000	1000
Bank interest	0	0	0	0	0	1018	3549	4649	3150	910	216	0
Business tax on land	100	100	100	100	100	100	100	100	100	100	100	100
Total cash outflow	41100	27100	27100	21100	21100	28118	32649	63749	61250	52010	51316	51100
Opening balance	100	29000	81900	55800	36100	15200	(12718)	(44367)	(58116)	(39366)	(11376)	(2692)
Net cash flow	28900	52900	(26100)	(19700)	(20900)	(27918)	(31649)	(13749)	18750	27990	8684	8900
Closing bank balance	29000	81900	55800	36100	15200	(12718)	(44367)	(58116)	(39366)	(11376)	(2692)	6208

> **Activity 23.5**
>
> Read the case study on page 288.
>
> **a** Why is cash flow forecasting important to managers such as Manuel?
> **b** Who else, apart from Manuel, is likely to be interested in a cash flow forecast for Gardener's Green? Give reasons for your answer.
> **c** Why do some costs stay the same each month? Use examples to explain your answer. Why do some costs vary each month? Use examples to explain your answer.
> **d** Manuel has just been informed that his supplier of plants and trees will raise prices by 10 per cent in July. Explain how the cash flow forecast for Gardener's Green will be affected.
> **e** Manuel wants to improve the cash flow of his business. Suggest **three** ways of improving the cash flow of Gardener's Green. Explain the advantages and disadvantages of each. Recommend which way he should choose.

The concept and importance of working capital

Definitions to learn

Working capital is the capital available to a business in the short term to pay for day-to-day expenses.

The term **working capital** refers to the amount of capital which is readily available to a business. That is, working capital is the difference between resources in cash or readily convertible into cash and the short-term debts of the business. After studying Chapter 26, you will understand that:

Working capital = Current assets − Current liabilities

Working capital is the life-blood of a business. Having enough working capital assists in raising the credit reputation of a business.

No business can run effectively without a sufficient quantity of working capital. It is crucial to retain the right level of working capital.

A business enterprise with ample working capital is always in a position to take advantage of any favourable opportunity, either to buy raw materials being offered at a discount or to implement a customer's special order.

Working capital may be held in different forms:

» Cash is needed to pay day-to-day costs and buy inventories.
» The value of a firm's debtors is related to the volume of production and sales. To achieve higher sales there may be a need to offer additional credit facilities.
» The value of inventories is also a significant part of working capital. Not having enough inventories may cause production to stop. On the other hand, a very high inventory level may result in high opportunity costs.

The overall success of a business depends upon its working capital position. So, it should be handled properly because it shows the efficiency and financial strength of company.

International business in focus

Dealing with cash flow issues in different ways

Two businesses in different industries have approached potential cash flow problems in different ways. Kodak – formerly the world's biggest supplier of camera film – has cut its workforce by 47 000 as demand for traditional film collapsed as a result of the 'digital revolution'. It also obtained a $950 million loan facility from Citicorp to give it the cash to keep it going. Kodak now still manufactures film but not digital cameras. It also produces print systems, inkjet systems, 3D printing and packaging, and software for printing, thereby increasing cash inflows from alternative products.

Kier Group is a huge construction company based in Europe. The end of a property boom meant that construction companies had less work and were having to wait longer for payment from customers. Kier started to manage its operations to minimise cash outflows. The business has over 80 different suppliers for a typical large building project. Kier now holds no or very low inventories and demands that all of its suppliers deliver goods and equipment on the day they are needed – or very shortly before. This means that valuable cash is not held up in inventories that will not be used for weeks.

Discussion points

- Explain how the following had an impact on cash flows:
  - Technological change for Kodak.
  - Ending of the property boom for Kier Group.
- Explain the different ways these businesses tried to resolve a potential cash flow problem.

Exam-style questions: Short answer and data response

1 Bruno manages a hotel. Most of the hotel bedrooms are occupied during the main tourist season, which lasts for seven months. The hotel's main cash outflows are the same each month but food costs and some employee costs increase when there are more tourists. Bruno plans to have the hotel redecorated but he does not know whether the cost of this will mean the hotel exceeds its overdraft limit. The hotel's bank account is overdrawn for several months of each year.
   a Define 'cash outflows'. [2]
   b Identify **two** likely cash outflows for Bruno's hotel. [2]
   c Outline **two** effects on Bruno's hotel if he offers hotel guests credit of one month following a stay in the hotel. [4]
   d Explain **two** likely benefits to Bruno of producing a cash flow forecast. [6]
   e Explain the advantages and disadvantages of any **two** ways in which Bruno could improve the cash flow position of the hotel. Which way would you advise him to use? Justify your answer. [6]

2 Abbas Manufacturing produces wheels for cars. It holds high inventory levels so that one-off orders from major car manufacturers can be satisfied quickly. The world's big car manufacturers demand long credit periods from their suppliers of three months. Abbas Manufacturing has prepared the following cash flow forecast for the next three months:

$000	July	August	September
Cash inflows			
Cash from debtors' payments	550	475	545
Sale of old equipment	0	0	50
Total cash in	550	475	595
Cash outflows			
Materials purchased	160	175	170
Employee costs	185	185	190
New computers	0	145	0
Other costs	155	125	135
Total cash out	500	630	495
Opening bank balance	(75)	(25)	(180)
Net cash flow	50	(155)	x
Closing bank balance	(25)	(180)	y

   a Define 'net cash flow'. [2]
   b Identify **two** reasons why Abbas Manufacturing needs high amounts of cash or working capital. [2]
   c Calculate the values for x and y in the cash flow forecast. Show your working. [4]
   d Amend the cash flow forecast for July assuming cash from debtors and material costs are going to be 10 per cent higher than originally forecast. Show your working. [6]
   e Using the cash flow forecast above, suggest **two** ways Abbas Manufacturing can reduce its bank overdraft (negative closing balance). Recommend the best one to choose. Justify your advice. [6]

Revision checklist

In this chapter you have learned:

✔ the importance of cash to a business
✔ what is meant by cash flow, cash inflow and cash outflow
✔ the difference between the profit made by a business and its cash flow position
✔ what the cash flow cycle is and how a business might improve its cash flow position
✔ to understand and amend a cash flow forecast.
✔ what working capital means and why it is important to a business.

NOW – test your understanding with the revision questions in the Student etextbook and the Workbook.

24

Income statements

This chapter will explain:

★ how a profit is made
★ the importance of profit to private sector businesses, for example, reward for risk taking/enterprise, source of finance
★ the difference between profit and cash
★ the main features of an income statement, for example, revenue, cost of sales, gross profit, profit and retained profit
★ how to use simple income statements in decision making based on profit calculations.

What are accounts and why are they necessary?

 Case study

Shazad Nidal has been in business for ten months. He is a tailor making expensive suits. He operates as a sole trader.

Imagine what could happen to his business if he failed to keep a written record of all financial transactions, such as purchases and sales.

- He could sell goods on credit to customers without keeping a record of the sale. As a result, he might forget that customers still owed him money.
- He might order too many raw materials because no record was kept of previous orders.
- He might pay all of the business costs, for example, electricity, raw materials and wages, on the same day and then find out that there was no money in the bank.
- The profits or losses of the business could not be calculated.
- The government tax collector would not be able to check how much tax Shazad owed – a heavy fine could be charged if the tax is not paid.
- Without written financial records, the business would soon be in deep trouble.

Definitions to learn

Accounts are the financial records of a firm's transactions.
Accountants are the professionally qualified people who have responsibility for keeping accurate accounts and for producing the final accounts.
Final accounts are produced at the end of the financial year and give details of the profit or loss made over the year and the worth of the business.

The financial records of a business are called its **accounts.** They should be kept up to date and with great accuracy – this is the responsibility of the **accountants** working in the Finance department.

At the end of each financial year, the accountant will produce the **final accounts** of the business. These will record the main financial results over the year and the current worth or value of the business.

Limited companies are required by law to publish their final accounts and these are much more detailed than those required from non-company businesses, such as sole traders and partnerships.

Recording accounting transactions

In most businesses, there are so many transactions each year that it would be very time-consuming to record them all by hand in accounting books. This is one reason most organisations now use computers. Computer files store records of all the sales, purchases and other financial transactions made by a firm and the information can be retrieved or printed out when required.

293

How a profit is made

Profit is an objective for most businesses. In simple terms, profit is calculated by:

Profit = Revenue − Cost of making products

This simple formula introduces the idea that profit is a 'surplus' that remains after business costs have been subtracted. If these costs exceed the revenue, then the business has made a loss. The profit formula also suggests that this surplus can be increased by:

1 increasing revenue by more than costs
2 reducing the cost of making products
3 a combination of 1 and 2.

Why profit is important to private sector businesses

Profit is important to private sector businesses for several reasons:

Why profit is important	Explanation
Reward for enterprise	Successful entrepreneurs have many important qualities and characteristics and profit gives them a reward for these.
Reward for risk taking	Entrepreneurs and other investors take considerable risks when they provide capital to a business – profits reward them for taking these risks by allowing payments to be made (for example, dividends to shareholders).
	These payments provide incentives: to business owners to try to make their business even more profitable; to investors to put more capital into profitable businesses.
Source of finance	Profits after payments to the owners (retained profits) are a very important source of finance for businesses – this allows for expansion (see Chapter 22).
Indicator of success	When some businesses are very profitable, other businesses or new entrepreneurs are given a signal that investment into producing similar goods or services would be profitable. If all businesses in an industry are making losses, this would not be a good signal to set up in that industry!

In public sector or state-owned businesses, profit might also be important. The government might set profit as one of the targets to be achieved for these businesses. These surpluses could also be used as a source of finance to develop the state-owned business or make it more efficient.

In social enterprises (see Chapter 5), profit also has an important role to play. Social enterprises cannot usually survive unless they make a surplus from their operations **but** profit is not their only objective. The managers of social enterprises will want to balance profit-making with other aims, such as protecting the environment and benefiting disadvantaged groups in society.

Difference between profit and cash

Do you recall from Chapter 23 that profit and cash are not necessarily the same? Re-read page 283.

Q: Why is it important to remember this distinction when looking at a business's final accounts?

A: Just because a business records a profit does not mean it has plenty of cash. In fact, it could have no cash at all!

Attempt the following activity to confirm that you understand this important point.

Activity 24.1

Copy and complete the following table.

Business transaction	Profit/loss	Impact on cash
a Sells 5000 items for cash @ $2. Each item cost the business $1.50 but it has not yet paid its suppliers	$2500 (5000 items × $0.50)	
b Sells 25 000 items on credit @ $3. Pays cash to suppliers ($2 per item)		Outflow of $50 000 (sales on credit but cash paid for supplies)
c Sells 8000 items for cash @ $4. Suppliers paid in cash ($2 per item)	$16 000	

Main features of an income statement

Income statements (also known as profit and loss accounts) are important financial statements. They indicate to managers, business owners and other account users whether the business has made a profit or loss over a period of time. This time period is usually one year but income statements could be constructed monthly too.

If the business is making a profit, managers will want to ask themselves:

» Is it higher or lower than last year?
» If lower, why is profit falling?
» Is it higher or lower than other similar businesses?
» If lower, what can we do to become as profitable as other businesses?

If the business is making a loss, managers will want to ask themselves:

» Is this a short- or long-term problem?
» Are other similar businesses also making losses?
» What decisions can we take to turn losses into profits?

You can begin to realise why income statements are so important.

Revenue

This is the amount made by the business from the sales of its goods or services. It is calculated by multiplying price by the amount sold. For example, if the price = $10 and 1000 products are sold, then **revenue** = $10 000. Ways of increasing revenue were considered in the marketing chapters, such as Chapter 13 on price and Chapter 15 on promotion.

Cost of sales

Cost of sales is also sometimes known as cost of goods sold. It is the variable cost of production for the goods or services sold by a business. This includes the cost of the materials used in creating the good plus the direct labour costs of producing the good. In a retail business it will be the cost of the inventory sold by the shop. It excludes fixed cost expenses such as distribution costs and sales staff costs.

Gross profit

What information do income statements contain? Before we can answer this, we need to consider an important concept known as **gross profit** – which is profit calculated before fixed costs are considered. Here is an example:

If a business bought $270 000 worth of goods during the year and sold them for $450 000, the gross profit would be $180 000.

Gross profit = Revenue – Cost of sales

It is important to note the following:

» Gross profit does not make any allowance for overhead costs or expenses.
» Cost of sales is not necessarily the same as the total value of goods bought by the business.

How is this information presented on an income statement?

The following table shows a simple example with some notes to explain each item. It is for a limited company, as these are the only businesses that have to publish their accounts.

Income statement for XYZ Limited		The business/company name should be shown clearly
For the year ending 31/10/18	$000	The time period covered by the income statement must be shown
Revenue	450	This is the value of goods sold during the year. For example, 900 000 items @ 50 cents each
Cost of sales	270	This is the variable cost (materials and labour, for example) of making the goods sold. For example, 900 000 items costing 30 cents each
Gross profit	180	This is the profit made before expenses = $450 000 – $270 000

This section of the income statement is often referred to as the **trading account**. It shows the gross profit made from the normal trading activities of the business. Why do you think it is not a complete income statement? There are several important items missing from this example, namely:

» other costs of running the business apart from the variable labour and material costs, for example, fixed costs
» taxes on profit paid by the company
» payment of a share of the profits to owners/shareholders.

Case study

City Café Co. buys cans of drink from a wholesaler for $1 each. It sells them for $2 each. City Café Co. started the year with 200 cans in stock (opening inventories). It bought in 1500 cans. At the end of the year it had 300 left (closing inventories).
1 How many cans did the business sell during the year?
2 What was the cost to the business of the goods sold?
3 What was the gross profit?
The answers to these questions are as follows:
1 Add together the opening inventory and the cans bought during the year:
200 + 1500 = 1700 cans.
The business could have sold 1700 cans during the year. We know that it did not sell this many. How? Because there were closing inventories of 300. Therefore, the business must have sold 1400 cans.
Goods sold = Opening inventories + Purchases – Closing inventories
2 As the goods were all bought by the business for $1 each, the cost of goods sold was $1400.
3 Remember:
Gross profit = Revenue – Cost of sales
In this example, revenue = $2 × 1400 cans sold = $2800
Gross profit = $2800 – $1400 = $1400

Activity 24.2

Copy and complete the following table (all figures in $).

Revenue	Cost of sales	Gross profit
a 3000	1500	
b 25 000	16 000	
c 80 000		20 000
d	25 000	50 000

Activity 24.3

Copy and complete this table.

Cost per unit	Opening inventories	Purchases of goods	Closing inventories	Cost of sales
a $3	500	3000	200	$9900
b $2	1000	5000	500	
c $5	100	400	300	
d $1	2000	60 000	2000	

 Case study

This is an example of a typical trading account section of an income statement.
ABC Ltd. For year ending 31/3/2018

Revenue	$55 000
Opening inventories	$10 000
Purchases	$25 000
Total inventory available	$35 000
Less closing inventories	$12 000
Cost of sales	$23 000
Gross profit	$32 000

It is important to note that in a manufacturing business, rather than a retailing one, the labour costs and production costs directly incurred in making the products sold will also be deducted before arriving at the gross profit total.

The gross profit is not the final profit for the business because all the other expenses have to be deducted. Costs such as salaries, lighting and rent of the buildings need to be subtracted from gross profit.

Net profit (also known as 'profit')

Net profit is calculated by deducting all expenses and overheads of the business from gross profit. Unlike gross profit, net profit will also include any non-trading income, such as the rent from an apartment above a shop.

Depreciation is the fall in the value of a fixed asset over time. This is included as an annual expense of the business. For example, a new truck bought by a building firm will fall in value with age and use. Each year, this fall in value or depreciation is recorded as an expense on the income statement.

Case study example

Newtown Garden Nursery Ltd. Income statement for year ending 31/3/2018

Gross profit	$32 000
Non-trading income	$5000
	$37 000
Less expenses:	
Wages and salaries	$12 000
Electricity	$6000
Rent	$3000
Depreciation	$5000
Selling and advertising expenses	$5000
	$31 000
Net profit	$6000

Retained profit

The **retained profit** is the profit left, or reinvested back into the business, after all payments have been deducted.

The income statement for limited companies will also contain:

» corporation tax paid on the company's net profits
» the dividends paid out to shareholders (in some years, dividends might be zero)
» the retained profits left after these two deductions
» results from the previous year to allow for easy comparisons.

Case study

Here is a typical income statement for a public limited company (plc). It is in a simplified form to help understanding.

Income statement for Ace Engineering plc for the year ending 31/3/2018

	2018	2017
	($000)	($000)
Revenue	1250	1300
Cost of sales	900	900
Gross profit	350	400
Expenses including interest paid	155	160
Net profit	195	240
Corporation tax	35	40
Profit after tax	160	200
Dividends	120	130
Retained profit for the year	40	70

Activity 24.4: ABC's retained profit

a) Using the same pattern as the typical income statement shown above, calculate the retained profits of ABC plc for the year ending 31/3/2018 from the following data (which is not in the correct order!).

	($000)
Revenue	280
Tax paid	40
Operating expenses	30
Cost of sales	100
Interest paid	15
Dividends	25

b Explain why retained profit is important to ABC's future success.

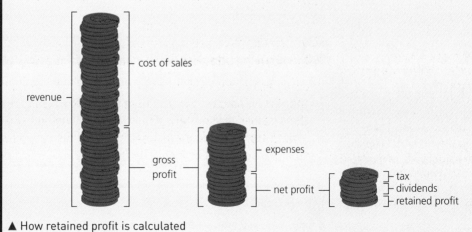

▲ How retained profit is calculated

Study tips

You must remember the important differences between gross profit, net profit and retained profit.

REVISION SUMMARY

Income statements

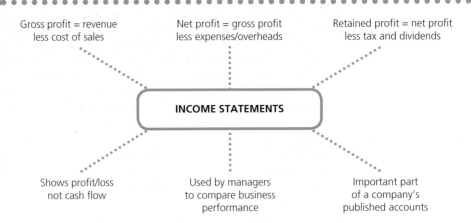

Gross profit = revenue less cost of sales

Net profit = gross profit less expenses/overheads

Retained profit = net profit less tax and dividends

INCOME STATEMENTS

Shows profit/loss not cash flow

Used by managers to compare business performance

Important part of a company's published accounts

Using income statements in decision making

Managers can use the structure of income statements to help them in making decisions based on profit calculations. If a manager has to choose which of two new products to launch, one way of making this decision is to construct two forecasted income statements.

Case study

Asif has to decide on which location would be best for a new shop. He has undertaken market research and forecasted the costs of these two locations. The information he has collected is shown below:

Forecasted information for next year	Location A	Location B
Revenue	$40 000	$60 000
Cost of sales	$16 000	$24 000
Gross profit	$24 000	$36 000
Rent	$10 000	$16 000
Other expenses	$5000	$8000
Net profit	$9000	$12 000

Case study

Asif also considered other factors before making the final decision:

- Annual rent at Location B is fixed for five years, but for only two years at Location A.
- A new housing estate is planned to be built just six kilometres away from Location B.
- A potential competitor has just closed a shop near Location A.

Asif finally selected Location B for the new shop.

Activity 24.5

Read the case studies above.

Do you think Asif made the right decision? Justify your answer.

Key info

The decision to retain profit for prospective profitable investment projects rather than pay higher dividends to shareholders is unlikely to affect the company share price. However, if lower profits are predicted this is likely to lead to a lower share price.

Case study

Joe is the new product manager at a chain of takeaway food stores. He is planning to introduce a new type of 'fast food' – a pizza or a curry. He has two product options but the business can only afford to buy the equipment and advertising material needed for one of these options.

He has undertaken some market research and forecasted the main costs for the two product options. He has asked you to help him complete the following income statements:

Forecasts for one year	Pizza option	Curry option
Revenue	50 000 units @ $3	40 000 units @ $5
Cost of sales	Unit cost of $1 each	Unit cost of $2 each
Gross profit		
Annual equipment costs	$13 000	$12 000
Annual advertising costs	$15 000	$20 000
Other expenses	$13 000	$15 000
Net profit		

Study tips

Business managers often have to use calculations as part of their job – don't be afraid of business calculations! This book explains a number of calculations – practise all of the examples. Take a calculator into the examination with you!

Activity 24.6

Read the case study above.

a Write out the two income statements.
b Fill in the totals for revenue and cost of sales.
c Calculate the gross profit and net profit of each product options.
d Explain **two** other factors Joe should consider before making this decision.

e Joe finally decides on the curry option. After one year, he finds that profit from this product is much lower than expected. Evaluate **two** ways which Joe could use to try to increase profits from this product.

International business in focus

Sun Resorts, revenue and net profit up

In 2017, Sun Resorts hotel group, the large leisure group operating in Mauritius and the Maldives, announced that its net profits for the second quarter was Rs 219.4 million as compared to only 4.6 million in the same period for the previous financial year. This impressive increase in profit was due to the new strategy and pricing policy adopted by the group.

The Mauritian company has set up a five-year plan to secure profitable growth.

- Firstly, increasing prices in the group's hotels was part of this plan and happily the occupancy rate has stayed high, reaching 87.7 per cent with a 22 per cent increase in revenue per available room.
- Secondly, all the hotels of the group are operating, which has not happened for more than two years. Indeed, the 5* hotel Kanuhura, in the Maldives, re-opened recently after nearly 18 months of renovations. However, the high costs of relaunching the hotel could affect the yearly profit of the group. Seasonality of the Mauritian hotel industry also affects profit at certain times of the year when room occupancy is lower and revenue is lower.

Discussion points

- Why are profits important to a large hotel group such as Sun Resorts?
- Explain why the company increased profits in 2017.
- Explain why Sun Resorts may not enjoy the same increase in profit in the future.

Exam-style questions: Short answer and data response

1 Ikram is a hairdresser. His revenue was 10 per cent higher this year than last year. He earned revenue of $50000 last year. He charged an average of $5 for each customer last year and has not increased prices. He buys in materials such as shampoo and hairspray and has calculated that the cost is an average of $2 for each customer. He estimates that his overhead expenses are $10000 this year.

  a Define 'revenue'. [2]

  b Calculate Ikram's revenue this year. Show your working. [2]

  c Identify **four** costs likely to be included in Ikram's annual overhead expenses. [4]

  d Calculate Ikram's net profit this year (using your result from **b**). Show your working. [6]

  e Ikram thinks that his net profit next year will be higher if he increases average prices to $6 per customer. Do you agree? Justify your answer. [6]

2 Sue develops new computer games. She has developed two new games but she only has the capital to launch one of these.

• Game A is aimed at young children of around 6–10 years old.

• Game B is targeted at teenagers of around 13–18 years old.

She has forecast the following financial information:

Forecasts for next year	Game A	Game B
Revenue	3000 units @$5	2000 units @$10
Cost of sales	$1.50 per unit	$3 per unit
Expenses	$4000	$9000

  a Define 'cost of sales'. [2]

  b Identify **two** reasons why retained profit of a company is not the same as its (net) profit. [2]

  c Outline **two** ways in which Sue could try to increase revenue for any one of her existing games. [4]

  d Explain **two** other pieces of information that Sue would find useful before making a choice between Game A and Game B. [6]

  e Advise Sue which game she should launch. Use calculations to support your answer. [6]

Revision checklist

In this chapter you have learned:

✔ what is meant by accounting information and why it is important

✔ why profit is important to businesses and investors – and that it is not the same as cash

✔ to explain the differences between such concepts as gross profit, net profit and retained profit

✔ what the main features of income statements are and how these statements can be useful to managers when taking decisions.

NOW – test your understanding with the revision questions in the Student etextbook and the Workbook.

Statement of financial position

Statement of financial position

Definitions to learn

The **statement of financial position** shows the value of a business's assets and liabilities at a particular time.

In the previous chapter, we learned how a manager can calculate whether the business is making a profit or a loss. This is clearly of great importance. However, by itself, the income statement does not tell us how much the business is worth. Business owners would be very interested to know how much their business is worth. This information, together with other details, is given on the **statement of financial position**.

The statement of financial position is very different from the income statement. The income statement records the income and expenses of a business, and the profit or loss it makes, over a period of time – usually one year. The statement of financial position records the value or worth of a business at just one moment in time – usually at the end of the financial year.

A personal statement of financial position example will help to introduce the basic concept of this account.

> **Case study:** A personal statement of financial position
>
> Sanchez plans to start his own business. A government business adviser asked him 'How much money can you put into the business?' and Sanchez had to admit, he did not really know!
>
> The adviser asked him for an approximate value of everything he owned including any bank accounts – as well as any debts or loans that he had.
>
> Together they made these two lists:
>
> | All items *owned* by Sanchez | All debts *owed* by Sanchez |
> |---|---|
> | House $50 000 | Loan on house (mortgage) $18 000 |
> | Car $4500 | Bank loan on car $3000 |
> | Savings $3000 | Owes brother $1500 |
> | Bank account $500 | |
> | **Total $58 000** | **Total $22 500** |
>
> The adviser told Sanchez: 'The total value of what you own is $35 500 more than the value of what you owe. This difference is called "equity" and means that you could, theoretically, invest this much of your own capital into your new business. Unfortunately, it is not all in a cash form!'

Business statements of financial position follow exactly the same principles. They list and give a value to all of the **assets** and **liabilities** of the business. It is important to understand these terms before the layout of the statement of financial position is explained.

» Assets are those items of value which are owned by the business. Land, buildings, equipment and vehicles are examples of non-current or fixed assets. They are likely to be kept by the business for more than one year. Most non-current (fixed) assets, apart from land, depreciate over time so the value of these will fall on the statement of financial position from one year to the next. Intangible assets are those that do not exist physically but still have a value – such as brand names, patents and copyrights. Cash, inventories (stocks) and accounts receivables (debtor customers who owe money to the business) are only held for short periods of time and are called current assets.

» Liabilities are items owed by the business. Again, there are two main forms of these. Non-current liabilities (or long-term liabilities) are long-term borrowings which do not have to be repaid within one year. Current liabilities are amounts owed by the business which must be repaid within one year, for example, bank overdraft and accounts payable (suppliers/creditors owed money by the business).

What is the importance of these terms? Refer again to the case study on page 303 giving details of Sanchez's own personal finances. The value of his assets is greater than the value of his debts or liabilities, so he owns wealth. In the case of a business, this wealth belongs to the owners; in the case of companies, it belongs to the shareholders. This is why the statement of financial position is so important to the users of the accounts (the owners of the business). It shows how much wealth or equity the owners have invested in the business. They would obviously like to see this increase year by year.

Total assets – Total liabilities = Owners' equity (shareholders' funds in a limited company)

Explanation of statement of financial position terms

» **Non-current** and **current assets**, **current** and **non-current liabilities** (see above).
» Total assets less total liabilities is always equal to total shareholders' funds or equity – otherwise the statement of financial position would not balance!
» Shareholders' equity (or shareholders' funds) is the total sum of money invested into the business by the owners of the company – the shareholders. This money is invested in two ways:
  • Share capital is the money put into the business when the shareholders bought newly issued shares.
  • Reserves arise for a number of reasons. Profit and loss reserves are retained profits from current and previous years. This profit is owned by the shareholders but has not been paid out to them in the form of dividends. It is kept in the business as part of the shareholders' funds.

Case study: Company statement of financial position

This is a typical statement of financial position, for Ace Machines Ltd. The previous year's figures are also usually shown to allow for easy comparisons. The terms that have not yet been explained are looked at in more detail below.

Ace Machines Ltd statement of financial position as at 31/3/2018 ($000)

ASSETS	2018	2017
Non-current (fixed) assets		
Land and buildings	450	440
Machinery	700	600
	1150	1040
Current assets		
Inventories	80	50
Accounts receivable (debtors)	50	60
Cash	10	15
	140	125
TOTAL ASSETS	**1290**	**1165**
LIABILITIES		
Current liabilities		
Accounts payable (creditors)	65	40
Bank overdraft	65	60
	130	100
Non current (long-term) liabilities		
Long-term bank loan	300	245
Total liabilities	**430**	**345**
TOTAL ASSETS – TOTAL LIABILITIES	**860**	**820**
Shareholders' equity (shareholders' funds)		
Share capital	520	500
Profit and loss account reserves	340	320
TOTAL SHAREHOLDERS' FUNDS/EQUITY	**860**	**820**

Study tips

There is more than one accounting term used for many statement of financial position items (some of these are given in brackets).

The Cambridge International syllabus uses the standard international terminology as used in this chapter – but may give other terms as well to aid your understanding.

Activity 25.1: Understanding the statement of financial position

A Managing Director of a company is trying to write out the statement of financial position for the business. The following items have been listed. You have been asked to help the Managing Director by putting them all under their correct heading. Copy out the table and tick the correct box for each item.

	Current assets	Non-current assets	Current liabilities	Non-current liabilities	Share capital	Reserves
Company vehicles						
Cash in the till						
Ten-year bank loan						
Ordinary share capital						
Money owed by customers						
Unsold goods						
Factory building						
Retained profit						
Amounts owed to suppliers						
Tax owed to government						

Interpreting the statement of financial position data

» Shareholders can see if 'their' stake in the business has increased or fallen in value over the last 12 months by looking at the 'total equity' figures for two years.
» Shareholders can also analyse how expansion by the business has been paid for – by increasing non-current liabilities (such as long-term loans); from retained profits or by increasing share capital (sale of shares). If inventories or stocks have been sold off to provide capital for business expansion then this will be clear by this figure declining on the statement of financial position.
» Working capital can be calculated from statement of financial position data. This is a very important concept (see also Chapter 23). It is also known as net current assets. It is calculated by the formula:

Working capital = Current assets – Current liabilities

» No business can survive without working capital. It is used to pay short-term debts. If these debts cannot be paid because the business does not have enough working capital, the creditors could force the business to stop trading.
» Capital employed can also be calculated by using data from the statement of financial position. The following formula is used:

Capital employed = Shareholders' funds + Non-current liabilities

This is the total long-term and permanent capital of the business which has been used to pay for the assets of the business.

» The statement of financial position data can also be used to calculate ratios which are used to assess business performance – see Chapter 26.

Case study: Using a statement of financial position

Refer to the statement of financial position for Ace Machines Ltd on page 305. Ace Machines Ltd manufactures washing machines and vacuum cleaners. Over the period shown by the statements of financial position, the business invested heavily in new IT-based equipment for its production line. The retained profits of the business have been falling in recent years.

Some shareholders were studying the company's 2018 statement of financial position and the following questions were raised:

Q: The business increased the value of non-current (fixed) assets last year, but how was this financed?

A: The business increased its bank loans, sold new shares and retained profit within the business.

Q: The value of inventories increased this year. Is this good?

A: Probably not if it resulted from not being able to sell a higher level of output to customers.

These inventories have to be financed somehow – and there is an opportunity cost to this!

The money tied up in inventories could have been used in other ways within the business.

REVISION SUMMARY

Statement of financial position

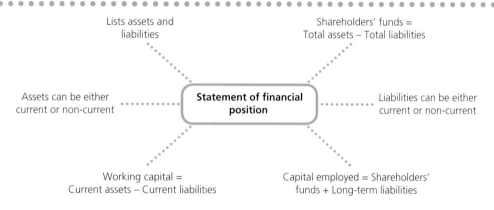

Lists assets and liabilities

Shareholders' funds = Total assets – Total liabilities

Assets can be either current or non-current

Statement of financial position

Liabilities can be either current or non-current

Working capital = Current assets – Current liabilities

Capital employed = Shareholders' funds + Long-term liabilities

Study tips

A statement of financial position is useful to many stakeholder groups – to help analyse the performance and financial strength of a business.

It can also be compared with statements of financial position from previous years or other businesses. See Chapter 26 for more detail of how business accounts can be analysed.

Activity 25.2: Using the statement of financial position data

Refer to Ace Machines Ltd's statement of financial position on page 305.

a Calculate the change in working capital between the two years shown.
b Comment on your result.
c Which source of finance provided most capital during 2018: loans, share issues or retained profit? Explain your answer.
d Do you think that this business should reduce the value of its inventories? Explain your answer.
e Do you think the shareholders of Ace Machines Ltd should be pleased with the statement of financial position data? Explain your answer.

Activity 25.3: Comparing statement of financial position data

KL Co. Ltd and HK Co. Ltd are two businesses that manufacture gifts bought by tourists – such as pottery and wooden carvings. The following table contains a summary of the two companies' statements of financial position for the year ending 31/10/18.

	KL Co. Ltd ($000)	HK Co. Ltd. ($000)
Non-current assets	50	120
Current assets:		
Inventories	12	50
Accounts receivable	8	16
Cash	1	4
Total assets	x	190
Current liabilities	18	70
Non-current liabilities	20	30
Total liabilities	38	100
Total assets – Total liabilities	y	90
Shareholders' equity:		
Share capital	20	75
Retained profit reserves	13	z
Total shareholders' equity	33	90

a Calculate the values for x, y and z.
b Identify **two** types of non-current assets that these businesses are likely to own.
c Identify **three** items that are likely to be held as inventories by these businesses.
d Which company seems to be in a stronger financial position? Use the data above to support your answer.

International business in focus

Hayley's statement of financial position

Hayley's is one of Sri Lanka's largest public limited companies. It is a very diversified business with divisions operating in agriculture, transport, consumer products and aviation. A summary of the Hayley Group statement of financial position is shown below.

All figures in rupees, '00 000	As at 31/3/17	As at 31/3/16
Non-current assets	38 864	38 155
Current assets	8202	8248
Total assets	47 066	46 403
Non-current liabilities	11 769	15 451
Current liabilities	11 276	9132
Total liabilities	23 045	24 583
Total equity (shareholders' funds)	24 021	21 820

Discussion points

● Suggest **two** non-current (fixed) assets that the transport division of Hayley's is likely to own.

● Suggest why the company reduced non-current liabilities (long-term loans) in the period shown above.

● Do you think that the shareholders in Hayley's would be pleased with the 2017 statement of financial position? Explain your answer.

Exam-style questions: Short answer and data response

1 An extract from Acme Builders Ltd's latest statement of financial position is shown below. During the period shown the government increased interest rates – the cost of borrowing money. A competitor business is for sale. The owners have asked the directors of Acme Builders if they wish to buy the business for $4 million.

Extract from Acme Builders Ltd's statement of financial position

	As at 31/9/2018 ($m)	As at 31/3/2017 ($m)
Non-current assets	67	58
Current assets	23	15
Non-current liabilities	12	6
Total equity (shareholders' funds)	57	50

a Define 'non-current assets'. [2]
b Identify **two** current assets likely to be held by Acme Builders Ltd. [2]
c Outline **two** possible reasons why the company increased its value of total equity (shareholders' funds) during the period shown. [4]
d Explain **two** ways in which the increase in non-current liabilities (long-term loans) might have been used by the company. [6]
e Consider how useful the information above would be to the directors of Acme Builders Ltd when they decide whether or not to take over the competing business for $4 million. Justify your answer. [6]

2 An extract from Penang Garages plc's latest statement of financial position is shown below. The garage company sells cars and repairs old vehicles. It has many competitors.

Extract from Penang Garages plc's statement of financial position

All figures in $m	As at 31/12/18	As at 31/12/17
Non-current assets	96	90
Current assets	23	25
Non-current liabilities	35	40
Current liabilities	28	25
Total equity (shareholders' funds)	56	50

a Define 'total equity' (or shareholders' funds). [2]
b Identify **two** current liabilities Penang Garages is likely to have. [2]
c Outline **two** possible reasons why the value of current assets has fallen during the period shown. [4]
d Explain the usefulness of **two** pieces of information, other than the data above, that a potential shareholder might need to analyse before investing in Penang Garages plc. [6]
e Do you think that the shareholders of Penang Garages plc would be pleased with the information shown above? Justify your answer. [6]

Revision checklist

In this chapter you have learned:

✔ what the main parts of a statement of financial position are
✔ what the main classifications of assets and liabilities are and how to illustrate these using examples
✔ about interpreting a simple statement of financial position and the judgements which can be made regarding the financial activities of a business.

NOW – test your understanding with the revision questions in the Student etextbook and the Workbook.

26 Analysis of accounts

This chapter will explain:

★ the concept and importance of profitability and liquidity
★ how to interpret the financial performance of a business by calculating and analysing profitability ratios and liquidity ratios: gross margin; (net) profit margin; return on capital employed; current ratio; acid test
★ the needs of different users of accounts and ratio analysis
★ how users of accounts and ratio results might use information to help make decisions, for example, whether to lend to or invest in the business.

Analysis of published accounts

The company accounts or financial statements we have studied contain a great deal of information. These published accounts of limited companies are made available to all those interested in the performance of the business. There are many stakeholders who will analyse company accounts. We must now look at how these accounts can be used and analysed to give the information these groups need.

Q: What is meant by 'analysis of accounts'?

A: It means using the data contained in the accounts to make some useful observations about the performance and financial strength of the business.

Without 'analysis of accounts' it is often impossible to tell whether a business is:

>> performing better this year than last year
>> performing better than other businesses.

Case study

Consider these results for two food retailing companies:

	Freshfoods plc	Foodstore plc
Net profit (2018)	$300 000	$30 000

What conclusions can be drawn from these figures?

- Is Freshfoods plc much more successful than Foodstore plc? You may think so just from these figures.
- Is the management of Freshfoods plc ten times more efficient than the management of Foodstore plc?
- Is Freshfoods plc making much better use of its assets than its competitor is?
- Is the profit margin made on each item sold much higher in one company than the other?

Definite answers to these questions cannot be given unless other information is considered. Take, for example, the total value of **capital employed** by both of these businesses:

	Freshfoods plc	Foodstore plc
Capital employed (2018)	$900 000	$60 000

Which company seems to have made more efficient use of the capital invested? We need to compare net profit made with capital employed in each company.

Foodstore plc has made $30 000 profit from an investment of $60 000 and Freshfoods plc has made $300 000 profit from an investment of $900 000. By comparing two figures from the accounts, Foodstore plc appears to have achieved a better performance even though its overall level of profits is lower.

▲ It is impossible to tell which of these businesses is more profitable without analysing their accounts

This example shows how important it is to use more than one figure from the accounts when trying to assess how a business is performing. Comparing two figures from the accounts in this way is called ratio analysis. This is a very important way of analysing the published accounts.

There are many ratios which can be calculated from a set of accounts. This chapter concentrates on five of the most commonly used. These ratios are used to measure and compare profitability (or performance) and **liquidity** of a business.

The concept and importance of profitability

Profit is an amount of money the business has made after all costs have been taken off revenue. However, **profitability** is different to profit, although it is related. It is the measurement of the profit made relative to either:

>> the value of sales achieved
>> the capital invested in the business.

Profitability is measured in percentage form. Profitability is therefore a measure of efficiency and can be used to compare the business's performance over a number of years and also to compare its performance with that of other businesses. It is important to:

>> investors when deciding which business to invest in
>> directors and managers of the business to assess if the business is becoming more or less successful over time. This might lead to the directors or managers needing to change the operations of the business to improve profitability.

Profitability ratios

Three commonly used profitability ratios are:

1 Return on capital employed (ROCE).

This is calculated by the formula:

$$\frac{Net\ profit}{Capital\ employed} \times 100$$

Case study

ABC Computing Ltd made a net profit of $280 million in 2018 and its capital employed was $1065 million. Its return on capital employed in 2018 was:

$$\frac{Net\ profit}{Capital\ employed} \times 100$$

$$= \frac{\$280}{\$1065} \times 100$$

$$= 26.3\%$$

This means that, in 2018, the company made a return on the capital employed in the business of 26.3 per cent. The higher this result, the more successful the managers are in earning profit from capital used in the business. If this percentage increases next year, it means that the managers are running the business more efficiently – making higher profits from each dollar invested in the business.

This result should now be compared with other years and other companies to see if the managers are running the business more efficiently or not.

2 Gross profit margin.

This is calculated by the formula:

$$\text{Gross profit margin (\%)} = \frac{Gross\ profit}{Revenue} \times 100$$

 Case study

ABC Computing Ltd made a gross profit in 2018 of $400 million. Revenue was $1300 million.

$$\text{Gross profit margin (\%)} = \frac{\$400}{\$1300} \times 100$$

$$= 30.8\%$$

This means that on every $1 worth of goods sold, the company made on average 30.8 cents gross profit. Do not forget that this is before other expenses have been deducted and is not the final profit of the company. Again, this result needs to be compared with other years and other companies.

If this percentage increases next year it would suggest that:

* prices have been increased by more than the cost of sales has risen

or that

* costs of sales has been reduced. Possibly a new supplier is being used or managers have negotiated lower cost prices.

3 Net profit margin (also known as profit margin).

This is calculated by the formula:

$$\text{Net profit margin (\%)} = \frac{Net\ profit}{Revenue} \times 100$$

Case study

ABC Computing Ltd made a net profit of $280m in 2018.

$$Net\ profit\ margin = \frac{\$280}{\$1300} \times 100$$

$$= 21.5\%$$

The company made 21.5 cents net profit on each $1 worth of sales. This is lower than the gross profit margin because all other expenses including interest have been deducted from gross profit to arrive at net profit before tax. The higher this result, the more successful the managers are in making net profit from sales. What could this result be compared with? Again, it should be compared with other years and other companies.

Profitability ratios – what do they tell us?

One profitability ratio result is not very useful. When a ratio result is compared with others, then some effective analysis can be done. Here are some examples taken from the same business:

Ratio results	Observation	Analysis
Gross profit margin: 2017 – 20% 2018 – 24%	This means that the gross profit on each $1 of sales has increased.	The business is more successful at converting sales into profit. Either the price of goods has increased (by more than costs) or the cost of sales has fallen (but price has not been reduced at all or not by as much).
Net profit margin: 2017 – 14% 2018 – 12%	This means that the net profit on each $1 of sales has fallen – even though gross profit margin has increased.	The business is less successful at converting sales into net profit. The overheads/fixed costs of the business must have increased significantly during the year – reducing the company's net profit compared to revenue.
Return on capital employed: 2017 – 10% 2018 – 6%	The profit made for each $1 invested in the business has fallen.	This must be because either net profit has fallen or capital employed has increased. If capital employed has increased, this could mean that the managers of the business have invested more, hoping to make higher profit in future.

Activity 26.1: ABC Computing Ltd – profitability

ABC Computing Ltd – 2017 accounts summary	$m
Revenue	1200
Gross profit	450
Net profit	220
Capital employed	965

a Using the 2017 accounting information above for Ace Computing Ltd calculate:
  • return on capital employed
  • gross profit margin
  • net profit margin.

b Refer to your results and the case studies on page 313. Do you feel that the company performed better in 2017 or 2018? Give reasons for your answer.

The concept and importance of liquidity

This measures a very important feature of a business. Liquidity is the ability of a business to pay back its short-term debts. If a business cannot pay its suppliers for materials that are important to production or if the business cannot repay an overdraft when required to, it is said to be **illiquid**. The businesses it owes money to may force it to stop trading and sell its assets so that the debts are repaid.

Liquidity ratios

Two commonly used liquidity ratios are:

1 Current ratio

This is calculated by the formula:

$$Current\ ratio = \frac{Current\ assets}{Current\ liabilities} \times 100$$

 Case study

ABC Computing Ltd had current assets valued at $125 million in 2018 and current liabilities of $100 million at the end of 2018.

$$Current\ ratio = \frac{125}{100} \times 100$$

This result means that the business could only just pay off all of its short-term debts from current assets. 1.25 is an acceptable result but a really 'safe' current ratio would be between 1.5 and 2. If the current ratio is less than 1, it would mean that the business could have real cash flow problems. It could not pay off its short-term debts from current assets.

More effective analysis of liquidity is possible if results for previous years and other similar businesses are available. If the current ratio is very high, say over 2.0, it could mean that too much working capital is tied up in unprofitable current assets.

The current ratio is useful but it assumes that all current assets could be turned into cash quickly. This is not always the case. For example, it might be very difficult to sell all inventories in a short period of time. For this reason a second liquidity ratio is used.

2 Acid test ratio

This is calculated by the formula:

$$Acid\ test\ ratio = \frac{Current\ assets - Inventories}{Current\ liabilities} \times 100$$

 Case study

ABC Computing Ltd had $50 million of inventories at the end of 2018. Its acid test ratio can now be calculated:

$$Acid\ test\ ratio = \frac{125 - 50}{100} \times 100$$

A result of 1 would mean that the company could just pay off its short-term debts from its most liquid assets. This is usually considered to be an acceptable acid test result. This result of 0.75 means that ABC Computing cannot do this. This might be worrying for the management and steps may have to be taken to improve the liquidity of the business – for example, reduce the level of inventories by selling some for cash.

Liquidity ratios – what can they tell us?

One liquidity ratio result is not very useful. When a ratio result is compared with others, then some effective analysis can be done. Here are some examples taken:

Ratio results	Observation	Analysis
Current ratio 1.0 – 2018 Current ratio 1.5 – 2017	The current ratio has fallen between 2017 and 2018.	This could be because the business has bought and used many more supplies, but not yet paid for them. It could also be because the business has used cash to pay for fixed assets. The business has low liquidity and needs to increase current assets or reduce current liabilities.
Current ratio 1.75 – 2018 Acid test ratio 0.5 – 2018	The current ratio is acceptable and much higher than the acid test ratio in 2018.	The acid test ratio might be too low – the business might be at risk of not being able to pay its short-term debts from its liquid assets – cash and accounts receivable (debtors). The great difference between the two results is because of a relatively high level of inventories.

Activity 26.2: ABC Computing Ltd – liquidity

ABC Computing Ltd – 2017 accounts summary	$m
Current assets	135
Inventories	40
Current liabilities	95

a Using the information above for ABC Computing Ltd, calculate the following ratios for 2017:
  • current ratio
  • acid test ratio.
b Do you think the management of ABC Computing should be satisfied with the liquidity of the company? Justify your answer using your results from **a** and the 2018 results on page 315.

Why and how accounts are used

Who uses the accounts of a business? Which groups would analyse a company's accounts, such as by calculating ratios? As it is only the accounts of public limited companies that have to be published, we shall concentrate on the uses and users of these. The following groups have an interest in a public limited company's accounts and the ratios based on them.

User of accounts	What they use the accounts for
Managers: they will be able to have much more detailed and frequent accounting information than any of the other groups	They will use the accounts to help them keep control over the performance of each product or division of the business. Managers will be able to identify which parts of the business are performing well or poorly. Accounting data will help in decision making, for example whether to expand the business, change price levels or close down a product or division that is not doing well.

User of accounts	What they use the accounts for
	Managers will calculate accounting ratios too. Ratios are very useful and a quick way for managers to compare their company's profit performance and liquidity. Ratio results may be compared with: ● other years ● other businesses. It is important to compare accounting ratios in these ways. One ratio result on its own means very little. Consider this example: Hurtwood Trading Co. Ltd return on capital employed 2018: 12%. Is this a good or a bad result? This question can only be answered by managers looking at past results and those of other companies. For example, here is some additional information: Hurtwood Trading Co. Ltd return on capital employed 2017: 5.8% Westbay Trading Co. Ltd return on capital employed 2018: 20%. Now the managers of Hurtwood Trading can make realistic comparisons. Their company is performing more effectively than in the previous year but it still needs to improve further to equal the performance and profitability of one of the company's closest rivals.
Shareholders: limited companies are owned by shareholders and they have a legal right to receive the published accounts each year	Shareholders – and potential investors – want to know, from the income statement, how big a profit or loss the company made. The profitability ratio results will be compared with last year's. The higher the profitability ratio results are, the more likely shareholders are to want to invest by buying more shares in the company. They will want to know, from the statement of financial position, if the business is worth more at the end of the year than it was at the beginning. They will also assess the liquidity of the business – they do not want to invest in a company with serious cash or liquidity problems.
Creditors: these are other businesses which have supplied goods to the company without yet receiving payment	The statement of financial position will indicate to creditors the total value of debts that the company has to pay back and the cash position of the company. Liquidity ratios, especially when compared with the previous year, will indicate the ability of the company to pay back all of its creditors on time. If these results suggest the company has a liquidity problem, suppliers may refuse to supply goods on credit.
Banks: these may have lent money to the company on a short- or long-term basis	They will use the accounts in a similar way to creditors. If the business seems to be at risk of becoming illiquid, it is unlikely that a bank will be willing to lend more.
Government	The government and the tax office will want to check on the profit tax paid by the company. If the company is making a loss, this might be bad news for the government's control of the whole economy, especially if it means that workers' jobs may be lost.
Workers and trade unions	Workers and trade unions will want to assess whether the future of the company is secure or not. In addition, if managers are saying that 'they cannot afford to give workers a pay rise' it would be useful for workers and unions to assess whether the profits of the company are increasing or not.
Other businesses – especially those in the same industry	The managers of other companies may be considering a bid to take over the company or they may just wish to compare the performance of the business with that of their own. Businesses will compare their performance and profitability with others in the same industry.

All of these users of accounts need to remember that ratio analysis does not provide 'all the answers' to the many questions they have about the performance and financial strength of a business.

Limitations of using accounts and ratio analysis

»» Managers will have access to all accounts data – but external users will only be able to use the published accounts, which contain only data required by law.
»» Ratios are based on past accounting data and may not indicate how a business will perform in the future.
»» Accounting data over time will be affected by inflation (rising prices), and comparisons between years may be misleading.
»» Different companies may use slightly different accounting methods, for example in valuing their fixed assets. These different methods could lead to different ratio results, therefore making comparisons difficult.

Business accounts

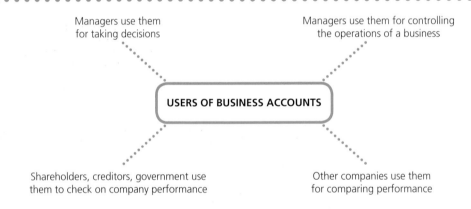

Managers use them for taking decisions

Managers use them for controlling the operations of a business

USERS OF BUSINESS ACCOUNTS

Shareholders, creditors, government use them to check on company performance

Other companies use them for comparing performance

Case study: Using ratios to help make decisions

Gloria Hotels is a public limited company that owns three hotels in the capital city. The tourist industry in the country is expanding but there are many competing hotel companies in the capital city. The company accountant has calculated the following ratio results from the latest published accounts:

Gloria Hotels plc	2018	2017
Return on capital employed	13%	17%
Gross profit margin	35%	30%
Net profit margin	12%	16%
Current ratio	1.2	1.4
Acid test ratio	0.6	1.0

Financial information and financial decisions: end-of-section case study

➡ Fruity Smoothies

Fruity Smoothies is a public limited company which produces a range of fruit smoothies drinks. The business operates in many different countries around the world. Fruity Smoothies is a successful company but the Directors want to increase its market share of the fruit smoothies global market.

The following two ways of increasing market share have been identified:

- Option 1: Increase sales of its most popular brand of smoothies by selling it in five new countries. The investment required to get the smoothies launched into new markets is estimated to be $80 million. This includes market research, marketing campaigns and building factories to produce the fruit smoothies in the other countries.
- Option 2: Take over a competitor that sells a different range of brands of smoothies. The cost of the takeover to buy all the shares in the company is estimated to be $160 million.

➡ Appendix 1

Summary of financial information for Fruity Smoothies 2018

Existing business	$m per year
Capital employed	800
Revenue	1600
Gross profit	1200
Net profit	200
Option 1	**$m per year**
Predicted revenue from five more countries	400
Additional fixed costs	160
Variable costs for additional sales	220
Option 2	**$m per year**
Predicted revenue from competitors' sales	400
Fixed costs of competitor	120
Variable costs of competitor	220

Appendix 2

Information on Country X and Country Y

	Country X	Country Y
Average income per head	$6000	$40 000
Population	20 million	20 million
Competitors' sales	$20 million per year	$200 000 per year
Climate	Seasons (hot in summer and cold in winter)	Hot all year round
Average wage rate	$2 per hour	$20 per hour
Unemployment rate	24%	4%
Rents	low	high

Exam-style questions: Case study

1 a Explain, using examples, the difference between fixed costs and variable costs for Fruity Smoothies. [8]

  b Using the information in Appendix 1, consider the **two** options for increasing the market share of Fruity Smoothies. Recommend which option the Directors should choose. Justify your choice using appropriate calculations of profitability ratios. [12]

2 a Both Option 1 and Option 2 require capital for the expansion. Explain **four** suitable sources of finance the Directors of Fruity Smoothies could use. [8]

  b Fruity Smoothies might take over a competitor which sells fruit smoothies. Consider how important the competitors' statement of financial position and income statement would be in helping the Directors of Fruity Smoothies decide whether to take over the competitor. Justify your answer. [12]

Optional questions

3 a The Directors of Fruity Smoothies want to increase its market share. Explain **two** other aims the Directors might have for the business. [8]

  b If Fruity Smoothies tries to sell its smoothies in several new countries it will have a number of problems to overcome. Consider **three** problems for the business when entering a new market in a different country. Do you think each of these problems can be easily overcome? Justify your answer. [12]

4 a Fruity Smoothies sells a wide range of branded smoothies. Explain **two** ways that Fruity Smoothies could create a brand image for a new fruit drink aimed at teenagers. [8]

  b Fruity Smoothies is considering building a new factory to produce and sell fruit smoothies in one of the two countries shown in Appendix 2. Consider the advantages and disadvantages of each of the **two** countries. Recommend which country it should choose to build the new factory. Justify your choice. [12]

SECTION 6

External influences on business issues

Chapters

27 Economic issues
28 Environmental and ethical issues
29 Business and the international economy

Economic issues

The wider economy and how it can affect businesses

What happens in the wider economy will affect businesses either directly or via their customers. Some of these external changes will be due to factors such as the business cycle, or as a result of government policy such as changes in interest rates. The effect of these changes in the economy will not be under the control of businesses themselves but they can decide how they will react to these effects, such as changes in exchange rates or the rates of unemployment.

The main stages of the business cycle

Economic growth may not be achieved steadily every year – there are often years when the economy does not grow at all or when the value of **Gross Domestic Product (GDP)** actually falls. This pattern is shown on the trade cycle diagram on page 327.

>> *Growth* – This is when GDP is rising, unemployment is generally falling and the country is enjoying higher living standards. Most businesses will do well at this time.
>> *Boom* – This is caused by too much spending. Prices start to rise quickly and there are shortages of skilled workers. Business costs will be rising and businesses will become uncertain about the future.
>> *Recession* – Often caused by too little spending. This is a period when GDP actually falls. Most businesses will experience falling demand and profits. Workers may lose their jobs.
>> *Slump* – A serious and long-drawn-out recession. Unemployment reaches very high levels and prices may fall. Many businesses will fail to survive this period.

These four main stages of the business cycle (sometimes known as the trade cycle) are shown on the diagram.

> **Definitions to learn**
>
> **Gross Domestic Product (GDP)** is the total value of output of goods and services in a country in one year.

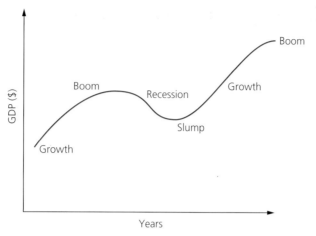

▲ A business cycle diagram

Clearly, governments will try to avoid the economy moving towards a **recession** or a slump, but will also want to reduce the chances of a boom. A boom with rapid inflation and higher business costs can often lead to the conditions that result in a recession.

Impact on businesses of changes in employment levels, inflation and GDP

Changes in economic indicators will have an impact – either positive or negative – on most businesses.

» Changes in employment levels will affect the ability of the business to recruit new employees and also the incomes of customers. If unemployment goes up then it may be easier to recruit employees as there are more people to choose from. Customers may have lost their jobs and so income levels may have fallen, therefore reducing the amount of sales made by the business. However, some businesses that sell cheaper products may see sales increase as customers cut back on spending and buy cheaper alternatives.

» Rising inflation may result in business costs increasing. Prices of products may have to be increased, leading to falling sales for the business. Rising prices of essential products may also mean consumers have less income available for the purchase of non-essential products. So the effect of increasing inflation on businesses may depend on the type of products they sell.

» Increasing GDP means that the economy is growing. Generally businesses will benefit from increasing sales as more people have jobs and have more income to spend buying products. It may start to get more difficult to recruit new employees if unemployment starts to fall at the same time.

Government economic objectives

Most governments have the following objectives for the economy:

» low **inflation**
» low **unemployment**
» **economic growth**
» **balance of payments** between imports and exports.

Low inflation

Inflation occurs when there is a rise in average prices over a period of time. Low inflation is an important objective. When prices rise rapidly it can be serious for the whole country. These are the problems a country will have if there is rapid inflation:

» Workers' wages will not buy as many goods as before. This means that people's **real incomes** will fall. Real income is the value, in terms of what can be bought, of an income – if a worker receives a 6 per cent wage increase but prices rise by 10 per cent in the same year, then the worker's real income has fallen by 4 per cent. Workers may demand higher wages so that their real incomes increase.

» Prices of the goods produced in the country will be higher than those in other countries. People may buy foreign goods instead. Jobs in the country will be lost.

» Businesses will be unlikely to want to expand and create more jobs in the near future. The living standards are likely to fall.

Therefore low inflation can encourage businesses to expand and it makes it easier for a country to sell its goods and services abroad.

Key info

Inflation in Venezuela is said to be 720 per cent. The minimum wage was increased by 454 per cent to take account of inflation. $1000 in savings in 2013 would now be worth less than $5.

Definitions to learn

Real income is the value of income, and it falls when prices rise faster than money income.

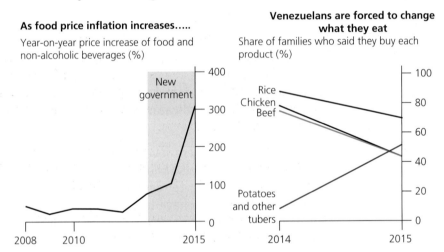

As food price inflation increases.....
Year-on-year price increase of food and non-alcoholic beverages (%)

Venezuelans are forced to change what they eat
Share of families who said they buy each product (%)

Source: Encuesta Sobre Condiciones de Vida en Venezuela, Instituto Nacional de Estadistica

▲ High rates of inflation reduce real incomes and lead consumers to change their spending patterns

Low unemployment

When people want to work but cannot find a job, they are unemployed. These are the problems unemployment causes:

» Unemployed people do not produce any goods or services. The total level of output in the country will be lower than it could be.

» The government pays unemployment benefit to those without jobs. A high level of unemployment will cost the government a great deal of money. This cannot be spent on other things such as schools and hospitals.

Therefore, low unemployment will help to increase the output of a country and improve workers' living standards.

▲ Youth unemployment reduces the country's economic growth

Economic growth

An economy is said to grow when the total level of output of goods and services in the country increases. The value of goods and services produced in a country in one year is called gross domestic product (GDP). When a country is experiencing economic growth, the standard of living of the population is likely to increase.

When a country's GDP is falling there is no economic growth. The problems this causes include the following:

» As output is falling, fewer workers are needed and unemployment will occur.
» The average standard of living of the population – the number of goods and services they can afford to buy in one year – will decline. In effect, most people will become poorer.
» Business owners will not expand their business as people will have less money to spend on the products they make.

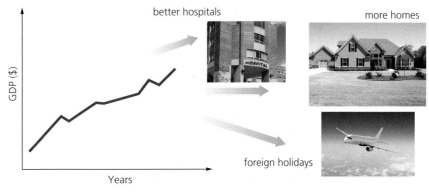

▲ Economic growth, makes a country richer and allows living standards to rise

Balance of payments

Exports are goods and services sold by one country to people and businesses in another country. These bring money (foreign currency) into a country. **Imports** are goods bought in from other countries. These must be purchased with foreign currency so these lead to money flowing out of a country. Governments will aim to achieve equality or balance between these over a period of time. The difference between a country's exports and imports is called the balance of payments.

Definitions to learn

The **exchange rate** is the price of one currency in terms of another, for example, £1 : $1.5.
Exchange rate depreciation is the fall in the value of a currency compared with other currencies.

If the value of a country's imports is greater than the value of its exports then it has a balance of payments deficit.

These are the problems that could result:

» The country could 'run out' of foreign currencies and it may have to borrow from abroad.
» The price of the country's currency against other currencies – the **exchange rate** – will be likely to fall. This is called **exchange rate depreciation**. The country's currency will now buy less abroad than it did before depreciation. Exchange rates are explained further in Chapter 29.

▲ A balance of payments deficit can lead to major problems for a country

Activity 27.1

a The GDP of Country A was $500 million in 2017. The population was 1 million. The average income per person was therefore $500. By 2018, as a result of economic growth, GDP was $1500 million. The population had also risen, to 2 million. What was the average income per person in 2018?

b Joe earned $20 000 in 2017. He had a pay rise of 10 per cent in 2018. Inflation was 15 per cent in 2018.
  i How much did Joe earn in 2018?
  ii Did his real income rise or fall in 2018? Explain your answer.

c For Country A, identify which of the following are imports or exports:
  i Washing machines purchased from Country B
  ii Cars made in Country A's factories and sold to a garage in Country B
  iii Machines sold to Country A from Country B
  iv Tourists from Country B who spend two weeks on holiday in a hotel in Country A.

REVISION SUMMARY   Economic objectives of government

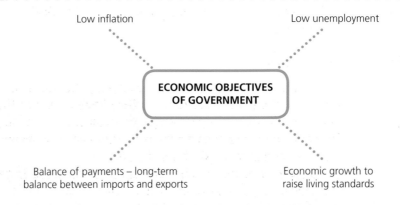

Low inflation

Low unemployment

ECONOMIC OBJECTIVES OF GOVERNMENT

Balance of payments – long-term balance between imports and exports

Economic growth to raise living standards

Government economic policies

Governments have a great deal of economic power. They raise taxes and spend this money on a wide range of services and state benefits. It is not unusual for governments to have control over 40–50 per cent of a country's GDP through the taxes they raise. Governments use this power to try to achieve the objectives we have just looked at. The decisions made by government can have a great effect on all businesses in a country. Business managers need to know how their business could be affected by government economic decisions. The main ways in which governments can influence the economy – sometimes called economic policies – are:

» **fiscal policy** – taxes and government spending
» monetary policy – interest rates
» supply side policies.

Fiscal policy: taxes and government spending

All governments spend money. They spend it on schools, hospitals, roads, defence, and so on. This expenditure is very important to some businesses. For example:

» Construction businesses will benefit from a new road-building scheme.
» Defence industries will gain if the government re-equips the army.
» Bus manufacturers will benefit from government spending on public transport.

Q: Where do governments raise this money from?
A: Mainly from taxes on individuals and businesses.
Q: What are the main types of taxes?
A: **Direct taxes** on the income of businesses and individuals, and **indirect taxes** on spending.
Q: How do these taxes affect business activity?
A: In a number of different ways.
We will look at these effects by studying the impact of four common taxes:

» income tax
» profits tax or corporation tax
» indirect taxes, for example, Value Added Tax (VAT)
» import tariffs.

Income tax

This is a tax on people's incomes. Usually, the higher a person's income, the greater will be the amount of tax they have to pay to the government. Income tax is set at a certain percentage of income, for example, 25 per cent of income. In many countries, income tax is progressive. This means that the rich pay tax at a higher percentage rate than the poor.

How would businesses be affected by an increase in the rate of income tax? Individual taxpayers would have a lower **disposable income**. They would have less money after tax to spend and save. Businesses would be likely to see a fall in sales. Managers may decide to produce fewer goods as sales are lower. Some workers could lose their jobs.

▲ Income tax flowchart

Which businesses are likely to be most affected by this increase in income tax rates? Businesses which produce luxury goods which consumers do not have to buy are likely to be the most affected. Businesses producing essential goods and services will be less affected. Consumers will still have to buy these products.

 Case study

The government of Country A has set the following rates of income tax:

Income level	Tax rate paid to government
$1–$5000 per year	20%
More than $5000 per year	30%

How much tax would John, earning $10 000 per year, pay to the government? The answer is $2500. This is worked out as follows:

   20 per cent of the first $5000 = $1000

   30 per cent of the next $5000 = $1500

How much income has John left to spend or save after tax? The answer is $7500. This is called the taxpayer's disposable income. John can now 'dispose' of it (spend it or save it) as he chooses.

Activity 27.2

Here are eight products:

- bread
- petrol
- TVs
- foreign holidays
- cooking oil
- jewellery
- salt
- home computers.

The sales of four of these products are likely to fall following an increase in income tax rates. Sales of the other four will not be much affected. Identify the four products likely to be most affected.

Study tips

When a question asks about the impact of tax or interest rate changes on a business, always refer to the type of good or service the business produces.

Profits tax (or corporation tax)

This is a tax on the profits made by businesses – usually companies.

How would an increase in the rate of corporation tax affect businesses? There would be two main effects:

» Businesses would have lower profits after tax. Managers will therefore have less money or finance to put back into the business. The business will find it more difficult to expand. New projects, such as additional factories or shops, may have to be cancelled.

» Lower profits after tax is also bad news for the owners of the business. There will be less money to pay back to the owners who originally invested in the business. Fewer people will want to start their own business if they consider that the government will take a large share of any profits made. Companies' share prices could fall.

Key info

The top rate of income tax in Belgium is 64 per cent, while company tax is 34 per cent. In Mongolia income tax is 10 per cent and company tax is the same rate. However, in Kuwait both income tax and company tax is 0 per cent.

Indirect taxes

Indirect taxes, such as Value Added Tax (VAT), are added to the prices of the products we all buy. They obviously make goods and services more expensive for consumers. Governments often avoid putting these taxes on really essential items, such as food, because this would be considered unfair, especially to poorer consumers.

How would businesses be affected by an increase in an indirect tax? Again, there would be two main effects:

>> Prices of goods in the shops would rise. Consumers may buy fewer items as a result. This will reduce the demand for products made by businesses. However, not all businesses will be affected in the same way. If consumers need to buy a product such as a new battery for their alarm clock, then the price increase is unlikely to stop them doing so. However, they might buy fewer ice creams as their prices have risen and they are hardly essential to anyone!
>> As prices rise so the workers employed by a business will notice that their wages buy less in the shops. It is said that their real incomes have declined. Businesses may be under pressure to raise wages, which will force up the costs of making products.

Key info

Indirect tax in Denmark is 25 per cent, in Mauritius is 15 per cent, Taiwan is 5 per cent, 0 per cent in Hong Kong.

Import tariffs and quotas

Many governments try to reduce the import of products from other countries by putting special taxes on them. These are called **import tariffs** and they raise money for the government. Many international organisations, such as the World Trade Organization, are trying to reduce the number of governments which do this.

How would businesses in a country be affected if the government put tariffs on imports into the country? There are three possible effects:

>> Businesses will benefit if they are competing with imported goods. These will now become more expensive, leading to an increase in sales of home-produced goods.
>> Businesses will have higher costs if they have to import raw materials or components for their own factories. These will now be more expensive.
>> Other countries may now take the same action and introduce import tariffs too. This is called retaliation. A business trying to export to these countries will probably sell fewer goods than before.

Definitions to learn

An **import tariff** is a tax on an imported product. An **import quota** is a physical limit on the quantity of a product that can be imported.

Key info

The import tariff for importing luxury cars into China ranges from 0 to 200 per cent, depending on which country they have come from.

Another method a government can use to limit imports is to introduce an **import quota** or physical limit on the quantity of a product that can be brought in. Quotas can be used selectively to protect certain industries from foreign competition that may be seen as unfair or damaging to jobs.

Changes in government spending

Governments in most countries spend the tax revenue they receive on programmes such as:

>> education
>> health
>> defence
>> law and order
>> transport – roads and railways.

When governments want to boost economic growth, they can increase their spending on these programmes. This will create more demand in the economy, more jobs and GDP will increase.

If governments want to save money, for example, if they have over-borrowed, they will often cut government spending. These cuts could have a considerable impact on businesses which, for example:

» produce equipment for schools, hospitals and defence equipment
» build roads, bridges and railways.

REVISION SUMMARY

Government taxes and spending

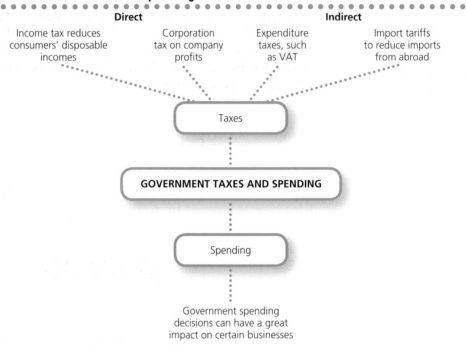

Direct

Income tax reduces consumers' disposable incomes

Corporation tax on company profits

Indirect

Expenditure taxes, such as VAT

Import tariffs to reduce imports from abroad

Taxes

GOVERNMENT TAXES AND SPENDING

Spending

Government spending decisions can have a great impact on certain businesses

Monetary policy – interest rates

> **Definitions to learn**
>
> **Monetary policy** is a change in interest rates by the government or central bank, for example, the European Central Bank.

An interest rate is the cost of borrowing money. In most countries, the level of interest rates is fixed by the government or the central bank via **monetary policy**. In some societies, the charging and the payment of interest is against the customs and traditions of the population. In most countries, however, businesses and individuals can borrow money, from a bank for example, and they will have to pay interest on the loan.

The following are likely to be the main effects of higher interest rates:

» Firms with existing variable interest loans may have to pay more in interest to the banks. This will reduce their profits. Lower profits mean less is available to distribute to the owners and less is retained for business expansion.
» Managers thinking about borrowing money to expand their business may delay their decision. New investment in business activity will be reduced. Fewer new factories and offices will be built. Entrepreneurs hoping to start a new business may not now be able to afford to borrow the capital needed.

Key info

Interest rates on loans in 2017 were lowest in Germany at 0.89 per cent. In the same year interest rates were: Malaysia 4.5 per cent, Uganda 20 per cent, Venezuela 24 per cent, and the highest were in Argentina where they varied between 33 and 62 per cent.

If consumers have taken out loans such as mortgages to buy their houses, then the higher interest payments will reduce their available income. Demand for all goods and services could fall as consumers have less money to spend.

» In addition to the point above, if a business makes expensive consumer items like cars or if it builds houses, then it will notice that consumer demand will fall for another reason. Consumers will be unwilling to borrow money to buy these expensive items if interest rates are higher. These businesses may have to reduce output and make workers redundant.

» Higher interest rates in one country will encourage foreign banks and individuals to deposit their capital in that country. They will be able to earn higher rates of interest on their capital. By switching their money into this country's currency they are increasing the demand for it. The exchange rate will rise – this is called **exchange rate appreciation**. This will have the effect of making imported goods appear cheaper and exports will now be more expensive. The opposite effect, if the exchange rate of a currency declines, is called an exchange rate depreciation.

Interest rates

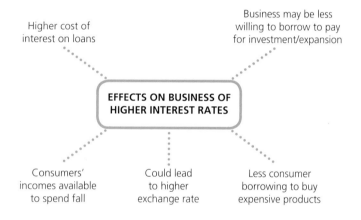

Supply side policies

In recent years many governments have tried to make the economy of their countries more efficient. They aim to increase the competitiveness of their industries against those from other countries. This would allow their businesses to expand, produce more and employ more workers. Some of the policies which have been used to achieve these aims are listed below – they are called **supply side policies** because they are trying to improve the efficient supply of goods and services.

Definitions to learn

Supply side policies try to increase the competitiveness of industries in an economy against those from other countries. Policies to make the economy more efficient.

» *Privatisation* – privatisation is now very common. The aim is to use the profit motive to improve business efficiency.

» *Improve training and education* – governments plan to improve the skills of the country's workers. This is particularly important in those industries such as computer software which are often very short of skilled staff.

» *Increase competition in all industries* – this may be done by reducing government controls over industry or by acting against monopolies.

► Activity 27.3: Impact of economic policies

You are the Managing Director of the largest computer manufacturing company in your country. Your business sells products at home and in foreign markets. Materials are imported from abroad. You employ hundreds of skilled workers to develop, assemble and test the computers. Your business is planning a major expansion programme.

The government of your country has recently announced the following policies. Explain the likely impact of each of these policies on your business:

a A reduction in income tax rates for high-income earners
b Lower corporation/profit tax rates
c Higher import tariffs on all imports
d Higher interest rates
e Higher expenditure taxes on luxury goods
f New training colleges to increase the supply of qualified workers
g Strict controls on monopoly businesses to encourage new businesses to be formed.

REVISION SUMMARY   **Government economic policies**

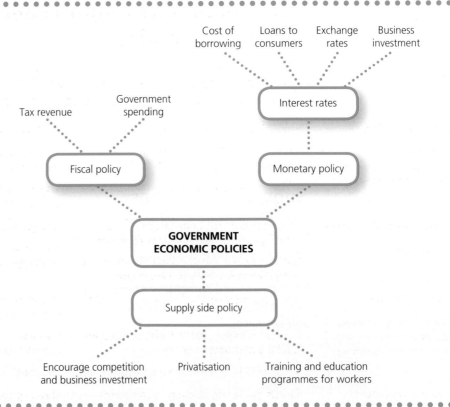

Case study: High levels of unemployment in Spain

The unemployment rate in Spain fell to 17.2 per cent in 2017. This is the lowest rate unemployment has been since the worst year of 2013 when it was 27 per cent. Spain still has the second highest unemployment rate of all the European Union (EU) countries. However, GDP has increased by 3.1 per cent in 2017 and living standards are improving for those in employment in Spain.

▶ Demonstration by unemployed workers in Spain

Activity 27.4

Read the case study above.

a Explain what is meant by 'GDP has increased by 3.1 per cent'.
b Explain how improving living standards could affect:
   ● a farm producing milk
   ● a manufacturer of leather goods.
c Explain two reasons why the Spanish government might aim to reduce the level of unemployment.

How business might react to changes in economic policy

The following table explains how businesses might react to some major changes in government economic policy. The business decisions and effects could be reversed if the government decided to reduce taxes, government spending or interest rates.

Government policy change	Possible business decision	Problems with this decision
Increase income tax – this reduces the amount consumers have to spend	Lower prices on existing products to increase demand	Less profit will be made on each item sold (reduces gross profit margin)
	Produce 'cheaper' products to allow for lower prices	The brand image of a product might be damaged by using cheaper versions of it
Increase tariffs on imports	Focus more on the domestic market as locally produced goods now seem cheaper	It might still be more profitable to export
	Switch from buying imported materials and components to locally produced ones	Foreign materials and components might be of higher quality
Increase interest rates	Reduce investment so future growth will be less	Other companies might still grow so market share will be lost
	Develop cheaper products that consumers will be better able to afford	Depends on the product but could consumers start to think that the quality and brand image are lower?
	Sell assets for cash to reduce existing loans	The assets might be needed for future expansion
Increase government spending	Switch marketing strategy to gain more public-sector contracts e.g. building or equipping schools and hospitals	May be great competition if other businesses take same action

You will notice that all of these business decisions could have both negative and positive effects. The overall impact of these decisions may depend on:

» how big the changes are in government policy
» what actions competitors take in response to these policies.

International business in focus

Bangladesh motorbike industry ready to power ahead

The rapidly developing motorbike industry in Bangladesh could win a significant portion of the growing Asian market. Major stakeholders in the industry – manufacturers, component importers and dealers – have encouraged the government to introduce policies to help encourage local motorbike assembly. In particular the government has:

● placed import tariffs on motorbikes

● provided more government spending on roads and other infrastructure

● provided low interest rate business loans.

India has overtaken China as the dominant Asian motorbike producer with total annual sales of 20 million units (2017). Demand from most Asian countries is growing as economies continue to benefit from growth and rising incomes. Africa is also seen as a growing market for the export of motorbikes from Bangladesh.

Discussion points

● Why is the demand for motorbikes growing in Asia as local economies continue to grow?

● Explain how each of the government policy measures is likely to benefit the Bangladesh motorbike industry.

Exam-style questions: Short answer and data response

1 The economy of Country A is growing rapidly. Unemployment is falling and the incomes of most consumers are rising. However, inflation increased to 8 per cent last year. Many business owners are worried that the government could increase interest rates.

   a Define 'inflation'. [2]

   b Identify **two** likely economic objectives of the government of Country A. [2]

   c Outline **two** types of taxes that a government can use to raise revenue. [4]

   d Explain **two** ways in which an increase in interest rates could affect businesses in Country A. [6]

   e Do you think all businesses within a country benefit when the economy grows? Justify your answer. [6]

2 The government in Country B is planning to increase taxes. It will use the revenue raised to build more roads and airports in an attempt to reduce unemployment and increase economic growth. The rate of inflation was very high last year but it has now started to fall. ADC produces exclusive branded fashion goods. Managers within ADC are planning to respond to the government policy of higher taxes.

   a Define 'economic growth'. [2]

   b Identify **two** effects on business of increased unemployment. [2]

   c Outline **two** effects on businesses of high inflation. [4]

   d Explain **two** ways in which a business producing luxury products could respond to higher taxes. [6]

   e Do you think that increased government spending on more roads and airports is a good idea? Justify your answer. [6]

Revision checklist

In this chapter you have learned:

✔ about growth, boom, recession and slump, which make up the the main stages of the business cycle

✔ about the effects employment levels, inflation and GDP have on a business

✔ about identifying government economic objectives

✔ about changes in taxes and government spending, and the impact these have

✔ about the impact of changes in interest rates.

NOW – test your understanding with the revision questions in the Student etextbook and the Workbook.

Environmental and ethical issues

This chapter will explain:

★ how business activity can impact on the environment, for example, global warming
★ the concept of externalities; possible external costs and external benefits of business decisions; sustainable development – how businesses' activity can contribute to this
★ how and why business might respond to environmental pressures and opportunities e.g., pressure groups
★ the role of legal controls over business activity affecting the environment, for example, pollution controls
★ ethical issues a business might face; conflicts between profits and ethics
★ how business might react and respond to ethical issues, for example, child labour.

How business activity can impact on the environment

Consider these two statements by different factory managers:

>> Manager A: 'I know that my factory pollutes the air and the river with waste products but it is very expensive to use cleaner methods. We make a profit from making cheap products and these are what consumers want.'
>> Manager B: 'We recently spent $10 million on new low energy boilers that produce 90 per cent less pollution than the old ones. We now recycle 75 per cent of our waste – consumers prefer businesses that are aware of their **social responsibility**.'

Business activity aims to satisfy customers' demand for goods and services – but it often has an impact on the **environment**. The 'environment' means our natural world.

Definitions to learn

Social responsibility is when a business decision benefits stakeholders other than shareholders, for example, a decision to protect the environment by reducing pollution by using the latest and 'greenest' production equipment.
Environment is our natural world including, for example, pure air, clean water and undeveloped countryside.

▲ Air pollution damages the environment

▲ Dirty rivers are expensive to clean up

▲ Road transport creates noise and air pollution and adds to global warming

Here are some examples of how business activity impacts on the environment:

» Aircraft jet engine **emissions** damage the atmosphere.
» **Pollution** from factory chimneys reduces air quality.
» **Waste disposal** can pollute rivers and seas.
» **Transport of goods** by ship and trucks burns fossil fuels such as oil, which create carbon emissions and may be linked to **global warming** and climate change.

Do these negative impacts on the natural environment matter? Many people believe they do – but other people think that all business should be worried about is satisfying customer demand as cheaply as possible.

Did you find yourself agreeing with one of the two managers on page 340? Whether businesses should be concerned about environmental issues is a major current argument. Which side do you come down on?

Let's look at both sides of the argument:

Argument A: Business should produce goods and services profitably and not worry about the environment	Argument B: Businesses have a social responsibility towards the environment and this can benefit them too
Protecting the environment can be expensive. Reducing waste, recycling waste and reducing polluting smoke all cost businesses money and this reduces profits	Global warming and global pollution affect us all and businesses have a social responsibility to reduce these problems
Firms might have to increase prices to pay for 'environmentally friendly' policies	Using scarce natural resources which are non-renewable, such as rainforest timber, leaves less for future generations and raises prices
This could make firms uncompetitive and they could lose sales to businesses, perhaps located in other countries, that are not environmentally friendly	Most scientists and environmentalists believe that business activity can damage the environment permanently
Consumers will buy less if they have to pay higher prices	Consumers are becoming more socially aware – they are increasingly demanding products from 'environmentally friendly' businesses, and this can become a marketing advantage
If pollution is a problem, then governments should pay to clean it up	If a business damages the environment, then **pressure groups** could take action to harm the business's reputation and sales
Some business owners claim there is not enough proof that business activity is doing permanent damage to the environment	

The concept of externalities

Most business activities – such as locating a factory or producing goods and services – lead to many different costs and benefits. It is important to distinguish between private costs and benefits and external costs and benefits. The following case study explains these differences.

Case study: Chemical firm expands

A business producing chemicals plans to open a new factory. It has chosen a site which it believes is the most profitable one. In coming to this decision, the managers considered only the costs and benefits to the business itself. These are called the **private costs** and **private benefits**. These are likely to be as follows:

Private costs	Private benefits
Cost of land	The money made from the sale of the chemical products
Cost of construction	
Labour costs	
Costs of running the plant when it has been built	
Transport costs of materials and completed products	

Definitions to learn

Private costs of an activity are the costs paid for by a business or the consumer of the product.
Private benefits of an activity are the gains to a business or the consumer of the product.

Unfortunately, the site chosen is near a housing estate. It is currently part of a park used by local residents. Waste products from the factory will be tipped into local rivers or quarries. The factory will create a lot of noise and fumes. The area is one with a high level of unemployment – people's incomes are below the national average.

Before deciding whether or not to grant planning permission the government will also consider the **external costs** and **external benefits** – that is, the impact on the rest of society other than the business itself.

External costs	External benefits
Waste products will cause pollution	Jobs will be created
Smoke and fumes may damage the health of residents	Other businesses may move into the area to provide services to the chemical company
Parkland cannot now be used by local residents	The chemical factory will pay taxes – government might increase spending on social projects, e.g. more hospitals
Noise from the factory will disturb the local neighbourhood	

Definitions to learn

External costs are costs paid for by the rest of society, other than the business, as a result of business activity.
External benefits are the gains to the rest of society, other than the business, as a result of business activity.

The government will try to give a value to all of these costs and benefits. This is called cost–benefit analysis. This is not easy to do. For example, what is the cost of losing parkland for children to play on? Estimates are made and then the total costs and benefits of the decision are added up:

» Private costs, added to external costs, give a total **social cost**.
» Private benefits, added to external benefits, give a total **social benefit** figure.

If the total social benefit is greater than the total social cost, the scheme is likely to be accepted. If, however, the total social cost is greater than the total social benefit, the government will probably refuse permission.

Definitions to learn

Social cost = external costs + private costs.
Social benefit = external benefits + private benefits.

Activity 28.1

Read the case study above.

a Define 'external costs'.
b Explain why any **two** stakeholder groups will be worried about the external costs from a new chemical factory.
c Explain why any **two** stakeholder groups will benefit from the possible external benefits from the new chemical factory.
d Assume you are the government minister responsible for planning decisions. Would you allow the new chemical factory to be built, or not? Explain your answer.

Sustainable development

Look at the following information about the world's demand for energy and carbon dioxide emissions:

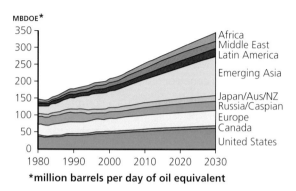

million barrels per day of oil equivalent

▲ World energy demand

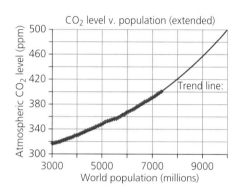

▲ Global population and carbon dioxide emissions since 1900 with predictions for the future

Definitions to learn

Sustainable development is development which does not put at risk the living standards of future generations.

These graphs show some of the problems that world economic and population growth is resulting in. Many economists and environmentalists argue that this rapid rate of energy use and pollution cannot continue if the world is to enjoy the same living standards as we have today. Using up scarce resources at a very fast rate will mean that there may be many fewer resources in the future. Creating so much pollution may lead to health and climate problems that put at risk the wellbeing of millions of people.

Sustainable development means trying to achieve economic growth but without damaging the environment and society for future generations.

Sustainable development: what can business do?

1 **Use renewable energy** – by fitting solar panels or buying energy that uses renewable sources such as wind or tidal power.
2 **Recycle waste** – by re-using water and other products that would otherwise be wasted or disposed of, total use of resources is reduced.
3 **Use fewer resources** – lean production (see Chapter 18) is about managing production so efficiently that the minimum quantity of resources is used.
4 **Develop new 'environmentally friendly' products and production methods**, for example, replacing drink cans and bottles with biodegradable packaging that will not damage the environment.

By using these production methods which allow for sustainable development businesses respond positively to environmental pressures and opportunities.

Case study: Tunweni Drinks, Namibia

This company was the first in Namibia to adopt the country's Zero Emissions Research Initiative (ZERI). Examples of sustainable development initiatives at the Tunweni site include:

- Fibres from grain used in the production process are recycled and used in cultivating mushrooms.
- Methane gas is produced from waste using a biodigester – the gas is used as energy within the plant.
- Waste water is used to farm fish in a newly constructed pond.

'This makes our business much more sustainable and gives us a competitive edge,' said the Chief Executive of Tunweni Drinks.

Activity 28.2

Read the case study above.

a Define 'sustainable development'.
b Explain why the **three** initiatives taken by Tunweni Drinks make the business 'more sustainable'.
c Explain why the Chief Executive believes that the business now has a 'competitive edge'.

How and why business might respond to environmental pressures and opportunities

How can society make business give the environment a higher priority? There are three main influences:

>> consumers
>> pressure groups
>> government, through legal controls.

Consumers

Bad publicity is bad news! If a business is reported as destroying an important natural site or dumping waste in the sea, then many consumers will stop buying its products. An increasing proportion of consumers are becoming concerned about the environment. Businesses obviously want to sell goods profitably. If sales of a product fall because consumers think it is harmful to nature, then the business may have to quickly change its products or its production methods.

Pressure groups

Pressure groups are becoming increasingly powerful. They can take some very effective actions against businesses that are not socially responsible. Pressure groups such as Greenpeace and Earth First! have tried to block up businesses' waste pipes or organise **consumer boycotts**.

 Definitions to learn

Pressure groups are groups of people who act together to try to force businesses or governments to adopt certain policies. A **consumer boycott** is when consumers decide not to buy products from businesses that do not act in a socially responsible way.

Pressure group activity is likely to change business actions when:

» it has popular public support and receives much media coverage
» consumer boycotts result in much reduced sales for the business
» the group is well organised and financed.

Pressure group activity is unlikely to result in a change in business actions when:

» what the firm is doing is unpopular but not illegal, such as testing drugs on animals
» the cost to the business of changing its methods is more than the possible cost of poor image and lost sales
» the business sells to other businesses rather than to consumers – public pressure will be less effective.

The role of legal controls over business activity affecting the environment

Governments can make business activities illegal. For example:

» locating in environmentally sensitive areas such as national parks
» dumping waste products into rivers or the sea – though it is sometimes difficult to prove which business is responsible for this
» making products that cannot easily be recycled.

▲ It is often difficult for governments to find out which firms are responsible for dumping chemical waste

Manufacturers often complain that these laws make it more expensive for them to produce. This raises prices to consumers. For this reason some governments do not pass strict laws on the environment, hoping that this will encourage firms to produce in their country to create jobs. Do you think it is socially responsible for a business to locate in a country that does not have strict laws on protecting the environment?

Governments can impose financial penalties on businesses, such as pollution permits

Pollution permits are licences to pollute up to a certain level. Governments can sell a permit to a factory that produces pollution. If it produces more pollution than the permit allows, it must either buy more permits from 'clean' businesses or pay large fines. Either way, the costs of the business increase. Businesses producing much less pollution can sell their permits to 'dirty' factories. This encourages businesses to produce goods in less polluting ways. Other financial penalties could be additional taxes on goods or factories that create pollution.

These three influences help to explain why many businesses now respond to environmental pressures. Being 'environmentally friendly' can create a positive public opinion of a business and lead to opportunities for sustainable growth.

Case study: Should governments use laws to protect the environment?

In Country X, there are very few government controls on business activity. The government of Country X wants to encourage businesses to start up and grow. A government minister said that: 'Legal controls over pollution and disposal of waste add to business costs. This will discourage production in our country.' Country X sells many products, such as cars, clothing and chemicals, in world markets at very low prices.

In Country Y, the government has very strict laws to control the ways in which businesses dispose of their waste, how much pollution they can produce and where new factories are located. A minister in the government said: 'We believe that businesses have a social responsibility to our community not to damage the environment. These laws have encouraged businesses to use much cleaner production methods. They have also developed products that pollute the environment much less than cheaper products. Many consumers in the world today will only buy "environmentally friendly" products.'

Activity 28.3

Read the case study above.

a Define 'social responsibility'.
b Explain **two** possible reasons why the government in Country X does not have strict controls on business activity that affects the environment.
c Explain **two** ways in which business activity can damage the environment. Use examples from your own country.
d Do you think that the government of Country Y is right to use strict laws against businesses that damage the environment? Justify your answer.

REVISION SUMMARY   **Environmental constraints**

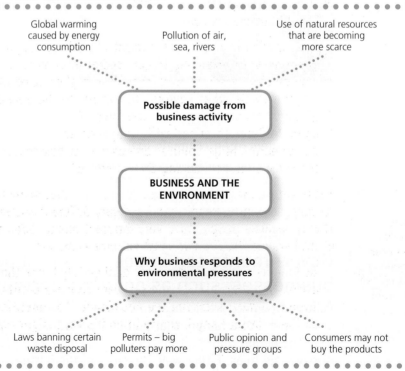

Case study: Achme Oil Company

For years Achme Oil Co. had been dumping waste products in the sea. The company argued that the dumping was far out at sea, and so it harmed no one. It was a much cheaper method of getting rid of the waste than buying equipment to treat the waste. Low costs helped the company to keep down prices for consumers.

Environmental pressure groups had taken some action but it was ineffective. Then, one day, thousands of dead fish and sea birds started to be washed up on the east coast. After examination it was found that they contained dangerous levels of oil-based poisons. Achme Oil denied all responsibility and blamed a recent oil spill from another business's tanker. Environmental pressure groups started to blockade Achme's petrol filling stations. They gained great support from the public. Achme's sales fell but it refused to change its policy. Foreign news reporters followed the story closely.

The Chief Executive was suddenly replaced and a press conference was announced for the following week. Perhaps the company was about to change its environmental policy after all?

▶ Activity 28.4

Read the case study above.

a Define 'pressure group'.
b Why was Achme Oil unwilling to change its dumping policy after the fish and birds were washed ashore?
c Explain **two** reasons why pressure groups might be successful in changing the business's decision in this case.
d Do you think that Achme Oil should stop dumping waste and buy equipment to treat it? Give reasons for your answer.

Ethical issues a business might face

Should businesses always 'do the right thing'? Should businesses always take decisions that are fair and moral?

Should businesses ever:

» take or offer bribes to government officials or people working for other businesses, for example, to gain secret information?
» employ child workers, even though it might not be illegal in some countries?
» buy in supplies that have led to damage to the environment, for example, wood obtained from cutting down rainforests?
» agree to 'fix high prices' with competitors?
» pay directors large bonuses and owners of businesses large profit payouts at the same time as reducing the workforce?

> **Definitions to learn**
>
> **Ethical decisions** are based on a moral code. Sometimes referred to as 'doing the right thing'.

These are all examples of **ethical decisions** that many businesses have to face up to very frequently. People can have very different answers to the questions above. This is because people have very different moral codes and therefore different ethical standards. The two most extreme views are:

1 'As long as a business does not deliberately break the law then any decision it makes is acceptable. Businesses want to make profits, after all.'
2 'Even if certain activities are not illegal, it is unethical and therefore wrong to do them despite any increase in profits that might occur.'

How businesses might react and respond to ethical issues

Assume a large multinational clothing business – Company X – bought clothes from a factory in a low-income country. The managers of Company X know that the factory employs child labour – it is not illegal to employ workers as young as 12 years old in the country it is based in.

Another business – Company Y – only buys clothes from suppliers who guarantee not to employ children and pay reasonable wages and offer good working conditions. Company Y managers check that suppliers keep to these standards. What is the potential impact on Company Y of this ethical decision?

Potential benefits of ethical decisions – Company Y	Potential limitations of ethical decisions – Company Y
Consumers may be against buying clothing products made by children and increase purchases from Company Y and reduce purchases from Company X	Higher costs – adult workers will be paid more than child workers and good working conditions add to business costs too
Good publicity about Company Y's ethical decisions will provide 'free promotion' – Company X may suffer from bad publicity	Company Y's prices might have to be set higher than those of Company X because of higher costs
Long-term profits of Company Y could increase	If consumers are only interested in low prices – and not how products are made – then sales of Company Y could fall
Some workers and investors may want to be linked to an 'ethical' business – Company Y may find it easier to recruit the best workers and raise capital from investors	Short-term profits of Company Y might fall
There is less risk of legal action being taken against Company Y	It could be argued that, in some countries, if children are not employed the incomes of their families will fall to very low levels

➡ Case study: Pay gap widens in India! How much is your director taking home?

In 2017, a report stated that there was a huge difference in pay between the directors of many large Indian companies and the employees. Some of the largest companies gave top executives salary packages of up to 1200 times the average pay of employees. The average pay of employees has fallen or stayed the same over the previous year while directors continued to be given very large pay increases. These figures are mainly for the 30 largest traded companies on the Mumbai (Bombay) stock exchange. Many people believe that this pay gap is unacceptable and unethical. 'How is it fair that a director earns in one day what a worker takes several years to earn?' is one criticism that is often heard.

This is similar in many countries across the world. Another example is South Africa: while it was normal for directors to earn a lot more than ordinary workers, the ratio 30 years ago was around 50 : 1. In 2017 it is 500 : 1. For example, if a director earns 2 million rand a month then the worker might be earning 4000 rand. The companies in South Africa paying enormous amounts to directors are often the same ones negotiating with trade unions to convince workers to accept lower wages. Workers feel this is unfair because it is their labour that creates all this wealth. Is this an example of an unethical decision or not?

Directors of some companies are not paid such high pay packages and claim that the great pay gap in other companies leads to low worker morale and loyalty. In addition, many consumers feel that the prices they pay are too high because of very high directors' salaries and bonuses. However, many directors argue that it is essential to pay very high incomes to 'the best and most talented' managers so that the companies can be more successful in the future.

Activity 28.5

Read the case study on page 348.

a What is meant by 'an unethical decision'?
b Explain **two** likely reasons why directors are paid more than workers in most companies.
c Is it right that directors can be paid up to 1200 times more than average workers? Explain your answer by considering the advantages and disadvantages of this situation.

International business in focus

Airbus reduces environmental cost of air travel

▲ Fuel-saving planes are popular with airlines

Airbus Industries, the world's largest manufacturer of passenger aircraft, is producing a new range of planes. These planes are more efficient than the existing models in order to save fuel – they are 20 per cent more economical. They are also much quieter than earlier models. Many airlines want to buy these planes even though they are expensive. The airlines will save fuel and also improve their image of 'social responsibility'.

Plane makers and airlines are worried by Greenpeace pressure group activity. This organisation claims that aircraft will cause 20 per cent of the world's air pollution by 2020. It is asking governments to put high taxes on aircraft fuel to make air travel more expensive. Airbus hopes that the new range of planes will reduce the need for such taxes.

Discussion points

● Does all business activity lead to environmental damage?

● Why do businesses often want to seem to be 'socially responsible'?

● When do you think businesses should respond to pressure from groups such as Greenpeace?

Exam-style questions: Short answer and data response

1 Jean-Luc is the Chief Executive of a furniture factory. He promotes his business as supporting 'sustainable development', as wood is better than plastic or metal for the environment. His company's furniture is sold in many countries. Wood is bought from the cheapest sources – Jean-Luc thinks it comes from rainforests that are being cut down but he does not ask the suppliers about this. Furniture is transported by trucks and ships. Waste wood is burnt as this is cheaper than sending it for processing into other products. Air quality in Jean-Luc's country is very poor but the government does not know which the major polluters are. Jean-Luc's business employs 200 workers.

  a Define 'sustainable development'. [2]

  b Identify **two** ways in which Jean-Luc's business impacts on the environment. [2]

  c Outline **two** ways in which Jean-Luc's business might be encouraged to be more 'environmentally friendly'. [4]

  d Explain **two** possible benefits to Jean-Luc's business of it becoming more 'environmentally friendly'. [6]

  e Do you think it is right for Jean-Luc to promote his business as a supporter of 'sustainable development'? Justify your answer. [6]

2 MST is a large steel-making business. Sales and profits have fallen recently. The directors are under pressure from the owners to make the business much more profitable. One director has paid a bribe to a government official to make sure MST gains a government contract. MST has closed two steel works this year and opened a huge new works in a low-income country. Pollution controls are very weak in this country. Wages are low and some children are employed in the steel production process – but in non-dangerous jobs. 'Profits must be increased as a priority,' said Marie, the Chief Executive of MST, 'ethical decisions can come later'.

  a Define 'ethical decisions'. [2]

  b Identify **two** ways in which MST could be said to be operating 'unethically'. [2]

  c Outline **two** possible benefits to the company of operating in these ways. [4]

  d Explain **two** possible drawbacks to MST caused by paying bribes and employing children. [6]

  e Do you agree with Marie when she said: 'Profits must be increased as a priority, ethical decisions can come later'? Justify your answer. [6]

Revision checklist

In this chapter you have learned:

✔ how business activity can damage the environment and lead to externalities

✔ ways in which business can respond to the threats and opportunities of environmental issues, such as aiming for 'sustainable development'

✔ the role of pressure groups in influencing business decisions

✔ what 'ethical decision making' means and why some businesses consider this important.

NOW – test your understanding with the revision questions in the Student etextbook and the Workbook.

29 Business and the international economy

The concept of globalisation and reasons for it

In many ways the world is becoming one large market rather than a series of separate national markets. The same goods and services can be found in many countries around the world. Workers are finding it easier to move between countries and capital (finance) is also moving more freely from country to country. There are several reasons for this increase in global trade and movement of products, people and capital (**globalisation**).

>> Increasing numbers of **free trade agreements** and economic unions between countries have reduced protection for industries. Consumers can purchase goods and services from other countries with few or no import controls such as tariffs.
>> Improved and cheaper travel links and communications between all parts of the world have made it easier to transport products globally. In addition the internet allows easy price comparisons between goods from many countries. Online or e-commerce is allowing orders to be placed from anywhere in the world.
>> Many 'emerging market countries' are industrialising very rapidly. China and countries in South-east Asia used to import many of the goods they needed. Now their own manufacturing industries are so strong they can export in large quantities – at very competitive prices.

Opportunities and threats of globalisation for business

Increasing free trade and the rising mobility of labour and capital, for example, the growth of multinational corporations (MNCs), are having many effects on businesses all over the globe. Some of these effects are positive – opportunities – and some are potentially negative – threats.

Globalisation: potential opportunities for businesses

Opportunity	Impact on businesses
Start selling exports to other countries – opening up foreign markets	This increases potential sales, perhaps in countries with fast-growing markets. Online selling allows orders for goods to be sent in from abroad
	But it can be expensive to sell abroad and will foreign consumers buy products, even if they were popular 'at home'?
Open factories/operations in other countries (become a multinational)	It could be cheaper to make some goods in other countries than 'at home'
	But will the quality be as good? Might there be an ethical issue (for example, over poor working conditions)? It is expensive and/or difficult to set up operations in other countries
Import products from other countries to sell to customers in 'home' country	With no trade restrictions it could be profitable now to import goods and services from other countries and sell them domestically
	But the products will need maintenance and, perhaps, repairs – will the parts and support be available from the producer in the foreign country?
Import materials and components from other countries – but still produce final goods in 'home' country	It could be cheaper to purchase these supplies from other countries now that there is free trade – this will help to reduce costs. These supplies could be purchased 'online'
	But will the suppliers be reliable? Will the greater distance add too much to transport costs?

Globalisation: potential threats to businesses

Threat	Impact on businesses
Increasing imports into home market from foreign competitors	If these competitors offer cheaper products (or of higher quality) sales of local business might fall
	But the increased competition could force the local businesses to become more efficient
Increasing investment from multinationals to set up operations in home country	This will create further competition – and the multinational may have economies of scale and be able to afford the best employees
	But some local firms could become suppliers to these multinationals and their sales could increase
Employees may leave businesses that cannot pay the same or more than international competitors	In some professions, employees will now have more choice about where they work and for which business – businesses will have to make efforts to keep their best employees
	But this might encourage local businesses to use a range of motivational methods to keep their workers

Key info

Globalisation has not benefited everyone. Since the 1970s, lower-skilled European and American workers have had a major fall in the real value of their wages, which dropped by more than 20 per cent by 2017. Workers in these developed countries also suffered more spells of unemployment.

Definitions to learn

An **import tariff** is a tax placed on imported goods when they arrive into the country.
An **import quota** is a restriction on the quantity of a product that can be imported.
Protectionism is when a government protects domestic businesses from foreign competition using tariffs and quotas.

Globalisation has led to more choice and lower prices for consumers. It has forced businesses to look for ways of increasing efficiency. Inefficient producers have gone out of business. Many firms have merged with foreign businesses to make it easier to sell in foreign markets. This is one of the reasons behind the growth of multinational organisations.

This process of more and more free trade does lead to some problems. Many production workers, often in the richest countries, have lost their jobs owing to globalisation. Big foreign corporations can often produce goods more cheaply and efficiently, so other countries' workers lose out. As governments can no longer 'protect' their own industries against foreign competition, this process can lead to serious economic and social problems.

Why governments might introduce import tariffs and import quotas

In Chapter 27, **import tariffs** were explained as being one form of taxes that governments can use to raise revenue. There is another important reason why governments might introduce tariffs and **quotas** on imports.

They are forms of **protectionism** – to protect domestic industries from competition that might otherwise close them down. Foreign competitors might be able to produce products much more cheaply and if they were allowed to import without any restriction then local companies might be forced out of business. This would reduce employment and incomes.

» An import tariff is a tax put on the imported goods when they arrive into the country. They usually lead to the price of the imported goods being increased, making them less competitive than locally produced goods.
» An import quota is a regulation which limits the import of a good to a certain fixed quantity. This reduces the amount of these goods that can be imported and often leads to an increase in the price of imported goods as they become less available. Both these effects are likely to lead to domestically produced goods having increasing sales.

This is a simple argument to understand – **but** many economists believe it is wrong. They believe it is better to allow local consumers to buy imported goods as cheaply as possible (to increase their living standards) and for local businesses to produce and export goods and services in which they have a competitive advantage. In this way, living standards across the globe can be increased. This is the free trade argument.

➡ Case study: IBM takes advantage of globalisation

IBM is one of the largest corporations in the world, manufacturing and selling computer hardware and software. It has taken full advantage of the opportunities offered by globalisation. Not only are its products sold in nearly every country but it has invested in factories and other operations in many low-cost countries with skilled IT employees – such as Romania and India. Most of the computers that it assembles in the USA use low-cost imported components. The company is well positioned to take advantage of growth in emerging market countries such as Brazil and Vietnam. However, IBM faces huge competition from newly developing computer businesses in China and India. IBM cannot ask the US government to protect its US market with tariffs because of free trade agreements.

Multinational businesses

It is important to remember that a **multinational business** (or multinational corporation – MNC) is not one which just sells goods in more than one country. To be called a multinational, a business must produce goods or services in more than one country.

Multinational businesses are some of the largest organisations in the world. They include:

» oil companies: for example, Shell, BP, Exxon Mobil
» tobacco companies: for example, British American Tobacco, Philip Morris
» car manufacturers: for example, Toyota, General Motors.

Benefits to a business of becoming a multinational and the impact on its stakeholders

Some benefits to a business from becoming a multinational are that it is able to:

» produce goods in countries with low costs, such as low wages. For example, most sports clothing is produced in Southeast Asia because wages are lower than in Europe
» extract raw materials which the company may need for production or refining. For example, crude oil from Saudi Arabia is needed to supply oil refineries in the USA
» produce goods nearer the market to reduce transport costs. For example, tiles and bricks are expensive to transport so the producer sets up a factory near the market in another country
» avoid barriers to trade put up by countries to reduce the imports of goods. For example, sales of cars made in Japan are restricted in Europe. Japanese manufacturers now make cars in Europe too
» increase market share and expand into different market areas to spread risks. For example, if sales are falling in one country the business may move to another country where sales are rising
» remain competitive with rival businesses which may be expanding abroad
» gain government grants given to the business to set up operations in particular countries.

The impact on its stakeholders of a business becoming a multinational

›› Shareholders are likely to receive increased dividends from higher profit.
›› Employees may have increased opportunities to gain promotion as the business gets larger and has operations across many countries; opportunity to live and work abroad.
›› Suppliers may have increased or decreased sales to the multinational depending where it operates and is located.
›› Government may gain higher tax revenue if profits from operations abroad are repatriated, or it may lose tax revenue if the multinational locates its head office elsewhere.

So, there is no doubt that businesses gain from becoming multinational. But what is the impact on the countries they operate in? There are both advantages and disadvantages to countries as a result of multinationals operating there.

Potential benefits to a country's economy where a multinational operates

›› Jobs are created, which reduces the level of unemployment.
›› Increased investment – new investment in buildings and machinery increases output of goods and services in the country. New technology can benefit the country by bringing in new ideas and methods.
›› Increased exports – some of the extra output may be sold abroad, which will increase the exports of the country. Also, imports may be reduced as more goods are now made in the country.
›› Taxes are paid by the multinationals, which increases the funds to the government.
›› Increased consumer choice – there is more product choice for consumers and more competition.

Potential drawbacks to a country's economy where a multinational operates

›› The jobs created are often unskilled assembly-line tasks. Skilled jobs, such as those in research and design, are not usually created in the 'host' countries receiving the multinationals.
›› Reduced sales for local businesses – local firms may be forced out of business. Multinationals are often more efficient and have lower costs than local businesses.
›› Repatriation of profits – profits are often sent back to a multinational's 'home' country and not kept in the country where they are earned.
›› Multinationals often use up scarce and non-renewable primary resources in the host country.
›› As multinational businesses are very large they could have a lot of influence on both the government and the economy of the host country. They might ask the government for large grants to keep them operating in the country – threatening to leave the country with big job losses if these are not paid by the government.

Key info

Nike factories located in Indonesia face increased costs after an increase in the minimum wage. Nike may raise productivity through mechanisation and reduce its workforce. Many workers want Nike factories to be exempt from the new minimum wage as many workers would prefer to receive less than the legal minimum wage rather than suffer the loss of their jobs.

REVISION SUMMARY   **Advantages and disadvantages of multinational businesses**

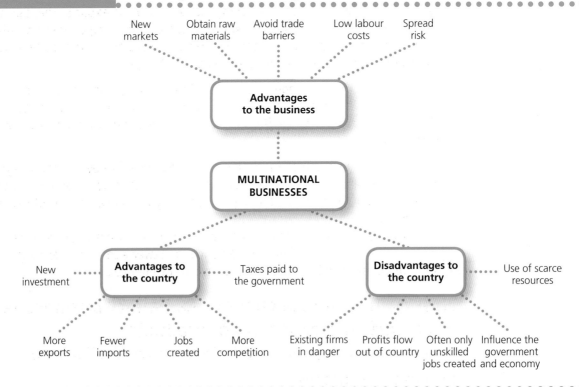

Exchange rates

If you have ever travelled abroad then you will know that it is usually necessary to change your money into foreign currency. Every country has its own currency and to be able to buy things in other countries you have to use the local currency. How much of another currency do you get in exchange for your own country's money? This will depend on the **exchange rate** between your currency and the foreign currency you wish to buy.

Assume that the exchange rate between the euro (€) and the US$ is €1 : $1.5. This means that for each €1 being changed into dollars, $1.5 would be received in exchange. In effect, this exchange rate is the price of one currency in terms of another.

How exchange rates are determined and depreciation and appreciation of an exchange rate

Most currencies are allowed to vary or float on the foreign exchange market according to the demand and supply of each currency. For example, if the demand for €s was greater than the demand for $s, then the price of the € would rise. Compared to the exchange rate in the first example, the new rate might now be €1 : $1.75. Each € now buys more $s than before.

Depreciation of the exchange rate is when the exchange rate is worth less against other currencies, for example, if the euro falls from €1 = $1.50 to €1 = $1. It means the currency (€) buys less of the other currency ($). The effect of this is to:

»» make exports cheaper, for example, exports from Europe sell for a lower price in America as it takes fewer dollars to buy each euro. People in America do not have to spend as many dollars buying euros to buy the exports from Europe
»» imports are more expensive and do the opposite, for example, imports into Europe now cost more to buy from America, as more euros have to be given to buy the dollars needed for the same amount of imports.

Appreciation of the exchange rate is when the exchange rate is worth more against other currencies, for example, if the euro rises from €1 = $1 to €1 = $1.50. It means the currency (€) buys more of the other currency ($). The effect of this is to:

»» raise the price of exports, for example, exports from Europe sell for a higher price in America as it takes more dollars to buy each euro. People in America have to spend more dollars buying euros to buy the same amount of exports from Europe
»» import prices fall and demand for them might rise, for example, imports into Europe now cost less to buy from America, as fewer euros have to be given to buy the dollars needed for the same amount of imports.

How exchange rate changes can affect businesses as importers and exporters of products

Changes in the exchange rate affect businesses in several different ways.

Exporting businesses

In the following case study example, consider the impact of changing exchange rates on an exporting business – one which sells goods and services abroad.

The change in the exchange rate described in the case study on page 358 is called a $ **appreciation** because the value of the $ has increased. Exporters have a serious problem when the currency of their country appreciates as they become less competitive in foreign markets and may lose sales, revenue and/or profit.

> **Definitions to learn**
>
> **Currency appreciation** occurs when the value of a currency rises – it buys more of another currency than before.

Case study

Lion Trading Co. produces washing machines. The retail price of these machines is $300. The company exports many machines to France and the price there has to be in euros (€). The current exchange rate is $1 : €1.6. The business will therefore set a price of €480 for its machines in France (ignoring additional distribution and marketing costs).

Assume that the exchange rate for $s now rises compared to the euro and $1 is now worth €2. The Marketing Manager for Lion Trading now has two main options:

- To keep the price in France at €480 – this will mean that each machine is earning the business only $240, not $300 as previously.
- To raise the price in France to €600 and continue to earn $300 from each machine. This higher price in France could lead to fewer sales and exports to France are likely to fall.

Definitions to learn

Currency depreciation occurs when the value of a currency falls – it buys less of another currency.

Key info

The £ depreciated by nearly 20 per cent after the 2016 vote to leave the EU, making UK goods more competitive in overseas markets. In 2017, Britain's biggest car manufacturer, Jaguar Land Rover (JLR), had a record year of sales, with the highest sales in China and North America. JLR is one of the UK's largest exporters, with about 80 per cent of its £24 billion annual revenues in 2017 from exports.

 ## Case study example: Exchange rate changes

A business currently sells men's coats for $100. It also exports them to Japan. It sells them there for 8000 yen as the exchange rate is currently $1 : 80¥.

- The exchange rate for the $ now appreciates to $1 : 100¥. The new ¥ selling price for the coats, assuming that the Marketing Manager wishes to earn the same amount of $ from each coat, will be: 10000¥.
- What might be the effect if the exchange rate for $ fell? This is called a **currency depreciation**. The new ¥ price if $1 falls to 60¥, assuming that the same amount of $ is earned from each coat, will now be 6000¥.

Importing businesses

Now consider how an importing business – one which buys goods and services from abroad – might be affected by changing exchange rates.

Case study

Nadir Imports Co. is based in the UK and buys fruit from other countries to sell to supermarkets. One tonne of bananas from abroad costs $250 and at the exchange rate of £1 : $2.5 this costs Nadir £100 for the imports.

If the value of the £ were now to depreciate, what would happen to Nadir Imports' costs? Assume that the value of the £ now falls to £1 : $2, how much will a tonne of bananas now cost? The answer is £125, which is a substantial increase in costs for the importing firm.

Study tips

Do not worry about exchange rate calculations. But you will have to remember what happens to import and export prices when currencies appreciate or depreciate in value.

Activity 29.4

Read the case study above.

a Explain what would happen to the cost of Nadir Imports' sales and the possible effect on profitability if the £ depreciated.
b Explain what would happen to the cost of Nadir Imports' sales and the possible effect on profitability if the £ appreciated.

We have shown that an importing firm will have higher costs if the exchange rate of its currency depreciates, but will have lower costs if the exchange rate appreciates. However, an exporting firm will be able to reduce its prices with a currency depreciation, but might have to raise prices with a currency appreciation.

You can now see how seriously businesses can be affected by exchange rate movements. This helps to explain why some international organisations such as the European Union (EU) have tried to reduce exchange rate movements. In the case of the EU, it has introduced a common currency (the euro) which removes the need for separate currencies and exchange rates between member countries.

REVISION SUMMARY **Exchange rates**

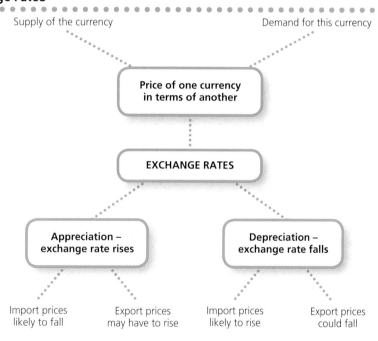

International business in focus

Starbucks to change Argentina's café culture

Since arriving in 2008, Starbucks has been opening new locations in Argentina at a rate of approximately 12 cafés per year. The company opened its 111th café in 2017, reflecting the shift of consumers in rural Argentina towards global brands. Some people in Argentina have very mixed feelings about the growth of this huge multinational in their own country. A local newspaper listed some effects of this expansion:

Positives: 1) Starbucks' employees here have an American customer service approach which is cheerful and helpful. 2) Your coffee is normally ready very quickly, and prepared using the correct method. 3) The opening of a Starbucks often leads to local competing cafés improving in areas such as cleanliness, service, and pricing.

Negatives: 1) Buenos Aires has a deeply rooted traditional café culture, and Starbucks may threaten this. 2) Branches are practically identical to Starbucks everywhere in the world. 3) All major decisions, such as new investments, are taken outside of Argentina.

Discussion points

- Explain why Starbucks is referred to as a 'multinational'.

- Would you prefer to use a local café or one operated by Starbucks? Ask everyone in your class this question and see what the results are.

- On balance, do you think the expansion of Starbucks is good for countries such as Argentina?

Exam-style questions: Short answer and data response

1 PaintCo manufactures specialist paints for aircraft. It has taken advantage of globalisation. The research department recruits scientists from several countries. Until ten years ago it only had one large factory in Europe. Now PaintCo has four factories in low-cost countries. Raw materials are imported and the paints are exported to aircraft manufacturers in the USA, Brazil and China.

   a Define 'globalisation'. [2]

   b Identify **two** reasons for increased globalisation. [2]

   c Outline **two** possible threats from globalisation to PaintCo. [4]

   d Explain **two** benefits of globalisation to PaintCo. [6]

   e Do you think PaintCo should build its next factory in Europe or in a low-cost country? Justify your answer. [6]

2 Beema is a successful business that makes shoes in Country B. It imports some of the leather and the machines it uses, and exports 30 per cent of its output. Recently the currency of Country B has fallen in value (depreciated). Beema's managers are planning to open a second factory. This will be located in Country C which already has several shoe manufacturers. Country C has just agreed to stop using protectionism by removing trade barriers such as import tariffs. Many of its industries are inefficient.

   a Define 'exchange rate'. [2]

   b Define 'exports'. [2]

   c Outline **two** likely reasons why Beema is planning to become a multinational business. [4]

   d Explain **two** effects on Beema of a depreciation of Country B's currency. [6]

   e Do you think the government of Country C should encourage businesses such as Beema to start operations in its country? Justify your answer. [6]

Revision checklist

In this chapter you have learned:

✔ what globalisation is and the threats and opportunities for businesses it causes

✔ what import tariffs and quotas are and why governments might introduce them

✔ why a business might become a multinational and how would this impact its stakeholders

✔ what benefits and drawbacks a multinational business might bring to a country

✔ that exchange rates are subject to depreciation and appreciation and how that affects businesses as importers and exporters.

NOW – test your understanding with the revision questions in the Student etextbook and the Workbook.

External influences on business activity: end-of-section case study

→ FirstElectricity

FirstElectricity is a large company that generates electricity. The company has ten power stations that use coal and two power stations that use water to produce electricity. The directors of FirstElectricity are considering building a new power station near Main City.

Main City is the capital of Country Z. It has been growing rapidly over the last five years as new businesses have set up and existing businesses have expanded. The population of the city also has grown as people from surrounding towns and villages have moved into Main City in search of jobs. Wages of skilled workers have been rising but unemployment for unskilled workers is high. The supply of electricity has become a problem, with more and more power cuts occurring.

FirstElectricity is planning to build a dam across a wide river near the capital city if it gets permission from the government. A dam blocks a river and creates a reservoir of water. Electricity is made as the water passes through the dam. This new power station would provide all the electricity needed by Main City and would be very profitable.

The reservoir behind the dam, if built, will be used by FirstElectricity to provide leisure facilities for people from Main City. They are considering having either the hire of rowing boats or swimming facilities in the reservoir.

→ Appendix 1

port

sea

area of agricultural land

proposed FirstElectricity dam

reservoir

main river

Main City

main road

▲ Map of the proposed area for the dam

Appendix 2

Extract from *Main City Times*, 3 November 2017

Will we benefit from the new power station?

Environmental groups have been protesting as FirstElectricity plans to build a dam over the country's wide river. If the dam is not built then the government claims there will be more power cuts. Businesses may lose a lot of output and profit if they cannot manufacture products. Environmental groups claim the dam will destroy thousands of acres of excellent agricultural land and food supplies will be reduced. Food imports will increase and this will have a negative effect on Country Z's exchange rate.

Many people will be forced to leave their homes and move to another area. A government spokesperson said the future growth of the country could be reduced if the dam is not built. Multinational companies may be put off locating in Country Z if the power station is not built.

Exam-style questions: Case study

1 a Explain **two** external costs and **two** external benefits of building the dam. [8]

b Do you think the government should encourage the location of a multinational company in Country Z? Justify your answer. [12]

2 a Explain **two** effects on a business in Country Z if its exchange rate rises (appreciates). [8]

b FirstElectricity is considering offering bribes to government employees to get permission to build the dam. Is this right? Justify your answer. [12]

Optional questions

3 a FirstElectricity will need to recruit construction workers to build the dam. Outline **four** stages of the recruitment and selection process FirstElectricity will need to follow to employ these workers. [8]

b Using all of the information available to you from the case study, consider the advantages and disadvantages of building the dam. Recommend whether the dam will be beneficial to Country Z. Justify your answer. [12]

4 a Identify **four** stakeholder groups affected by the building of the dam. For each of the stakeholder groups identified, explain how they would be affected by the building of the dam. [8]

b FirstElectricity plans to use the reservoir behind the dam to provide either the hire of rowing boats or swimming facilities for the people of Main City. Consider the advantages and disadvantages of primary research and secondary research to find out which activity will be the most popular. Recommend which research method it should use. Justify your choice. [12]

Index

Page numbers in *italics* refer to activities

A

absenteeism 64
accounts *see* analysis of accounts
acid test ratio 315
added value 7–9, *9*
advertising 132, 158, 165, 166, 185, 186–90
  below-the-line 191
  budgets 194
  internet 189, 197–8
  jobs 96–8
  marketing strategy 206
  market segments 137–8
  media 187–90, *189, 190*
after-sales service 191
agents 180
analysis of accounts 311–24, *319*
  capital employed 311
  defining 311–12
  limitations of using 318
  ratio analysis 312, 317, *319*
    liquidity 33, 312, 315–16, *316*
    profitability 312–14, *314*
  users of accounts 316–18
Annual General Meetings (AGMs) 43
Articles of Association 40
assets 304–6
  sale of existing 267–8
autocratic leadership 85–6, 87, 119
autonomous work groups 73
average cost 229–30

B

backward vertical integration 28, 29, 31
balance of payments 329–30
banks
  accounts data 317
  and business plans 22
  and cash flow 285, 287
  loans 269, 270–1, 273, 278, 287
  objectives of 54, 55
  overdrafts 272
batch production 221–2, 223
bonus payments 69
branding/brand image 160, 162–3
  advertising 185
  localising existing brands 209–10, *210*
  and price 170–1, 174
Brazil 14
break-even charts 233–8, 237
break-even point 238, *238*
buffer inventory level 217
business activity 2–10
business cycle 326–7
business growth 28–33, *30*
  as a business objective 52, 56, 57
business objectives 51–61, 54

changing 54
  for different businesses 51–3
  marketing 203
  stakeholders 54–5, 56–8, *57*
business organisations *see* private
    sector businesses; public sector
    organisations
business plans 22–5, *24–5*
business size 25–7, *27*
  businesses staying small 32, *32*

C

capital 3, 4, 6, 270
  and private sector businesses 16, 40, 42
  risk and gearing 276
  start-up 266
  value of capital employed 26
  working capital 266, 289
capital employed 311, 313
capital expenditure 266–7
capital-intensive production 26, 215
cash flows 33, 281–90, 282, 283
  forecasts 284–8, *286, 289*
  inflows and outflows 281–2
  insolvency 283, 284
  and profit 283, 295
  short-term problems 287
cell production 220
CEOs (Chief Executive Officers) 96
chains of command 78, 79–80, *80*
charities 348
China 14, 22, 47
choice, and limited resources 3–4
classification of businesses 11–18
climate, and business location 250, 253
closed shops 88
commanding 82
commission 70
communication 114–28, 232
  barriers 125–7, *127*
  and business location 250
  direction of 125
  feedback 116
  formal and informal 124–5
  internal and external 114–16, *115, 116*
  methods 118–24, *123, 124*
    medium of 116, 126
  one-way and two-way 117–18, *118*
  process of effective 116–17
  receiver of 116, 126
  transmitter/sender of 116, 126
communities, and business objectives
    54, 55, 56, 57, 58
competitive pricing 172, 175
conglomerate merger/integration 29, 30,
    31, 33
consumer protection 206–8
consumers 132

distribution channels 179
  and e-commerce 199
  and environmental issues 341, 344
  goods and services 159, *160*
  and interest rates 335
  objectives of 54, 55, 57
  see also customers
contactless payment 224–5
controlling 82
coordination 82, 232
corporation tax 332
cost-plus pricing 171–2, 172, 175
costs 135, 228–40, 233
  and added value 7, 8
  break-even charts 233–8
  business costs 228–30
  and business growth 28, 31
  economies and diseconomies of
      scale 231–3
  environmental 342
  and prices 158
  and product development 162
  production 218
crowdfunding 271
currency appreciation 357
currency depreciation 358
current ratio 315
customers 132
  and business growth 52
  and distribution channels 182
  expectations of quality 241–2
  needs and requirements 133–4,
      135, *136*
  objectives of 54, 55, 58
  and service sector location 251–2
  see also consumers

D

debentures 269, 275
debt factors 269
de-industrialisation 14
delegation 83–4
democratic leadership 86, 87, 119
developed economies 13, 14
developing countries 13, 214–15
directors
  objectives of 57
  and organisation structure 80, 81
  private limited companies 39
  public corporations 47
  public limited companies 43, 44
diseconomies of scale 231–3
dismissal 92
distribution channels 158, 178–83
diversification 29
dividends 43, 52, 70
division of labour *see* specialisation
dynamic pricing 174, 199

E

economic growth 329
economic issues 326–39
  and the business cycle 326–7
  changes in employment levels 327
  the economic problem 2–4
  governments
    economic objectives 327–30, *330*
    economic policies 330–8, *332, 336, 337*
  stages of economic activity 11–12
  see also international economy
economic sectors, classification of
    11–17, *12, 13, 14*
economies of scale 52, 231–3
  and location decisions 249–50
emerging market countries 351
employees *see* workers
employment levels, changes in 327
enterprise and entrepreneurship 3, 6,
    19–25
  benefits and disadvantages of 19–20
  and the economic problem 3, 4
  entrepreneurs 3, 19, 20–2, *25*
  government support for 25
environmental issues 340–7, 349
  externalities 341–2, *342*
  FirstElectricity 362–3
  impact of business activity 340–1
  responses to 344–7, *346*
  sustainable development 343–4
ethical issues 347–9
European Union (EU) 359
exchange rates 330, 356–8, *356–9*
  appreciation 335
  depreciation 330
exports 329–30, 352, 357–8
external costs/benefits 342
external finance 269–72
external growth 28–30, 31
externalities 341–2
external recruitment 96–8, *97*
external stakeholders 54, 55

F

factors of production 3, 6, 7
failure of businesses 32–3, *33*
finance 265–324
  analysis of accounts 311–24
  business plans 23
  departments 265
  marketing budgets 144, 194
  needs of business 265–7, *267*
  poor financial management 33
  sources of 267–79, *268, 271*
  statement of financial position 303–10
  see also capital; cash flows; income
    statements
financial economies 231, 233
financial rewards 68–71

fiscal policy 331–4
fixed costs 228–9
flow production 222–3, 232
  and location 248
forward vertical integration 28, 29, 31
franchising *46, 47,* 209
free trade 351, 353
fringe benefits 71, 73

G

GDP (gross domestic product) 326, 327,
    329, 330, 337
gifts and sales promotion 191–2
globalisation 351–3
global marketing 135, 194–5, 208–10
  relocating businesses 256–8
global warming 341
governments
  accounts data 317
  and business location 250, 259
  and business objectives 54, 55, 58
  economic objectives 327–30
  economic policies 330–8, *332, 336, 337*
  and environmental issues 345–6
  Job Centres 96
  and multinational businesses 354
  and the private sector 15
  and privatisation 15–16, *16*
  and public corporations 47–8
  and the public sector 15, *15*
  statistics 148
  support for business start-ups 25
  and trade unions 88
gross profit margin 313

H

health and safety 92
Herzberg's motivation theory 66–7,
    67, 72
hierarchy 76
horizontal merger/integration 28, 29, 31
Human Resources department 92

I

imports 329–30, 352, 358–9
import tariffs/quotas 333, 353
incomes 328
income statements 293–302, *297, 299,*
    300, 301
  accounts and accountants 293
  cost of sales 296
  profit 267, 295, 296, 298–9
  revenue 294, 295
  use in decision making 300–1, *301*
income tax 331–2, *332*
incorporated businesses 39, 42
India
  business organisations 37, 47, 49
  economic sectors *13, 14*

pay gap 348
  social enterprises 53
industrial relations 92
industry sectors *see*
    economic sectors
inflation 327, 328
informative advertising 186
integration of businesses
    28, 28–31
interest rates 334–5
internal finance 267–8
internal growth 28
internal recruitment 95–6, 97
internal stakeholders 54, 55
international economy 351–61
  exchange rates 330, 356–8, *356–9*
  globalisation 351–3
  multinational businesses 352, 353,
    354–5, *356*
internet
  advertising/promotion
    189, 197–8
  and crowdfunding 271
  dynamic pricing 174–5
  e-commerce 135, 181, 198–201
  and location decisions 252, 253
  marketing and online sources 149
  online surveys 145, 146
interviews 145, 146
inventories 217, 218
  and finance 266, 268,
    275, 289
  JIT systems 220, 222, 248

J

job analysis and description 93–4, 95
Job Centres 96
job enrichment 72, 73
job production 221, 223
  and location 248
job rotation 72, 73
job satisfaction 71–5, *74,* 88, 222, 225
job specification 93, 94–5
joint ventures *47, 47,* 209
just-in-time (JIT) systems 220,
    222, 248

K

Kaizen principles 218, 219–20, *219*

L

labour
  availability of 250, 252, 257
  and business activity 6
  division of 6
  and the economic problem 3, 4
labour-intensive production methods
    26, 215
laissez-faire leadership 86, 87

land 3, 4, 6
leadership styles 85–7, 87
  and communication 119
leaflets 189
lean production 218–21, 219
leasing 273
LEGO 8
liabilities 304–6
  and capital employed 311
limited companies
  private 16, 38, 39–41, 41, 43, 45, 49
  public 41–5, 275
  published accounts of 311
limited liability 36, 39, 40, 41, 42, 45, 45
limited resources 3–4, 5–6
line managers 81
liquidity 33, 312, 315–16, 316
liquidity ratios 316
LLPs (Limited Liability Partnerships) 39
loans
  bank loans 269, 270–1, 273, 278, 287
  and interest rates 334–5
local government services 47
local newspapers 96, 97
location 248–61
  legal controls on location decisions
    259, 259
  manufacturing businesses 248–51, 251
  service sector businesses 251–6, 254

M

magazine advertisements 98, 188
managerial economies 231, 233
managers
  and accounts data 316–17, 318
  and the communication process 125
  and economic issues 330–1, 334
  lack of management skills 32
  objectives of 54, 55, 57, 58
  Operations department 215
  and organisation structure 81
    chains of command 79
    delegation 83–4
    importance of good managers 85
    leadership 85–7, 87
    role and functions of 81–3, 83
  public corporations 47
  public limited companies 42, 43
  and worker motivation 64, 65
manufacturing businesses 13, 14, 16
  location 248–51, 251
marketing 132–212
  budgets 144, 194
  departments 132–3, 135
  economies 231, 233
  understanding market changes 134–5
marketing mix 158–202
  the four Ps 158–59
  and marketing strategy 203, 204–5
  and technology 197–202, 197, 198

  see also place; price; products; promotion
marketing strategy 22, 203–12, 204
  extension strategy 166, 167–8, 203
  foreign markets 208–10
  legal controls on marketing 206–8
  recommending and justifying 205–6, 205
market research 132, 143–57
  agencies 149
  market-/product-oriented businesses
    144, 144
  methods 144–53, 149, 150
  presentation of data from 154–5, 155
  role of 143
markets
  and business plans 22
  and location decisions 249
  size of 32
market segments 137–41, 140
market share 53, 56, 134, 134, 172
  increasing 203, 354
Maslow's hierarchy of needs 64–5, 65, 67, 72
mass marketing 136, 137
Memorandum of Association 40
mergers 28, 28–30, 31
micro-finance 270–1
mixed economies 15–16, 15
monetary policy 334–5
money 2
motivation 63–75, 222
  benefits of a well-motivated workforce
    63–4
  job satisfaction 71–5
  methods 71
    financial rewards 68–71, 73
    non-financial factors 71–4, 74
  theories 64–7, 65, 66, 67
  why people work 63
multinational businesses 352, 353,
    354–5, 356

N

names of businesses 35
national newspapers 96, 97
needs 2, 2, 3
  marketing 133–4, 135
  Maslow's hierarchy of 64–5, 65
net profit 298
net profit margin 313–14
new businesses, failure of 33
newly industrialised countries 14
newspapers
  advertising in 188
    job advertisements 96, 97
  and market research 148
niche marketing 137

O

online recruitment sites 96
operations management 213–63

location 247–61
production 214–27
quality 8, 241–7
opportunity cost 3, 4, 6
organisational structure 76–81, 76
  chain of command and span of control
    79–80, 80
  changing to expand 76, 77
  marketing department 132–3
  roles, responsibilities and
    inter-relationships 80–1, 80
  trade unions 87–8, 88
  see also managers
organisation charts 76, 78, 80–1, 82
  direction of communication 125
output 214–15, 216
  break-even level of 233–4
  and business size 26
outsourcing 96
owners of businesses
  objectives of 54, 55, 57, 58
  small businesses 32

P

packaging 163–5, 164
partnership agreements 37
partnerships 37–9, 40, 43, 45, 275
  LLPs (Limited Liability Partnerships) 39
penetration pricing 172–3
people 6, 7
  and business size 26
  organising 82
  roles, responsibilities and
    inter-relationships 80–1, 81
  see also motivation; workers
persuasive advertising 186
piece rate payments 68–9
place 158, 159, 178–84
  distribution channels 158, 178–83, 181,
    182
  and new technology 197
planning 81–2
pressure groups 344–5
price 2, 158, 159, 170, 170–7
  and added value 8, 9
  and economic policies 333
  increasing share price 52
  and inflation 328
  marketing strategy 206
  and new technology 197
  and product life cycle 165
  sales promotions 192
  strategies/methods 170–1, 175
price elasticity of demand 176
price skimming 165, 173, 174, 175
primary market research 146–7, 150
primary sector 11, 12, 12, 13, 13, 14, 14,
    16, 17
private costs/benefits 342
private sector businesses 15–16, 35–47

advantages and disadvantages 16
franchising 46, 47
joint ventures 47, 47, 209
objectives of 51–3, 56
partnerships 37–9, 40, 43, 45
private limited companies 16, 38,
    39–41, 41, 43, 45, 49
and profit 294
public limited companies 41–5, 275
small businesses 32
sole traders 16, 35–7, 38, 38, 39, 43, 44, 45
privatisation 15–16, 16, 336
producer goods/services 159, 160, 194
production 214–27
    factors of 3
    inputs and outputs 214–15, 216
    inventories 217, 218, 220
    lean production 218–21, 219
    methods 220–3, 223
        and location decisions 248–49
        and new technology 223–6, 225
    operations department 215
    quality 241–7
    stages of 11–12
productivity 216–17, 216
    and worker motivation 65–6, 72
product-oriented businesses 143–4, 144
product placement 185
products 158–69
    branding 162–3
    development 135, 161, 162, 165
    life cycle 165–8, 167, 194
    marketing strategy 203–12
    market segmentation 137–41, 140
    and new technology 197
    packaging 163–5, 164
    product decisions 159–61, 161
profit 206, 294–5
    and added value 7, 8
    as a business objective 52, 54, 55, 56
    and cash flow 283, 295
    and income statements 267, 295, 296,
        298–299
profitability 312–14, 314
profitability ratios 314
profit and loss accounts see income
    statements
profit margin 313–14
profit sharing 70
profits tax 332
promotion 158, 159, 185–96
    aims of 186
    in the Marketing department 132–3
    marketing strategy 206
    and new technology 197–8, 198
    and the product life cycle 165
    sales promotion 185, 191–3, 193, 194
    see also advertising
promotional pricing 173, 175
protectionism 353
psychology and pricing decisions 174

public corporations 47–8
public limited companies 41–5, 275
public relations 195
public sector organisations 15–16, 47–9
    key industries/activities 15
    objectives of 55–6
    and profit 294
purchasing economies 231, 233

Q
quality 8, 241–7
quality assurance 243, 245–6
quality control 242–3
questionnaires 145–6, 150, 152–3, 153, 155

R
radio advertising 187
ratio analysis 312
raw materials, and location decisions 249
real incomes 328
recruitment and selection 92–101
    definitions 92
    external recruitment 96–8, 97
    Human Resources department 92, 93
    internal recruitment 95–6, 97
    job analysis and description 93–4, 95
    job specification 94–5
    summary of the process 93
redundancy (retrenchment) 92
resources see limited resources
retailing businesses 215
    distribution channels 179–80
    location 254–5, 256
    technology 224–5
retained profit 267, 298–9
revenue 294, 295
revenue expenditure 266–7

S
salaries 69, 92
sales 132
    and business size 26
    commission 70
    cost of 296
sales promotion 185, 191–3, 193, 194
sampling 147, 150
scarcity 2, 3, 7
secondary market research 148–9, 150
secondary sector 12, 12, 13, 13, 14, 14,
    16, 17
services 6, 7, 13, 14
    location 251–6, 254
    objectives 56
shareholders
    and accounts data 317, 318
    dividends 43, 52, 70
    equity 304
    finance from 269, 273–4, 275, 278, 287
    private limited companies 39–40, 41
    public limited companies 42, 43, 45

returns to 52, 56
shops see retailing businesses
size see business size
small businesses 32, 137
social enterprises 53, 294
social media 114, 115, 197–8
social objectives 56
sole traders 16, 35–7, 38, 38, 39,
    43, 44, 45
    finance 275
Somalia 14
South Korea 14
span of control 79–80, 80
specialisation 5–6, 6, 7, 9, 82
sponsorship 195
staff managers 81
stakeholders
    multinational businesses 354–5, 356
    objectives 54–5, 56–8, 57
        conflict of 57
start-ups
    and cash flow 285
    finance for 265–6
    government support for 25
statement of financial position 303–10,
    306, 307
    assets and liabilities 304–6
    comparing data 308
strikes 64, 88
supervisors 81
supply side policies 335–6
survival of businesses 52, 56
sustainable development 343–4

T
takeovers 28–30, 31
tariffs 333, 351
taxes 331–3, 353
Taylor's motivation theory 64, 65–6, 66, 67
teamworking 73
technical economies 232, 233
technology 134, 135, 141, 168
    accounting transactions 293
    and communications 121
    and location 252
    and the marketing mix 197–202,
        197, 198
    production methods 223–6, 225
    see also internet
television advertising 187, 194
tertiary sector 12, 12, 13, 13, 14, 14, 16
time rate payments 68
total cost 229–30
TQM (Total Quality Management) 243–5, 245
trade 7
    barriers to 257
    free trade 351, 353
    global 351, 352
    and tariffs 333, 351
    see also exports; imports

trade associations 149
trade credit 272–3
trade unions 87–8, 88, 317
training 73, 92
transport
    and business location 250
    environmental impact of 340, 341

U

unemployment 328–9, 337
unincorporated businesses 38
unlimited liability 36
USP (unique selling point) 162

V

variable costs 228–9
VAT (value added tax) 333
verbal communication 118, 120
vertical merger/integration 28, 29, 31
visual communication 119, 122–3, 124
voluntary work 63

W

wages 6, 7, 68, 92
    and inflation 328

wants 2, 2, 3, 6
wholesalers 179–80
workers
    accounts data 317
    in large businesses 232
    objectives of 54, 55, 57, 58
    specialisation 5–6, 6, 7, 9, 82
    trade unions 87–8, 88, 317
    training and education 336
    see also motivation; recruitment
        and selection
working capital 266, 289
written communication 119, 121–2

Acknowledgements

The Publishers would like to thank the following for permission to reproduce copyright material. Every effort has been made to trace all copyright holders, but if any have been inadvertently overlooked the Publishers will be pleased to make the necessary arrangements at the first opportunity.

p.1 © Rudy Balasko/Shutterstock.com; **p.4** *tl* © Romolo Tavani/stock.adobe.com, *tm* © Hamik/stock.adobe.com, *tr* © naughtynut/stock. adobe.com, *bl* © Maksim Toome/stock.adobe.com, *bm* © mbongo/stock.adobe.com, *br* © Mark Winfrey/Shutterstock.com; **p.7** *l* © withGod – Fotolia, *m* © snapfoto105 – Fotolia, *r* © artush – Fotolia; **p.9** © Paul Brown/REX/Shutterstock; **p.11** *t* © Kadmy/stock.adobe.com, *m* © Stasique/stock.adobe.com, *b* © Elnur/stock.adobe.com; **p.12** *l* © forcdan – Fotolia, *m* © KeystoneUSA-ZUMA/REX/Shutterstock, *r* © frans lemmens/Alamy Stock Photo; **p.17** © Sara Berdon – Fotolia; **p.20** *l* © Sipa Press/REX/Shutterstock, *ml* © Henry Lamb/Photowire/BEI/REX/ Shutterstock, *mr* © Adam Orchon/Everett Collection Inc/Alamy Stock Photo, *r* © ZUMA Press, Inc./Alamy Stock Photo; **p.27** *l* © svedoliver – Fotolia, *r* © gemenacom – Fotolia; **p.30** © Adrian Bradshaw/EPA/REX/Shutterstock; **p.33** *l*, 59, 242 *bl* © P Cox/Alamy Stock Photo; **p.33** *m* © Robyn Beck/AFP/Getty Images, *r* © Bhushan Koyande/Hindustan Times/Getty Images; **p.36** © wesleyguijt – Fotolia; **p.44** © Zhang jiahan/ Alamy Stock Photo; **p.48** *l* © line-of-sight – Fotolia, *m* © janniswerner – Fotolia, *r* © Marzena Hmielewicz/AdventurePictures/Alamy Stock Photo; **p.49** © TORSTEN BLACKWOOD/AFP/Getty Images; **p.53** © www.Rangsutra.com; **p.61** © JackF – Fotolia; **p.62** © VadimGuzhva/stock. adobe.com; **p.74** © Janie Airey/ Photodisc/Getty Images; **p.89** © Ian Kington/AFP/Getty Images; **p.104** © Highwaystarz/stock.adobe.com; **p.105** © Rawpixel.com/stock.adobe.com; **p.131** © Helene Rogers/Art Directors & TRIP/Alamy Stock Photo; **p.134** © Richard Levine/Alamy Stock Photo; **p.139** *l* © Rafael Ben-Ari – Fotolia, *ml* © Dave J. Anthony/ Photodisc/Getty Images, *mr* © Jaak Nilson/Alamy Stock Photo, *r* © WP Simon/Photodisc/Getty Images; **p.140** *tl* © Evox Productions/Drive Images/Alamy Stock Photo, *tr* © Chatchai Somwat/Alamy Stock Photo, *bl* © Michael Doolittle/Alamy Stock Photo, *br* © VDWI Automotive/Alamy Stock Photo; **p.141** *l* © fergregory– Fotolia, *ml* © Goir/stock.adobe.com, *m* © Nikolai Sorokin – Fotolia, *mr* © Ian Hooton/Science Photo Library/Alamy Stock Photo, *r* © Samsung; **p.145** © The Image Works/TopFoto; **p.147** © WavebreakMediaMicro/stock.adobe.com; **p.148** © Connel/Shutterstock.com; **p.149** © bloomicon/stock.adobe.com; **p.156** © Anton Gvozdikov/stock.adobe.com; **pp.164**, 191 *b*, 192 *m* © Kellog's; **p.168** © Karl Denham/Alamy Stock Photo; **p.170** *l* © Bright/stock.adobe.com, *r* © Martin Lee/Alamy Stock Photo; **p.181** © Enigma/Alamy Stock Photo; **p.186** © Cobalt/stock.adobe.com; **p.187** *t* © Tomispin/stock.adobe. com, *b* © Alexandra/stock.adobe.com; **p.188** *t* © Gina Sanders/stock.adobe.com, *tm* © Ninami/stock.adobe.com, *bm* © Yashnov Fedor - Fotolia, *b* © Ewais/stock.adobe.com; **p.189** *t* © Helene Rogers/Art Directors & TRIP/Alamy Stock Photo, *b* © Cath Harries/Alamy Stock Photo; **p.191** *t* © imabase – Fotolia; **p.192** *t* © Craig Stephen/Alamy Stock Photo, *tm* © Jaak Nilson/Alamy Stock Photo, *mb* © Dennis MacDonald/Alamy Stock Photo, *b* © Ted Foxx/Alamy Stock Photo; **p.193** © Barbie; **p.210** *t* © McDonalds, *b* © Moving Moment/stock.adobe.com; **pp.213, 224** *t* © xieyuliang/Shutterstock.com; **p.215** *l* © photocrew – Fotolia, *m* © M.studio – Fotolia, *r* © mr.markin – Fotolia; **p.221** *t* © bst2012 – Fotolia, *b* © alephcomo1 – Fotolia; **p.222** © industrieblick – Fotolia; **p.224** *b* © jutaphoto/stock.adobe.com; **p.226** © Colin C. Hill/Alamy Stock Photo; **p.241** © Alexander Babich – Fotolia; **p.242** *tl* Sorge/Agencja Fotograficzna Caro/Alamy Stock Photo, *tm* © Amanda Hall/Robertharding/Getty Images, *tr* © jim forrest/ Stock Photo, *bm* © Ton koene/Alamy Stock Photo, *br* © Mike Hewitt/Getty Images; **p.244** © Christopher Barnes/ Alamy Stock Photo; **p.245** *t* © British Standards Institution (BSI), *b* © International Organization for Standardization (ISO); **p.246** © Paul Brown/REX/Shutterstock; **p.248** © Nataliya Hora/Shutterstock.com; **p.249** © kustov – Fotolia; **p.250** © Paylessimages – Fotolia.com; **p.252** © WavebreakMediaMicro/stock.adobe.com; **p.253** © Oleg Zhukov/stock.adobe.com; **p.254** © danr13/stock.adobe.com; **p.255** © Mick Sinclair/ Alamy Stock Photo; **p.257** *t* © Joanna Kearney/Alamy Stock Photo, *b* © marilyn barbone – Fotolia; **p.260** © cynoclub – Fotolia; **p.262** © Rob Pitman – Fotolia; **p.264** © Jirapong Manustrong/Shutterstock.com; **p.270** Courtesy of Farmers Friend Organization (FFO); **p.271** © Maurice Savage/Alamy Stock Photo; **p.279** © Divyakant Solanki/epa/REX/Shutterstock; **p.290** © Finnbarr Webster/Alamy Stock Photo; **p.301** © Sun Properties & Resort; **p.308** © Travelib sri lanka/Alamy Stock Photo; **p.312** *l* © Iain Masterton/Alamy Stock Photo, *r* © Kees Metselaar/Alamy Stock Photo; **p.319** © markhall70 – Fotolia; **p.323** © tashka2000 – Fotolia; **p.325** © Corepics/stock.adobe.com; **p.328** Reprinted with permission of The Financial Times; **p.329** *t* Allsorts Stock Photo/Alamy Stock Photo, *ml* © Sam Spiro/stock.adobe.com, *mr* © itsallgood/stock.adobe.com, *b* © Dell/stock.adobe.com; **p.337** © Pablo Blazquez Dominguez/Getty Images; **p.338** © James Hardy/PhotoAlto sas/Alamy Stock Photo; **p.340** *l* © corepics – Fotolia, *m* © Martin Diebel/Getty Images, *r* © mihi – Fotolia; **p.345** © kobah/123 RF; **p.349** © Ralph Mortimer/REX/Shutterstock; **p.360** © David Gee/Alamy Stock Photo; **p.362** © Zechal – Fotolia.

t = top, *b* = bottom, *l* = left, *r* – right, *m* - middle